CW01022945

Led Zeppelin
Day by Day

Led Zeppelin
Day by Day

Marc Roberty

**Backbeat
Books**

An Imprint of Hal Leonard Corporation

Published in 2016 by Backbeat Books
An Imprint of Hal Leonard Corporation
7777 West Bluemound Road
Milwaukee, WI 53213

Trade Book Division Editorial Offices
33 Plymouth St., Montclair, NJ 07042

All images are from the author's collection, unless otherwise noted.

Printed in the United States of America

Book design by Kristina Rolander

Library of Congress Cataloging-in-Publication Data is available upon request.

ISBN 978-1-6171-3584-2

www.backbeatbooks.com

Contents

Introduction

A lot of fantasy has been written about Led Zeppelin over the years. Of course, we all like a good story or two, but when people start believing the myth rather than the reality, that's when history changes and becomes fact for many. The truth is far more simple. Led Zeppelin were a bunch of talented young guys who were not prepared, or equipped, for the massive fame and wealth that came their way in a relatively short period of time. Were they choirboys? Of course not, but they were no worse than any other major touring band of the time. Lots of groupies and drugs were freely available, and let's not forget that the '60s and '70s were all about experimentation, especially in places like Los Angeles. They were young and everything they asked for was provided for them on a platter, and after a while it became pretty easy to lose touch with reality. When it comes to wild tales about being on the road, Led Zeppelin are always the first to get mentioned because they were the biggest band of the decade and everybody has heard of them. In reality, history has shown that other bands behaved just as badly, but they are now just forgotten names hardly even worth a footnote in the history of popular music. So it goes.

Perhaps the most ludicrous Led Zeppelin stories are reserved for Jimmy Page and his interest in the occult. Most creative people in the '60s and '70s were fascinated by Aleister Crowley and his teachings. He was even included among the figures on the front cover of the iconic Beatles *Sgt. Pepper* album sleeve. It was really all about new esoteric understandings of magic and following your "true will." In other words, each of us should know and act from our own will. Jimmy Page had mentioned in an early interview that he admired Crowley, which resulted in numerous ill-informed journalists writing erroneous fantasy stories of Jimmy performing satanic rituals and the casting of evil spells. Crowley was not a Satanist, although it suited many religious groups to claim he was as a way of discrediting him. All he really wanted was for people to have the free will to denounce religious slavery if they chose to. Page made the right decision in keeping his feelings on Crowley largely to himself as people were all too ready to accept what the media was saying.

So this book will deal with the music and the live phenomenon that was Led Zeppelin. That means looking at the good as well as the bad.

Today, Led Zeppelin members are very much part of the establishment, and although they have earned many awards over the years, one of the most emotional was when Heart performed a mind-blowing version of "Stairway To Heaven" at the Kennedy Center Awards in 2012 with John Bonham's son, Jason, on drums. The band were being honored at the show, and during Jack Black's speech he called Led Zeppelin "the greatest rock 'n' roll band of all time" before humorously reminding everyone that they wrote songs about "love, Vikings, and Vikings making love." "Stairway To Heaven" was performed with a full choir and orchestra, and there was not a dry eye in the house by the song's conclusion. Present were Jimmy Page, Robert Plant and John Paul Jones, who looked on from the balcony. As the camera panned in on their faces, you could not help but wonder what was going through their minds. They were there; they created it and lived through it all. It was a very emotional moment, not least seeing Jason Bonham behind the kit. His dad would have been so proud, and rightly so. Led Zeppelin captured the imaginations of young people like no other band at the time. Their live shows were legendary, with lengthy performances and intricate light and laser shows incorporated into the act. The volume levels were ear shattering. Their music was as epic as it was dynamic, mood building with beautiful textural arrangements, all aimed at the young generation who could relate to the sounds of the time and turned Led Zeppelin into the greatest rock band of the '70s.

What made Led Zeppelin so special? They all brought their own style and influences to the table and the fit was perfect. Their charisma and artistic talent was there in abundance from the beginning. John Paul

Jones was an exceptional arranger and seasoned session player. Jimmy Page was also a much-in-demand hired hand, and both he and John Paul Jones knew their way around a recording studio. John Bonham, well respected as one of the best rock drummers on the scene, pushed and drove the band to captivating highs. Robert Plant was the perfect up-front guy with a voice that delivered conviction and emotion. Anyone who saw them in those early days knew they were witnessing greatness in the making. Before long the doors to the USA that had been opened by Cream were blown clean off by Led Zeppelin. On those early tours in America, they slayed any bill-topper who dared go on after them.

Led Zeppelin
Day by Day

1 The Birth of Led Zeppelin

The Yardbirds were a popular R&B band who are now best remembered for being the launching pad for three of the world's most iconic guitar players—Eric Clapton, Jeff Beck, and Jimmy Page. The core band consisted of Keith Relf on vocals, Paul Samwell-Smith on bass, Chris Dreja on guitar, and Jim McCarty on drums. The band had many ups and downs during their relatively short life. Eric Clapton wanted to have more control over the musical direction, and he was eventually asked to leave after every other band member voted for him to be sacked, having gotten fed up with his unpredictable mood swings. Jimmy Page was offered the chance of joining the band but declined, suggesting Jeff Beck instead. In came Jeff Beck, with whom the band arguably reached their most creative and critical peak. Perhaps inevitably, Beck would outgrow the band and head off to pursue a successful solo career. Before that happened, however, Jimmy Page accepted a second invitation to join and was brought in on bass in June 1966 to replace a departing Paul Samwell-Smith. He had grown tired of the long tours as well as Keith Relf's unreliability and wanted to concentrate on production instead. Page at this point was fed up with playing studio sessions and was starting to feel a bit stale; he desperately wanted to play live in front of an audience as part of a band. The idea was for Chris Dreja to learn how to play bass, with Page taking over as second lead guitarist alongside Beck. In August 1966, Beck collapsed onstage during a US tour due to tonsillitis, and for the remainder of the tour Page had to play guitar and Chris Dreja bass, albeit a bit earlier than planned. A recuperated Beck returned for a UK package tour with headliners the Rolling Stones in September 1966. Now the band had

two remarkable lead guitarists whose intricate weaves would prove hugely popular with the audiences that were lucky enough to catch this lineup. Beck and Page were very much in tune with each other, and for a short time it seemed that the band were destined for massive success with this formula. It was not to be. Beck flew over to America with the band for a tour, but his unreliability and inconsistency were simply too much for the other members. He was fired, and the Yardbirds continued on as a four-piece with Page easily taking care of all the guitar duties.

The Yardbirds' then manager, Simon Napier-Bell, sold his stake in the Yardbirds to producer Mickie Most, who had formed RAK Music Management with producer Peter Grant. RAK now took over their management, which turned out to be perfect timing. The band were unhappy and tired of struggling financially due to poor management decisions, not to mention feeling disgruntled and road weary. So for them a change in management could only be a good thing. Peter Grant was streetwise and a highly motivated individual who made sure that his artists were looked after. He was "old school," having been taught management skills by Don Arden. By 1964, he was already successfully managing acts as diverse as Ray Cameron, the She Trinity, the New Vaudeville Band, Jeff Beck, and Terry Reid. RAK's management offices operated out of 155 Oxford Street in London's West End.

One of the first things he organized for the Yardbirds was a short US tour, followed by an Australasian tour that actually earned the band some money. Billed as "The Big Show 1967," the band found themselves on a bill with Roy Orbison, the Walker Brothers, and

Johnny Young. On their return to England, they went to Olympic Studios in Barnes to record their first single with new producer Mickie Most. Although Page was familiar with Most's production, having played on various sessions for him in the past, he was not that pleased to have him as their new producer. He had no choice, though, as this was part of the arrangement made by Simon Napier-Bell and RAK. The A-side was called "Little Games," and Most brought in session players John Paul Jones to play bass and Dougie Wright on drums, refusing to allow Dreja and McCarty to play on the record. John Paul Jones was also given the job of cello arrangement. Bringing session musicians in to achieve a particular sound was common practice at the time. Page had himself been brought in many times to add his guitar work to save embarrassing the bands whose skills were not up to the job. The B-side, "Puzzles," actually did feature the whole band with some double-tracked guitar by Page, as well as his first recording of bowed guitar.

The single was a typical overtly commercial Mickie Most production but surprisingly did not do well, only reaching #51 in America, and it did not even chart in the UK. Despite poor sales, the band was given an opportunity to record a new album. Sessions started at De Lane Lea Studios in London at the end of March and continued on and off until early May. All in all they were not allowed more than five days in the studio by Most. As a result, many of the numbers on the album had a demo-like quality to them. The album did have many engaging well-written songs and good musicianship; however, it did not do well sales-wise in the US and was not even released in the UK as EMI felt it would not sell. Maybe if they had been given more time, the album could have sounded more polished. Page told *ZigZag* magazine in December 1972, "On half the tracks we didn't even hear the playbacks. . . . They were first takes. That's how it used to be done; we would spend time on singles, but Mickie Most thought that LPs were nothing—just something to stick out after a single." The band was very different in concert, blowing away its studio pop sound and delivering a high-energy psychedelic show. They all looked the part and Page's guitar acrobatics mesmerized fans. One of his trademarks was playing the guitar with a violin bow during a number called "I'm Confused," which was basically a rearrangement of a Jake Holmes number called "Dazed And Confused" that was found on his *The Above Ground*

Sound Of Jake Holmes album. Jimmy and the Yardbirds took Holmes's low-key acoustic version and gave it a heavy vibe with Middle Eastern tinges and new lyrics. The *Man From U.N.C.L.E.* star David McCallum's father, also called David McCallum, suggested this unorthodox method of playing to him at a studio session in 1966. He just happened to be a violinist and leader of Annunzio Mantovani's orchestra at the time. Although other players have laid claim to being pioneers of this practice, it is Page who turned it into a spectacular showpiece event in the live arena with both the Yardbirds and later Led Zeppelin.

By the middle of 1968 Jimmy had grown dissatisfied with the band. While they all got on pretty well socially, the onstage chemistry was a different story and apathy had set in. Jimmy was a consummate professional and was fed up with Keith Relf's apparent lack of enthusiasm for singing certain numbers as well as his overindulgence in various substances. There were other problems with members in the band wanting to head off in a softer direction, whereas Jimmy wanted to go with a heavier guitar sound. It became clear that the end was inevitable. Jimmy Page explained to *Go* magazine in the 27 December 1968 issue the reason the Yardbirds split: "They were too much into their own bag. They were great at experimenting, allowing me to move in and out of the expression every good musician needs—but then they started to get erratic. Sometimes we would play at concerts and the audience would want to hear some of our older songs—the ones that were hits—but the guys didn't want to do them. They just wanted to do their own stuff, solos and the like."

When the Yardbirds broke up after one last US tour, Jimmy had a vision of the new band he wanted to form, a dynamic rock band. The two main things high on his request list were good musicianship and reliability. Still onboard originally was bassist Chris Dreja, who along with Jimmy and other ex-members of the band, had equal shares in Yardbirds Ltd, and was invested in forming a new band with him. Jimmy's first choice of vocalist was Terry Reid. He recalled hearing Reid's lead vocals when he was in a band called Peter Jay and the New Jay Walkers, who along with the Yardbirds, supported the Rolling Stones and Ike and Tina Turner on a UK tour in September 1966. Page felt he would be an ideal choice for the position of lead singer in the New Yardbirds. But by 1968 Terry was about to start a solo career and enter the recording studio for his first album, which had already been booked. The thought of joining a band that had not even been formed yet as opposed to a potentially successful solo career meant he had to decline the offer of joining Page's new band. He did recommend another hot young singer whose name was Robert Plant, who he had gotten to know when he saw him singing in a group called the Band of Joy in the mid-'60s. They were a good band but ahead of their time locally, playing a mixture of West Coast numbers mixed in with more ethnic influences from Africa and India. By 1968 Robert was with a band called Obs-Tweedle, which included Bill Bonham, who was future Led Zeppelin drummer John Bonham's cousin. Another good band, but not exactly setting the musical world on fire. Plant was disenchanted, feeling that nobody wanted to listen to what he had to offer and even considered giving up on the music business.

Jimmy, accompanied by Peter Grant and Chris Dreja, went to see the Obs-Tweedle in action on 20 July 1968 at Walsall College on the outskirts of Birmingham. After listening to their set, Jimmy was confident that they had found their new singer. Chris Dreja, who had been more familiar with Keith Relf's style, was less, viewing Plant as an uncouth shrieker. Peter Grant trusted Page's instinct and in the next few days after the gig tried to contact Plant several times by phone to no avail. Eventually, a telegram had to be sent to him at his Beechdale Estate flat in Walsall asking him if he would be interested in joining the Yardbirds. After some fast soul searching, he said yes and Jimmy invited him to come and stay with him and his American girlfriend at his Pangbourne home to see how they would get on musically and on a personal level. Plant recalled how it all happened in a March 1969 interview with the *International Times*:

> The Yardbirds singer had just left. I knew they had done a lot of work in America, which to me meant audiences who *did* want to know what I'd got to offer, so naturally I was very interested. It was the real desperation scene, man, like I had nowhere else to go. I went down to Pangbourne where Jimmy lives. There I was with my suitcase getting off the train and suddenly this old woman starts slapping my face and shouting about my hair. Well, I was staggered, so I called a cop and he says it was my own fault for having long hair. So much for British justice! Anyway I got to Jimmy's and we found we had exactly the same tastes in music.

Robert had already been seduced by Indian music as well as ska, jazz, and blues. This melting pot of exotic sounds would later influence him in his songwriting with Jimmy Page and beyond. A search for a drummer had been going on at the same time, and Chris Dreja had already contacted Paul Francis, who had drummed for people as diverse as Rolf Harris and Tony Jackson and the Vibrations and who was now in a soul group about to tour in Germany. He was interested in joining the new band but would have to honor his commitment to the soul group and contact Chris on his return. Jimmy did not particularly want to wait and went ahead and contacted a couple of players he knew and played with on various studio sessions in the past. Clem Cattini was considered but decided to keep to the safety of his regular session work. Jimmy had worked with Procol Harum's B. J. Wilson on a Joe Cocker session earlier in 1968, and he was also offered the job but declined, as he was happy with the already successful Procol Harum.

Robert Plant came up with a suggestion in John Bonham, his mate and drummer from the old Band of Joy who was now playing in Tim Rose's band and touring the UK. He had a good reputation in the music community and was very much in demand as a drummer. Jimmy, along with Chris and Peter, went to the Hampstead Country Club, located at 210A Haverstock Hill, on 31 July 1968 to see Bonham in action with Tim Rose. They were all impressed and did not hesitate to offer him the job. Like the other drummers, he did not jump at the chance of joining the new band as he was already committed to a US tour with Tim Rose as well as considering recent job offers from Joe Cocker and Chris Farlowe. John's wife was also putting pressure on him not to leave a job that was bringing in money on a regular basis. However, over a period of one week, Peter Grant and Robert Plant were able to persuade him that he would have a great future if he did join. The only sure way to prove that was to offer him more money than he was getting with Tim Rose. Knowing how good a singer Robert Plant was from their days together in the Band of Joy, also helped him make his mind up.

Just as it looked like the band was ready, Chris Dreja lost enthusiasm and decided to bow out and concentrate on his real passion, which was photography. It was something he had been toying with for sometime and decided that now the time was right. When on the road on the last Yardbirds US tour, he had taken every opportunity to take shots of the amazing scenery in between dates. After telling Page he wanted out, he headed to New York to do an apprenticeship with Irving Penn, an American photographer known for his fashion photography, portraits, and still lifes. One of Chris's first professional jobs as a photographer was to shoot the back cover of Led Zeppelin's first album.

John Paul Jones, another seasoned session player and a versatile musician and arranger, was pretty much waiting in the wings, having heard about the new band Jimmy was putting together. More importantly, he was Jimmy Page's musical equal, and the two of them knew and respected each other, having played together on numerous sessions in the past. John Paul Jones was happy to leave the session scene behind him and join a band, just as Jimmy had the year before. Both musicians knew their way around the recording studio, which would prove to be a huge advantage in the future. When the new band first got together, they decided to call themselves the Yardbirds in the short term as a way of fulfilling some contractual commitments of the old band to tour in Scandinavia. Obviously the name would offer some continuity, as it was already an established one. In readiness for their dates in Scandinavia, the first rehearsals took place in the middle of August in a basement at 39 Gerrard Street in London's Soho. The basement was originally the location of Ronnie Scotts Jazz Club before becoming a rehearsal space for hire when Ronnie moved his club to nearby Frith Street. The band played several versions of "Train Kept A Rollin'"as well as further rock 'n' roll and blues standards. Everyone in the band knew the chemistry was right and a setlist was prepared for the upcoming tour.

As the initial concerts were billed as the Yardbirds, it made sense to play one of their big hits, "For Your Love." Ironically, Jimmy had not yet joined the Yardbirds when it was released in 1966. Also, the original hit not only featured Eric Clapton, but the single was also the reason for Clapton's departure from the band due to his supposed displeasure at the commercial sound of the song.

On his return from the Scandinavian gigs in September 1968, Jimmy Page spoke with *Melody Maker*'s Chris Welch and explained to him what the new band was all about musically: "It's blues, basically, but not Fleetwood Mac style. I hate that phrase 'progressive blues.' It sounds like a hype, but it's more

or less what the Yardbirds were playing at the end, but nobody knew about it because they never saw us. We're starting work on an LP and we're going to the States in early November. I'm hoping the Marquee will be a good scene. Robert can get up and sing against anybody. He gets up and sings against Terry Reid! Those two are like brothers together."

The band also spent time at Jimmy's home, the Thames Boathouse, which was located at 2 Shooters Hill in Pangbourne, Berkshire, writing and rehearsing material for their first album, some of which had been premiered on the tour. Before the band actually started recording their first album, they participated in a session for P. J. Proby in early September 1968. John Paul Jones was already committed to the session and suggested that the other members in the band came to the session as a way of getting a bit of cash, as well as getting to know themselves in a studio environment. Although various members appear on different tracks, all four appear together on "Jim's Blues/ George Wallace Is Rollin' In This Mornin'" and "Mery Hoppkins Never Had Days Like These," the latter being a funky seven-minute jam that can only be found on the B-side single of "The Day That Lorraine Came Down." Even on these two numbers you can already hear the future sound of Led Zeppelin. The band entered Olympic Studios in Barnes on 27 September 1968 to start sessions for their first album. It became apparent early on in the sessions that they really had nothing in common with the "old" Yardbirds sound and it would be wise to change the name. However, the Yardbirds name did get them bookings in the UK. It would have been harder for an unknown band to get choice bookings such as at the Marquee. The ex-members of the Yardbirds were upset that the name was being used past the old contracted dates that had been booked originally under their name. Now, there was no excuse to use it.

The name Led Zeppelin, although not liked by everyone, was certainly one that gave the impression of heaviness and the band's albums would be located in the hip "underground" section in record stores. It was a name that first came up during a secret session in May 1966 with Jeff Beck for his "Beck's Bolero" single that featured Keith Moon, Nicky Hopkins, John Paul Jones, and Jimmy Page. Someone at the session half-joked that they should all form a band and record an album. Keith Moon, or possibly John Entwistle, said that they would go down like a lead Zeppelin! It seemed appropriate to use the name for the new group. They changed it to Led Zeppelin to avoid pronunciation problems with the American market. That, coupled with the striking artwork featuring the iconic photo of the *Hindenburg* exploding as it came into land at Lakehurst Naval Air Station, meant that it grabbed any self-respecting music fan's attention. It deservedly stood out. Best of all was the actual music, powerful, mysterious, and dynamic. It was obvious Led Zeppelin were destined to be huge from that moment on.

The band formed a publishing company, Superhype Company Limited, which was incorporated on 22 October 1968. The registered address was in the City of London at 91 Tabernacle Street, London EC2. Manager Peter Grant flew over to the US in August 1968 to start talking to various record labels with a view of getting a record deal for his new charges. He returned in October to sign with Jerry Wexler at Atlantic Records, who issued the following press release:

ATLANTIC RECORDS SIGNS ENGLAND'S HOT NEW GROUP, LED ZEPPELIN, IN ONE OF THE BIGGEST DEALS OF THE YEAR

Atlantic Records has signed the hot new English group, Led Zeppelin, to a long term, exclusive recording contract. Although the exact terms of the deal are secret, it can be disclosed that it is one of the most substantial deals Atlantic has ever made. Agreement for the group's services was made between Jerry Wexler, Executive Vice President of Atlantic Records, and Peter Grant, manager of the group.

Led Zeppelin consists of four of the most exciting musicians performing in Britain today. They are Jimmy Page, leader of the group and lead guitarist; John Paul Jones, bassist, pianist, organist, arranger; John Bonham, drums; and Robert Plant, lead vocal and harmonica.

Jimmy Page is a former member of the Yardbirds, the group that spawned the careers of two other great musicians, Eric Clapton and Jeff Beck. Page joined the Yardbirds in 1966 and stayed with the group until it disbanded in the summer of 1968. Prior to joining the Yardbirds he was one of the busiest session men in London.

John Paul Jones is considered one of England's finest arrangers as well as an outstanding bass player. He is the arranger of Donovan's "Mellow Yellow," "Sunshine Superman," and "Hurdy Gurdy Man," and of the Rolling Stones' "She's a Rainbow." Drummer John Bonham created

a sensation with his drum solos, while accompanying Tim Rose on his British tour in early 1968. Vocalist Robert Plant is considered one of England's outstanding young blues singers, and has been involved in singing blues since he was 15. All of the members of the group are in their early 20s.

The pulsations surrounding Led Zeppelin have intensified ever since the group recorded its first (and as yet unreleased) album, which was produced by Jimmy Page, just a month ago in London. Top English and American rock musicians who have heard the tracks have called Led Zeppelin the next group to reach heights achieved by Cream and Hendrix. This Led Zeppelin LP will be released by Atlantic early in January.

Led Zeppelin is the eighth British group to be signed by Atlantic during the past 24 months. The others are Cream, Bee Gees, Julie Driscoll—Brian Auger & Trinity, The Crazy World of Arthur Brown, The Marbles, The Magic Lanterns, and Jimmy James & The Vagabonds.

YARDBIRDS SCANDINAVIAN TOUR
7 SEPTEMBER 1968–15 SEPTEMBER 1968

The band were contracted to play for thirty minutes. Although the exact setlists are not known, they would likely have been drawn from the following: "The Train Kept A-Rollin', "Dazed And Confused," "Communication Breakdown," "White Summer," "Flames" (written by Elmer Gantry), "As Long As I Have You" (a Garnett Mimms song), "I Can't Quit You Babe," "You Shook Me," "For Your Love," "How Many More Times." There were many complaints about the band being too loud and even some criticism that this was done as a gimmick to disguise the fact that they were not good. Although the band were a little under-rehearsed, these dates gave them plenty of experience as well as the opportunity to get their chops together before entering the studio to record the all-important first album.

66 They don't cheer too madly there, you know? We were really scared, because we only had about fifteen hours to practice together. It was sort of an experimental concert to see if we were any good. I guess. 99

—JIMMY PAGE (From a *Melody Maker* interview from December 1968 talking about the Scandinavian audiences)

The Yardbirds (Led Zeppelin)—first live appearance at the Teen Club, Club 45, in Gladsaxe, Denmark. (Jorgen Angel/Getty Images)

7 September 1968, Teen Club, Egegård School, Gladsaxe, Copenhagen, Denmark (5:30 p.m. Billed as Yardbirds. Support from Fourways and Bodies)

7 September 1968, Brondby Pop-Club, Norregardenhallen, Brondby, Denmark (7:30 p.m. Billed as the Yardbirds. Support from Day of the Phoenix, the Eyes and Ham)

❝ The English group YARDBIRDS had been rehearsing their new set most of the afternoon. So by the time they came on stage they were really hot to get started and give it their all. Their performance and their music were absolutely flawless, and the music continued to ring nicely in the ears for some time after the curtains were drawn after their show. Let me in particular give my praise to JIMMY PAGE who has made a great job with the 3 new men. They really succeeded and in particular the guitar solos by Jimmy Page created huge applause. We can therefore conclude that the new YARDBIRDS are at least as good as the old ones were. ❞

—BENT LARSEN (*Review in Teen Club Nyt* [Gladsaxe Teen Club's monthly members' magazine], October 1968)

Advert for the Yardbirds appearance at the Teen Club, Club Box 45, in Gladsaxe, Denmark.

Advert for the Yardbirds appearance at the Brondby Pop Club in Copenhagen, Denmark.

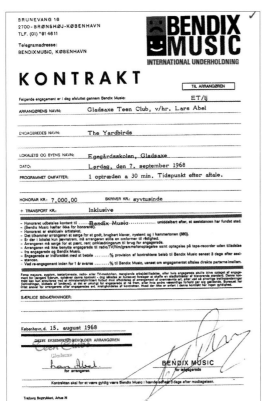

Contract for the Yardbirds (Led Zeppelin)—first live appearance at the Teen Club, Club 45, in Gladsaxe, Denmark.

Advert for the Yardbirds (Led Zeppelin) appearance at the Stora Grona Lund Amusement Park in Stockholm, Sweden.

Advert for the Yardbirds (Led Zeppelin) appearance at the Inside Club in Stockholm, Sweden.

8 September 1968, Reventlowparken, Nykobing, Lolland, Denmark (4:00 p.m. The band play the first of three scheduled shows today. The distance between clubs/towns is quite short. Billed as Yard-Birds. Support from the Beatniks and the Ladybirds)

8 September 1968, Fjordvilla, Roskilde, Denmark (6:30 p.m. Billed as Yard Birds. Support from the Ladybirds and Beauty Fools)

8 September 1968, Koge Popklub, Teaterbygningen, Koge, Denmark (7:30 p.m. Canceled, the band never made it to the show)

12 September 1968, Gröna Lund, Stora Scenen, Stockholm, Sweden (9:30 p.m. Billed as Yardbirds)

13 September 1968, Inside Club, Stockholm, Sweden (Billed as Yardbirds. Support from Atlantic Ocean)

66 The members have changed and the Yardbirds currently touring Sweden have very little in common with the original line-up. It is not only the line-up that has changed. The style of music is different, as is the quality—only the name is the same. Friday night they played the Inside. They were so loud it almost hurt. Sometimes playing loud has an important role in pop, but here it was just a superficial effect. 99

—REVIEW IN THE *STOCKHOLM DAILY NEWS*

(14 September 1968)

Advert for the Yardbirds appearance at Angby Park, Knivsta, Sweden.

14 September 1968, Ängby Park, Knivsta, Sweden (11:00 p.m. Billed as the Yardbirds with Kenneth Staggs and Hayati Kafe)

15 September 1968, Liseburg Amusement Park, Strjarnscenen, Gothenburg, Sweden (7:30 p.m. Billed as Yardbirds pop band)

17 September 1968, Folkets Park, Malmo, Sweden (canceled)

20 September 1968, Tivoli Gardens, Stockholm, Sweden (canceled)

21 September 1968, Tivoli Gardens, Stockholm, Sweden (canceled)

22 September 1968, Bergen, Norway (canceled)

23 September 1968, Oslo, Norway (canceled)

23 September 1968, Oslo, Norway (canceled)

YARDBIRDS / LED ZEPPELIN UK TOUR
4 OCTOBER 1968–20 DECEMBER 1968

4 October 1968, the Mayfair Ballroom, Newcastle Upon Tyne (8:00 p.m. Billed as the Yardbirds (featuring Jimmy Page). (Support from Terry Reid's Fantasia, Junco Partners, and Downtown Fraction)

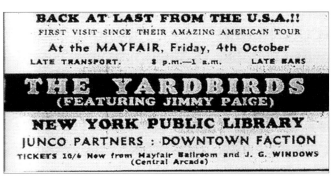

BACK AT LAST FROM THE U.S.A.!!
FIRST VISIT SINCE THEIR AMAZING AMERICAN TOUR
At the MAYFAIR, Friday, 4th October
LATE TRANSPORT.   8 p.m.—1 a.m.   LATE BARS
THE YARDBIRDS
(FEATURING JIMMY PAIGE)
NEW YORK PUBLIC LIBRARY
JUNCO PARTNERS : DOWNTOWN FACTION
TICKETS 10/6 Now from Mayfair Ballroom and J. G. WINDOWS
(Central Arcade)

Press advert for Led Zeppelin's appearance at the Mayfair Ballroom in Newcastle, England.

17 October 1968, Lafayette Club, Wolverhampton, West Midlands, UK (unconfirmed date and venue)

18 October 1968, Marquee Club, Wardour Street, London (11:30 p.m. Billed as the British Debut of the Yardbirds. Support from Sleepy)

66 The New Yardbirds, originally a 'Marquee group,' also re-appear this month, on Friday, 18th October. Fittingly their British debut is at the club. The personnel has changed since the early days and now features Jimmy Page (lead guitar), John Paul Jones (bass guitar), John Bonham (drums) and Robert Plant (vocals). Incidentally Jimmy is now playing a specially built Fender 6 pedal steel guitar as well as the more usual lead guitar. 99

—**FROM A MARQUEE FLYER TALKING ABOUT THE YARDBIRDS RETURN TO THE CLUB** (October 1968)

66 Led Zeppelin, the re-grouped Yardbirds, made their Marquee debut last week. They are now very much a heavy music group, with singer Robert Plant leading and ably holding his own against a powerful backing trio of John Paul Jones (bass), John Bonham (drums), and Jimmy Page (guitar). . . . One of the best numbers of the set was 'Days of Confusion' (Dazed and Confused), featuring interesting inter-play of Plant's voice and Page's guitar on which he used a violin bow creating an unusual effect. 99

—**TONY WILSON** (Review in *Melody Maker*, December 1968)

19 October 1968, Mountford Hall, Liverpool University, Liverpool (The press report that this will be the Yardbirds' last appearance under that name. They will be known as "Led Zeppelin" from Sunday, 20 October 1968, onwards)

25 October 1968, Great Hall, University of Surrey, Battersea Park Road, Battersea, London (Although billed as the New Yardbirds on the poster advertising the show, this is Led Zeppelin's official debut and is reported as such in the press)

26 October 1968, Bristol Boxing Club, Bristol (support from the Deviants)

NOVEMBER 1968

9 November 1968, the Roundhouse, Camden, London (10:30 p.m. Billed on adverts as "Yardbirds now known as Led Zeppelin." Support from John Lee Hooker, the Deviants, John James, Tyres, and music by DJ Jeff Dexter)

16 November 1968, Faculty of Technology Union, Manchester University, Manchester

23 November 1968, Students Union, Sheffield University, Sheffield

29 November 1968, the Crawdaddy Club, Richmond Athletic Ground, Richmond, Surrey(Billed as Led Zeppelin [formerly Yardbirds])

DECEMBER 1968

10 December 1968, Marquee Club, Wardour Street, London (7:30 p.m. Billed as Led Zeppelin [nee the Yardbirds]. Support from Bakerloo Blues Line)

13 December 1968, Bridge Place Country Club, Cantebury, Kent (Although billed as the Yardbirds on the handbills, Led Zeppelin was the name given on press advertisements)

16 December 1968, Bath Pavilion, Bath, Somerset (7:30 p.m. Support from Yellow Brick Road. Led Zeppelin performed as a replacement for the Jeff Beck Blues Group [who was the headliner] after they canceled)

19 December 1968, Civic Hall, Exeter, Devon (Support from the Deviants and Empty Vessels [who later went on to become Wishbone Ash]. This was a Christmas Ball for the Exeter Art College students)

20 December 1968, Bourne Hall, Fishmongers Arms, Wood Green, London (7:30 p.m. Billed as Led Zeppelin [formerly Yardbirds]. Support from Closed Cell Sponge)

LED ZEPPELIN FIRST US TOUR

26 DECEMBER 1968–15 FEBRUARY 1969

Led Zeppelin had signed with Atlantic Records in America on a worldwide basis with Grant and Page as "Superhype," but retained UK rights for the band. Perhaps surprisingly, England's initial response to the band was lukewarm at best. Agents and labels had not really wanted to know them in the UK as the Yardbirds were viewed as has-beens with no recent chart hits. It was a real struggle for them in their home country. So Grant and Page told Atlantic that the UK should be included as part of their deal. It made commercial sense to concentrate on the lucrative US market first as they had far more suitable venues than those in England, and the album-buying public was also far larger than that in Europe and England. On top of that, Jimmy Page's popularity in America was also far greater than back home, thanks to the exciting live performances undertaken by the Yardbirds there. It is worth noting that Cream had pretty much set the

Led Zeppelin onstage at the Marquee Club in London. (Rex)

template for English bands in the US and Jimmy Page saw the huge potential straight away.

Their first date was a hastily arranged support slot for Vanilla Fudge and Spirit in Denver. It was so hastily arranged that the band were not even billed! Their first US tour was basically supporting the likes of Vanilla Fudge, Iron Butterfly, and Country Joe and the Fish, all of whom were well-established artists at the time. The band spent Christmas and the New Year touring in America, which showed how committed they were to being successful. On the road in the harsh American winter was hard for any artist, not to mention dangerous, traveling long distances in treacherous snowstorms. It certainly helped bond everyone, and friendships developed with members of the other bands. John Bonham and Carmine Appice, drummer with Vanilla Fudge, were inseparable on that tour. In fact, it was Appice who was instrumental in getting Bonham an endorsement deal with the Ludwig drum company during the tour.

As for the gigs, Led Zeppelin were quick to show their musical prowess onstage. Like Cream before them, they embraced spontaneity and the art of improvisation thanks to Jimmy Page. By the time they hit LA, the band played the now infamous Whiskey a Go Go alongside Alice Cooper. This was the start of the great love affair between the band and LA. They loved each other. And with that came the whole LA groupie scene, which some members of the band embraced very quickly! As their debut album had not been released yet, the band were playing a largely unknown setlist, although advance white-label promo copies of the album were quickly distributed to all the influential FM radio stations that were starting to build up in the US. This helped the band to get better known, especially in some of the smaller cities in the US. Ultimately, though, it was talk of their amazing live performances that got the band noticed. From LA, the band moved to San Francisco to play at the prestigious Fillmore West, where they played two shows a night. This was their first turning-point event, impressing the hip audiences of San Francisco. The Fillmore West, operated by promoter Bill Graham, had a relatively open policy to the length of time the bands could play. This gave Led Zeppelin an opportunity to experiment more than they had so far on the tour. The crowds loved it and the band realized for the first time that things could take off in a big way for them.

Bizarrely, the popular *Rolling Stone* magazine took a dislike to the band, giving their concerts and albums unfavorable reviews. They had already crucified Eric Clapton and Cream in May 1968 and now saw fit to do the same to Led Zeppelin. It would not be until 1975 that they finally relented and gave the band the positive credit they deserved.

Another turning point for the band was when they played the other venue owned by Bill Graham, the Fillmore East in New York. The first of two shows was a showcase for them with the Atlantic hard hitters present in the audience. Despite being a supporting act, and putting up with the usual disadvantages associated with that, Led Zeppelin pulled out all the stops and floored the place along with Bill Graham and everyone from Atlantic Records in attendance. They were brought back for an unprecedented two encores. The crowd just did not want them to leave the stage. It was an evening that reverberated in rock circles for years. Headliners Iron Butterfly had the unenviable task of trying to follow them.

Led Zeppelin's first US tour ended on 15 February 1969 in Miami, after which the band headed home in an optimistic frame of mind. They might not have taken America over by storm quite yet, but their future now looked decidedly bright.

26 December 1968, Auditorium Arena, Denver, Colorado (Led Zeppelin's first ever US concert was as an un-billed support slot opening for Vanilla Fudge and Spirit)

For their first US appearance, Led Zeppelin's name was not even mentioned on the adverts for the gig in Denver. It was a show featuring Spirit and Vanilla Fudge, who were co-headlining. Concert promoter Barry Fey recalled getting a phone call from Vanilla Fudge's booking agent, Ron Terry, about a week before the show, asking him to add another group to the already sold-out Denver date. Not surprisingly, Fey refused. Terry tried again and explained that the group, Led Zeppelin, was going to be huge and it would be good business to offer them an opening slot. Fey still refused to budge. In a last-bid

Press advert for Led Zeppelin's appearance at the Seattle Center Arena in Seattle, Washington.

effort, Terry called him one last time to explain that Vanilla Fudge had agreed to take $750 of the money Fey was going to pay them and give it to Led Zeppelin if he agreed pay them $750 too. Fey figured that if Vanilla Fudge was prepared to offer a band nobody had heard of a part of their fee, this band must be something that's worth looking at. So he made the deal with Terry and booked Led Zeppelin for their first North American show for a mere out-of-pocket sum of $750!

❝ I introduced the band to a smattering of polite applause. Then Robert Plant let it rip and everybody in the audience was stunned. Frankly, I don't know how Spirit went on after that. You don't have to be a genius to know Zeppelin was going to be a smash. People were going crazy! The next morning I got a call from Max Floyd, the program director at the Denver FM rock station, KLZ. 'Who did you have on last night? Our phone lines are jammed!' The band had given me a white-label copy of their album, which hadn't been released yet. I took it to the radio station and they played it continuously, all day. ❞
—PROMOTER BARRY FAY (In his autobiography, *Backstage Past*)

❝ Blues oriented (although not a blues band), hyped electric, the full routine in mainstream rock—done powerfully, gustily, unifiedly, inventively and swingingly by the end of their set. Singer Robert Plant—a cut above average in style, but no special appeal in sound. Guitarist Jimmy Page of Yardbirds fame—exceptionally fine. Used a violin bow on the guitar strings in a couple of tunes with resultant interesting, well integrated effects. Bassist John Paul Jones—solid, involved, contributing. John Bonham—a very effective drummer, but uninventive, unsubtle and unclimactic, just an uneventful solo. ❞
—REVIEW IN THE *DENVER POST* (29 December 1968)

27 December 1968, Seattle Center Arena, Seattle, Washington (8:00 p.m. Led Zeppelin and Floating Bridge provided support for Vanilla Fudge)

28 December 1968, Pacific Coliseum, Vancouver, British Columbia, Canada (7:00 p.m. Led Zeppelin and the Trials of Jason Hoover provided support for Vanilla Fudge)

29 December 1968, Portland Civic Auditorium, Portland, Oregon (7:30 p.m. Billed as Special Guest: Led Zeppelin, featuring Jimmy Paige, opening for Vanilla Fudge. At this stage of their career, Led Zeppelin were still unknown and spelling mistakes were a common occurrence)

Press advert for Led Zeppelin's appearance at the Kennedy Pavilion in Spokane, Washington.

30 December 1968, John F. Kennedy Memorial Pavilion, Gonzaga University, Spokane, Washington (8:00 p.m. Apparently a band called Len Zefflin opened for Vanilla Fudge. It was clear that the company who put the advert together did not know the band)

SETLIST: The Train Kept A Rollin' / I Can't Quit You Baby / As Long As I Have You (including Fresh Garbage, Bags' Groove, Mockingbird) / Dazed And Confused / White Summer / How Many More Times (including The Hunter) / Pat's Delight

To date this is the only known audience recording of Led Zeppelin from 1968. The quality is surprisingly good for the era and gives the listener a rare opportunity to hear the raw power and intensity of the band who were only a few days into their first ever US tour. Robert Plant explains to the audience that due to the very cold conditions in Spokane, the band's equipment had to be heated up with portable heaters!

2   1968 Recording Sessions

GUEST SESSIONS FOR P. J. PROBY

LANSDOWNE STUDIOS
Lansdowne House, Lansdowne Road, Holland Park, London W11

Front sleeve of P. J. Proby's *Three Week Hero* album with members of Led Zeppelin appearing on various tracks. The band were still called the Yardbirds at this stage.

AUGUST 1968

Great opportunity to hear Led Zeppelin's first studio session as guest artists for P. J. Proby's *Three Week Hero* album. John Paul Jones had been hired by producer Steve Rowland to do arrangements and play bass. Rowland also agreed he could bring along members of the new band to play on various tracks. Jones ended up playing bass on the entire album as well as arranging ten of the album's twelve tracks. Jimmy Page plays on at least six numbers. But the real attraction here are the two numbers with pretty much the whole of Led Zeppelin, the medley "Jim's Blues/George Wallace Is Rollin' In This Mornin'," which is the last track on side two of the album. The medley is a blues jam with Led Zeppelin as the backing band, featuring Robert Plant on harmonica and P. J. Proby on vocals. The other track with Led Zeppelin did not actually make the album, but was a B-side to "The Day Lorraine Came Down." Titled "Mery Hoppkins Never Had Days Like These," which is basically an extended instrumental jam with P. J. Proby and Steve Rowland overdubbing spoken vocals over the top of it.

Jimmy Page plays acoustic guitar, electric guitar, and pedal steel guitar on the album and appears on "The Day That Lorraine Came Down," "Empty Bottles," "It's Too Good To Last," and "Today I Killed A Man." The medley "Jim's Blues/George Wallace Is Rollin' In This Mornin'" features all four members, with Robert Plant playing harmonica and tambourine. The single's B-side, "Mery Hoppkins Never Had Days Like These," which was edited down from twelve minutes, also includes the band.

The *Three Week Hero* album, as well as the single's B-side, "Mery Hoppkins Never Had Days Like These," are fascinating pieces of musical history that are worthy of attention for anyone wanting to hear the band in its embryonic stage a few weeks away from going to the studio to record their first album.

MERY HOPPKINS NEVER HAD DAYS LIKE THESE (Steve Rowland) Available on B-side of "The Day That Lorraine Came Down" 7-inch single (Liberty LBF15152 released November 1968) / *Your Time Is Gonna Come: Roots of Led Zeppelin* CD (Sanctuary label, released August 2007).

66 P. J. Proby's new single, 'Mery Hoppkins Never Had Days Like These,' is a spoof of the popular singer recorded by Proby and some of his friends; it has been cut down from twelve minutes to seven and a half. 99

—*DISC AND MUSIC ECHO* (12 October 1968)

JIM'S BLUES/GEORGE WALLACE IS ROLLIN' IN THIS MORNIN' AVAILABLE ON THREE WEEK HERO ALBUM (Liberty LBS 83219 released April 1969) / CD BGOBGOCD87 released October 1993) / *Your Time Is Gonna Come: Roots of Led Zeppelin* CD (Sanctuary label, released August 2007).

PRODUCER: STEVE ROWLAND
ENGINEER: MIKE WEIGHELL

66 As Jim (P. J. Proby) is a good friend of mine and has been for many years, producing this album for him was a real pleasure. We had many laughs during the time we spent in the studio. My group, The Family Dogg, did all the vocal backing. As a matter of fact, we used one of the tracks from our album in order for Jim to record his Johnny Cash impression. It was released as a single in Holland and went to number one in the Dutch charts.

All the guys that would later become Led Zeppelin played on the entire album. John Paul Jones did most of the arrangements. I had been using all the guys on most of my previous productions. They all played on the Family Dogg album, *A Way of Life*.

As far as *Three Week Hero* goes, the sessions with Jim Proby, Jimmy Page, John Paul Jones, John Bonham, and Robert Plant were one of the most enjoyable recording sessions ever. It brought back memories of the good old days in Hollywood with P. J. Proby, then known as Jett Powers. Great times were had by all. 99

—**STEVE ROWLAND** (Producer)

66 Lansdowne was one of the best of London studios at that time, liked by producers and musicians alike. Consequently I considered myself privileged to be there, working with and listening to the cream of session musicians while getting paid. We had met and worked with Jimmy Page and John Baldwin (John Paul Jones) many times on all sorts of sessions over the years, both at Lansdowne and other studios, so to see them on this album was no surprise. As you will see on the album notes, Steve Rowland had booked the best available, Alan Parker and Clem Cattini included.

I was familiar with Steve's ways of working, having just recently recorded his Family Dogg album; he knew what he wanted and how to achieve that. Both sessions were recorded on 8-track. There were two separate albums, Family Dogg first and multi-session for both of them. I can't tell you how many sessions altogether. We would have recorded music first, then instrumental overdubs, then vocal tracks. These guys were all supreme at what they did, just listen to the album! I saw them as session musicians, not members of a

supergroup. After all the first Led Zeppelin album was released at the end of March '69 and this one on 8 April '69, so we had no time to consider what Led Zeppelin were up to. 99

—**MICHAEL WEIGHELL** (Engineer)

66 When I got to the studio that day, there was what they called 'the New Yardbirds.' There was Jimmy Page, lead guitar player, a great lead guitar player by now, and John Bonham and another guy, John Paul Jones. Anyway, we recorded that album, I think it was in two days. We even undershot, we recorded it with about thirty-five minutes left over, and so Rowland yelled down, 'Why don't you all busk it? We shouldn't waste the studio time.' I told the boys, 'Y'all start picking and I'll write as you pick.' So the three last numbers on the album [the medley], I just made up as the boys played. 99

—**P. J. PROBY** (Unknown interview)

66 I was committed to doing all the arrangements for the album. As we were talking about rehearsing at the time, I thought it would be a handy source of income. I had to book a band anyway, so I thought I'd book everybody I knew. 99

—**JOHN PAUL JONES** (Talking to Chris Welch of *Melody Maker*)

LED ZEPPELIN SESSIONS

OLYMPIC SOUND STUDIOS
Studio 1, 117 Church Road, Barnes, London, SW13

27 SEPTEMBER 1968-18 OCTOBER 1968

Olympic Studios were located in what had been a large derelict television studio previously owned by Guild TV. Located at 117-123 Church Road, Barnes, the building was redeveloped by renowned recording engineers Keith Grant and Dick Swettenham in 1966 after their old premises in Carton Street were due for demolition. Grant saw the new building as the ideal recording venue, and the new Olympic company duly purchased it. The architecturally attractive early-20th-century Byfeld Hall building had in the past been both a theater and a cinema at different times. The new Olympic recording studios interior was built to be the best and compete with the best in the world, both of which were certainly achieved. Many classic albums were recorded here by some of the biggest names in the music industry. Jimmy was familiar with the studios, and he knew what sounds he would be able to achieve there. It made sense for Led Zeppelin to record their first album here. It was mainly recorded in Studio 1, a large room measuring 60" x 40' x 30', which had been the cinema space in the early days of the building. The room floor was polished wood with hessian cloth draped over the ceiling, giving great acoustics. The vocal booth was located on one side of the studio floor, and the control room, which was the old projection room of the cinema, overlooked Studio 1. The control room housed the 24' x 8' x 8' channel recorder.

The band entered the studio very well prepared and ready to record. They had perfected most of the numbers on tour as well as at rehearsals before and after the tour at Jimmy Page's home in Pangbourne. As Page was financing the sessions, they had to be well prepared to minimize the expensive studio costs. That preparation paid off as in the

Iconic front cover of Led Zeppelin's debut album. A few of the first copies came out with turquoise lettering and quickly disappeared after being replaced with the more common orange lettering.

end the album was recorded in less than 40 hours over a period of a few weeks at a cost of around £2000, which was still a lot of money in 1968. The album was essentially cut live with only a few overdubs and a handful of takes for each number. The sessions were so concise that only a few tracks were left over. In answer to a *Melody Maker* reader's question (9 November 1968, issue), Jimmy Page explained how he achieved his guitar sounds: "The sustain is achieved by volume combined with the use of a Tone Bender. It is virtually a standard model, but with a few modifications carried out by it's inventor, Gary Hurst, which provide more sustain and a harmonic overtone. My guitar is a Fender Telecaster, given to me by Jeff Beck. I have wired the pick-ups together, creating a different sound, which cannot be obtained on the new models. I use an ordinary violin bow on the guitar, giving a little more tension on the horsehair than one would employ for violin playing, plus lots more rosin." Page played his guitar through

a 12-inch speaker Supro amplifier for the recording of *Led Zeppelin 1*.

Jimmy Page asked Glyn Johns if he would be interested in engineering the session for the first album. He agreed, but as there would not be a producer in the control room, Glyn felt he would end up producing some of the album as a matter of course, and as such wanted a percentage of retail price royalties. This was normal practice at the time for producers, but he was hired as the engineer and no formal agreement was drawn up to say the contrary. When the album was released, Jimmy Page took the production credit and Glyn was paid for his engineering work. In fairness, Jimmy did not need a producer, as he was the one with the vision and had all the required production capabilities. So, as creative as the sessions were, there were occasions when Jimmy and Glyn locked horns over production decisions, at which point Jimmy had to remind Glyn who was producing the sessions and who was engineering them.

Olympic Studio logs from 27 September 1968 show that they initially recorded under the name of the Yardbirds. Some of the first numbers recorded were "Babe I'm Gonna Leave You" and "You Shook Me." Final master mixes were done at a later date in October and used for *Led Zeppelin I*. Although Page used his Fender Telecaster throughout the sessions, he did use a borrowed Gibson Flying V, which he used on "You Shook Me." You can hear the fatter tone clearly on the recording. He used another borrowed guitar, a Gibson J-200 acoustic belonging to Mickie Most, on "Black Mountain Side" and "Babe I'm Gonna Leave You." Throughout the album, Jimmy Page showed his guitar mastery, whether it be on acoustic, pedal steel, or electric.

How good was this album? Well, the fact that today it still sounds as fresh and exciting as it did on the day of its release in 1968 really says it all. Led Zeppelin were never going to be a band with a two-dimensional sound. The scene was already full of those types of bands. Instead, they would pursue a more textural path with many layers.

27 September 1968

BABE I'M GONNA LEAVE YOU (Anne Bredon / Jimmy Page / Robert Plant) Originally released on 12 January 1969 on *Led Zeppelin.*

> JIMMY PAGE: MID-'60S GIBSON J-200 ACOUSTIC GUITAR, FENDER TELECASTER GUITAR, PEDAL STEEL GUITAR
> ROBERT PLANT: VOCALS
> JOHN PAUL JONES: BASS
> JOHN BONHAM: DRUMS

YOU SHOOK ME (Willie Dixon) Originally released on 12 January 1969 on *Led Zeppelin.*

> JIMMY PAGE: GIBSON FLYING V GUITAR, FENDER TELECASTER GUITAR
> ROBERT PLANT: VOCALS, HARMONICA
> JOHN PAUL JONES: BASS, HAMMOND ORGAN
> JOHN BONHAM: DRUMS

3 October 1968

YOUR TIME IS GONNA COME (Jimmy Page / John Paul Jones) Originally released on 12 January 1969 on *Led Zeppelin.*

> JIMMY PAGE: MID-'60S GIBSON J-200 ACOUSTIC GUITAR, FENDER 800 PEDAL STEEL GUITAR, FENDER TELECASTER GUITAR
> ROBERT PLANT: VOCALS
> JOHN PAUL JONES: BASS, HAMMOND ORGAN
> JOHN BONHAM: DRUMS

SUGAR MAMA (Jimmy Page / Robert Plant) Available on the companion disc of the super-deluxe edition box set of *Coda* released July 2015.

> JIMMY PAGE: FENDER TELECASTER GUITAR
> JOHN PAUL JONES: BASS
> JOHN BONHAM: DRUMS

A MAN I KNOW (later re-titled "Good Times Bad Times") (Jimmy Page / John Paul Jones / John Bonham) Originally released on 12 January 1969 on *Led Zeppelin.*

> JIMMY PAGE: FENDER TELECASTER GUITAR, BACKING VOCALS
> ROBERT PLANT: LEAD VOCALS
> JOHN PAUL JONES: BASS, BACKING VOCALS
> JOHN BONHAM: DRUMS, BACKING VOCALS

BABE I'M GONNA LEAVE YOU (Anne Bredon / Jimmy Page / Robert Plant) (Overdubs) Originally released on 12 January 1969 on *Led Zeppelin.*

> JIMMY PAGE: MID-'60S GIBSON J-200 ACOUSTIC GUITAR, FENDER TELECASTER GUITAR, PEDAL STEEL GUITAR
> ROBERT PLANT: VOCALS
> JOHN PAUL JONES: BASS
> JOHN BONHAM: DRUMS

TOO GOOD (later re-titled "Communication Breakdown") (Jimmy Page / John Paul Jones / John Bonham) Originally released on 12 January 1969 on *Led Zeppelin.*

> JIMMY PAGE: FENDER TELECASTER GUITAR
> ROBERT PLANT: VOCALS
> JOHN PAUL JONES: BASS, ORGAN
> JOHN BONHAM: DRUMS

HOW MANY MORE TIMES (Jimmy Page / John Paul Jones / John Bonham) Originally released on 12 January 1969 on *Led Zeppelin.*

> JIMMY PAGE: FENDER TELECASTER GUITAR, VIOLIN BOW
> ROBERT PLANT: VOCALS
> JOHN PAUL JONES: BASS, ORGAN BASS
> JOHN BONHAM: DRUMS

DAZED AND CONFUSED (Jimmy Page) Originally released on 12 January 1969 on *Led Zeppelin.*

> JIMMY PAGE: FENDER TELECASTER GUITAR, BOW
> ROBERT PLANT: VOCALS
> JOHN PAUL JONES: BASS
> JOHN BONHAM: DRUMS

BLUES I unreleased

> JIMMY PAGE: FENDER TELECASTER GUITAR
> JOHN PAUL JONES: BASS
> JOHN BONHAM: DRUMS

10 October 1968

One of the final sessions was done on this day. The song was originally recorded in honor of the American songwriter and producer Bert Berns, who had died in December 1967. Jimmy had known him well during his days as a session guitarist and respected him. "Tribute to Bert Burns" (note that the spelling of "Burns" is the one used on the original tape box in 1968) is based on a song he had written for Hoagy Lands in 1964 called "Baby Come On Home." Solomon Burke also released the song in 1965. The band later changed/corrected the name to the original title, giving Berns a writing credit. Robert Plant shows a more mellow side and the number has a very soulful groove that fitted the Atlantic label very well. Jimmy Page plays a Leslie guitar and John Paul Jones plays piano and a Hammond organ. Plant also records background vocals. It was left off the album, perhaps wisely as it did not really sit well with the other material. It was eventually officially released on the *Led Zeppelin Remasters Box Set 2* and was also included exclusively on the extended version of *Coda* found in the *Complete Studio Recordings* box set in September 1993.

TRIBUTE TO BERT BURNS (aka "Baby Come On Home") (Jimmy Page / Robert Plant / Bert Berns) (Take 1) unreleased

TRIBUTE TO BERT BURNS (aka "Baby Come On Home") (Jimmy Page / Robert Plant / Bert Berns) (Take 2) unreleased

BABY COME ON HOME (Jimmy Page / Robert Plant / Bert Berns) (Take 1, instrumental with count-in, stopped at 1:12) unreleased

BABY COME ON HOME (Jimmy Page / Robert Plant / Bert Berns) (Take 2, instrumental with count-in, stopped at 1:07) unreleased

BABY COME ON HOME (Jimmy Page / Robert Plant / Bert Berns) (Take 3, completed master with vocals) *Led Zeppelin Remasters Box Set 2* Atlantic label 7567-82477-2 released September 1993 / also included exclusively on the version of *Coda* found in the *Complete Studio Recordings* box set Atlantic label 7 82526-2 released September 1993. Worth noting that the regular version of *Coda* sold independently of the box does not have any bonus tracks. Available on the companion disc of the super-deluxe edition box set of *Coda* released July 2015.

15 October 1968

BLACK MOUNTAIN SIDE (Jimmy Page) Originally released on 12 January 1969 on *Led Zeppelin*

JIMMY PAGE: MID-'60S GIBSON J-200 ACOUSTIC GUITAR
VIRAM JASANI: TABLAS

I CAN'T QUIT YOU BABY (Willie Dixon) Originally released on 12 January 1969 on *Led Zeppelin*

JIMMY PAGE: FENDER TELECASTER GUITAR
ROBERT PLANT: VOCALS
JOHN PAUL JONES: BASS
JOHN BONHAM: DRUMS
PRODUCER: JIMMY PAGE
ENGINEER: GLYN JOHNS

During the session for their first album, Jimmy Page used Supro amps, along with a Fender 800 pedal steel, the violin bow, a Vox wah-wah, and a Sola-Sound Tone-Bender fuzzbox.

3   Establishing a Reputation

JANUARY 1969

1 January 1969, Salem Armory Auditorium, Salem, Oregon (show canceled because of bad weather conditions)

2 January 1969, Whisky a Go Go, Los Angeles, California (Show billed as Led Zeppelin featuring: Jimmy Page formerly of the Yardbirds. Co-headliner was Alice Cooper)

66 I think we ended up flipping a coin before the shows to see who would go on first. . . . That's how unknown we both were. 99

—ALICE COOPER

3 January 1969, Whisky a Go Go, Los Angeles, California (Show billed as Led Zeppelin featuring: Jimmy Page formerly of the Yardbirds. Co-headliner was Alice Cooper)

4 January 1969, Whisky a Go Go, Los Angeles, California (Show billed as Led Zeppelin featuring: Jimmy Page formerly of the Yardbirds. Co-headliner was Alice Cooper)

5 January 1969, Whisky a Go Go, Los Angeles (Show billed as Led Zeppelin featuring: Jimmy Page formerly of the Yardbirds. Co-headliner was Alice Cooper)

SETLIST: As Long As I Have You (including Fresh Garbage, Summertime Blues, Bag's Groove, Mockingbird) / I Can't Quit You Baby / The Train Kept A Rollin' / Babe I'm Gonna Leave You / Dazed And Confused / Killing Floor (including Blues With A Feeling) / For Your Love

A recording of this intimate show circulates and reveals the band playing in a less improvisational way than they would in the future. Page has certainly got his chops together despite having been very ill with flu and does experiment with certain effects during the show. The whole band is on form but had to cancel the remaining shows scheduled at the Whisky due to several band members coming down with the flu.

Poster for Led Zeppelin's four-night appearance at the Fillmore West in San Francisco. The band pretty much sealed their reputation on the West Coast during these shows, receiving standing ovations at each concert.

Press advert for Led Zeppelin's appearances at Bill Graham's Fillmore East in New York on 31 January 1969 and 1 February 1969.

66 We got here [Los Angeles] and did the Whisky and I was really, really ill. In fact the doctor said I was insane to do the set. The first night I did it I had a temperature of 104, but he'd given me the shots and things so I was able to make it. We managed to finish the whole engagement without letting the guy down, but of course he docked us money because we only did one long set each night, we couldn't do two. It's not the greatest paying job in the world anyway, and he knocked money off, we were all really down about that, as you can imagine. 99

—JIMMY PAGE

(Interviewed in *Rock* magazine, October 1970)

9 January 1969 Fillmore West, San Francisco, California (Two shows. Taj Mahal opens followed by Led Zeppelin and headliners Country Joe & the Fish. Introductions by Bill Graham)

Like Cream before them, San Francisco's Fillmore West sealed Led Zeppelin's reputation. The crowd at each show was beyond ecstatic and it was clear that the band had "arrived." Luckily some fans made recordings at the shows and are now part of the band's rich musical history. The recordings reveal how much they had grown in a relatively short span of time. Page was using two Rickenbacker Transonic TS200 amps on this tour, and these expensive amps had a pretty

unique sound, so it's easy to recognize any recordings from this period. Although the Rickenbacker was arguably a better amp than Fender and Vox for live work at the time, they could not compete with the awesome power of Jim Marshall's amps, which would be Page's new choice at the end of the US tour.

10 January 1969, Fillmore West, San Francisco, California (2 shows. Taj Mahal opens followed by Led Zeppelin and headliners Country Joe & The Fish. Introductions by Bill Graham)

SETLIST FOR SET 1: The Train Kept A Rollin' / I Can't Quit You Baby / As Long As I Have You (including Fresh Garbage, Bags' Groove) / Dazed And Confused / How Many More Times (including a guitar improvisation based on San Francisco theme, Dream Lover, The Hunter, Tobacco Road)

SETLIST FOR SET 2: White Summer / Killing Floor (including improvisations based on What Is And What Should Never Be and Bring It On Home that would later be recorded for Led Zeppelin II) / You Shook Me / Pat's Delight / Babe I'm Gonna Leave You / Communication Breakdown / For Your Love

Press advert for Led Zeppelin's appearance at the Boston Tea Party, Boston, Massachusetts.

Among the many highlights is a rousing ten-minute version of the Yardbirds classic "For Your Love." Robert Plant shows he has a sense of humor by introducing the number as "a thing Keith Relf had something to do with. Do you remember him? Works for Hammersmith Council now!" Ouch!

11 January 1969, Fillmore West, San Francisco, California (Two shows. Taj Mahal opens followed by Led Zeppelin and headliners Country Joe & the Fish. Introductions by Bill Graham)

Recordings of the show exist and you can hear that there were quite a few technical issues this evening resulting in long pauses between songs. Plant is showing signs of strain in his vocals, but it does not seem to impair his abilities surprisingly, or his humor when he tells the crowd, "I tell you what. This is the third night and we've decided that we're gonna come and live here, 'cos you're so nice! If we don't make it, then the police in England would rather we'd stay there!"

SETLIST FOR SET 1: I Can't Quit You Baby (including Don't Know Which Way To Go) / Dazed And Confused / You Shook Me / How Many More Times / Communication Breakdown

12 January 1969, Fillmore West, San Francisco, California (Two shows. Taj Mahal opens followed by Led Zeppelin and headliners Country Joe & the Fish. Introductions by Bill Graham)

SETLIST FOR SET 1: As Long As I Have You (including Fresh Garbage, Mockingbird, Bags' Groove, Baby Please Don't Go) / I Can't Quit You Baby (Don't Know Which Way To Go) / Dazed And Confused / Babe I'm Gonna Leave You / Communication Breakdown / You Shook Me

SETLIST FOR SET 2: White Summer / Black Mountain Side / The Train Kept A Rollin' / Pat's Delight / How Many More Times (including The Hunter) / Killing Floor (including The Lemon Song)

13 January 1969, Fox Theatre, San Diego, California (no evidence that this show took place)

15 January 1969, Iowa Memorial Union, Main Lounge, Iowa City, Iowa (8:00 p.m. Support from the Mother Blues Band. The concert was organized at a fairly late stage as a replacement for Count Basie, who had to cancel. It was a bad winter and Led Zeppelin encountered a snowstorm on their way to the show. As a result, they were late to arrive at the venue. On top of that, their equipment had not arrived, but they had most of their instruments except

John Bonham's drum kit, which was stuck in the equipment truck. They had to borrow the Mother Blues Band's equipment.)

SETLIST NOT KNOWN BUT PROBABLY CONSISTED OF THESE NUMBERS: Train Kept A Rollin' / I Can't Quit You Baby / Dazed And Confused / Killing Floor / White Summer / Black Mountain Side / Communication Breakdown / How Many More Times

" I called Jimmy out in Iowa this week, prior to his first university date in that state. The group had been completely hemmed in by snow and ice, making the 100-mile drive from the closest airport a dangerous trek across treacherous roads. 'Yeah, really, it's been incredible,' he said. 'We're all so knocked out. All the kids keep telling us they've heard the album and how quickly can they get it and all that. And we haven't even done half the tour yet!'"
—JUNE HARRIS (New Musical Express, January 1969)

16 January 1969, New Orleans, Louisiana (no evidence that this show took place)

17 January 1969, Grande Ballroom, Detroit, Michigan (8:30 p.m. Spelling mistakes were still happening on the adverts. Tonight's show was billed erroneously as Led Zeptlin. Support from Linn County and Lawrence Blues Band)

SETLIST NOT KNOWN BUT PROBABLY CONSISTED OF THESE NUMBERS: Train Kept A Rollin' / I Can't Quit You Baby / Dazed And Confused / Killing Floor / White Summer / Black Mountain Side / Communication Breakdown / How Many More Times

18 January 1969, Grande Ballroom, Detroit, Michigan (8:30 p.m. Spelling mistakes were still happening on the adverts. Tonight's show was billed erroneously as Led Zeptlin. Support from Target)

SETLIST NOT KNOWN BUT PROBABLY CONSISTED OF THESE NUMBERS: Train Kept A Rollin' / I Can't Quit You Baby / Dazed And Confused / Killing Floor / White Summer / Black Mountain Side / Communication Breakdown / How Many More Times

19 January 1969, Grande Ballroom, Detroit, Michigan (Once again the band's name is misspelled as Led Zeptlin. Support from Wind)

SETLIST NOT KNOWN BUT PROBABLY CONSISTED OF THESE NUMBERS: Train Kept A Rollin' / I Can't Quit You Baby / Dazed And Confused / Killing Floor / White Summer / Black Mountain Side / Communication Breakdown / How Many More Times

❝ When the first tune was over ('Train Kept a Rollin'), there wasn't much reaction. As they went through 'I Can't Quit You Baby,' we could sense something lacking. The next one took our minds off the playing, through Jimmy Page's use of the bow on his guitar. The sound was weird and mind-bending and yet somehow marvelously controlled. During 'Killing Floor,' the real problem became evident. Each member of the group was on a separate riff, not at all together. At times, Jimmy's guitar and Robert's voice blended beautifully enabling the music to really communicate, but other than that, they were playing different things simultaneously. Jimmy later played a solo, 'White Summer,' after a change of guitars. It was melodious and resembled sitar playing at points, but was in no way as spectacular or complicated as made to look. A great favorite of mine, 'Communication Breakdown,' didn't nearly equal the quality of the album. After hearing the album, I was even further disappointed in the Zeppelin's performance. The album is together and far superior to their live performance. The set finished, but the lights were turned back off and they played one last slow bluesy number that was finally together. ❞

— **PAT BRENT** (Review in *Creem* magazine, March 1969)

20 January 1969, Wheaton Youth Centre, Wheaton, Maryland (No evidence that this show took place.)

21 January 1969, Hunt Armory, Pittsburgh, Pennsylvania (No evidence that this show took place.)

22 January 1969, Cleveland, Ohio (No evidence that this show took place.)

23 January 1969, Boston Tea Party, Boston, Massachusetts (Two sets. Support from the Raven. MC Charie the Masterblaster Daniels introduced both acts.)

SETLIST FOR SET 1: The Train Kept A Rollin' / I Can't Quit You Baby / As Long As I Have You (including Fresh Garbage, Bag's Groove) / Dazed And Confused / You Shook Me / How Many More Times (including The Hunter)

As soon as "The Train Kept A Rollin'" finished, Jimmy Page had to change a string on his guitar. Robert Plant took the time to chat to the crowd: "It's great to be in Boston. According to Jimmy, it's one of the best places he's ever played! I think, right now, in the shops there's an album called *Led Zeppelin*. I don't know whether it's out here yet. Is it out? You see, in one place it comes out one day and another place, three weeks later. On this album we've tried to do a cross section of everything we've got into and we've included some blues because that's where it all comes from!"

24 January 1969, Boston Tea Party, Boston, Massachusetts (Two sets. Support from the Raven. MC Charie the Masterblaster Daniels introduced both acts.)

25 January 1969, Boston Tea Party, Boston, Massachusetts (Two sets. Support from the Raven. MC Charie the Masterblaster Daniels introduced both acts.)

26 January 1969, Boston Tea Party, Boston, Massachusetts (Two sets. Support from the Raven. MC Charie the Masterblaster Daniels introduced both acts.)

SETLIST FOR SET 1: The Train Kept A Rollin' / I Can't Quit You Baby / Killing Floor (including The Lemon Song) / Dazed And Confused (including Shapes Of Things) / You Shook Me / Communication Breakdown

SETLIST FOR SET 2: White Summer / Black Mountain Side / Babe I'm Gonna Leave You / Pat's Delight / How Many More Times (including For Your Love)

Also probably played: Long Tall Sally / Something Else / C'mon Everybody / I Saw Her Standing There / Please Please Me / Roll Over Beethoven / Johnny B. Goode

One of the best shows from 1969. The band are on fire and the crowd is wildly responsive. This show has become legendary over the years with rumors stating that the show lasted around four hours. Seems highly unlikely, but they probably did play an extra-long encore consisting of various cover versions. Until a complete tape surfaces, we will never know for sure.

27 January 1969, Municipal Auditorium, Springfield, Massachusetts (there is no evidence that this show took place)

29 January 1969, Electric Factory, Philadelphia, Pennsylvania (there is no evidence that this show took place)

31 January 1969, Fillmore East, New York City, New York (Two shows at 8:00 p.m. and 11:30 p.m. Porter's Popular Preachers are the support this evening followed by Led Zeppelin. Headliners are Iron Butterfly. Bill Graham introduced all the acts. The Move had originally been billed as the opening act, but had to cancel. Iron Butterfly canceled their second show tonight and were replaced by the Edwin Hawkins Singers.

SETLIST FOR SET 1: The Train Kept A Rollin' / I Can't Quit You Baby / Dazed And Confused / White Summer / Black Mountain Side / Pat's Delight / How Many More Times (including The Hunter) / You Shook Me / Communication Breakdown

FEBRUARY 1969

1 February 1969, Fillmore East, New York City, New York
(Two shows at 8:00 p.m. and 11:30 p.m. Porter's Popular
Preachers are the support this evening followed by Led
Zeppelin. Headliners are Iron Butterfly. Bill Graham
introduced all the acts. The Move had originally been billed
as the opening act, but had to cancel. The first show was
delayed because John Paul Jones had forgotten to take
his bass guitar from his hotel room. The band had to start
without him and open with Jimmy Page's solo piece "White
Summer.")

SETLIST FOR SET 1: White Summer / Black Mountain Side /
The Train Kept A Rollin' / I Can't Quit You Baby / Pat's Delight
/ How Many More Times (including Dazed And Confused, The
Hunter) / Communication Breakdown

SETLIST FOR SET 2: The Train Kept A Rollin' / I Can't Quit
You Baby / Dazed And Confused / Pat's Delight / How
Many More Times (including The Hunter) / You Shook Me /
Communication Breakdown

Press advert for Led Zeppelin's appearance at Steve Paul's Scene
club in New York.

Advert for Led Zeppelin's appearance at Toronto's Rock Pile Club.

After Bill Graham's introduction, the first show started
unusually with an announcement from Robert Plant.
"We're sorry about the delay but because we're all a
bit stupid, we forgot the bass player's guitar! Would
you believe that! So we're gonna open up without the
bass player. We're gonna feature Jimmy Page. This is
a thing that was very popular when he was with The
Yardbirds." Jimmy then played his solo pieces, "White
Summer" / "Black Mountain Side" by which point
John Paul Jones' bass has arrived and the band kick the
show into gear with an explosive version of "The Train
Kept A Rollin'." The band are in top form, so much
so that an audience member has to shout out, "Who
gives a shit about the Butterfly?" Iron Butterfly were
headlining, so it can't have been pleasant for them.
The second set was even better and the band are super
tight and powerful.

2 February 1969, The Rock Pile, Toronto, Ontario, Canada
(Two sets from 8:00 p.m. Billed as Led Zeppelin featuring
Jimmy Page. Support from Teegarden and Van Winkle.
Ritchie Yorke introduced all the acts and the light show was
provided by Catharsis.)

SETLIST: The Train Kept A Rollin' / I Can't Quit You Baby / Dazed And Confused / You Shook Me / Killing Floor (including The Lemon Song, Think You Need A Shot [The Needle] / How Many More Times (including Fever, The Hunter, Money [That's What I Want])

66 Advance airplay and reviews of the debut Led Zeppelin album (to be issued on Atlantic shortly) brought over 1,200 people to the Rock Pile. They expected a lot, and few were disappointed. Considering the group was only formed a few months back, it's remarkably tight and together. Led Zeppelin is not Cream, nor will it fill the spot left behind by Cream. Nobody will. But the Zeppelin outfit has a thing going of its own and there's little doubt that thing is going to be very successful. Page came off as the finest group guitarist to emerge since Clapton. Already, he is way above Jeff Beck, Mike Bloomfield and Elvin Bishop. His spotlighted work, including riffs with the violin bow, was executed expertly, without pomp or pretension. Singer Plant is from the English blues school—hard, angry, defiant, gutsy. He could well develop into one of the big name group singers of the year.

The concert is introduced by Richie York, 'Led Zeppelin is going to be doing two sets tonight . . . in between we've got Teegarden and Van Winkle. Next Friday and Saturday night—Albert King, don't forget and B.B. King at Massey Hall on February 14th . . . but right now . . . their first Canadian appearance, and there's going to be a lot more of them . . . Atlantic recording stars—Led Zeppelin!' The band then proceed to rip the place apart with their dynamic playing. All members are playing to the height of their abilities and received the appropriate crowd response. 99

—RICHIE YORKE

(Review in "Pop Scene," *G&M,* February 1969)

3 February 1969, Steve Paul's the Scene Club, New York City, New York (Billed as Jimmy Paige [spelling as on advert] and England's most exciting new group Led Zeppelin, and on a second add as Lead Zeppelin [again, wrong spelling as on advert]. The show was canceled because John Bonham had to return to England because his son, Jason, was ill.)

4 February 1969, Steve Paul's the Scene Club, New York City, New York (Billed as Jimmy Paige [spelling as on advert] and England's most exciting new group Led Zeppelin, and on a second add as Lead Zeppelin. The show was canceled because John Bonham had to return to England because his son, Jason, was ill.)

5 February 1969, Steve Paul's the Scene Club, New York City, New York (Billed as Jimmy Paige [spelling as on advert] and England's most exciting new group Led Zeppelin, and on a second add as Lead Zeppelin. The show was canceled because John Bonham had to return to England because his son, Jason, was ill.)

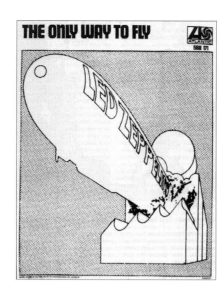

UK press advert announcing the release of *Led Zeppelin,* the band's debut album.

6 February 1969, Steve Paul's the Scene Club, New York City, New York (Billed as Jimmy Paige [spelling as on advert] and England's most exciting new group Led Zeppelin, and on a second add as Lead Zeppelin. The show was canceled because John Bonham had to return to England because his son, Jason, was ill.)

7 February 1969, Kinectic Playground, Chicago, Illinois (8:00 p.m. Billed with incorrect spelling again as Led Zepelin. Sharing bill with Vanilla Fudge and Jethro Tull. Jethro Tull played first followed by Led Zeppelin and then headliner Vanilla Fudge.)

SETLIST WOULD HAVE BEEN TAKEN FROM THE FOLLOWING: Train Kept A Rollin' / I Can't Quit You Baby / Dazed and Confused / As Long As I Have You / Killing Floor / White Summer / Black Mountain Side / Babe I'm Gonna Leave You / You Shook Me / How Many More Times / Communication Breakdown / Pat's Delight

8 February 1969, Kinectic Playground, Chicago, Illinois (8:00 p.m. Billed with incorrect spelling again as Led Zepelin. Sharing bill with Vanilla Fudge and Jethro Tull. Jethro Tull played first followed by Led Zeppelin and then headliner Vanilla Fudge.)

SETLIST WOULD HAVE BEEN TAKEN FROM THE FOLLOWING: Train Kept A Rollin' / I Can't Quit You Baby / Dazed and Confused / As Long As I Have You / Killing Floor / White Summer / Black Mountain Side / Babe I'm Gonna Leave You / You Shook Me / How Many More Times / Communication Breakdown / Pat's Delight

10 February 1969, Memphis State University, Memphis, Tennessee

SETLIST WOULD HAVE BEEN TAKEN FROM THE FOLLOWING: Train Kept A Rollin' / I Can't Quit You Baby / Dazed and Confused / As Long As I Have You / Killing

Floor / White Summer / Black Mountain Side / Babe I'm Gonna Leave You / You Shook Me / How Many More Times / Communication Breakdown / Pat's Delight

14 February 1969, Thee Image Club, Miami, Florida (Two sets from 8:30 p.m. Support from Broadway Park)

SETLIST FOR SET 1: The Train Kept A Rollin' / I Can't Quit You Baby / Dazed And Confused (including Sugartime) / Killing Floor (including The Lemon Song, Think You Need A Shot [The Needle], You'll Be Mine) / Babe I'm Gonna Leave You (including Reflection On My Mind) / How Many More Times (including Roll Over Beethoven)

SETLIST FOR SET 2: White Summer / Black Mountain Side / As Long As I Have You (including Fresh Garbage, Mockingbird, Bag's Groove) / You Shook Me / Pat's Delight

The band played two high-powered sets at the small Thee Image Club. The last set ended with John Bonham's solo piece "Pat's Delight." Throughout the sets, Robert Plant sang with raw passion and Jimmy Page wailed on the guitar. John Paul Jones and John Bonham provided their usual solid rhythm backing that the two front men had grown to depend on.

15 February 1969, Thee Image Club, Miami, Florida (Two sets from 8:30 p.m. Support from Broadway Park)

SETLIST WOULD HAVE BEEN TAKEN FROM THE FOLLOWING: Train Kept A Rollin' / I Can't Quit You Baby / Dazed and Confused / As Long As I Have You / Killing Floor / White Summer / Black Mountain Side / Babe I'm Gonna Leave You / You Shook Me / How Many More Times / Communication Breakdown / Pat's Delight

Danish television program listing, showing a broadcast date of 19 May 1969 for Led Zeppelin's appearance at Studio 5 TV-Byen in Gladsaxe, Denmark.

16 February 1969, Baltimore Civic Center, Baltimore, Maryland (Vanilla Fudge is the headliner supported by Led Zeppelin, the Gun, Paul Butterfield Blues Band, the Procreation, the Lemon Lime. An eye-witness reports that Led Zeppelin played beyond their allocated time, leaving Vanilla Fudge only 20 minutes to play before the curfew)

SETLIST WOULD HAVE BEEN TAKEN FROM THE FOLLOWING: Train Kept A Rollin' / I Can't Quit You Baby / Dazed and Confused / As Long As I Have You / Killing Floor / White Summer / Black Mountain Side / Babe I'm Gonna Leave You / You Shook Me / How Many More Times / Communication Breakdown / Pat's Delight

LED ZEPPELIN SECOND UK TOUR

1 MARCH 1969–13 MARCH 1969

The band start the year with a surprise birthday party for John Bonham's wife at the Lafayette Club in Wolverhampton before undertaking a busy schedule of concert dates in England, Scandinavia, and Europe. As a way of increasing their profile in these countries, they also decided to make several television appearances. It was something that they had always felt reluctant to do due to the poor sound delivered by the medium. However, most kids watching the shows would not have cared too much as the band were so visual. Not only that, as soon as they bought the band's first album, they would know how great the sound was. Some of the television shows were mimed and others were done live. Luckily some of the better shows have survived and were included on the *Led Zeppelin* DVD in 2003.

After playing in some great venues in America, the band undertake their second UK tour in small clubs and pubs. But the lack of decent venues in England did not diminish their popularity there, which had grown in just a few short months from their previous tour. They had been on the radio playing some sessions for the BBC and their first album was released to coincide with the tour. The only downside of being back in the UK was that their improvisational pieces were too long. So they had to revert back to the original length of the songs to avoid overrunning their stage time. The other problem was the lack of decent money in the UK because they were only playing to audiences of 300 to 400, even if the venues were sold out.

24 February 1969 Lafayette Club, Wolverhampton, West Midlands (Support from Galliard. Led Zeppelin made a private special appearance onstage to celebrate John Bonham's wife's twenty-first birthday party. The gig was arranged by John Bonham via Pat Bonham's sister, who was working at the Lafayette Club.)

MARCH 1969

1 March 1969, Van Dike Club, Plymouth, Devon (8:00 p.m. Billed as Led Zeppelin [ex-Yardbirds])

3 March 1969, *Top Gear*, Playhouse Theatre, Northumberland Avenue, London WC2 (BBC Radio recording session took place between 2:00 p.m. and 6:00 p.m. The resulting session was broadcast on John Peel's *Top Gear* show on Radio One between 3:00 p.m. and 5:00 p.m. on 23 March 1969. It was re-broadcasted on the *Tommy Vance Friday Rock Show* on 2 February 1979. "Dazed And Confused," "You Shook Me," and "I Can't Quit You Baby" were released on the *Led Zeppelin BBC Sessions* CD in 1997. The band were exceptionally tight, having played these in concert over the past few months. These live in-the-studio versions are a remarkable snapshot of how the band sounded like during this period as well as showing how much they had grown since recording these for the first album back in October 1968.)

SETLIST:

YOU SHOOK ME (Willie Dixon / J. B. Lenoir) Broadcast on 23 March 1969 / Available on *BBC Sessions* CD Atlantic 7567-83061-2 released November 1997.

JIMMY PAGE: FENDER TELECASTER GUITAR, SLIDE
ROBERT PLANT: LEAD VOCALS, HARMONICA
JOHN PAUL JONES: ORGAN
JOHN BONHAM: DRUMS

COMMUNICATION BREAKDOWN (Jimmy Page / John Paul Jones / John Bonham) Broadcast on 23 March 1969 / unreleased

JIMMY PAGE: FENDER TELECASTER GUITAR, SOME OVERDUBBED GUITAR
ROBERT PLANT: LEAD VOCALS, OVERDUBBED BACKING VOCALS ON CHORUS
JOHN PAUL JONES: BASS
JOHN BONHAM: DRUMS

I CAN'T QUIT YOU BABY (Willie Dixon) Broadcast on 23 March 1969 / Available on *BBC Sessions* CD Atlantic 7567-83061-2 released November 1997.

JIMMY PAGE: FENDER TELECASTER GUITAR
ROBERT PLANT: LEAD VOCALS
JOHN PAUL JONES: BASS
JOHN BONHAM: DRUMS

DAZED AND CONFUSED (Jimmy Page) Recorded at the same session but not broadcast at the time. It was eventually broadcast on *Tommy Vance's Friday Rock Show* on 2 February 1979 / Available on *BBC Sessions* CD Atlantic 7567-83061-2 released November 1997.

JIMMY PAGE: FENDER TELECASTER GUITAR, BOWED GUITAR
ROBERT PLANT: LEAD VOCALS
JOHN PAUL JONES: BASS
JOHN BONHAM: DRUMS
BBC PRODUCER: BERNIE ANDREWS
BBC ENGINEER: PETE RITZEMA

5 March 1969, Top Rank Ballroom, Cardiff, Wales

7 March 1969, Bluesville 69 Club, Hornsey Wood Tavern, Manor House, London (Billed as Led Zeppelin—Back From Their Sensational American Tour!)

13 March 1969, De Montfort Hall, Leicester, East Midlands (Led Zeppelin play the University's Rag Week Pyjama Dance with Ferris Wheel and Decoys as support.)

LED ZEPPELIN SCANDINAVIAN TOUR
14 MARCH 1969–17 MARCH 1969

The band are in magical form on this short Scandinavian tour. There was now no doubt at all about them becoming a huge success. Everyone knew it and the band's confidence onstage made them irresistible to fans who were hungry for something new. Led Zeppelin delivered that in spades and more. Anyone who witnessed these shows all confirm how spectacular the playing was. Luckily, thanks to Danish Television we have a thirty-minute snapshot of the band during this tour. We also get a fabulously wild version of "Dazed And Confused" recorded the day after their Scandinavian tour on the *Supershow* film.

14 March 1969, Kram television show, Sveriges Radio TV Studios, Oxenstiernsgatan, Stockholm, Sweden (The start of a busy day for the band as they record their segment for a TV show in the afternoon. They mime to "Communication Breakdown" for a program called Kram. Filmed in black and white, it was broadcast on 31 March 1969. John Bonham is using a double-bass drum kit. The whole video was used for Early Days—The Very Best of Led Zeppelin Volume 1 in 2000 and on the Led Zeppelin DVD in 2003.)

14 March 1969, Konserthuset, Stockholm, Sweden (evening set at 7:30 p.m. sharing a bill with Country Joe & the Fish. The show is broadcast on a program called *Rock från underjorden* (*Rock from Underground*) in 1982 and 1985.

Jimmy Page has some string problems on his guitar during "Train Kept A Rollin'" and has to change a string after the number ends. While he does that, the rest of the band play a version of Otis Rush's "I Gotta Move.")

SETLIST: The Train Kept A Rollin' / I Gotta Move / I Can't Quit You Baby / Dazed And Confused / White Summer / Black Mountain Side / How Many More Times (including Communication Breakdown, The Hunter)

66 Even though Country Joe & The Fish was the big name at Friday night's concert in Stockholm, Led Zeppelin did a much more interesting performance. Unfortunately, some of the group's equipment was left at a TV recording studio that day, but it was hardly noticeable. The band plays in a very hard and intensive blues style. Its music has room for much experimenting and is, to a great extent, built on an exciting dialogue between former Yardbirds guitarist Jimmy Page and singer Robert Plant. 99
   —**REVIEW FROM** *THE SWEDISH DAILY NEWS* (15 March 1969)

66 The Concerthouse was almost sold-out. Led Zeppelin first impressed me because they played so hard and loud; not in that typical thin English way. They had an almost American heaviness and depth to their music. But the group is just a few months old and they haven't found their place yet. The guitarist Jimmy Page is good, a skillful and imaginative soloist. His bassist was good too and the drummer was promising. The singer I didn't like. He mostly screamed and the lyrics he was screaming were banal. 99
   —**REVIEW FROM** *THE STOCKHOLM DAILY NEWS* (15 March 1969)

14 March 1969, Lecture Hall, Uppsala University, Uppsala, Sweden (late-evening show due to start at 10:00 p.m. The band arrive onstage around 11:00 p.m. and again share the bill with Country Joe & the Fish)

SETLIST: The Train Kept A Rollin' / I Can't Quit You Baby / Dazed And Confused / You Shook Me / White Summer / Black Mountain Side / Babe I'm Gonna Leave You / How Many More Times

15 March 1969, Teen-Clubs Box 45, Egegårdskolen, Gladsaxe, Denmark (early show 7:30 p.m. Billed as Led Zeppelin (Yardbirds). Support from the Ox and Uffe Sylvesters Badekar)

SETLIST: The Train Kept A Rollin' / I Can't Quit You Baby / As Long As I Have You (including Fresh Garbage, Bag's Groove) / You Shook Me / Communication Breakdown

The audience recording reveals how incredibly powerful the band are at this show. The whole set is a highlight, but the standouts are a concise version of "As Long As

I Have You" with visits to Spirit's "Fresh Garbage" and Miles Davis's "Bag's Groove." Due to time constraints, "Dazed and Confused" was not played.

15 March 1969, Brøndby Pop-Club, Nørregardshallen, Brøndby, Denmark (late show 7:30 p.m., but the band played much later. Support from the Keef Hartley Blues Band, Ham, and Made in Sweden)

SETLIST: The Train Kept A Rollin' / I Can't Quit You Baby / Dazed And Confused / You Shook Me / White Summer / Black Mountain Side / Pat's Delight / Babe I'm Gonna Leave You / How Many More Times

16 March 1969, Tivolis Koncertsal, Copenhagen, Denmark (Billed as Super Session. Two shows at 4:00 p.m. and 7:00 p.m. Support from Country Joe & the Fish and the Keef Hartley Blues Band.)

17 March 1969, "Led Zeppelin—New English supergroup in the TV studio." Danmarks Radio (national Danish TV), Studio 5, TV-Byen, Mørkhøjvej 500, 2860 Søborg, Gladsaxe, Denmark (Afternoon recording session for a program simply called "Led Zeppelin—New English supergroup in the TV studio." The band fly home to the UK after the filming. During the sound check for the actual show, an elderly lady walked in and started to complain loudly about the name Led Zeppelin. Turns out the lady in question was Eva Von Zeppelin, a descendant of Count Ferdinand von Zeppelin (creator of the famous airship) and she did not like the idea of her family name being used by a bunch of long-haired scruffs. Jimmy approached her and together they went to see the TV director, Niels-Jørgen Kaiser. The matter was discussed over a cup of tea and she was introduced to the whole band. She could see that they were actually nice guys and allowed them to carry on. Unfortunately, as she was walking out after the show, she noticed a backdrop with Led Zeppelin's first album cover featuring a Zeppelin on fire. Well, that did it for her. She came back into the studio and went ballistic and threatened legal action. When the band returned to Copenhagen on 28 February 1970, they were prepared to play their show as "The Nobs" to avoid being sued. Nothing more was heard about it after that and Led Zeppelin happily carried on. The television show was originally going to be aired on Danish TV on 19 May 1969. However, it was brought forward to 18 May between 8:50 and 9:20 p.m. This was done due to avoid any legal problems with Eva von Zeppelin, who would not have had time to get an injunction prepared for the next day. The full show was aired only once in the UK on BBC2 on 1 January 1990. The whole video can now be found on the *Led Zeppelin* DVD that was released in 2003.)

SETLIST: Communication Breakdown / Dazed And Confused / Babe I'm Gonna Leave You / How Many More Times (including The Hunter)

The thirty-two-minute television broadcast captures Led Zeppelin at an exciting transitional time in their history. Still fresh and clearly enjoying themselves, the band go all out, and no audience can fail to be impressed with the dynamic performances the band are giving. Luckily, the performance survived in exceptional quality.

LED ZEPPELIN THIRD UK TOUR

18 MARCH 1969–17 APRIL 1969

Led Zeppelin return to the UK for a week of high-profile filming and television appearances as well as a BBC Radio session. These were followed by their third UK tour, interrupted only by a lightning two-day visit to Holland and Germany for more television appearances.

17 March 1969, Colston Hall, Bristol, Somerset (canceled due to additional television appearance in Scandinavia)

18 March 1969, Staines Linoleum Factory, Norris Road, Staines, Middlesex (Led Zeppelin play a powerful version of "Dazed And Confused" in a haze of atmospheric dry ice. The Linoleum Factory ceased manufacturing in Staines in early 1969 and the premises were converted into warehouses. Colourtel transformed one of these spaces into a film studio and Supershow was filmed there over two days. The whole show was filmed and audio was recorded on the Pye Mobile Studio on 8-track tape machines. As well as producing a film, the plan was to release a double album of the event subject to the various clearances.)

SETLIST: Dazed And Confused

Director: John Crome
Producer: Tom Parkinson
Recorded by: Pye Mobile on eight track
Recording engineer: Brian Stott

The idea behind this project was to assemble the best musicians from the world of pop, rock, jazz, and blues and let them jam together over two days in the old Staines Linoleum Factory in Norris Road, located near the banks of the River Thames in Staines, Surrey. The main room had a small stage surrounded by tables to give the impression this was being filmed in a small club. The first day of filming and recording took place on Tuesday 18 March 1969 and featured

Steve Stills, Buddy Miles, Dallas Taylor, Jack Bruce, Buddy Guy, Chris Mercer, Dick Heckstall-Smith, and Led Zeppelin. Led Zeppelin did not partake in any jamming other than their own in an intensely powerful version of "Dazed And Confused" from their debut album. Jimi Hendrix, who was recording in New York, was also due to come, but missed his flight. The recording dates for *Supershow* have always been wrongly attributed to 25 and 26 March 1969.

66 We performed 'Dazed And Confused' with what seemed to be a pretty experienced production team, as the camera angles appeared interesting at the time. They also used some dry ice, which was quite vibey, and we were just part of a number of artists that were to appear on this show—some of whom had not yet recorded and were due to arrive at the building. There was definitely a timeslot for us to do another number, especially as the other artists hadn't arrived, and I suggested to the director that maybe it would be a good opportunity to do 'Communication Breakdown' as a second number, but they declined the offer and said it wasn't necessary! 99

—**JIMMY PAGE** (From his website)

66 Supershow was filmed on 18 and 19 March 1969. As far as I know, all the unused footage was dumped way back in 1969 or thereabouts. The company that made the film, Colourtel, went into liquidation. I personally gave the audio masters to Shel Talmy in 1970 to see what he could do with them. I have contacted Shel via his ex-wife Jenny who lives in the US. He can't remember anything about them.

There was also a mono mix made at EMI, I think, and a rough audio/visual version put together as we shot by the PA, which might still exist. I think the film was processed at Humphries Labs, which no longer exists, but all their material must have been moved to somewhere. Nick Hague, the line producer, and I bought the material from the liquidator and subsequently licensed to Virgin and then Eagle Rock.

There was no significance in the show being filmed at the 'lino factory,' it was just an affordable studio which had in the past been a lino factory. I don't think we were the only people to use it. *The Rolling Stones R&R Circus*, the Coloutel film shot just before *Supershow*, was shot at Wembley. Vic Gardner, managing director of Colourtel (he went on to be MD of LWT), had been a senior executive at Rediffusion TV, so he knew the independent TV scene very well. I remember that the deal at West London Studios was the best available.

Both the Stones film and *Supershow* were shot on 16mm film using a unique French system which we imported for the purpose. The cameras were mounted on typical peds. (Vintens) and

transmitted images to a scanner as in OB shoots. The cameras simultaneously photographed on film. There were 3–4 cameras shooting film, which were turned on and off from the scanner. Some were left to run. I communicated with the cameras via headsets from the scanner. At the same time the PA made an edited version. Ted Hooker was the film editor. Brian Stott recorded on 8-track using the mobile unit from Pye Studios. He also made a mono back-up.

Zep did only play 'Dazed.' I don't remember how they came to be in the show, but they played and left and hardly spoke to anyone. They notoriously refused all TV offers except ours. The number was filmed just once and performed live. Page's violin bow on guitar strings solo went on too long and some of it was way off key, so the editor Ted Hooker (not me) cut a lump out. When Zep bought the segment to put in their DVD, they wanted to reinstate the lost footage, but we couldn't find it. The present version of *Supershow* does not have the Zep number in it. But Eagle, who have licensed it, are trying to put it back. 99

—**JOHN CROME** (Director of *Supershow*)

19 March 1969, *Rhythm & Blues*, BBC Maida Vale Studio 4, Delaware Road, London W9 (Recording session between 5:30 p.m. and 9:00 p.m. Originally broadcast on Alexis Korner's *Rhythm & Blues* show on the BBC World Service, 14 April 1969. This was their second BBC session this month, recorded in the BBC's Maida Vale Studio 4, which was a small studio with a vocal booth and balcony. The real rarity here is a one-off performance of a number titled "Sunshine Woman," which Jimmy Page has said was just the band mucking around a tune he had written earlier in the day. At the time of putting this book together, it was confirmed that the session master tapes are still missing from the BBC archives. The only circulating tapes from this session are taken from an off-air recording in sub-standard quality.)

SETLIST:

I CAN'T QUIT YOU BABY (Willie Dixon) Broadcast 14 April 1969

JIMMY PAGE: FENDER TELECASTER GUITAR
ROBERT PLANT: LEAD VOCALS
JOHN PAUL JONES: BASS
JOHN BONHAM: DRUMS

YOU SHOOK ME (Willie Dixon / J. B. Lenoir) Broadcast 14 April 1969

JIMMY PAGE: FENDER TELECASTER GUITAR
ROBERT PLANT: LEAD VOCALS. HARMONICA
JOHN PAUL JONES: ORGAN
JOHN BONHAM: DRUMS

SUNSHINE WOMAN (Jimmy Page) Broadcast 14 April 1969

JIMMY PAGE: FENDER TELECASTER GUITAR
ROBERT PLANT: LEAD VOCALS, HARMONICA
JOHN PAUL JONES: PIANO
JOHN BONHAM: DRUMS
PRODUCER: JEFF GRIFFIN
ENGINEER: JOE YOUNG

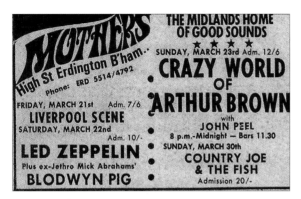

Press advert for Led Zeppelin's appearance at Mothers' club in Erdington, Birmingham.

21 March 1969, *How Late It Is*, Studio G, BBC Lime Grove Studios, Lime Grove, Shepherds Bush, London W12 (The band have to be ready for a recording session at 5:45 p.m. The original series was called *How It Is*, hosted by John Peel, and ran from July to December 1968 on BBC1. By 1969 the name changed to *How Late It Is* to reflect it's later time slot. The second episode of the popular arts discussion program featured Led Zeppelin playing "Communication Breakdown." Although several music clips from the series have survived, the Led Zeppelin segment appears to have been wiped or lost. The show was aired at 10:50 p.m. that night on BBC1 and was introduced by Michael Wale. Both series were produced by acclaimed filmmaker Tony Palmer, but was axed after ten episodes in 1969 after being classed as too controversial for an increasingly nervous BBC, who caved in to pressure from the "Clean Up TV Campaign" led by Mary Whitehouse. Led Zeppelin supposedly also appeared on *How It Is* in 1968 at John Peel's instigation, but no documentation has been found to confirm this at the time of researching this book.)

22 March 1969, Mothers Club, Erdington, Birmingham, West Midlands (8:00 p.m. with support from Blodwyn Pig. Witnesses say that John Bonham was worse for wear at the show and Blodwyn Pig's drummer, Ron Berg, took over the drum duties for the encore.)

SETLIST WOULD HAVE BEEN TAKEN FROM THE FOLLOWING: Train Kept A Rollin' / I Can't Quit You Baby / Dazed And Confused / As Long As I Have You / Killing Floor / White Summer / Black Mountain Side / Babe I'm Gonna Leave You / You Shook Me / How Many More Times / Communication Breakdown / Pat's Delight

23 March 1969, The Argus Butterfly, Peterlee, County Durham (Support from Middle Earth)

SETLIST WOULD HAVE BEEN TAKEN FROM THE FOLLOWING: Train Kept A Rollin' / I Can't Quit You Baby / Dazed And Confused / As Long As I Have You / Killing Floor / White Summer / Black Mountain Side / Babe I'm Gonna Leave You / You Shook Me / How Many More Times / Communication Breakdown / Pat's Delight

26 March 1969, *Jam* television show, Tros TV, Holland (*Jam* was a hugely popular teenage music magazine for television. Led Zeppelin mime to "Good Times Bad Times." The tapes of the show are probably wiped.)

27 March 1969, *Beat Club*, Radio Bremen Studios, Studio 3, Bremen, Germany (The band mime to two songs. Although recorded on 27 March 1969, the producers were not enamored with what was filmed and only used a collage of what was recorded as a backdrop for a studio version for "Whole Lotta Love" in 1970, which was a huge hit in the German charts at the time. First aired on *Beat Club* episode #53 on 28 March 1970. The original videos of "Babe I'm Gonna Leave You" and "You Shook Me" were eventually broadcast forty years later.)

SETLIST: Babe I'm Gonna Leave You / You Shook Me

28 March 1969, Marquee Club, Wardour Street, London (7:30 p.m. Support from the Eyes of Blue.)

SETLIST WOULD HAVE BEEN TAKEN FROM THE FOLLOWING: Train Kept A Rollin' / I Can't Quit You Baby / Dazed And Confused / As Long As I Have You / Killing Floor / White Summer / Black Mountain Side / Babe I'm Gonna Leave You / You Shook Me / How Many More Times / Communication Breakdown / Pat's Delight

Peter Grant had approached the producers of the popular BBC television show *Colour Me Pop* to come and film the band's concert this evening. They had already produced some exciting shows for the Small Faces and the Move, among others. Grant felt that they would do a good job in capturing the band in action on their home turf. According to Grant the company did not turn up on the night and did not have the courtesy to tell them they would not be coming and never apologized after the fact. This tainted the way Grant would view television companies in the future.

Atlantic Records released a press release on 26 March to promote the Marquee show as well as announce the forthcoming second US tour and how well Led Zeppelin's debut album had done in the US:

66 Led Zeppelin, the most talked about (and raved about) British group of the moment, plays London's famous Marquee Club on Friday night, March 28th.

All eyes are on Led Zeppelin following the fantastic success of their first album (Atlantic 588 171), which in a matter of weeks in America climbed rapidly into the upper limits of Billboard, Cashbox and Record World charts. This album, entitled simply 'Led Zeppelin,' was recently released in Britain and seems destined for similar success.

Led Zeppelin features two of Britain's top young musicians; Jimmy Page (guitar) and John Paul Jones (bass, organ)—plus drummer John Bonham and singer Robert Plant.

The group returns to America for a second tour shortly, starting on April 18th, when they will play New York University's Third Annual Jazz Festival, along with Dave Brubeck and Errol Garner. Other dates so far booked on this tour are San Francisco's Fillmore (April 24–27), Los Angeles (May 2, 3), Seattle (May 9), Vancouver (May 10), Portland (May 11), Detroit (May 16, 17), Minneapolis (May 18), Baltimore (May 23) and New York's Fillmore East. 99

—**ATLANTIC RECORDS PRESS RELEASE** (26 March 1969)

66 Jimmy Page, bent over his guitar and straining for unknown notes, listening hard because he's right there in the middle of that Led Zeppelin wall of sound, sweat oozing torrential down his face, and dripping off the ends of that long wavy hair down onto the guitar and one expects that guitar to fizz and steam because it's so near boiling point. John Bonham, wild on the drums looking over almost painful with effort at John Paul Jones, laying down such a heavy bass, and through it all is the power of that Robert Plant voice. Led Zeppelin at the Marquee—Led Zeppelin anywhere, for that's how they are onstage. Powerful, heavy and very good. 99

—*RECORD MIRROR* (Review of Marquee show, April 1969)

29 March 1969, Bromley College of Technology, Bromley Common, Kent (7:30 p.m. Support from the Maddening Crowd.)

SETLIST WOULD HAVE BEEN TAKEN FROM THE FOLLOWING: Train Kept A Rollin' / I Can't Quit You Baby / Dazed And Confused / As Long As I Have You / Killing Floor / White Summer / Black Mountain Side / Babe I'm Gonna Leave You / You Shook Me / How Many More Times / Communication Breakdown / Pat's Delight

30 March 1969, Farx Blues Club, Northcote Arms, Southall, Middlesex (7:30 p.m. Support from Smokey Rice, Pale Green Limousine, light show, and heavy sounds by Andy Dunkley.)

SETLIST WOULD HAVE BEEN TAKEN FROM THE FOLLOWING: Train Kept A Rollin' / I Can't Quit You Baby / Dazed And Confused / As Long As I Have You / Killing Floor / White Summer / Black Mountain Side / Babe I'm Gonna Leave You / You Shook Me / How Many More Times / Communication Breakdown / Pat's Delight

31 March 1969, Cooks Ferry Inn, Edmonton, London

SETLIST WOULD HAVE BEEN TAKEN FROM THE FOLLOWING: Train Kept A Rollin' / I Can't Quit You Baby / Dazed And Confused / As Long As I Have You / Killing Floor / White Summer / Black Mountain Side / Babe I'm Gonna Leave You / You Shook Me / How Many More Times / Communication Breakdown / Pat's Delight

APRIL 1969

1 April 1969, Klooks Kleek Railway Hotel, West Hampstead, London (Support from the End with Pale Green Limousine, light show and DJ Pat B.)

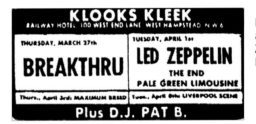

Press advert for an appearance by Led Zeppelin at Klooks Kleek, London.

SETLIST WOULD HAVE BEEN TAKEN FROM THE FOLLOWING: Train Kept A Rollin' / I Can't Quit You Baby / Dazed And Confused / As Long As I Have You / Killing Floor / White Summer / Black Mountain Side / Babe I'm Gonna Leave You / You Shook Me / How Many More Times / Communication Breakdown / Pat's Delight

2 April 1969, the Progressive Blues Night, Top Rank Suite, Cardiff, Wales (Support from Kimla Taz, the Eyes of Blue, and DJ Bob McClure. The concert was in aid of the Biafran Relief Organisation.)

SETLIST WOULD HAVE BEEN TAKEN FROM THE FOLLOWING: Communication Breakdown / I Can't Quit You Baby / Dazed And Confused / As Long As I Have You / Killing Floor / White Summer / Black Mountain Side / Babe I'm Gonna Leave You / You Shook Me / How Many More Times

5 April 1969, Village Blues Club, Dagenham Roundhouse, London (Support from the Further)

SETLIST WOULD HAVE BEEN TAKEN FROM THE FOLLOWING: Train Kept A Rollin' / I Can't Quit You Baby / Dazed And Confused / As Long As I Have You / Killing Floor / White Summer / Black Mountain Side / Babe I'm Gonna Leave You / You Shook Me / How Many More Times / Communication Breakdown / Pat's Delight

6 April 1969, Boat Club, Nottigham, Leicestershire

SETLIST WOULD HAVE BEEN TAKEN FROM THE FOLLOWING: Train Kept A Rollin' / I Can't Quit You Baby / Dazed And Confused / As Long As I Have You / Killing Floor / White Summer / Black Mountain Side / Babe I'm Gonna Leave You / You Shook Me / How Many More Times / Communication Breakdown / Pat's Delight

7 April 1969, Bay Hotel, Whitburn, Sunderland, County Durham (Canceled)

8 April 1969, Bluesville '69 Club's, the Cherry Tree, Welwyn Garden City, Hertfordshire (7:30 p.m.)

SETLIST WOULD HAVE BEEN TAKEN FROM THE FOLLOWING: Train Kept A Rollin' / I Can't Quit You Baby / Dazed And Confused / As Long As I Have You / Killing Floor / White Summer / Black Mountain Side / Babe I'm Gonna Leave You / You Shook Me / How Many More Times / Communication Breakdown / Pat's Delight

9 April 1969, Toby Jug, Tolworth, Surrey

SETLIST WOULD HAVE BEEN TAKEN FROM THE FOLLOWING: Train Kept A Rollin' / I Can't Quit You Baby / Dazed And Confused / As Long As I Have You / Killing Floor / White Summer / Black Mountain Side / Babe I'm Gonna Leave You / You Shook Me / How Many More Times / Communication Breakdown / Pat's Delight

13 April 1969, Kimbells Blues Club, Southsea, Portsmouth, Hampshire (8:00 p.m.)

SETLIST WOULD HAVE BEEN TAKEN FROM THE FOLLOWING: Train Kept A Rollin' / I Can't Quit You Baby / Dazed And Confused / As Long As I Have You / Killing Floor / White Summer / Black Mountain Side / Babe I'm Gonna Leave You / You Shook Me / How Many More Times / Communication Breakdown / Pat's Delight

14 April 1969, the Place, Stoke-On-Trent, Staffordshire (Show canceled with no reason given. No refunds were given, but Led Zeppelin honored the booking by agreeing to play the Place at a later date. That date happened to be in 1971 and by that point the band were huge and there was no way that the Place could have dealt with the demand to see the band. Instead, it was agreed to move the gig to Trentham Gardens with a bigger capacity of 3,500.)

17 April 1969, Lafayette Club, Wolverhampton, West Midlands

SETLIST WOULD HAVE BEEN TAKEN FROM THE FOLLOWING: Train Kept A Rollin' / I Can't Quit You Baby / Dazed And Confused / As Long As I Have You / Killing Floor / White Summer / Black Mountain Side / Babe I'm Gonna Leave You / You Shook Me / How Many More Times / Communication Breakdown / Pat's Delight

LED ZEPPELIN SECOND US TOUR

24 APRIL 1969–1 JUNE 1969

Jimmy Page had confirmed to *Record Mirror* in April 1969 that he was very pleased with Led Zeppelin's last UK tour and that the now apparent acceptance of the band was very encouraging. But he also admitted that America was where their main market was. "We're working every day here now—but before we went to the States nobody wanted to know. And it's not just London—it's all over the country. Very pleasing reaction. I still reckon the States is our main market, though."

To that end, the band headed back to the US at the end of April for their second tour there. The tour opened in California and their popularity had grown so much that instead of playing four shows at the Fillmore West, two nights had to be moved to the larger Winterland in San Francisco due to high demand for tickets.

18 April 1969, New York University Jazz Festival, New York City, New York (canceled)

24 April 1969, Fillmore West, San Francisco, California (Two sets. Support from Julie Driscoll, Brian Auger & the Trinity, and the Colwell-Winfield Blues Band. Bill Graham introduced all the acts.)

SETLIST: As Long As I Have You (including Fresh Garbage, Shake, Mockingbird, You Can't Judge A Book By The Cover, Suzie Q) / Killing Floor / White Summer / Black Mountain Side / Babe I'm Gonna Leave You / Pat's Delight

A near-professional recording circulates from this show. Bill Graham often taped the shows at his venues and this one no doubt comes from that source. The sound is exceptional, especially for the era. The set opens with one of the best versions of "As Long As I Have You" that is available on circulating recordings. Unfortunately halfway through the number, John Paul Jones's bass cabinet blows up. Robert Plant can't help himself and sings some ad-libbed lyrics about the problems they are having onstage. After the song he comments, "We seem to have a cock-up every time we've been here!"

25 April 1969, Winterland Ballroom, San Francisco, California (Two sets. Support from Julie Driscoll, Brian Auger & the Trinity, and the Colwell-Winfield Blues Band.)

SETLIST: The Train Kept A Rollin' / You Shook Me / Communication Breakdown / As Long As I Have You (including Fresh Garbage, Bag's Groove)

26 April 1969, Winterland Ballroom, San Francisco, California (Two sets. Support from Julie Driscoll, Brian Auger & the Trinity, and the Colwell-Winfield Blues Band.)

SETLIST FOR SET 1: Communication Breakdown / I Can't Quit You Baby / Dazed And Confused / You Shook Me / How Many More Times (includes Smokestack Lightning, Roll Over Beethoven, Girl From The North Country, The Hunter)

Ticket for Led Zeppelin show on 25 April 1969 at the Fillmore West in San Francisco replicating poster image. Tickets and handbills for Fillmore shows are prized items and are very valuable.

Ticket for Led Zeppelin show on 26 April 1969 at the Fillmore West in San Francisco replicating poster image. Tickets and handbills for Fillmore shows are prized items and are very valuable.

Ticket for Led Zeppelin show on 24 April 1969 at the Fillmore West in San Francisco replicating poster image. Tickets and handbills for Fillmore shows are prized items and are very valuable.

SETLIST FOR SET 2: White Summer / Black Mountain Side / Killing Floor (including The Lemon Song, That's Alright Mama) / Babe I'm Gonna Leave You / Pat's Delight / As Long As I Have You (including Fresh Garbage, Bag's Groove, Mockingbird) / Whole Lotta Love

These shows feature Led Zeppelin in full-blown improvisational psychedelic rock mode. Like Cream before them, they had a limited amount of material to play and decided to lengthen certain numbers and improvise to make the shows longer. These concerts were the beginning of Led Zeppelin stretching out and blowing everyone away in the process. They were one of the most exciting acts around. The West Coast was buzzing with creativity at this time and Led Zeppelin embraced it all. When you listen to these historic recordings, you hear a band in transition and about to take the music world over with sheer power and dynamics. They would never look back from this moment on. These shows are also historic for the first appearance of the theremin onstage during "Dazed And Confused" and, perhaps more significantly, the first-ever performance of "Whole Lotta Love." Again, from a historic perspective, it is fascinating to hear how much of the number had already been developed. Robert Plant's lyrics are pretty much what would end up on the album version. By now they had nearly finished the track, which had started it's life at Olympic Studios back in England and was now being finished in various US studios while on the road. It probably just needed a few more overdubs at this point. Jimmy Page does not use the theremin in the middle section yet. Instead he plays some slide for effect. You can tell the band are finding their feet on this one and it would be a few more weeks before it is perfected.

27 April 1969, Fillmore West, San Francisco, California (Two sets. Support from Julie Driscoll, Brian Auger & the Trinity, and the Colwell-Winfield Blues Band. Bill Graham introduced all the acts.)

SETLIST FOR SET 1: Train Kept a Rollin' / I Can't Quit You Baby / As Long As I Have You (including Fresh Garbage, Bag's Groove, Cat's Squirrel, No Money Down, I'm A Man) / You Shook Me / How Many More Times (including Feel So Bad, The Hunter, Here We Go Round The Mulberry Bush)

SETLIST FOR SET 2: Killing Floor (including Sweet Jelly Roll) / Babe I'm Gonna Leave You / White Summer / Black Mountain Side / Sitting And Thinking / Pat's Delight / Dazed And Confused / Communication Breakdown

Yet again, the band demonstrates why everyone at the time was talking about them. People simply had not heard anything like it before. This show is just incredible. The first set has the group in high-energy mode. The second set is far more bluesy, but still has bite and excitement in the performance. Opening with Howlin' Wolf's "Killing Floor," they set the tone. The highlight of the second show is a version of Buddy Guy's "Sitting and Thinking" with Page in amazing form. Even "Dazed And Confused" is bluesy tonight with ad-libbed lyrics from "I Can't Quit You Babe" thrown in. "I'm so glad you came tonight . . . but I think we're gonna leave this town for a little while . . . I don't want to leave you people . . . but I think we've got to leave San Francisco for a little while." The crowd loved it. One final encore of "Communication Breakdown" confirms that the band can do no wrong in San Francisco.

MAY 1969

1 May 1969, Crawford Hall, University of California, Irvine, California (8:00 p.m. Support from Lee Michaels. Initially the band planned to play two shows but the second was canceled.)

SETLIST NOT KNOWN BUT WOULD PROBABLY HAVE INCLUDED THE FOLLOWING: Train Kept A Rollin' / I Can't Quit You Baby / Dazed And Confused / You Shook Me / White Summer / Black Mountain Side / Babe I'm Gonna Leave You / You Shook Me / How Many More Times / Communication Breakdown

2 May 1969, Rose Palace, Pasadena, California (8:00 p.m. Support from Julie Driscoll, Brian Auger & the Trinity, and Elvin Bishop Group.)

SETLIST NOT KNOWN BUT WOULD PROBABLY HAVE INCLUDED THE FOLLOWING: Train Kept A Rollin' / I Can't Quit You Baby / Dazed And Confused / You Shook Me / White Summer / Black Mountain Side / Babe I'm Gonna Leave You / You Shook Me / How Many More Times / Communication Breakdown

3 May 1969, Rose Palace, Pasadena, California (8:00 p.m. Support from Julie Driscoll, Brian Auger & the Trinity, and Elvin Bishop Group.)

SETLIST NOT KNOWN BUT WOULD PROBABLY HAVE INCLUDED THE FOLLOWING: Train Kept A Rollin' / I Can't Quit You Baby / Dazed And Confused / You Shook Me / White Summer / Black Mountain Side / Babe I'm Gonna Leave You / You Shook Me / How Many More Times / Communication Breakdown

Press advert for Led Zeppelin's appearance at the Rose Palace in Pasadena, California.

> **66** The hottest new rock band from Britain stalked on stage at the Gardens Friday night and let loose an earthquake of sound and frenzy. Their music's loud, almost to the point of pain, but they don't use volume to cover up deficiencies. The volume is part of their attack. They don't titillate or tease audiences to share their inspiration. Instead, they blast out with raw, jagged power, enough to bust a new door into your brain. They use their instruments like a brush and palette, creating frenzied visions that tumble through space and time. **99**
>
> —**BOB HARVEY** (Review in the *Journal*, May 1969)

10 May 1969, PNE Agrodome, Vancouver, British Columbia, Canada (8:00 p.m. Support from Spring and Jaime Brockett, a last-minute replacement for Papa Bear's Medicine Show Band, who were left stranded in Alberta due to an Air Canada strike.)

SETLIST NOT KNOWN BUT WOULD PROBABLY HAVE INCLUDED THE FOLLOWING: Train Kept A Rollin' / I Can't Quit You Baby / Dazed And Confused / You Shook Me / White Summer / Black Mountain Side / Babe I'm Gonna Leave You / You Shook Me / How Many More Times / Communication Breakdown

11 May 1969, Green Lake Aqua Theater, Seattle, Washington (2:00 p.m. to 6:00 p.m. Support from Three Dog Night, Jaime Brockett, Spring, and Jimmy Winkler's Translove Airlines.)

5 May 1969, Civic Centre, Santa Barbara, California

SETLIST NOT KNOWN BUT WOULD PROBABLY HAVE INCLUDED THE FOLLOWING: Train Kept A Rollin' / I Can't Quit You Baby / Dazed And Confused / You Shook Me / White Summer / Black Mountain Side / Babe I'm Gonna Leave You / You Shook Me / How Many More Times / Communication Breakdown

8 May 1969, Thee Experience, Los Angeles (Led Zeppelin join Lord Sutch for a jam at the end of his set. They carried him out onstage in a coffin. Lord Sutch was backed by Noel Redding's Fat Mattress.)

9 May 1969, Edmonton Gardens, Edmonton, Alberta, Canada (8:00 p.m. Support from Angus Park Blues Band and Papa Bear's Medicine Show Band.)

SETLIST NOT KNOWN BUT WOULD PROBABLY HAVE INCLUDED THE FOLLOWING: Train Kept A Rollin' / I Can't Quit You Baby / Dazed And Confused / You Shook Me / White Summer / Black Mountain Side / Babe I'm Gonna Leave You / You Shook Me / How Many More Times / Communication Breakdown

Advert for upcoming shows at the Kinetic Playground in Chicago, including Led Zeppelin.

SETLIST NOT KNOWN BUT WOULD PROBABLY HAVE INCLUDED THE FOLLOWING: Train Kept A Rollin' / I Can't Quit You Baby / Dazed And Confused / You Shook Me / White Summer / Black Mountain Side / Babe I'm Gonna Leave You / You Shook Me / How Many More Times / Communication Breakdown

❝ The rock concert at the Aqua Theater yesterday afternoon was a smashing success. . . . The stars of the concert were Three Dog Night and Led Zeppelin. Both are brilliant bands. Zeppelin put on an instrumentally excellent performance. Jimmy Page is a superb guitarist and the rest of the group provides able backing too for his wild, fiery style. However, Three Dog Night stole the show. Their personality, their talent and their superb singing make them the hit of any show they play.❞

—**REVIEW IN** *SEATTLE TIMES* (12 May 1969)

13 May 1969, Honolulu Civic Auditorium, Honolulu, Hawaii (7:30 p.m.)

SETLIST NOT KNOWN BUT WOULD PROBABLY HAVE INCLUDED THE FOLLOWING: Train Kept A Rollin' / I Can't Quit You Baby / Dazed And Confused / You Shook Me / White Summer / Black Mountain Side / Babe I'm Gonna Leave You / You Shook Me / How Many More Times / Communication Breakdown

16 May 1969, Grande Ballroom, Detroit, Michigan (Two shows at 7:00 p.m. and 10:00 p.m. Support from Sun Ra and Golden Earring.)

SETLIST NOT KNOWN BUT WOULD PROBABLY HAVE INCLUDED THE FOLLOWING: Train Kept A Rollin' / I Can't Quit You Baby / Dazed And Confused / You Shook Me / White Summer / Black Mountain Side / Babe I'm Gonna Leave You / You Shook Me / How Many More Times / Communication Breakdown

17 May 1969, J-Prom Concert, Ohio University, Convocation Center, Athens, Ohio (8:30 p.m. The band are the support for Jose Feliciano, who headlines the show this evening. He was riding high in the charts with his "Light My Fire" single. He had wanted to meet Jimmy Page, but they somehow missed each other. Led Zeppelin were advertised as the "Special Added Attraction.")

18 May 1969, Tyrone Guthrie Memorial Theater, Minneapolis, Minnesota

SETLIST NOT KNOWN BUT WOULD PROBABLY HAVE INCLUDED THE FOLLOWING: Train Kept A Rollin' / I Can't Quit You Baby / Dazed And Confused / You Shook Me / White Summer / Black Mountain Side / Babe I'm Gonna Leave You / You Shook Me / How Many More Times / Communication Breakdown

❝ Led Zeppelin blitzed the Guthrie Sunday evening. It revealed not just four players of extraordinary talent, but a group which understood that ensemble playing implies communication and mutual stimulation among its members. It is the dialogue among the Zeppelin's members that distinguishes the group. Pairs of players Sunday were constantly getting together in stage corners to establish musical conversations of exciting imaginativeness. The concert's repertory was varied and provocative. Page starred in ['White Summer'], there was irresistible speed and explosion in 'You Shook Me' and there was anguish of a more traditional character in 'Babe I'm Gonna Leave You.'❞

—**P. ALTMAN** (Review in *Minneapolis Star*, May 1969)

23 May 1969, San Jose Pop Festival, Santa Clara City Fairgrounds, San Jose (canceled) The band would have shared the bill with the Jimi Hendrix Experience, Jefferson Airplane, Santana, Spirit, Eric Burdon, Canned Heat, and many others. The band apparently canceled their appearance at the festival because it would have clashed with two dates in Chicago. Despite Peter Grant stating that the promoter paid for a Lear jet to fly them to and from Chicago to attend the festival in the afternoon of 23 May, there is no reported evidence to support that, either with photographs or eye-witness reports.

23 May 1969, Kinetic Playground, Chicago, Illinois (8:00 p.m. Support from Pacific Gas & Electric Co. and Illinois Speed Press.)

SETLIST NOT KNOWN BUT WOULD PROBABLY HAVE INCLUDED THE FOLLOWING: Train Kept A Rollin' / I Can't Quit You Baby / Dazed And Confused / You Shook Me / White Summer / Black Mountain Side / Babe I'm Gonna Leave You / You Shook Me / How Many More Times / Communication Breakdown

24 May 1969, Kinetic Playground, Chicago, Illinois (8:00 p.m. Support from Pacific Gas & Electric Co. and Illinois Speed Press.)

SETLIST NOT KNOWN BUT WOULD PROBABLY HAVE INCLUDED THE FOLLOWING: Train Kept A Rollin' / I Can't Quit You Baby / Dazed And Confused / You Shook Me / White Summer / Black Mountain Side / Babe I'm Gonna Leave You / You Shook Me / How Many More Times / Communication Breakdown

25 May 1969, Merriweather Post Pavilion, Columbia, Maryland (8:00 p.m. Amazing double bill with the Who. Comedian Uncle Dirty opened the show. Led Zeppelin came on first and had to have their amps unplugged by a member of the Who's crew because they were playing over their allocated time.)

SETLIST: The Train Kept A Rollin' / I Can't Quit You Baby / As Long As I Have You (including Fresh Garbage) / Dazed And Confused / You Shook Me / How Many More Times (including The Hunter) / Whole Lotta Love

❝ At the Merriweather Post Pavilion in Columbia, MD, on Sunday night, comedian Uncle Dirty, Led Zeppelin and The Who performed to a packed hall, field and parking lot. Led Zeppelin played a fairly orthodox show, mostly using material off their first album. And although guitarist Jimmy Page once again proved himself a fine musician, there wasn't much more to be said about the act as a whole. He and singer Robert Plant launched into innumerable transgressions of tonal question-answer games, more conducive to boredom than musically induced languor. ❞

—RICHARD COWAN (Review from unknown publication)

26 May 1969, Boston Tea Party, Boston, Massachusetts (canceled)

27 May 1969, Boston Tea Party, Boston, Massachusetts (Support from Zephyr)

SETLIST: As Long As I Have You (including Fresh Garbage, Bag's Groove, Mockingbird) / I Can't Quit You Baby / Dazed And Confused (including Move On Down The Line) / You Shook Me / Pat's Delight / Babe I'm Gonna Leave You / How Many More Times (including For Your Love, The Hunter) / Drums, Bass, Harmonica Improvisation / Communication Breakdown

Another fabulous 1969 show that features the band in fiery mode. Plant is in top form vocally and the whole band are in the zone tonight, despite the fact that the crowd must be stoned as they are quite passive. Their improvisations are gathering momentum more and more from now on, and "Dazed And Confused" is particularly impressive tonight. Also worthy of mention are the opening "As Long As I Have You" and the lengthy "How Many More Times" jam, both of which are majestic in their execution. This show is among several that represent an audio-vérité of what the band sounded like during this period.

28 May 1969, Boston Tea Party, Boston, Massachusetts (Support from Zephyr)

Train Kept A Rollin' / I Can't Quit You Baby / Dazed And Confused / You Shook Me / White Summer / Black Mountain Side / Babe I'm Gonna Leave You / You Shook Me / How Many More Times / Communication Breakdown

29 May 1969, Boston Tea Party, Boston, Massachusetts (Support from Zephyr)

SETLIST NOT KNOWN BUT WOULD PROBABLY HAVE INCLUDED THE FOLLOWING: Train Kept A Rollin' / I Can't Quit You Baby / Dazed And Confused / You Shook Me / White Summer / Black Mountain Side / Babe I'm Gonna Leave You / You Shook Me / How Many More Times / Communication Breakdown

30 May 1969, Fillmore East, New York City, New York (Two shows at 8:00 p.m. and 11:30 p.m. Support from Woody Herman & His Orchestra and Delaney & Bonnie & Friends. Bill Graham introduced all the acts. Light show by the Joshua Light Show.)

SETLIST: The Train Kept A Rollin' / I Can't Quit You Baby / Dazed And Confused / You Shook Me / White Summer / Black Mountain Side / How Many More Times (including Boogie Chillun', The Hunter) / Communication Breakdown

The great thing about the Bill Graham–promoted shows at his Fillmore venues was the eclectic bill of artists that would appear in the same evening. Tonight was no different. Sets were on the short side at around sixty minutes to accommodate all artists. Led Zeppelin play a ferocious set, which sees all band members playing to the height of their capabilities. The New York crowd are certainly very appreciative.

Poster for the San Jose Folk Rock Festival, which included an appearance by Led Zeppelin on 23 May 1969.

31 May 1969, Fillmore East, New York City, New York (Two shows at 8:00 p.m. and 11:30 p.m. Support from Woody Herman & His Orchestra and Delaney & Bonnie & Friends. Bill Graham introduced all the acts. Light show by the Joshua Light Show.)

SETLIST: Train Kept A Rollin' / I Can't Quit You Baby / Dazed And Confused / You Shook Me / White Summer / Black Mountain Side / Babe I'm Gonna Leave You / You Shook Me / How Many More Times (including Roll Over Beethoven, Move On Down The Line) / Communication Breakdown

❝ The following evening (May 31), I went to the second performance again and had a few words with them before the show. They are in England now working on their new LP to be released shortly and they will do several appearances including the Royal Albert Hall. Their performance was to say the least just as spectacular as the night before. John Bonham did a fantastic drum solo. He is really something else to watch perform. During 'How Many More Times' they broke into some early rock numbers, 'Roll Over Beethoven' and 'Move On Down The Line' by the fabulous Jerry Lee Lewis. They received a tremendous ovation as usual and left the Fillmore audience paralyzed. ❞

—DENISE KELLY (Review in *World Countdown*, June 1969)

JUNE 1969

1 June 1969, Kiel Auditorium, St. Louis, Missouri (4:00 p.m. Canceled. Led Zeppelin had been scheduled to play with Joe Cocker and the Who at this show. The concert was advertised with Led Zeppelin as second on the bill. However, the band pulled out for unknown reasons.)

LED ZEPPELIN FOURTH UK TOUR

13 JUNE 1969–29 JUNE 1969

After returning from their successful US tour, the band finally got away from small clubs and pubs and played the larger town halls and civic centers around the UK to accommodate their increased popularity. Further radio sessions and a televison appearance in Paris were also made to continue their promotion in Europe.

13 June 1969, Birmingham Town Hall, Birmingham, West Midlands (7:30 p.m. Support from Liverpool Scene and Blodwyn Pig.)

Train Kept A Rollin' / I Can't Quit You Baby / Dazed And Confused / As Long As I Have You / White Summer / Black Mountain Side / Babe I'm Gonna Leave You / You Shook Me / How Many More Times / Pat's Delight / Communication Breakdown

15 June 1969, Free Trade Hall, Manchester, Lancashire (7:00 p.m.) Support from Liverpool Scene and Blodwyn Pig. This date had been previously scheduled for 22 June 1969.

SETLIST NOT KNOWN BUT WOULD HAVE PROBABLY INCLUDED THE FOLLOWING: Train Kept A Rollin' / I Can't Quit You Baby / Dazed And Confused / As Long As I Have You / White Summer / Black Mountain Side / Babe I'm Gonna Leave You / You Shook Me / How Many More Times / Pat's Delight / Communication Breakdown

16 June 1969, *Tasty Pop Sundae*, Studio 2, Aeolian Hall, 135-137 New Bond Street, London W1 (BBC Radio recording session from 7:30 p.m. to 11:00 p.m. Show was broadcast between 10:00 a.m. and 12:00 noon on *Chris Grant's Tasty Pop Sundae*, 25 July 1969. The session was originally going to be part of the more appropriate *Symonds On Sunday* program hosted by David Symonds, but ended up being replaced for the month of June by the rather lightweight *Tasty Pop Sundae*, which on this broadcast also featured sessions by Marmalade and Vanity Fare. The Led Zeppelin session includes a rare one-off recording of the Sleepy John Estes number "The Girl I Love She Got Long Black Wavy Hair." The other rarity was a cover of Eddie Cochran's "Something Else," a live favorite but never recorded in the studio until now. Jimmy had also acquired his 1958 Gibson Les Paul guitar to replace his well-worn Telecaster. This cover would certainly not have been out of place on *Led Zeppelin II*. Also recorded this day is a rather hilarious interview by a clearly out of his depth Chris Grant with Led Zeppelin. Not surprisingly, the interview was never broadcast but survives on bootleg. The majority of the broadcast, without interview and "What Is And What Should Never Be," was released on Led Zeppelin's *BBC Sessions* album in 1997.)

SETLIST:

THE GIRL I LOVE SHE GOT LONG BLACK WAVY HAIR
(Jimmy Page / Robert Plant / John Paul Jones / John Bonham / John Estes) Broadcast 22 June 1969 / Available on *BBC Sessions* CD Atlantic 7567-83061-2 released November 1997.

JIMMY PAGE: 1958 GIBSON LES PAUL GUITAR
ROBERT PLANT: LEAD VOCALS
JOHN PAUL JONES: BASS
JOHN BONHAM: DRUMS

COMMUNICATION BREAKDOWN (Jimmy Page / John Paul Jones / John Bonham) Broadcast 22 June 1969 / Available on *BBC Sessions* CD Atlantic 7567-83061-2 released November 1997.

> JIMMY PAGE: 1958 GIBSON LES PAUL GUITAR
> ROBERT PLANT: LEAD VOCALS, OVERDUBBED BACKING VOCALS ON CHORUS
> JOHN PAUL JONES: BASS
> JOHN BONHAM: DRUMS

SOMETHING ELSE (Sharon Sheeley / Bob Cochran) Broadcast 22 June 1969 / Available on *BBC Sessions* CD Atlantic 7567-83061-2 released November 1997.

> JIMMY PAGE: 1958 GIBSON LES PAUL
> ROBERT PLANT: LEAD VOCALS
> JOHN PAUL JONES: PIANO
> JOHN BONHAM: DRUMS

WHAT IS AND WHAT SHOULD NEVER BE (Jimmy Page / Robert Plant) Not broadcast and remains unreleased

> JIMMY PAGE: 1958 GIBSON LES PAUL GUITAR
> ROBERT PLANT: LEAD VOCALS
> JOHN PAUL JONES: BASS
> JOHN BONHAM: DRUMS
> PRODUCER: PAUL WILLIAMS
> ENGINEER: NOT KNOWN

18 June 1969, L'Antenne du Chapiteau du Kremlin-Bicêtre, Val de Marne, Paris (8:00 p.m. rehearsal for tomorrow's television recording.)

19 June 1969, L' Antenne du Chapiteau du Kremlin-Bicêtre, Val de Marne, Paris (Recording takes place between 4:00 p.m. and 8:00 p.m. The concert was professionally filmed for the popular *Tous En Scene* television show on the ORTF television channel. The show was broadcast on France's ORTF channel on 25 June 1969. It was re-broadcast on France's Canal Jimmy in 1991. Some song fragments from the show were used on the *Whole Lotta Love* promo video in 1997. An afternoon-rehearsal version of "Communication Breakdown" has survived and a mix of both versions along with a complete version of "Dazed And Confused" from the show can be found on the *Led Zeppelin* DVD, which was released in 2003.)

SETLIST: Communication Breakdown / Dazed And Confused

The filming of Led Zeppelin for *Tous En Scene* was done with two video cameras along with a further two 16mm film cameras. Led Zeppelin rehearsed all afternoon and played the concert in the evening in front of a Salvation Army Band in full uniform and looking somewhat bemused at these long-haired youths playing at very loud levels while they waited patiently for their turn to play. The main concern for Led Zeppelin, though, was the sound quality. The sound levels during the rehearsal had been perfect and well balanced, but were unfortunately changed by the sound engineer for the show in between the rehearsal and the actual show. This resulted in Robert Plant's vocals being very much up-front, to the detriment of the rest of the band who were now in the background. Both the rehearsal and evening concert were filmed.

> " On this day in 1969, I played the TV programme *Tous En Scene—Antenne Culturelle du Kremlin-Bicêtre*' in Paris with Led Zeppelin. The two songs that were featured in various TV shows and TV series to promote the band's work with reference to the first album were 'Communication Breakdown' and 'Dazed And Confused.' With some of these TV shows at the time, it became more obvious that wanting to perform our material live and the quality of the TV recording just wasn't working—like mixing oil and water. "
>
> **—JIMMY PAGE** (From his website)

20 June 1969, Barclay Records reception, Paris (Band reputedly play a thirty-minute set at around 1:00 a.m.)

20 June 1969, Newcastle City Hall, Newcastle, Newcastle Upon Tyne (7:30 p.m. Support from Liverpool Scene and Blodwyn Pig.)

SETLIST: The Train Kept A Rollin' / I Can't Quit You Baby / Dazed And Confused / White Summer / Black Mountain Side / You Shook Me (including The Lemon Song) / Pat's Delight / How Many More Times (including Over Under Sideways Down, There's A Mountain, The Hunter) / Communication Breakdown

Fabulous performance which luckily was recorded by an audience member allowing fans to hear a rare show from this UK tour in 1969. Page throws in some lines from Donovan's "There Is A Mountain" during "How Many More Times" and the band play a short instrumental jam ahead of "You Shook Me." The band and audience are clearly enjoying themselves as Robert Plant confirms, "You know we do a lot of work in America but I think this is the best night we've ever had in England."

21 June 1969, Colston Hall, Bristol, South West England (7:30 p.m.) Support from Liverpool Scene (Blodwyn Pig were unable to play that night. This date had been previously scheduled for 23 June 1969.

SETLIST NOT KNOWN BUT WOULD HAVE PROBABLY INCLUDED THE FOLLOWING: Train Kept A Rollin' / I Can't Quit You Baby / Dazed And Confused / As Long As I Have You / White Summer / Black Mountain Side / Babe I'm Gonna Leave You / You Shook Me / How Many More Times / Pat's Delight / Communication Breakdown

24 June 1969, *Top Gear*, BBC Maida Vale Studio 4, Delaware Road, London W9 (BBC Radio One recording session from 2:30 p.m. to 9:30 p.m. The session was broadcast between 7:00 p.m. and 9:00 p.m. on John Peel's *Top Gear* show on Radio One 29 June 1969. The influential *Top Gear*, hosted by John Peel, was aimed at fans of so-called underground music, so it fitted the bill perfectly for Led Zeppelin and their target audience. "Whole Lotta Love" obviously has none of the recording studio effects found on the *Led Zeppelin II* album, but the version here is still a smoldering anthem for the band with some killer wah-wah playing by Jimmy. Also played is a short but sweet version of "Communication Breakdown." Although the band had recorded a version of "What Is And What Should Never Be" at the previous BBC session, they had been unhappy with their performance of it. They redeem themselves with a much more confident and assured version at this session. The highlight has to be a their interpretation of Robert Johnson's "Travelling Riverside Blues" featuring some tasty slide work from Jimmy Page. A magnificent performance of a number that really that should have been revisited during sessions for their *Led Zeppelin II* album. Other bands in session were Pentangle, Savoy Brown Blues Band, and Idle Rice. The Led Zeppelin session was rebroadcast on Tommy Vance's *Friday Rock Show* on 2 February 1979. "Travelling Riverside Blues" was first released the *Led Zeppelin* box set in 1990.)

SETLIST:

WHOLE LOTTA LOVE (Jimmy Page / Robert Plant / John Paul Jones / John Bonham / Willie Dixon) Broadcast 29 June 1969 / Available on *BBC Sessions* CD Atlantic 7567-83061-2 released November 1997.

> JIMMY PAGE: 1958 GIBSON LES PAUL GUITAR
> ROBERT PLANT: LEAD VOCALS
> JOHN PAUL JONES: BASS
> JOHN BONHAM: DRUMS

COMMUNICATION BREAKDOWN (Jimmy Page / John Paul Jones / John Bonham) Broadcast 29 June 1969 / Available on *BBC Sessions* CD Atlantic 7567-83061-2 released November 1997.

> JIMMY PAGE: 1958 GIBSON LES PAUL GUITAR
> ROBERT PLANT: LEAD VOCALS, OVERDUBBED BACKING VOCALS ON CHORUS
> JOHN PAUL JONES: BASS
> JOHN BONHAM: DRUMS

WHAT IS AND WHAT SHOULD NEVER BE (Jimmy Page / Robert Plant) Broadcast 29 June 1969 / Available on *BBC Sessions* cd Atlantic 7567-83061-2 released November 1997.

> JIMMY PAGE: 1958 GIBSON LES PAUL GUITAR
> ROBERT PLANT: LEAD VOCALS
> JOHN PAUL JONES: BASS
> JOHN BONHAM: DRUMS

TRAVELLING RIVERSIDE BLUES (Jimmy Page / Robert Plant / Robert Johnson) Broadcast 29 June 1969 / Available on *BBC Sessions* CD Atlantic 7567-83061-2 released November 1997.

> JIMMY PAGE: DANELECTRO GUITAR
> ROBERT PLANT: LEAD VOCALS
> JOHN PAUL JONES: BASS
> JOHN BONHAM: DRUMS
> PRODUCER: JOHN WALTERS
> ENGINEER: TONY WILSON

Press advert for Led Zeppelin's UK summer 1969 tour.

66 We recorded this show at BBC's Maida Vale studio to promote *Led Zeppelin II*. In typical Led Zeppelin tradition, 'Travelling Riverside Blues' was made up on the spot from a riff I had on the electric twelve string. We had reached a point at the BBC where you could overdub a solo over the initial track of the song. This helped a lot to give a more complete rendition of our material and I must say the BBC engineer Tony Wilson did a really good job for us on this day. The BBC producer was John Walters. 99

—**JIMMY PAGE** (From his website)

26 June 1969, Portsmouth Guildhall, Portsmouth, Hampshire (7:30 p.m. Support from Liverpool Scene and Blodwyn Pig. This date had been previously scheduled for 27 June 1969.)

SETLIST NOT KNOWN BUT WOULD HAVE PROBABLY INCLUDED THE FOLLOWING: Communication Breakdown / I Can't Quit You Baby / Dazed And Confused / As Long As I Have You / White Summer / Black Mountain Side / Babe I'm Gonna Leave You / You Shook Me / How Many More Times

27 June 1969, *One Night Stand*, Playhouse Theatre, Northumberland Avenue, London WC2 (Led Zeppelin record their first live concert for the BBC, which was introduced by Alan Black. The concert recording session took place from 8:45 p.m. to 10:15 p.m. Rehearsal took place at 7:00 p.m. The session was broadcast between 8:00 p.m. and 9:00 p.m. on John Peel's *Top Gear*, 10 August 1969. The Led Zeppelin session was rebroadcast on Tommy Vance's *Friday Rock Show*, on 28 December 1979. In 2013, almost the entire show was rebroadcast on BBC Radio 6. "White Summer" / "Black Mountain Side" was released as a part of *Led Zeppelin* box set in late 1990. "Communication Breakdown," "I Can't Quit You Baby," "You Shook Me," and "How Many More Times" were released on the *BBC Sessions* album in 1997.

SETLIST:

COMMUNICATION BREAKDOWN (including "It's Your Thing") Broadcast 10 August 1969 / Available on *BBC Sessions* CD Atlantic 7567-83061-2 released November 1997. Copyright and royalty issues prevented ten seconds of Plant singing the Isley Brothers' "It's Your Thing" during "Communication Breakdown" from being issued on the official release.

I CAN'T QUIT YOU BABY BROADCAST 10 August 1969 / Available on *BBC Sessions* CD Atlantic 7567-83061-2 released November 1997.

JIMMY PAGE AND ROBERT PLANT INTERVIEW WITH ALAN BLACK BROADCAST 10 August 1969 / unreleased.

DAZED AND CONFUSED BROADCAST 10 August 1969 / unreleased

BATH FESTIVAL OF BLUES
RECREATION GROUND—PULTENEY STREET ENTRANCE

Saturday, June 28th

FEATURING

John Mayall - Fleetwood Mac
Led Zeppelin - 10 Years After
Nice
Chicken Shack
John Hiseman's Colosseum
Mick Abraham's Blodwyn Pig
Keef Hartley
Group Therapy
Liverpool Scene
Taste - Savoy Brown's Blues band
Champion Jack Dupre
Clouds   -   Babylon
Principal Edward's Magic Theatre
Deep Blues band - Just Before Dawn
Compére JOHN PEEL

| REFRESHMENTS AND HOT SNACKS WILL BE AVAILABLE ALL DAY | In case of bad weather there will be a substantial amount of under cover accommodation. 12 NOON—10.30 p.m. | IN ADVANCE All day 18/6. Eve only 14/6 ON DAY All day 22/6. Eve only 16/6 |

For further information regarding tickets please see over.

Handbill for the Bath Festival of Blues, which took place in Shepton Mallet, Somerset.

Poster for the Bath Festival of Blues which took place in Shepton Mallet, Somerset.

LIVERPOOL SCENE SKETCH (Adrian Henry / Mike Evans / Andy Roberts) Members of the Liverpool Scene, perform a short parody of television commercials during a break. Broadcast 10 August 1969 / unreleased.

WHITE SUMMER / BLACK MOUNTAIN SIDE BROADCAST 10 August 1969 Available on *Led Zeppelin* box set released in 1990 / *Coda* extended CD from the *Complete Studio Recordings* box set.

Press advert for Led Zeppelin's appearance at London's Royal Albert Hall.

YOU SHOOK ME BROADCAST 10 August 1969 / Available on *BBC Sessions* CD Atlantic 7567-83061-2 released November 1997.

HOW MANY MORE TIMES (including "The Hunter," "The Lemon Song") Broadcast 10 August 1969 / Available on *BBC Sessions* CD Atlantic 7567-83061-2 released November 1997.

JIMMY PAGE: 1958 GIBSON LES PAUL GUITAR / DANELECTRO (ON "WHITE SUMMER" / "BLACK MOUNTAIN SIDE")
ROBERT PLANT: LEAD VOCALS
JOHN PAUL JONES: BASS
JOHN BONHAM: DRUMS
PRODUCER: JEFF GRIFFIN
ENGINEER: TONY WILSON

28 June 1969, First Bath Festival of Blues and Progressive Music, Bath Recreation Grounds, Bath, Somerset (The festival started at 12:00 noon and featured Led Zeppelin playing on a bill with Fleetwood Mac, Ten Years After, John Mayall, the Nice, and Chicken Shack along with a host of other bands. 12,000 people attended the show, which was the largest audience Led Zeppelin had played to in the UK at that point.)

SETLIST NOT KNOWN BUT WOULD HAVE PROBABLY INCLUDED THE FOLLOWING: Communication Breakdown / I Can't Quit You Baby / Dazed And Confused / As Long As I Have You / White Summer / Black Mountain Side / Babe I'm Gonna Leave You / You Shook Me / How Many More Times

Souvenir program cover for the Pop Proms, which took place at London's Royal Albert Hall.

Press advert for Led Zeppelin's appearance at the Pop Proms, which took place at London's Royal Albert Hall.

Led Zeppelin onstage at the Pop Proms, which took place at London's Royal Albert Hall. (Rex)

EXIT

❝ Nobody had coerced the youth of England into becoming Zep freaks, but there they were, cheering Page, Jones, Bonham and Plant, as the drums thundered and the guitars roared. ❞
—**CHRIS WELCH** (*Melody Maker*, July 1969)

29 June 1969, Pop Proms, Royal Albert Hall, London (Two shows, 5:30 p.m. and 8:30 p.m. Support from Liverpool Scene, Blodwyn Pig and DJ Jeff Dexter. Members from the Liverpool Scene and Blodwyn Pig joined Led Zeppelin on their final encore, "Long Tall Sally."

SETLIST NOT KNOWN BUT WOULD HAVE PROBABLY INCLUDED THE FOLLOWING: Communication Breakdown / I Can't Quit You Baby / Dazed And Confused / As Long As I Have You / White Summer / Black Mountain Side / Babe I'm Gonna Leave You / You Shook Me / How Many More Times / Long Tall Sally

❝ When the group returned to the stage, they found the power had been switched off. 'Hey, put the power on,' demanded singer Robert Plant as the group stood bewildered. Stalemate, Plant took up a harmonica and let fly on that and all the others could do was clap until a few minutes later the flow of juice was resumed. With the first few bars of 'Long Tall Sally,' the audience was on its feet dancing in the aisles and in the boxes and there was incredible mayhem happening on and around the stage. The saxists from Blodwyn Pig and Liverpool Scene added their support in to the Zeppelin's rock. ❞
—*NEW MUSICAL EXPRESS* (Review, July 1969)

LED ZEPPELIN THIRD US TOUR

5 JULY 1969–31 AUGUST 1969

JULY 1969

5 July 1969, First Atlanta International Pop Festival, Atlanta International Raceway, Hampton, Georgia (2:00 p.m. Led Zeppelin shared the bill with the cream of US rock acts: Janis Joplin, Canned Heat, Sweetwater, the Paul Butterfield Blues Band, Delaney and Bonnie, Spirit, among many others.)

SETLIST NOT KNOWN, BUT WOULD HAVE PROBABLY INCLUDED THE FOLLOWING:
The Train Kept A Rollin' / I Can't Quit You Baby (including Your Good Thing [Is About To End]) / Dazed And Confused / You Shook Me / How Many More Times (including The Hunter, The Lemon Song) / Communication Breakdown

6 July 1969, Sixteenth Annual Newport Jazz Festival, Newport Festival Field, Newport, Rhode Island (1:00 a.m. The band headlined the fourth night of the festival. Other artists sharing the bill over the four days included Jeff Beck, Miles Davis, John Mayall, Savage Rose, Sly & the Family Stone, B.B. King, Johnny Winter, Herbie Hancock, among many others.)

SETLIST: The Train Kept A Rollin' / I Can't Quit You Baby (including Your Good Thing [Is About To End]) / Dazed And Confused / You Shook Me / How Many More Times (including The Hunter, The Lemon Song) / Communication Breakdown / Long Tall Sally

For an appearance that almost did not happen due to growing tensions between authorities and large groups of concert goers, the band put in a high-octane performance that just kills the audience. Maybe the band's annoyance at the misinformation given to the fans about one of the band being ill and having to cancel gave them an extra push to deliver an intense performance. Robert Plant informs the boisterous crowd, "A lot of people thought that we weren't gonna come here today. There was a lot of talk that

Front cover of Led Zeppelin tour program, which now commands high prices in the collectors market.

Press advert for Led Zeppelin's appearance at the Newport Jazz Festival, Rhode Island.

everyone was ill and bad. There was nothing wrong with us at all and we intended on playing. That's what we've come to America for. We were coming in the first place, so don't get any hassles about what we were gonna do and what we weren't. We hope you'll enjoy everything we do tonight and have a ball!"

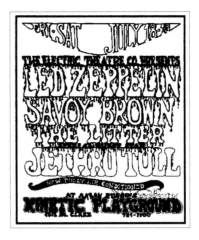

Press advert for Led Zeppelin's appearance at the Kinetic Playground in Chicago.

66 It also attracted the attention of the local authorities who, because of the tension and near riotous situation which prevailed on the same Friday night, demanded that Led Zeppelin be canceled from the final bill on Sunday, and subsequently revoked the permission given for the opening concert on the Blind Faith tour. Wein announced the Zeppelin would not appear owing to the illness of one of the group. They showed up on Sunday anyway, following a knockout performance at the Atlanta Pop Festival and at 1 a.m. Monday morning, proceeded to go on stage and completely destroy the audience. 99

—**J. HARRIS** (Review, July 1969)

8 July 1969, Miami Convention Center, Miami, Florida (There is no evidence that this show took place.)

9 July 1969, Tampa, Florida (There is no evidence that this show took place.)

10 July 1969, Jacksonville, Florida (There is no evidence that this show took place.)

11 July 1969, Laurel Jazz & Pop Festival, Laurel Race Course, Maryland (8:00 p.m. The band headlined. Shared bill with Savoy Brown, Frank Zappa & the Mothers of Invention, Buddy Guy, Jethro Tull, Johnny Winter, Ten Years After, Wilson Picket, among others.)

SETLIST NOT KNOWN BUT WOULD HAVE PROBABLY INCLUDED THE FOLLOWING: The Train Kept A Rollin' / I Can't Quit You Baby (including Your Good Thing [Is About To End]) / Dazed And Confused / You Shook Me / How Many More Times (including The Hunter, The Lemon Song) / Communication Breakdown

12 July 1969, Summer Pop Festival, the Spectrum, Philadelphia (8:00 p.m. Led Zeppelin headlined on the last day of the festival. Shared bill with Johnny Winter, Jeff Beck, Blood, Sweat & Tears, Al Kooper, Jethro Tull, Buddy Guy's Blues Band, and many others.)

SETLIST NOT KNOWN, BUT WOULD HAVE PROBABLY INCLUDED THE FOLLOWING: The Train Kept A Rollin' / I Can't Quit You Baby (including Your Good Thing [Is About To End]) / Dazed And Confused / You Shook Me / How Many More Times (including The Hunter, The Lemon Song) / Communication Breakdown

66 At the Spectrum Stadium in Philadelphia where a three-day festival was in progress, there was a strict rule that no artist could perform an encore—they each had a 30 minute spot and that was that. After Zep left the stage the audience went berserk and screamed for more. They continued demanding an encore and the organizers finally had to let them reappear. 99

—*TOP POPS* **REVIEW**

13 July 1969, Singer Bowl, Flushing Meadows, Queens, New York (Guest appearance. The band joined the Jeff Beck Group, along with Glenn Cornick of Jethro Tull and Alvin Lee of Ten Years After, onstage for an encore jam of "Jailhouse Rock." John Bonham had earlier joined Jeff Beck, playing drums on "Rice Pudding."

66 Sunday's (13th) Jeff Beck, Vanilla Fudge, Ten Years After, Edwin Hawkins Singers concert at Singer Bowl resulted in an unexpected jam amongst members of The Jeff Beck Group, Led Zeppelin and Jethro Tull. The music excited Zeppelin drummer John Bonham to the point where he started tearing his clothes off. He was carried offstage by friends before he could get past his underwear. 99

—**PRESS REVIEW**

15 July 1969, Rochester, New York (There is no evidence that this show took place.)

16 July 1969, Olympia Stadium, Detroit, Michigan (There is no evidence that this show took place.)

17 July 1969, Cincinnati, Ohio (There is no evidence that this show took place.)

18 July 1969, Kinetic Playground, Chicago, Illinois (8:30 p.m. Support from Savoy Brown and the Litter with special guest Jethro Tull.)

SETLIST NOT KNOWN BUT WOULD HAVE PROBABLY INCLUDED THE FOLLOWING: The Train Kept A Rollin' / I Can't Quit You Baby (including Your Good Thing [Is About To End]) / Dazed And Confused / You Shook Me / How Many More Times (including The Hunter, The Lemon Song) / Communication Breakdown

66 The ecstasy inherent in The Doors is due for the most part to Jim Morrison, but with Led Zeppelin it's all four of them; they all exude this tremendous energy force. John Bonham, the drummer, is excellent. Most drum solos tend to fall into monotony quickly and become boring, but his was able to keep the listener constantly involved, feeling each rhythm throughout one's whole body. Jimmy Page and John Paul Jones are also able to do this with their instruments. 99

—REVIEW IN THE *CHICAGO TRIBUNE* (JULY 1969)

19 July 1969, Kinetic Playground, Chicago, Illinois (8:30 p.m. Support from Savoy Brown and the Litter with special guest Jethro Tull.)

SETLIST NOT KNOWN, BUT WOULD HAVE PROBABLY INCLUDED THE FOLLOWING: The Train Kept A Rollin' / I Can't Quit You Baby (including Your Good Thing [Is About To End]) / Dazed And Confused / You Shook Me / How Many More Times (including The Hunter, The Lemon Song) / Communication Breakdown

20 July 1969, Musiccarnival, Warrensville Heights, Cleveland, Ohio (7:00 p.m. Support from the James Gang.)

SETLIST: The Train Kept A Rollin' / I Can't Quit You Baby / Dazed And Confused / White Summer / Black Mountain Side / You Shook Me / How Many More Times (including The Hunter, The Lemon Song, You Make Me Feel So Young) / Communication Breakdown

The intensity and concentration is let down tonight by equipment problems as Robert Plants reminds the crowd, "Once again, as last time in the state of Ohio, we find that the PA system is completely inaudible; but, nevertheless, we'd like to carry on. . . . I think I'd better get out of the way. . . . If we go up with a flash and a bang . . ." Plant jokingly sings a few lines of "You Make Me Feel So Young" during the "How Many More Times" medley. Jimmy Page strikes up a friendship with Joe Walsh, who is the guitarist in the James Gang.

66 Jimmy Page, former anchor man for the Yardbirds, received a standing ovation for his bluesy solo 'White Summer.' But the group hit their highest stride in the last part of their 10-minute 'Dazed and Confused' when Page, singer Robert Plant, drummer John Bonham and bass guitarist John Paul Jones sailed in a tight, together jam. Plant shakes and bumps like a burlesque headliner, swings the mike like a lariat, comes across with the funky finesse of a male Janis Joplin. The Atlantic group scored with encore 'Communication Breakdown.' A local group, the James Gang, also received a standing ovation. 99

—JANE SCOTT (Review in *Billboard*, July 1969)

21 July 1969, Schaefer Music Festival, Wollman Skating Rink Theater, Central Park, New York City, New York (Two shows at 7:00 p.m. and 9:30 p.m. Led Zeppelin headlined on the first day of the festival with B.B. King. The festival ran from

Press advert for Led Zeppelin's appearance at the Midwest Rock Festival, which took place at the State Fair Grounds in Milwaukee, Wisconsin.

21 July to 27 July and featured artists such as, Sly & the Family Stone, Joni Mitchell, and Tim Hardin, among others. It is reported that forty minutes of 16mm color film exists along with another 16mm full coat mag track with sound.)

SETLIST: The Train Kept A Rollin' / I Can't Quit You Baby / Dazed And Confused / You Shook Me (including Rock Me Baby) / White Summer / Black Mountain Side / How Many More Times (including Woody Woodpecker Song, For What It's Worth, The Hunter, The Lemon Song, You Make Me Feel So Young) / Communication Breakdown (including Just A Little Bit)

Another great 1969 show where the crowd and band are one. The energy the band had during this period is incredible. Their new album was pretty much finished, but they were not playing any new material just yet as Plant explained to the crowd, "We've got an album coming out in the second week in August, but at the moment there's a bit of delay in us getting the numbers together really for stage, because we're still doing the old ones." The band are in good spirits playing the "Woody Woodpecker" theme during the "How Many More Times" medley as well as "You Make Me Feel So Young."

66 Led Zeppelin practically brought the house down; no kidding. By the end of a four-encore musical colossus the beam and erector-set framework of the temporary stage (and adjoining walls) were creaking under the strain as performers and audience alike were swept into a rock 'n' roll bacchanalia that would have made the most cynical critic wilt. The accomplishment and spontaneity of John Paul Jones on bass and John Bonham on drums could have only been enhanced by a phenomenon like Jimmy Page. The apparently unimprovable gifts of the youthful virtuoso have, if possible, expanded since we saw him last. The subtlety and lyrical inventiveness for which Page has always been recognized seem to have gained a hitherto dormant passion equal to that of any flamenco gypsy, as he whipped through 'I Can't Quit You Babe,' 'Dazed and Confused,' and the incredible 'White Summer.' 99

—*CASH BOX* (Review, August 1969)

25 July 1969, Mid-West Rock Festival, Grand Stand, Wisconsin State Fair Park, West Allis, Wisconsin (5:00 p.m. The festival was spread over two days and featured groups such Pacific Gas & Electric, Blind Faith, Delaney & Bonnie, Taste, MC5, Joe Cocker & the Grease Band, and Jeff Beck Group, among others.)

SETLIST: The Train Kept A Rollin' / I Can't Quit You Baby / Dazed And Confused / White Summer / Black Mountain Side / How Many More Times (including The Hunter, Travelling Riverside Blues, The Lemon Song) / Communication Breakdown

Another incredible high-octane performance from Led Zeppelin. How did they manage to be generally so consistent in their playing during this period? Passion and youth were the main two ingredients at this stage. Those and the fact that they were fast becoming superstars.

26 July 1969, PNE Agrodome, Vancouver, British Columbia, Canada (8:30 p.m. Support from Vanilla Fudge.)

SETLIST NOT KNOWN, BUT WOULD HAVE PROBABLY INCLUDED THE FOLLOWING: The Train Kept A Rollin' / I Can't Quit You Baby / Dazed And Confused / You Shook Me / How Many More Times (including The Hunter, The Lemon Song) / Communication Breakdown

Poster for Led Zeppelin's appearance at the Fairgrounds Arena, Santa Barbara, California.

66 Led Zeppelin exists on the genius of lead guitarist Jimmy Page, whose baby face bellies his musical message, that of jarring and unnerving the listeners with a fortissimo yowl that never lets up, never allows time for recovery. . . . It is made up of four individual musical artists attuned to each other's whims, capable of ensemble performance as well as separate forays into the jungle of lonely escapades. How perfectly Led Zeppelin has assessed the hang-ups of their listeners is evident when Plant screams, 'Do you feel all right?' And seething mob below the platform screams back: 'Yes!' 99

—J. HESSE (Review in *Vancouver Sun*, July 1969)

27 July 1969, Seattle Pop Festival, Gold Creek Park, Woodinville, Washington (12:00 noon. Led Zeppelin share the bill with Chuck Berry, the Byrds, Chicago Transit Authority, Albert Collins, the Doors, Flying Burrito Brothers, It's a Beautiful Day, Santana, Spirit, Ten Years After, and Vanilla Fudge, among others.)

SETLIST NOT KNOWN, BUT WOULD HAVE PROBABLY INCLUDED THE FOLLOWING: The Train Kept A Rollin' / I Can't Quit You Baby / Dazed And Confused / You Shook Me / How Many More Times (including The Hunter, The Lemon Song) / Communication Breakdown

66 Sunday night was supposed to belong to The Doors but it was stolen right out from under them by the great English blues group, Led Zeppelin. Coming onstage about 11:30 p.m., immediately after the forced extravaganza of The Doors, the Zeppelin faced a jaded and uncomfortable audience that had been standing in the cold all evening. But the electricity of lead singer Robert Plant and guitarist Jimmy Page quickly warmed them up. Plant has a voice that is controlled hysteria. Anguish pours from his every note; his voice is an epitome of the blues. 99

—P. MACDONALD

(Review in *Seattle Post-Intelligencer*, July 1969)

29 July 1969, Main Hall, Kinsmen Field House, Edmonton, Alberta, Canada (Vanilla Fudge are co-headliners at this show and play last. Vanilla Fudge's drummer, Carmine Appice, and bassist Tim Bogert switched places with John Bonham and John Paul Jones in the middle of "How Many More Times," which evidently came as a surprise to Robert Plant and Jimmy Page.)

SETLIST NOT KNOWN, BUT WOULD HAVE PROBABLY INCLUDED THE FOLLOWING: The Train Kept A Rollin' / I Can't Quit You Baby / Dazed And Confused / You Shook Me / How Many More Times (including The Hunter, The Lemon Song) / Communication Breakdown

66 It would have been better if Vanilla Fudge had played first. Their music's more intellectual and more jazz-influenced than the gutsy Zeppelin's. Tuesday's show at the Kinsmen Field House was probably the best of the year and the size of the turnout probably caught the promoters—Concerts West of Seattle and Dick Lodmell—by surprise. There weren't enough chairs to go around the crowd of 5,000 but otherwise, the concert was the smoothest and best-organized rock show here in a long time. 99

—*EDMONTON JOURNAL* (Review, 1 August 1969)

30 July 1969, Terrace Ballroom, Salt Lake City, Utah (7:00 p.m. and 9:30 p.m. Vanilla Fudge are co-headliners at this show and play last.)

SETLIST NOT KNOWN, BUT WOULD HAVE PROBABLY INCLUDED THE FOLLOWING: The Train Kept A Rollin' / I Can't Quit You Baby / Dazed And Confused / You Shook Me / How Many More Times (including The Hunter, The Lemon Song) / Communication Breakdown

66 Both Zeppelin and Fudge are prominent hands on the 'heavy' scene. The British group Led Zeppelin was billed second to the well-known American group Vanilla Fudge. But Zeppelin went over noticeably better than Fudge. . . . Led by Jimmy Page, one time guitarist for the Yardbirds, Led Zeppelin's music is characterized by excellent, flashy vocals backed by creative and appropriate guitar work. Vanilla Fudge appeared as musical imposters when compared to a group like Zeppelin. The bass player for the Fudge even apologetically acknowledged this as he mounted the stage and said, 'There's no way we can follow that.' 99

—S. POULSEN (Review in *Summer Chronicle*, 1 August 1969)

31 July 1969, Eugene, Oregon (There is no evidence that this show took place.)

AUGUST 1969

1 August 1969, Samuel E. Kramer Arena, Earl Warren Showgrounds, Santa Barbara, California (7:30 p.m. Support from Jethro Tull and Fraternity of Man.)

SETLIST NOT KNOWN, BUT WOULD HAVE PROBABLY INCLUDED THE FOLLOWING: The Train Kept A Rollin' / I Can't Quit You Baby / Dazed And Confused / You Shook Me / How Many More Times (including The Hunter, The Lemon Song) / Communication Breakdown

2 August 1969, Albuquerque Civic Auditorium, Albuquerque, New Mexico (8:30 p.m. Co-headliner with Vanilla Fudge. Vanilla Fudge play first tonight.)

SETLIST NOT KNOWN, BUT WOULD HAVE PROBABLY INCLUDED THE FOLLOWING: The Train Kept A Rollin' / I Can't Quit You Baby / Dazed And Confused / You Shook Me / How Many More Times (including The Hunter, The Lemon Song) / Communication Breakdown

3 August 1969, Houston Music Hall, Houston, Texas (8:00 p.m.)

SETLIST NOT KNOWN, BUT WOULD HAVE PROBABLY INCLUDED THE FOLLOWING: The Train Kept A Rollin' / I Can't Quit You Baby / Dazed And Confused / You Shook Me / How Many More Times (including The Hunter, The Lemon Song) / Communication Breakdown

66 Lead guitarist Jimmy Page is the helium in the Zeppelin. Primarily responsible for the group's unique sound, he is almost a one-man, one-instrument rock band. Cross-fretting, picking, plunking, slapping, even bowing, Page utilizes the peculiarities of amplified guitar to produce dynamic contrasts, echo and simulated feedback effects.99

—*HOUSTON CHRONICLE* (Review from August 1969)

4 August 1969, Texas State Fair Coliseum, Dallas, Texas (8:00 p.m. Support from F.O.B.)

SETLIST NOT KNOWN, BUT WOULD HAVE PROBABLY INCLUDED THE FOLLOWING: The Train Kept A Rollin' / I Can't Quit You Baby / Dazed And Confused / You Shook Me / How Many More Times (including The Hunter, The Lemon Song) / Communication Breakdown

6 August 1969, Sacramento Memorial Auditorium, Sacramento, California

SETLIST NOT KNOWN, BUT WOULD HAVE PROBABLY INCLUDED THE FOLLOWING: The Train Kept A Rollin' / I Can't Quit You Baby / Dazed And Confused / You Shook Me / How Many More Times (including The Hunter, The Lemon Song) / Communication Breakdown

7 August 1969, Berkeley Community Theater, Berkeley, California (There is no evidence that this concert took place.)

Jimmy Page onstage at the State Fair Coliseum, Dallas, Texas. (Photo by Carl Dunn)

Robert Plant onstage at the State Fair Coliseum, Dallas, Texas. (Photo by Carl Dunn)

8 August 1969, Swing Auditorium, San Bernardino, California (8:00 p.m. Support from Jethro Tull and Trane.)

SETLIST: The Train Kept A Rollin' / I Can't Quit You Baby / I Gotta Move / Dazed And Confused / White Summer / You Shook Me / How Many More Times (including The Hunter, Everything I Do Gonna Be Funky, The Lemon Song, Schooldays, Hail Hail Rock 'n' Roll)

The intense heat causes tuning problems for Jimmy Page at various stages throughout the show. Plant, ever the professional, fills in for Page, "We're gonna carry on with a thing from the first album, which I better tell you a bit about as Jimmy's doing a quick string thing. We did an album called *Led Zeppelin One*, but we left the 'One' off, 'cos we didn't know what to call it at the time. You must bear with me, 'cos it's on-the-spot coordination, so if you're ready to take it, I can give it!" The group proceed to play a jam that sounds like "I Gotta Move," which they had done back in Stockholm on 14 March 1969. The delays caused by the guitar problems means the band ran out of time and could not play an extra encore after "How Many More Times."

Press advert for Led Zeppelin's appearance at the Texas State Fair, Dallas, Texas.

9 August 1969, Anaheim Convention Center Arena, Anaheim, California (8:00 p.m. Support from Fairport Convention and Jethro Tull.)

SETLIST NOT KNOWN, BUT WOULD HAVE PROBABLY INCLUDED THE FOLLOWING: The Train Kept A Rollin' / I Can't Quit You Baby / Dazed And Confused / You Shook Me / How Many More Times (including The Hunter, The Lemon Song) / Communication Breakdown

10 August 1969, San Diego Sports Arena, San Diego, California (8:00 p.m. Support from Surprise Package and Jethro Tull.)

SETLIST NOT KNOWN, BUT WOULD HAVE PROBABLY INCLUDED THE FOLLOWING: The Train Kept A Rollin' / I Can't Quit You Baby / Dazed And Confused / You Shook Me / How Many More Times (including The Hunter, The Lemon Song) / Communication Breakdown

❝ Last night at the International Sports Arena, the British supergroup Led Zeppelin created a kind of instant magic, the moment it appeared on stage. People began milling around when Robert Plant, the lead vocalist, went into his Janis Joplin dancing and screaming act. The group played well, exceptionally well, but all that instant charisma seemed rather preposterous. Jimmy Page, the old Yardbird, did a beautiful solo guitar number in 'White Summer' and the whole group jammed hard and right on 'Days of Confusion.'**❞**

—S.D. UNION (Review from 11 August 1969)

❝ Jethro Tull were great, playing to a sold-out audience who really appreciated their efforts. Led Zeppelin, ostensibly stars of the show, came on for the second half. They were awful. Loud, pretentious, no subtlety, no nuance, just multi-decibel riffs, echoed by Plant's frenzied 'singing.' He has obviously been watching Roger Daltrey. It would be nice if he listened to Roger Daltrey. And the crowd loved it! Perhaps I shouldn't blame Page and co. for performing undemanding material when all they have to do is stand there and whack out mediocrity to receive the reward of thunderous appreciation that greeted their every move.**❞**

—JUDY SIMS (*Disc*, UK music publication)

11 August 1969, Las Vegas Ice Palace, Las Vegas, Nevada (Support from Pinkiny Canandy)

SETLIST NOT KNOWN, BUT WOULD HAVE PROBABLY INCLUDED THE FOLLOWING: The Train Kept A Rollin' / I Can't Quit You Baby / Dazed And Confused / You Shook Me / How Many More Times (including The Hunter, The Lemon Song) / Communication Breakdown

13 August 1969, Civic Center Music Hall, Lubbock, Texas

SETLIST NOT KNOWN, BUT WOULD HAVE PROBABLY INCLUDED THE FOLLOWING: The Train Kept A Rollin' / I Can't Quit You Baby / Dazed And Confused / You Shook Me / How Many More Times (including The Hunter, The Lemon Song) / Communication Breakdown

14 August 1969, Austin Municipal Auditorium, Austin, Texas (Support from Flash and the Laughing Kind)

SETLIST NOT KNOWN, BUT WOULD HAVE PROBABLY INCLUDED THE FOLLOWING: The Train Kept A Rollin' / I Can't Quit You Baby / Dazed And Confused / You Shook Me / How Many More Times (including The Hunter, The Lemon Song) / Communication Breakdown

15 August 1969, Hemisfair Arena, San Antonio, Texas (8:00 p.m. Co-billed with Jethro Tull and Sweet Smoke.)

SETLIST NOT KNOWN, BUT WOULD HAVE PROBABLY INCLUDED THE FOLLOWING: The Train Kept A Rollin' / I Can't Quit You Baby / Dazed And Confused / You Shook Me / How Many More Times (including The Hunter, The Lemon Song) / Communication Breakdown

16 August 1969, Asbury Park Convention Hall, Asbury Park, New Jersey (Two shows at 7:30 p.m. and 10:00 p.m. Support from Joe Cocker. This date coincided with the now legendary Woodstock Festival in New York's Bethel. Joe Cocker flies to the festival site after playing the shows with Led Zeppelin, who had also been approached to play the festival, but Peter Grant turned down the offer.)

SETLIST NOT KNOWN, BUT WOULD HAVE PROBABLY INCLUDED THE FOLLOWING: The Train Kept A Rollin' / I Can't Quit You Baby / Dazed And Confused / You Shook Me / How Many More Times (including The Hunter, The Lemon Song) / Communication Breakdown

❝ Among Zeppelin's numbers were a rousing 'Dazed and Confused,' which seemed to please the audience immensely and featured Plant on vocals and choreography and Page's guitar; 'You Shook Me' and a solo by Page, which, according to Plant, the group 'still likes to call "White Summer"' and which demonstrated clearly Page's technical mastery of the electric guitar and showed just as clearly his search for a style. The audience at the last show, while happily attentive and receptive to Joe Cocker, seemed to be more followers of Led Zeppelin. ❞

—**J. PIKULA** (Review in *Asbury Press*, 18 August 1969)

17 August 1969, Oakdale Theatre, Wallingford, Connecticut (8:00 p.m. Support from the Mustard Family. The bands played on a revolving stage, which resulted in a very uneven sound.)

SETLIST: The Train Kept A Rollin' / I Can't Quit You Baby / Dazed And Confused / White Summer / Black Mountain Side / You Shook Me / How Many More Times (including The Hunter, The Lemon Song) / Communication Breakdown

18 August 1969, The Rock Pile, Toronto, Ontario (Two shows at 8:00 p.m. and 11:30 p.m. Support from Edward Bear.)

FIRST SHOW SETLIST: The Train Kept A Rollin' / I Can't Quit You Baby / Dazed And Confused / You Shook Me / How Many More Times (including The Hunter, The Lemon Song)

SECOND SHOW SETLIST: The Train Kept A Rollin' / I Can't Quit You Baby / Dazed And Confused / White Summer / Black Mountain Side / You Shook Me / How Many More Times (including The Hunter, Truckin' Little Mama, The Needle, The Lemon Song) / Communication Breakdown

The band are in good form for their first set, but are clearly keeping some energy back for the later second set, which was mind-blowing. The epic numbers from *Led Zeppelin I* are played with power and the crowd goes wild, showing its appreciation to an overwhelmed band. Led Zeppelin had a few problems with their appearance in Texas and are thrilled to be so warmly welcomed in Canada. Plant told the crowd about their problems: "It's very nice to be back, but we've got a lot of problems. We've just come from San Antonio in Texas, where all the geezers thought we should get our hair cut, and we've been through that and everybody's been feeling rather bad, so we're very pleased to be here one way or another. It's nice to be back. We'd like to say hello to anybody from the British Isles, including Scotland and two geezers who used to come from Birmingham in a group called the Yellow Rainbow. Nice to see you're still nicking gear! And so, if everybody can feel free and easy, we'd like to see what we can do." By the end of the show, the whole band are in great spirits. They know they have played a great set and have been rapturously received. Plant tells them, "We'd like to try to draw a conclusion to what's been a very hectic day. We'd like to tell you that Texas is still as it was when you last read about it and that England is still what it always will be, and we'd like to see you very shortly again, but if not you could all move to the Bahamas or something . . . on bass guitar, Hammond organ, and throne . . . King John Paul Jones, on drums

John Henry Bonham and on lead guitar and as many chicks as he can find . . . Jimmy Page!" John Bonham then takes the microphone and introduces Plant as coming "straight from the Labour club at Cradley Heath." The final encore is an uber-dynamic version of "Communication Breakdown," introduced as "an old number by Bing Crosby," which has the concrete floor of the venue vibrating to the heavy pulse of the PA.

66 Not only were the two shows completely sold out in advance, but at least 2,000 were turned away, the management reported. Led Zeppelin proved itself not only to be one conceivable replacement for Cream, but at times I doubt if even Clapton, Bruce and Baker could have topped what Zeppelin offered. At its tightest, Cream was the most exciting band of musicians in the history of rock 'n' roll, yet the Zeppelin came close to equaling it. 99

—RICHIE YORKE (Review in "Pop Scene," *G&M*, August 1969)

20 August 1969, Schenectady Aerodrome, Schenectady, New York (Two shows at 8:00 p.m. and 11:00 p.m. Support from Spyder and Last Thursday.)

SETLIST NOT KNOWN, BUT WOULD HAVE PROBABLY INCLUDED THE FOLLOWING: The Train Kept A Rollin' / I Can't Quit You Baby / Dazed And Confused / You Shook Me / How Many More Times (including The Hunter, The Lemon Song) / Communication Breakdown

21 August 1969, Carousel Theatre, Framingham, Massachusetts (Support from Orpheus. DJ J. J. Jackson introduced the band onstage. Robert Plant introduces "What Is And What Should Never Be" as a new song from their forthcoming album, which is played for the very first time in public.)

SETLIST NOT KNOWN, BUT WOULD HAVE PROBABLY INCLUDED THE FOLLOWING: The Train Kept A Rollin' / I Can't Quit You Baby / Dazed And Confused / What Is And What Should Never Be / You Shook Me / How Many More Times (including The Hunter, The Lemon Song) / Communication Breakdown

66 Most of the tunes came from the group's album. There was Willie Dixon's 'Down and Dirty Blues,' 'I Can't Quit You Babe,' featuring a fine Jimmy Page solo. Later came Page's own earthy 'Dazed and Confused,' to be greeted by a standing ovation. Next there was a zinging Indian-influenced solo tune by Page again; then 'What Is and What Should Never Be' (never before done on stage); and at last Dixon's 'You Shook Me.' The Zeppelin flew high all right, and therein may be its problem; it has a tendency to soar, rather than keep on a straight flight plan. 99

—THE *GLOBE* (Review from August 1969)

22 August 1969, Pirates World, Dania, Florida (Support from the Echo, Royal Ascots, and Brimstone. The band were staying at the Doral hotel in Miami and caught Little Richard and his band in the small cocktail lounge club in the hotel basement.)

SETLIST NOT KNOWN, BUT WOULD HAVE PROBABLY INCLUDED THE FOLLOWING: The Train Kept A Rollin' / I Can't Quit You Baby / Dazed And Confused / What Is And What Should Never Be / You Shook Me / How Many More Times (including The Hunter, The Lemon Song) / Communication Breakdown

23 August 1969, Pirates World, Dania, Florida (Support from the Echo, Royal Ascots, and Brimstone)

SETLIST NOT KNOWN, BUT WOULD HAVE PROBABLY INCLUDED THE FOLLOWING: The Train Kept A Rollin' / I Can't Quit You Baby / Dazed And Confused / What Is And What Should Never Be / You Shook Me / How Many More Times (including The Hunter, The Lemon Song) / Communication Breakdown

24 August 1969, Jacksonville Memorial Coliseum, Jacksonville, Florida

SETLIST NOT KNOWN, BUT WOULD HAVE PROBABLY INCLUDED THE FOLLOWING: The Train Kept A Rollin' / I Can't Quit You Baby / Dazed And Confused / What Is And What Should Never Be / You Shook Me / How Many More Times (including The Hunter, The Lemon Song) / Communication Breakdown

66 Led Zeppelin generated excitement to the crowd at the Jacksonville Coliseum. In fact, the four-piece powerhouse brought the audience out of its general admission seats to crowd around near the stage. The fans gave standing ovations to the group's last two songs, and when the performance was over people rushed the stage and Bob Plant—the group's secret weapon who generates emotion of blues—shook hands with fans. Plant simply yelled, 'You're fantastic!' and finally left the stage. 99

—*JACKSONVILLE JOURNAL* (Review from August 1969)

25 August 1969, Delano Motor Lodge, Monticello, New York (Two shows at 9:00 p.m. and 11:30 p.m.)

SETLIST NOT KNOWN, BUT WOULD HAVE PROBABLY INCLUDED THE FOLLOWING: The Train Kept A Rollin' / I Can't Quit You Baby / Dazed And Confused / What Is And What Should Never Be / You Shook Me / How Many More Times (including The Hunter, The Lemon Song) / Communication Breakdown

27 August 1969, Hampton Beach Casino Ballroom, Hampton Beach, New Hampshire (Two shows at 8:00 p.m. and 10:00 p.m.)

SETLIST NOT KNOWN, BUT WOULD HAVE PROBABLY INCLUDED THE FOLLOWING: The Train Kept A Rollin' / I Can't Quit You Baby / Dazed And Confused / What Is And What Should Never Be / You Shook Me / How Many More Times (including The Hunter, The Lemon Song) / Communication Breakdown

29 August 1969, the Pavilion at Flushing Meadows Park, Queens, New York (Billed as "Guitar Virtuoso Show." Support from Larry Coryell and Raven.)

SETLIST NOT KNOWN, BUT WOULD HAVE PROBABLY INCLUDED THE FOLLOWING: The Train Kept A Rollin' / I Can't Quit You Baby / Dazed And Confused / What Is And What Should Never Be / You Shook Me / How Many More Times (including The Hunter, The Lemon Song) / Communication Breakdown

❝ Page's style, with all its fury and passion, was an excellent complement to (previous act) Larry Coryell's and provided an excellent study in different approaches to the same instrument. At one point, Page played his guitar with a violin bow, and in addition to being a great gimmick and fabulous showmanship, it created a unique, very exciting sound. ❞
—*CASHBOX* (Review from September 1969)

30 August 1969, the Pavilion at Flushing Meadows Park, Queens, New York (Billed as "Guitar Virtuoso Show." Support from Buddy Guy and Raven.)

SETLIST NOT KNOWN, BUT WOULD HAVE PROBABLY INCLUDED THE FOLLOWING: The Train Kept A Rollin' / I Can't Quit You Baby / Dazed And Confused / What Is And What Should Never Be / You Shook Me / How Many More Times (including The Hunter, The Lemon Song) / Communication Breakdown

❝ On this night, I played in Flushing Meadows, New York, with Led Zeppelin who were on the bill with Buddy Guy and Larry Coryell. The legendary Bernard Purdie was playing drums in the house band that night. I made a point of going to hear Buddy Guy as this would be my first time of hearing him play live. I'd admired and had been moved by his playing, one of my earliest access points being his dynamic guitar playing and vocals on the *Folk Festival of the Blues* album on Chess Records. I had heard legendary stories of him when he had made a fleeting visit to England in 1965. Even to this day, Buddy Guy's guitar playing and vocals are something of a primeval force. ❞
—**JIMMY PAGE** (From his website)

Press advert for Led Zeppelin's appearance at the Anaheim Convention Center in Anaheim, California.

Press advert for Led Zeppelin's appearance at the Pavilion in Flushing Meadows Park, Queens, New York.

Press advert for the huge Texas International Pop Festival, which took place over Labor Day weekend at the Dallas International Motor Speedway. Led Zeppelin appear on the bill alongside artists such as Janis Joplin, Herbie Mann, Ten Years After, Delaney & Bonnie, Chicago Transit Authority, Canned Heat, B.B. King, Spirit, and other popular acts of the time.

Jimmy Page wows the crowd with his violin-bow section during "Dazed and Confused" at the Texas International Festival. (Photo by Carl Dunn)

31 August 1969, Texas International Pop Festival, Dallas International Motor Speedway, Lewisville, Texas (4 p.m. start. Led Zeppelin appeared on the second day of the three-day festival. Shared bill with Freddie King, Delaney & Bonnie & Friends, James Cotton Blues Band, Incredible String Band, Canned Heat, Herbie Mann, Chicago Transit Authority, Sweetwater, Ten Years After, Grand Funk Railroad, Spirit, and Janis Joplin, among many others.)

SETLIST: The Train Kept A Rollin' / I Can't Quit You Baby / Dazed And Confused / You Shook Me (includes Rock Me Baby) / How Many More Times (including Suzie Q, The Hunter, The Lemon Song, Eyesight To The Blind, Shake For Me) / Communication Breakdown

The last show of the US tour and a killer set is performed by the band. A soundboard recording of their set has been doing the rounds in collectors circles for years as well as being released on bootleg. This was the last date of the current tour as Plant informed the crowd, "This is the last date before we go back to England, so we'd really like to have a nice time. . . . And you can help us." Unfortunately, as was often the case in those days at festivals, there were delays in running times and Led Zeppelin had to cut short their set. Plant apologized, "We've got to say good night according to the program. Unfortunately, the program has got a little delayed but there's nothing we can do about it!"

Jimmy Page headed to New York to finish the mixing of *Led Zeppelin II* with Eddie Kramer. The rest of the band headed back to England for their holidays. As soon as he had finished mixing the final numbers, Page headed off for a well-deserved break in Spain and Morocco. In early October, the band played some dates in Europe and Scandinavia as a promotion for their forthcoming new album before heading back to America.

OCTOBER 1969

LED ZEPPELIN EUROPEAN TOUR

3 OCTOBER 1969–13 OCTOBER 1969

The band rehearsed at the Hanwell Community Centre for their forthcoming tour.

3 October 1969, Fortis Circustheater, Scheveningen, the Hague, Netherlands (Support from Steamhammer)

SETLIST NOT KNOWN, BUT WOULD HAVE PROBABLY INCLUDED THE FOLLOWING: Good Times Bad Times Intro / Communication Breakdown / I Can't Quit You Baby / Heartbreaker / You Shook Me / What Is And What Should Never Be / Dazed And Confused / How Many More Times

4 October 1969, De Doelen Grote Zaal, Rotterdam, Netherlands (Support from After Tea and George Cash)

SETLIST NOT KNOWN, BUT WOULD HAVE PROBABLY INCLUDED THE FOLLOWING: Good Times Bad Times Intro / Communication Breakdown / I Can't Quit You Baby / Heartbreaker / You Shook Me / What Is And What Should Never Be / Dazed And Confused / How Many More Times

5 October 1969, Concertgebouw, Amsterdam, Netherlands (Support from Steamhammer)

SETLIST NOT KNOWN, BUT WOULD HAVE PROBABLY INCLUDED THE FOLLOWING: Good Times Bad Times Intro / Communication Breakdown / I Can't Quit You Baby / Heartbreaker / You Shook Me / What Is And What Should Never Be / Dazed And Confused / How Many More Times

7 October 1969, Konserthuset, Stockholm, Sweden (Canceled and rescheduled for 26 February 1970.)

8 October 1969, Konserthuset, Göteborg, Sweden (canceled)

9 October 1969, Concertgebouw, Haarlem, Netherlands

Press advert announcing the much-anticipated release of *Led Zeppelin II*, the band's second album.

Robert Plant onstage at the Texas International Pop Festival. (Photo by Carl Dunn)

SETLIST NOT KNOWN, BUT WOULD HAVE PROBABLY INCLUDED THE FOLLOWING: Good Times Bad Times Intro / Communication Breakdown / I Can't Quit You Baby / Heartbreaker / You Shook Me / What Is And What Should Never Be / Dazed And Confused / How Many More Times

10 October 1969, L'Olympia, Paris, France (The concert was recorded professionally by Europe 1. The concert was originally aired on the *Musicorama* show on Europe 1 on 2 November 1969. It was also rebroadcast on Europe 2 on 7 December 2007 at 10:30 p.m. The concert was bootlegged, although "Moby Dick" was left off. An edited version of the complete concert was released with the deluxe reissue of *Led Zeppelin 1* in 2014.)

SETLIST:

GOOD TIMES BAD TIMES INTRO / COMMUNICATION BREAKDOWN Available on bonus disc in deluxe edition of *Led Zeppelin 1* released in 2014

I CAN'T QUIT YOU BABY Available on bonus disc in deluxe edition of *Led Zeppelin 1* released in 2014

HEARTBREAKER Available on bonus disc in deluxe edition of *Led Zeppelin 1* released in 2014

DAZED AND CONFUSED Available on bonus disc in deluxe edition of *Led Zeppelin 1* released in 2014

WHITE SUMMER / BLACK MOUNTAIN SIDE Available on bonus disc in deluxe edition of *Led Zeppelin 1* released in 2014

YOU SHOOK ME Available on bonus disc in deluxe edition of *Led Zeppelin 1* released in 2014

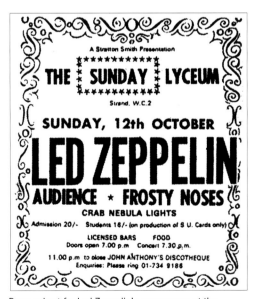

Press advert for Led Zeppelin's appearance at the Lyceum in London.

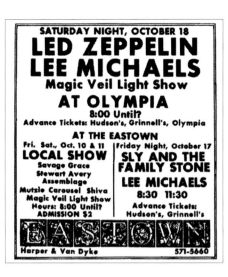

Press advert for Led Zeppelin's appearance at Olympia Stadium in Detroit.

MOBY DICK Available on bonus disc in deluxe edition of *Led Zeppelin 1* released in 2014

HOW MANY MORE TIMES (including Over Under Sideways Down, The Hunter, The Lemon Song, Boogie Chillun', Hideaway, Think You Need A Shot [The Needle]) available in edited form on bonus disc of Led Zeppelin 1 released in 2014

12 October 1969, Lyceum, London, England (Support from Frosty Noses and Audience)

❝ The group were in tremendous form. Robert Plant offered screaming vocals and Jimmy Page offered screaming guitar—a combination guaranteed to send audiences wild. But there was serious music on hand as well as Zeppelin's more wild moments. Jimmy Page played a superb acoustic guitar and John Bonham's drum solo was exceptional, drawing bursts of applause throughout, especially for his hand drumming interlude. Led Zeppelin don't do anything that is so revolutionary or new. They just do what the public want very well. They play heavy rock the best, and no arguing!❞
—**CHRIS WELCH** (Review in *Melody Maker*, October 1969)

❝ Having seen them both at the Marquee and the Albert Hall it seems the larger the venue the better it suits the Zeppelin's overpowering sound, although the Lyceum audience responded enthusiastically to everything they did. It was mainly the now familiar opening to their act—'Communication Breakdown' etc. that suffered, Robert Plant's voice being drowned by the sheer volume of sound. Jimmy Page's guitar solo midway through was deservedly well received and when the group came in again on 'You Shook Me' and 'What Is And What Should Never Be' there was something of an improvement. ❞
—**NICK LOGAN** (Review in *New Musical Express*, October 1969)

LED ZEPPELIN FOURTH US TOUR

17 OCTOBER 1969–8 NOVEMBER 1969

The band start their US tour in style by playing at the prestigious Carnegie Hall in New York.

17 October 1969, Carnegie Hall, Main Auditorium, New York City, New York (Two shows, first at 8:30 p.m. and second at midnight.)

SETLIST NOT KNOWN, BUT WOULD HAVE PROBABLY INCLUDED THE FOLLOWING: Good Times Bad Times Intro / Communication Breakdown / I Can't Quit You Baby / Heartbreaker / Dazed And Confused / White Summer / Black Mountain Side / You Shook Me / Moby Dick / How Many More Times

18 October 1969, Olympia Stadium, Detroit, Michigan (Support from Lee Michaels)

SETLIST NOT KNOWN, BUT WOULD HAVE PROBABLY INCLUDED THE FOLLOWING: Good Times Bad Times Intro / Communication Breakdown / I Can't Quit You Baby / Heartbreaker / Dazed And Confused / White Summer / Black Mountain Side / What Is And What Should Never Be / Moby Dick / How Many More Times

19 October 1969, Kinetic Playground, Chicago, Illinois (Afternoon and evening shows advertised with support from Santana and Lighthouse.)

SETLIST NOT KNOWN, BUT WOULD HAVE PROBABLY INCLUDED THE FOLLOWING: Good Times Bad Times Intro / Communication Breakdown / I Can't Quit You Baby / Heartbreaker / Dazed And Confused / White Summer / Black Mountain Side / What Is And What Should Never Be / Moby Dick / How Many More Times

20 October 1969, Paramount Theatre, Seattle, Washington

SETLIST NOT KNOWN, BUT WOULD HAVE PROBABLY INCLUDED THE FOLLOWING: Good Times Bad Times Intro / Communication Breakdown / I Can't Quit You Baby / Heartbreaker / Dazed And Confused / White Summer / Black Mountain Side / What Is And What Should Never Be / Moby Dick / How Many More Times

21 October 1969, Electric Factory, Philadelphia, Pennsylvania

Press advert for Led Zeppelin's appearance at the Public Auditorium in Cleveland, Ohio.

SETLIST NOT KNOWN, BUT WOULD HAVE PROBABLY INCLUDED THE FOLLOWING: Good Times Bad Times Intro / Communication Breakdown / I Can't Quit You Baby / Heartbreaker / Dazed And Confused / White Summer / Black Mountain Side / What Is And What Should Never Be / Moby Dick / How Many More Times

24 October 1969, Public Hall, Cleveland, Ohio (Support from Grand Funk Railroad)

SETLIST NOT KNOWN, BUT WOULD HAVE PROBABLY INCLUDED THE FOLLOWING: Good Times Bad Times Intro / Communication Breakdown / I Can't Quit You Baby / Heartbreaker / Dazed And Confused / White Summer / Black Mountain Side / What Is And What Should Never Be / Moby Dick / How Many More Times

25 October 1969, Boston Garden, Boston, Massachusetts (Billed as Narragansett's "First Tribal Rock Festival." Support from Johnny Winter and MC5.)

SETLIST NOT KNOWN, BUT WOULD HAVE PROBABLY INCLUDED THE FOLLOWING: Good Times Bad Times Intro / Communication Breakdown / I Can't Quit You Baby / Heartbreaker / Dazed And Confused / White Summer / Black Mountain Side / What Is And What Should Never Be / Moby Dick / How Many More Times

26 October 1969, Independence Coliseum, Charlotte, North Carolina

SETLIST NOT KNOWN, BUT WOULD HAVE PROBABLY INCLUDED THE FOLLOWING: Good Times Bad Times Intro / Communication Breakdown / I Can't Quit You Baby / Heartbreaker / Dazed And Confused / White Summer / Black Mountain Side / What Is And What Should Never Be / Moby Dick / How Many More Times

30 October 1969, Kleinhans Music Hall, Buffalo, New York
(Support from the James Gang)

SETLIST: Good Times Bad Times Intro / Communication Breakdown / I Can't Quit You Baby / Heartbreaker / Dazed And Confused / White Summer / Black Mountain Side / What Is And What Should Never Be / Moby Dick / How Many More Times (including The Hunter)

During "I Can't Quit You Baby," a member of the audience throws a bottle at Plant, causing him to change some of the lyrics now aimed at the culprit to "You're messing up a good concert, you silly fool! If you think you're really very smart, then come right up here and do that thing again!" At the number's conclusion, Plant goes on to say, "Thank you very much. Thank you. It's a great pleasure to be here tonight. And we'd like to welcome our friend. He's so used to throwing coconuts in the fairground, he doesn't really know. Thanks for the glass." Despite this, the show is a perfect example of how mesmerizing Led Zeppelin were onstage at this point. The sheer power was overwhelming.

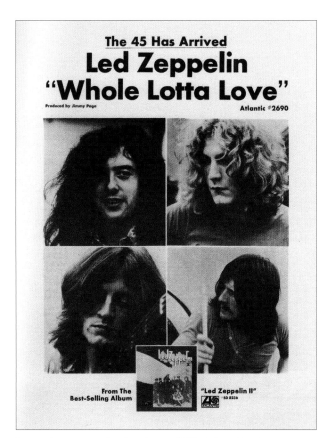

Press advert announcing the release of "Whole Lotta Love" as a single in the US.

66 The Led Zeppelin group came off better in person in Kleinhans Music Hall than they do on their albums. They were in true simplistic terms . . . good, excellent professional, top-quality and nice to listen to! The form this group seems to be best in is the media of the live performance. They are extremely professional in their concerts. They have sound men controlling every aspect of their music. Jimmy Page, though somewhat berated by many snobbish rock 'critics,' gave a fascinating technical display of guitar artistry that still sticks in my mind.99
—**BUFFALO NEWS** (Review from October 1969)

31 October 1969, Springfield Municipal Auditorium, Springfield, Massachusetts (Two shows at 7:00 p.m. and 9:30 p.m. Support from Taj Mahal.)

SETLIST NOT KNOWN, BUT WOULD HAVE PROBABLY INCLUDED THE FOLLOWING: Good Times Bad Times Intro / Communication Breakdown / I Can't Quit You Baby / Heartbreaker / Dazed And Confused / White Summer / Black Mountain Side / What Is And What Should Never Be / Moby Dick / How Many More Times

NOVEMBER 1969

1 November 1969, Onondaga War Memorial, Syracuse, New York

SETLIST NOT KNOWN, BUT WOULD HAVE PROBABLY INCLUDED THE FOLLOWING: Good Times Bad Times Intro / Communication Breakdown / I Can't Quit You Baby / Heartbreaker / Dazed And Confused / White Summer / Black Mountain Side / What Is And What Should Never Be / Moby Dick / How Many More Times

66 The Zeppelin didn't waste any time in making a good connection with the audience which kept applauding until the Zeppelin drowned the applause with their soul-stretching sounds. The James Gang set a pace and the Zeppelin had no trouble keeping it up and surpassing it. Zeppelin put on a better show than the Gang which helped them to make a better connection with the audience.99
—**SYRACUSE JOURNAL** (Review from November 1969)

2 November 1969, O'Keefe Centre, Toronto, Ontario, Canada (Two shows at 5:00 p.m. and 8:30 p.m. Support from Edward Bear.)

SETLIST: Good Times Bad Times Intro / Communication Breakdown (including Bluebird) / I Can't Quit You Baby / Heartbreaker / Dazed And Confused / White Summer / Black Mountain Side / Babe I'm Gonna Leave You (including Down By The River, Ramble On) / Moby Dick / How Many More Times (including The Hunter)

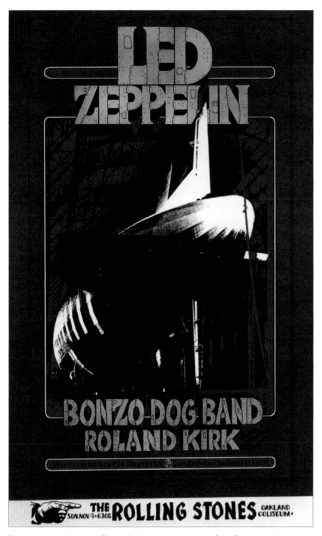

Poster advertising Led Zeppelin's appearances at San Francisco's Winterland over three nights on the 6th, 7th, and 8th of November 1969.

SETLIST: Good Times Bad Times Intro / Communication Breakdown / I Can't Quit You Baby / Heartbreaker / Dazed And Confused / What Is And What Should Never Be / How Many More Times

66 Jimmy Page is Led Zeppelin. He's not just a part of the group along with the three other members, singer Robert Plant, drummer John Bonham and bass guitarist John Paul Jones. He's it—the whole sound. He gives Led Zeppelin's rock its diamond hardness and his guitar splits through the heavy background and Plant's frantic singing light from a facet of a 30-carat stone. . . . 'Tonight was a very short set,' Page said after the 45-minute show. 'I didn't do my set because of the amplifier blowing and the drummer didn't do his set because he wasn't feeling well.' 99

—J. CLEMENTE
(Review from *Kitchener Record*, 5 November 1969)

5 November 1969, Memorial Hall, Kansas City, Kansas (Two shows at 7:00 p.m. and 9:30 p.m. Support from Morning Star, Bartok's Mountain, Spokesmen, Blues Garden, and Bill Zickos.)

SETLIST: Good Times Bad Times Intro / Communication Breakdown / I Can't Quit You Baby / Heartbreaker / Dazed And Confused / White Summer / Black Mountain Side / How Many More Times (including The Hunter, Boogie Chillun', Move On Down The Line)

Interesting show, which sees the band experimenting with some of their numbers, such as including part of Buffalo Springfield's "Bluebird" during "Communication Breakdown." Page teases the crowd by including snippets of the Yardbirds "Still I'm Sad" during his performance of "White Summer." Tonight's show is a typical Zeppelin 1969 concert, full of energy, and humor. Every night they seemed to find their groove and played spectacularly. Robert Plant, who was in a particularly great mood, joked with the crowd, "We intend to try to do as much of the *Led Zeppelin IV* album as possible, but we thought we'd cut it down by half and do *Led Zeppelin II*." A snippet of Neil Young's "Down By The River" is played during "Babe I'm Gonna Leave You." All in all, another amazing evening.

4 November 1969, Memorial Auditorium, Kitchener, Ontario, Canada (Support from Copper Penny)

Challenging evening for the band. All of their stage equipment and instruments had to be air-freighted ahead to San Francisco from their show in Ontario, Canada, the night before in readiness for their important headlining shows at the Winterland. They played on a rented PA, instruments and amps hired from Mission Music in Kansas. Eye-witness reports claim that the shows were lackluster and that there were problems getting the first-house people moved out to allow the second-house ticket holders to come in. John Bonham was also drunk by the time the second house made it in and did not help matters musically.

6 November 1969, Winterland Ballroom, San Francisco, California (Support from Roland Kirk and Isaac Hayes)

SETLIST: Good Times Bad Times Intro / Communication Breakdown / I Can't Quit You Baby / Heartbreaker / Dazed And Confused / White Summer / Black Mountain Side / What Is And What Should Never Be / Moby Dick / How Many More Times (including Over Under Sideways Down, The Hunter, Boogie Chillun', Move On Down The Line, Hideaway, Bottle It Up And Go, They're Red Hot, Cumberland Gap, The Lemon Song) / C'mon Everybody / Something Else

The setlist says it all really. Another high-octane performance with some killer jamming by the band. The band loved the West Coast.

7 November 1969, Winterland Ballroom, San Francisco, California

SETLIST: Good Times Bad Times Intro / Communication Breakdown / I Can't Quit You Baby / Heartbreaker / Dazed And Confused / White Summer / Black Mountain Side / Babe I'm Gonna Leave You / What Is And What Should Never Be / Moby Dick / How Many More Times (including The Hunter)

8 November 1969, Winterland Ballroom, San Francisco, California

SETLIST NOT KNOWN, BUT WOULD HAVE PROBABLY INCLUDED THE FOLLOWING: Good Times Bad Times Intro / Communication Breakdown / I Can't Quit You Baby / Heartbreaker / Dazed And Confused / White Summer / Black Mountain Side / Babe I'm Gonna Leave You / What Is And What Should Never Be / Moby Dick / How Many More Times (including The Hunter)

DECEMBER 1969

ONE-OFF CONCERT IN PARIS

6 December 1969, Piston 70, L'Ecole Centrale, Grande Voie des Vignes, Chatenay-Malabry, Paris, France

SETLIST: Good Times Bad Times Intro / Communication Breakdown / I Can't Quit You Baby / Heartbreaker / Dazed And Confused / White Summer / Black Mountain Side / You Shook Me / Moby Dick / How Many More Times (including The Hunter, Smokestack Lightning, Whole Lotta Love, Improvisation based on Good Times Bad Times theme, Wee Baby Blues, Hideaway, Move On Down The Line, Boogie Chillun')

This date was always a contentious one and the source of great debate as to whether it actually happened or not. A review in the well-respected French music magazine *Best* in February 1970 should have been proof enough. However, it was not until the sudden appearance of a recording from the show in the noughties along with photos of the gig that everyone agreed that it took place. As it turns out, it is one of the best gigs from 1969. The band are tight and are having a ball in this no-pressure environment.

4 1969 Recording Sessions

LED ZEPPELIN II SESSIONS

10 APRIL 1969–30 AUGUST 1969

OLYMPIC SOUND STUDIOS
Studio 1, 117 Church Road,
Barnes, London, SW13

14 APRIL–19 APRIL 1969

Inspired by his early love of rockabilly guitarists' big intros to songs, Jimmy first came up with the future "Whole Lotta Love" main riff toward the end of the summer of 1968 at his home in Pangbourne. He instinctively knew that the riff could be the driving force for a whole song. When he later played the riff to the other band members during rehearsals for their first album, they collectively knew that this had the potential to be a killer song due to the additive nature of the riff. As all the necessary material for their first album had already been rehearsed, they did not pursue the riff and put it aside with a view to revisit it for the second album.

When the time came to start recording their second album, in April 1969, the song had been honed and developed some more, both at home and on the road during some of their improvisations. Jimmy had a vision in his mind and was so excited about the prospect that it was decided to record this number first with a view of it opening the new album. Initial recording sessions for "Whole Lotta Love" began on 10 April 1969 at Olympic Sound Studios in Barnes. "What Is And Should Never Be" was also started at the same sessions. Both songs would have overdubs added at later dates in various studios in America

while on tour. Jimmy chose Studio 1 at Olympic, as he had done for the first album, the larger of the two studios at Olympic that used an 8-track recorder so that the drums could be miked properly for stereo.

Jimmy really wanted the drum sound to stand out, allowing every stick stroke to sound clear and natural. He knew that if the drums were recorded properly, the band could lay in everything else. The drums needed to sound impressive and dynamic, but the studio had a wooden floor rather than cement. To avoid any drum movement from transmitting rumble across the wooden floor to other mikes, George Chkiantz, who was the engineer at the session, placed the kit on a platform about 1½ feet off of the wooden studio floor. He hung a stereo mike on an 8-foot boom above the drums along with two distant side mikes, which gave the tom-toms edge. He also placed a huge AKG D30 mike about two feet from the bass drum.

Robert Plant was placed in a vocal booth to better isolate his vocals. He was in great form, adding little asides to see if they would work. Robert referenced Willie Dixon's "You Need Love" lyrics, which eventually resulted in Dixon having a songwriting credit. Everyone was pushing themselves to the limit. The whole band was in a very creative phase. When it came to the freeform section, Jimmy detuned the strings on his Les Paul and used some theremin for the eerie sounds.

Rough mixes were made and the tapes were then taken with Jimmy Page to the US in April to June 1969, where Led Zeppelin would be touring. In Los Angeles, they mainly used Mystic Sound Studios and A&M for recording additional songs and overdubs. The criteria for the studios used was that they had to be an 8-track facility. They also popped in to R&D

Recording Studios before playing a gig in Vancouver on 10 May 1969 to overdub vocals and a harmonica onto "Bring It On Home," which had been recorded on 4 May at Mystic Studios in Los Angeles. R&D Recording Studios is referred to as "the hut" in the liner notes due to its primitive state at the time. In New York they worked at Mira, Mayfair, Groove, A&R, and Juggy studios for yet more recording and overdubs. Quantum and Gold Star in Los Angeles were also used, but Page was unhappy with the sound and scrapped the session. Rough mixes of the album were done at Atlantic Studios in New York between 21 July and 24 July. A version of "Bring It On Home" from 24 July is available on the companion disc of the remastered *Coda* released in July 2015. The final mixing took place at A&R Sound in New York in August over just two days.

Jimmy Page and Eddie Kramer really showed how great they were at what they did. The album was recorded on the move at multiple studios with very different sounds, yet because of the mixing process the album sounds whole, like it had all been done at one studio. The recording console at A&R was fairly primitive, having only twelve channels with old-fashioned rotary dials to control all the track levels instead of the usual sliding faders. There were just two control knobs, which were used to send the sound from left to right channels.

Something unexpected happened during the mixing of "Whole Lotta Love" at A&R Studios. When Jimmy and Eddie listened to the playback where Plant wails the iconic "Way down inside . . . woman . . . you need . . . love," they heard a faint voiced Plant singing the lyric before the master vocal track. Turns out Plant had recorded separate vocals on two different tracks. So even when the volume was turned all the way down on the track they did not want to use, his voice had been so powerful that it ended up bleeding through the console and onto the master. The magic here is that it sounds like it was meant to be that way. A glorious mistake!

Jimmy Page was now using a '58 Gibson Les Paul Standard through a Marshall stack. He also occasionally used a couple of electric 12-string guitars, one a '65 Fender Electric XII and the other a '67 Vox Phantom XII. For effects pedals he used a Sola Sound Tone Bender MKII and a Vox Cry Baby, both

of which were modified by Roger Mayer who had worked wonders for Jimi Hendrix.

LA LA (John Paul Jones / Jimmy Page) (Basic track recorded.) Available for the first time on the bonus CD from the deluxe edition of *Led Zeppelin II*, which was released in June 2014.

WHOLE LOTTA LOVE (Jimmy Page, Robert Plant, John Paul Jones, and John Bonham) (Various takes and basic track recorded. Some overdubs were done at A&M Studios, Los Angeles, in April and the final mix made at A&R Studios in New York.)

WHAT IS AND WHAT SHOULD NEVER BE (Jimmy Page / Robert Plant) (Various takes and basic track recorded. Some overdubs were done at Mayfair Studios, New York, in June and the final mix made at A&R Studios in New York.)

PRODUCER: JIMMY PAGE
ENGINEER: GEORGE CHKIANTZ

GOLD STAR RECORDING STUDIOS
6252 Santa Monica Blvd.,
Los Angeles, California

(Gold Star Studios were located in the old Del-Fi studios where Richie Valens recorded "La Bamba" and Bobby Fuller recorded "I Fought The Law." The Addrisi Brothers, Little Caesar and the Romans, and Johnny Crawford are just some of the many other artists who recorded there.)

QUANTUM RECORDING STUDIOS
1425 Marcelina Avenue,
Torrance, California

A&M STUDIOS
1416 North LaBrea Avenue,
Hollywood, California

28 APRIL 1969-30 APRIL 1969

(Although Jimmy Page tried out Gold Star and Quantum recording studios, he preferred the sound and facilities at A&M before moving on to Mystic Sound.)

WHOLE LOTTA LOVE (Jimmy Page / Robert Plant / John Paul Jones / John Bonham) (Overdubs and master made.)

MYSTIC SOUND STUDIOS
6277 Selma Avenue and Vine, Hollywood, California

4 MAY 1969–5 MAY 1969

THE LEMON SONG (Jimmy Page / Robert Plant / John Paul Jones / John Bonham) (Basic track recorded. Overdubs recorded on 5 August at A&M Studios, Los Angeles.)

MOBY DICK (Jimmy Page / John Bonham / John Paul Jones) (Intro and outro recorded. Various drum solos were recorded later at Mayfair Studios in New York and edited into a final master.)

BRING IT ON HOME (Jimmy Page / Robert Plant) (Basic track. Overdubs made at R&D Studios in Vancouver on 10 May.)

66 I worked on the following tracks for *Led Zeppelin II*: Lemon Song, Moby Dick, Bring It On Home . . . and one other track, the title of which I cannot remember, although I think it had a 'working title' at the time. It is possible that the 'working title' number could have been 'La La.'99

—**CHRIS HUSTON** (Owner Mystic Sound and engineer)

R&D STUDIOS
West Broadway, Vancouver

10 MAY 1969

(The 8-track studio is referred to as "the hut" in the sleeve credits for *Led Zeppelin II*.)

Led Zeppelin had just arrived from Edmonton and would be playing the PNE Agrodome in Vancouver that same evening. Robert and Jimmy headed down to R&D Studios, a small local studio located above a post office on West Broadway, east of Cambie Street, in Vancouver to lay down harmonica and fix a vocal track for "Bring It On Home," which had distortion on it. They were told that the distortion they heard on the playback was just the speakers in the studio, but when they listened to it later they found it was on the master tape. They arranged to use R&D to fix the problem and recorded the one line that needed fixing and got the same distortion. Doug Gyseman, who owned R&D Studios and was engineering the session, was having problems recording Plant's vocals because he was singing too loud and they could not get a good take. He told everyone to take a break and put a second mike a couple of feet ahead of a dummy

mike, brought everyone back to the studio, and got the take, not telling anyone that the mike he was singing into was off and the one that was in front of the other one was on. The line in question was all way back in the mix and Doug Gyseman said they could have left it the way it was and no one would have noticed it.

BRING IT ON HOME (Jimmy Page / Robert Plant / Willie Dixon)

ROBERT PLANT: HARMONICA AND VOCAL OVERDUBS
PRODUCER: JIMMY PAGE
ENGINEER: DOUGLAS GYSEMAN

A&R STUDIOS
322 West 48th Street & 799 Seventh Avenue, New York

21 MAY 1969

HEARTBREAKER (Basic track. Overdubs made on 30 and 31 May 1969 at A&R Studios in New York.)

PRODUCER: JIMMY PAGE
ENGINEER: EDDIE KRAMER

GROOVE STUDIOS
240 West 55th Street, New York

1 JUNE 1969

WHAT IS AND WHAT SHOULD NEVER BE (Overdubs and final master made.)

RAMBLE ON (Basic track. Overdubs added at Juggy Sound in New York.)

JUGGY SOUND STUDIO
265 West 54th Street, New York

2 JUNE 1969

RAMBLE ON (Overdubs and master made.)

PRODUCER: JIMMY PAGE
ENGINEER: EDDIE KRAMER

MAYFAIR RECORDING STUDIOS
130 West 42nd Street, New York

3 JUNE 1969

MOBY DICK (Various drum solos recorded, which were later edited to make a master by Eddie Kramer at A&R Studios in New York.)

MORGAN STUDIOS
169–171 High Road,
Willesden Green, London NW10

25 JUNE 1969

During a short break in live work, the band record some more material for their next album in the UK. Although the original sleeve credits for the 1982 Coda album credit the version of "We're Gonna Groove" as being recorded this day, the version used was actually from the Royal Albert Hall concert on 9 January 1970 with overdubbed guitar at Page's Sol Studios in 1982. If indeed a studio version was recorded, and it probably was as it was so often played live, it remains unreleased. According to some bootlegs, another version of "Sugar Mama," originally recorded during Led Zeppelin I sessions, was also recorded at this session, this time with vocals.

LIVING LOVING MAID
THANK YOU
WE'RE GONNA GROOVE (Unreleased)
SUGAR MAMA (Unreleased)

A&M STUDIOS
1416 North LaBrea Avenue,
Hollywood, California

5 AUGUST 1969

THE LEMON SONG (Final overdubs and master made.)

A&R STUDIOS
322 West 48th Street &
799 Seventh Avenue, New York

29 AUGUST 1969–30 AUGUST 1969

Final mixing of *Led Zeppelin II*.

WHOLE LOTTA LOVE (5:34)
WHAT IS AND WHAT SHOULD NEVER BE (4:46)
THE LEMON SONG (6:18)
THANK YOU (4:47)
HEARTBREAKER (4:14)

LIVING LOVING MAID (She's Just A Woman) (2:38)
RAMBLE ON (4:24)
MOBY DICK (4:21)
BRING IT ON HOME (4:21)

PRODUCER: JIMMY PAGE
ENGINEER: EDDIE KRAMER

GUEST RECORDING SESSIONS

GUEST SESSION FOR LORD SUTCH

MYSTIC SOUND STUDIOS
6277 Selma Avenue and Vine,
Hollywood, California

7 MAY 1969–8 MAY 1969

WAILING SOUNDS (Jimmy Page / Lord Sutch) Available on *Lord Sutch and Heavy Friends* in US on Cotillion Records SD 9015 released February 1970 / UK Atlantic 2400 008 released March 1970 / remastered CD on Esoteric ECLEC 2405 released December 2013.

LORD SUTCH: VOCALS
JIMMY PAGE: GUITAR
JOHN BONHAM: DRUMS
DANIEL EDWARDS: BASS, LEAD GUITAR

'CAUSE I LOVE YOU (John Bonham / Daniel Edwards / Jimmy Page / Lord Sutch) Available on *Lord Sutch and Heavy Friends* in US on Cotillion Records SD 9015 released February 1970 / UK Atlantic 2400 008 released March 1970 / remastered CD on Esoteric ECLEC 2405 released December 2013.

LORD SUTCH: VOCALS
JIMMY PAGE: GUITAR
JOHN BONHAM: DRUMS
DANIEL EDWARDS: BASS, LEAD GUITAR

FLASHING LIGHTS (Jimmy Page / Lord Sutch) Available on *Lord Sutch and Heavy Friends* in US on Cotillion Records SD 9015 released February 1970 / UK Atlantic 2400 008 released March 1970 / remastered CD on Esoteric ECLEC 2405 released December 2013.

LORD SUTCH: VOCALS
JIMMY PAGE: GUITAR
JOHN BONHAM: DRUMS
DANIEL EDWARDS: BASS, LEAD GUITAR

THUMPING BEAT (Jimmy Page / Lord Sutch) Available on *Lord Sutch and Heavy Friends* in US on Cotillion Records SD 9015 released February 1970 / UK Atlantic 2400 008 released March 1970 / remastered CD on Esoteric ECLEC 2405 released December 2013.

> LORD SUTCH: VOCALS
> JIMMY PAGE: GUITAR
> JOHN BONHAM: DRUMS
> NOEL REDDING: BASS

UNION JACK CAR (Jimmy Page / Lord Sutch) Available on *Lord Sutch and Heavy Friends* in US on Cotillion Records SD 9015 released February 1970 / UK Atlantic 2400 008 released March 1970 / remastered CD on Esoteric ECLEC 2405 released December 2013.

> LORD SUTCH: VOCALS
> JIMMY PAGE: GUITAR
> JOHN BONHAM: DRUMS
> DANIEL EDWARDS: BASS, LEAD GUITAR

BABY, COME BACK (Jimmy Page and Lord Sutch) Available on *Lord Sutch and Heavy Friends* in US on Cotillion Records SD 9015 released February 1970 / UK Atlantic 2400 008 released March 1970 / remastered CD on Esoteric ECLEC 2405 released December 2013.

> LORD SUTCH: VOCALS
> JIMMY PAGE: GUITAR
> JOHN BONHAM: DRUMS
> DANIEL EDWARDS: BASS, LEAD GUITAR
> PRODUCER: JIMMY PAGE
> ENGINEER: TOMMY CACCETTA

66 The timing of the Lord Sutch sessions was the same 1969 period that the four tracks that I did with Led Zeppelin. Dave (Lord Sutch) was a friend of mine—I first met him when we, the Undertakers, played together at the Star Club, in Hamburg and then on the road in the UK—and, at the time, was down on his luck. We all agreed to do something to help him. Although I was there, I did not work on those sessions; instead Tommy Caccetta, who was my assistant, did them, with Jimmy Paige producing. Unfortunately, the whole album backfired. Dave was not a singer, he was a showman. All the help in the world, from world-class musicians couldn't change that fact. God bless him. 99

—**CHRIS HUSTON** (Owner Mystic Sound and engineer)

66 It was all fixed that I'd go down there and just do a bit, so we went down and played and I just did some backing tracks to numbers like 'Good Golly Miss Molly' and 'Roll Over Beethoven.' You've got the picture, right? I didn't do any solos, no solos at all. I did a little bit of wah-wah on one track, but I didn't do the solo in the middle, which isn't a wah-wah thing. Somebody else put that on. So, to cut a long story short, he rewrote all the tunes and he put another guitarist on over the top. But, and this is where the criminal side of it comes in, he didn't put 'Extra guitar: So and So' or 'Lead guitar played by so and so'; he put 'Guitar: Jimmy Page,' so everybody thought, 'Oh, Jimmy Page played that heap of crap,' and it became more than an embarrassment. He also wrote me in as producer, which was very nice of him [Jimmy laughs]. I wasn't interested in that, I just went down to have a laugh, playing some old rock and roll, a bit of a send-up. The whole joke sort of reversed itself and became ugly. 99

—**JIMMY PAGE** (From unknown interview 1970)

1970:
Rock Gods Go Acoustic

5

Another busy year ahead for the band, starting with a UK, European, and US tour that ended on 18 April 1970. After the tour, it was time for a well-earned break away from the madness of being on the road. Robert Plant recalled a place he had been to with his parents in Machynlleth, Wales, when he was younger and suggested to Jimmy Page that they go there and relax. Along with their respective partners and a couple of roadies, they headed to Bron-Yr-Aur, a secluded cottage in the Welsh countryside. The cottage was pretty primitive with no electricity and no obvious distractions other than the glorious scenery and views of the Welsh valleys. In the evenings out came the acoustic guitars and some inspired playing led to some new material being worked on around a crackling log fire. Some of it was just basic ideas and sketches of songs that would be used on later albums, such as "Down By The Seaside" and "Over The Hills And Far Away." But some, such as "The Boy Next Door" (later re-titled "That's The Way"), were pretty much completed at this time, although the lyrics would be altered slightly by the time of entering a recording studio.

By the end of their vacation it became clear to them that the new album would have potential to be more varied and pastoral in feel than Led Zeppelin's previous two releases. Other material was written at other times and others, like "Tangerine," found their origins all the way back to the Yardbirds days. Page had started the original song after a bad breakup and got as far as recording a basic track with the Yardbirds but never got finished. The title at the time was perhaps more appropriate for a breakup, "Knowing That I'm Losing You." Another track, "Gallows

Pole," had been a standard on the UK club circuit in 1965. Page had first heard it on a Folkways album by Fred Gerlach, who had interpreted it with heavy Leadbelly overtones. Page in turn used his version as a basis for Led Zeppelin's, but with a totally different arrangement.

In May, the whole of Led Zeppelin got together to rehearse material for their next album at Robert Plant's home, Jennings Farm in Blakeshall, Kidderminster. By the end of the month, they were ready to lay down some tracks at Olympic Studios in Barnes.

Recording sessions for the album that would eventually become *Led Zeppelin III* took place initially at Olympic Studios in December 1969 and January 1970, continuing in May and June 1970 at both Olympic in Barnes and Island Studios in Basing Street, London.

LED ZEPPELIN FIFTH UK TOUR
7 JANUARY 1970–17 FEBRUARY 1970

7 January 1970, Town Hall, Birmingham, West Midlands, England

SETLIST NOT KNOWN BUT WOULD HAVE PROBABLY INCLUDED THE FOLLOWING: We're Gonna Groove / I Can't Quit You Baby / Dazed And Confused / Heartbreaker / White Summer / Black Mountain Side / Since I've Been Loving You / Organ Solo / Thank You / Moby Dick / How Many More Times (including The Hunter, Boogie Chillun', Move On Down The Line, High Flyin' Mama, The Lemon Song) / Whole Lotta Love / Communication Breakdown (including Good Times Bad Times)

8 January 1970, Colston Hall, Bristol, England

SETLIST: We're Gonna Groove / I Can't Quit You Baby / Dazed And Confused / Heartbreaker / White Summer / Black Mountain Side / Since I've Been Loving You / Organ Solo / Thank You / Moby Dick / How Many More Times (including The Hunter, Boogie Chillun', Move On Down The Line, High Flyin' Mama, The Lemon Song) / Whole Lotta Love / Communication Breakdown (including Good Times Bad Times)

9 January 1970, Royal Albert Hall, London, England (Jimmy Page's twenty-sixth birthday)

SETLIST: We're Gonna Groove / I Can't Quit You Baby / Dazed And Confused / Heartbreaker / White Summer / Black Mountain Side / Since I've Been Loving You / What Is And What Should Never Be / Moby Dick / How Many More Times (including The Hunter, Boogie Chillun', High Flyin' Mama, Leave My Woman Alone, The Lemon Song, That's Alright Mama) / Whole Lotta Love / Organ Solo / Thank You / Communication Breakdown / C'mon Everybody / Something Else / Bring It On Home / Long Tall Sally (including Bye Bye Baby, Move On Down The Line, Whole Lotta Shakin' Goin' On)

The show is filmed by Peter Whithead and 8-track audio recorded by the Pye Mobile Studio by Vic Maile.

13 January 1970, Guildhall, Portsmouth, England (8:00 p.m.)

SETLIST NOT KNOWN BUT WOULD HAVE PROBABLY INCLUDED THE FOLLOWING: We're Gonna Groove / I Can't Quit You Baby / Dazed And Confused / Heartbreaker / White Summer / Black Mountain Side / Since I've Been Loving You / Organ Solo / Thank You / Moby Dick / How Many More Times (including The Hunter, Boogie Chillun', Move On Down The Line, High Flyin' Mama, The Lemon Song) / Whole Lotta Love / Communication Breakdown (including Good Times Bad Times)

15 January 1970, City Hall, Newcastle Upon Tyne, England (8:00 p.m.)

SETLIST NOT KNOWN BUT WOULD HAVE PROBABLY INCLUDED THE FOLLOWING: We're Gonna Groove / I Can't Quit You Baby / Dazed And Confused / Heartbreaker / White Summer / Black Mountain Side / Since I've Been Loving You / Organ Solo / Thank You / Moby Dick / How Many More Times (including The Hunter, Boogie Chillun', Move On Down The Line, High Flyin' Mama, The Lemon Song) / Whole Lotta Love / Communication Breakdown (including Good Times Bad Times)

16 January 1970, Oval Hall, City Hall, Sheffield, South Yorkshire, England (8:00 p.m.)

UK poster advertising Led Zeppelin tour dates.

SETLIST NOT KNOWN BUT WOULD HAVE PROBABLY INCLUDED THE FOLLOWING: We're Gonna Groove / I Can't Quit You Baby / Dazed And Confused / Heartbreaker / White Summer / Black Mountain Side / Since I've Been Loving You / Organ Solo / Thank You / Moby Dick / How Many More Times (including The Hunter, Boogie Chillun', Move On Down The Line, High Flyin' Mama, The Lemon Song) / Whole Lotta Love / Communication Breakdown (including Good Times Bad Times)

24 January 1970, the Refectory, Leeds University, Leeds, West Yorkshire

SETLIST NOT KNOWN BUT WOULD HAVE PROBABLY INCLUDED THE FOLLOWING: We're Gonna Groove / I Can't Quit You Baby / Dazed And Confused / Heartbreaker / White Summer / Black Mountain Side / Since I've Been Loving You / Organ Solo / Thank You / Moby Dick / How Many More Times (including The Hunter, Boogie Chillun', Move On Down The Line, High Flyin' Mama, The Lemon Song) / Whole Lotta Love / Communication Breakdown (including Good Times Bad Times)

FEBRUARY 1970

7 February 1970, Usher Hall, Edinburgh, Scotland (7:30 p.m. The show was canceled as Robert Plant was involved in a head-on car collision. The concert was rescheduled for February 17, 1970.)

17 February 1970, Usher Hall, Edinburgh, Scotland (7:30 p.m. Rescheduled from February 7, 1970.)

SETLIST NOT KNOWN BUT WOULD HAVE PROBABLY INCLUDED THE FOLLOWING: We're Gonna Groove / I Can't Quit You Baby / Dazed And Confused / Heartbreaker / White Summer / Black Mountain Side / Since I've Been Loving You / Organ Solo / Thank You / Moby Dick / How Many More Times (including The Hunter, Boogie Chillun', Move On Down The Line, High Flyin' Mama, The Lemon Song) / Whole Lotta Love / Communication Breakdown (including Good Times Bad Times)

LED ZEPPELIN SCANDINAVIAN / EUROPEAN TOUR

23 FEBRUARY 1970–12 MARCH 1970

23 February 1970, Aalto Hall, Kulttuuritalo, Helsinki, Finland

SETLIST (INCOMPLETE): We're Gonna Groove / I Can't Quit You Baby / Dazed And Confused / Heartbreaker / White Summer / Black Mountain Side / Since I've Been Loving You / Organ Solo / Thank You / Moby Dick / How Many More Times (including The Hunter, Boogie Chillun', Move On Down The Line, Hideaway, Cocaine Blues, CC Rider, The Lemon Song, Be-Bop-A-Lula) / Whole Lotta Love

25 February 1970, Konsethuset, Gothenburg, Sweden

SETLIST NOT KNOWN BUT WOULD HAVE PROBABLY INCLUDED THE FOLLOWING: We're Gonna Groove / I Can't Quit You Baby / Dazed And Confused / Heartbreaker / White Summer / Black Mountain Side / Since I've Been Loving You / Organ Solo / Thank You / Moby Dick / How Many More Times (including The Hunter, Boogie Chillun', Move On Down The Line, High Flyin' Mama, The Lemon Song) / Whole Lotta Love / Communication Breakdown (including Good Times Bad Times)

26 February 1970, Konserthuset, Stockholm, Sweden (7:00 p.m. The concert was booked to replace the canceled date on 7 October 1969. During their stay in Stockholm, the band received Gold Disc awards for Swedish sales of *Led Zeppelin II*.)

SETLIST NOT KNOWN BUT WOULD HAVE PROBABLY INCLUDED THE FOLLOWING: We're Gonna Groove / I Can't Quit You Baby / Dazed And Confused / Heartbreaker / White Summer / Black Mountain Side / Since I've Been Loving You / Organ Solo / Thank You / Moby Dick / How Many More Times (including The Hunter, Boogie Chillun', Move On Down The Line, High Flyin' Mama, The Lemon Song) / Whole Lotta Love / Communication Breakdown (including Good Times Bad Times)

27 February 1970, Concertgebouw, Amsterdam, Holland (There is no evidence that this show took place.)

28 February 1970, K. B. Hallen, Copenhagen, Denmark (The 1969 Danish television-show backstage encounter with Eva von Zeppelin comes back to haunt the band when they are threatened with legal action should they go on as Led Zeppelin. To avoid any potential trouble, for one night only they are prepared to go on as the Nobs.)

SETLIST: We're Gonna Groove / I Can't Quit You Baby / Dazed And Confused / Heartbreaker / White Summer / Black Mountain Side / Since I've Been Loving You / Organ Solo / Thank You / Moby Dick / How Many More Times (including The Hunter, Boogie Chillun', Move On Down The Line, Cocaine Blues, Bottle It Up And Go, They're Red Hot) / Whole Lotta Love / Communication Breakdown / C'mon Everybody / Something Else / Bring It On Home / Long Tall Sally

This has gone on to become quite a legendary show. Maybe their frustration at the possibility of having to change their name for one evening was channeled into the music. Whatever the reason, the band, and especially Jimmy Page, are in amazing form. "Dazed

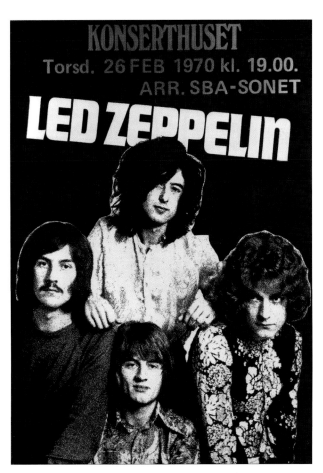

Press advert for Led Zeppelin's concert at the Konserthuset in Stockholm, Sweden.

And Confused" and "Heartbreaker" are glorious versions. You can always tell when the band are enjoying themselves when they throw in some of their favorite rock 'n' roll covers. Tonight the crowd was treated to two numbers from Eddie Cochran during the extra encores after "How Many More Times." Before the final encore, Plant tells the crowd, "We'd like to say thank you very much for receiving us back again, after last time we came here with Country Joe and the Fish. We've gotta say that I don't think we've changed much, but an incredible change in playing. We'd like to dedicate this to the wonderful clubs in Copenhagen, and until we come back again this is how we'd like you to remember us." In the end, the band went on as Led Zeppelin, although they had been prepared to go on as the Nobs if any legal action was threatened. In the end it never was.

7 March 1970, Montreux Casino, Montreux, Switzerland (Claude Knobs, the Montreux Jazz Festival organizer, introduces the band. He would later represent Atlantic Records in Switzerland.)

SETLIST: We're Gonna Groove / I Can't Quit You Baby / Dazed And Confused / Rice Pudding Intro / Heartbreaker / White Summer / Black Mountain Side / Since I've Been Loving You / Organ Solo / Thank You / What Is And What Should Never Be / Moby Dick / How Many More Times (including The Hunter, Boogie Chillun', Move On Down The Line, Hideaway, Bottle It Up And Go, They're Red Hot, Cumberland Gap, My Baby Left Me, Jenny Jenny, The Lemon Song) / Whole Lotta Love

Another high-energy show full of highlights. Page plays Jeff Beck's "Rice Pudding" riff before launching into one of the best ever versions of "Heartbreaker." Luckily for collectors and fans, the majority of the

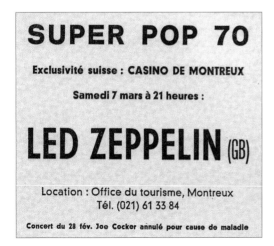

Press advert for Led Zeppelin's appearance at the famous Montreux Casino on 7 March 1970.

show was taped and circulates freely all over the web, and not so freely as a bootleg.

8 March 1970, Circus Krone, Munich, Germany (10:15 p.m.)

SETLIST NOT KNOWN BUT WOULD PROBABLY HAVE CONSISTED OF: We're Gonna Groove / I Can't Quit You Baby / Dazed And Confused / Heartbreaker / White Summer / Black Mountain Side / Since I've Been Loving You / Organ Solo / Thank You / Moby Dick / How Many More Times / Whole Lotta Love / Communication Breakdown

9 March 1970, Konzerthaus, Vienna, Austria (A fairly low-key gig that is not helped by equipment problems at various times throughout the show.)

SETLIST: We're Gonna Groove / I Can't Quit You Baby / Dazed And Confused / Rice Pudding Intro / Heartbreaker / White Summer / Black Mountain Side / Since I've Been Loving You / Moby Dick / How Many More Times (including The Hunter, Boogie Chillun', Move On Down The Line, Hideaway, Bottle It Up And Go, Cumberland Gap, They're Red Hot, The Lemon Song) / Whole Lotta Love

10 March 1970, Kongresshalle, Frankfurt, Germany (The concert was canceled because riots had taken place at the venue on 21 February after an appearance by Jethro Tull. Instead, the band added an extra date at the Musikhalle in Hamburg for the same day. Riots were common place in Europe at this period with many people objecting to having to pay to attend concerts. France and Germany were the worst affected.)

10 March 1970, Musikhalle, Hamburg, Germany (8:00 p.m. Rescheduled from the canceled Kongresshalle, Frankfurt, show.)

SETLIST: We're Gonna Groove / I Can't Quit You Baby / Dazed And Confused / Heartbreaker / White Summer / Black Mountain Side / Since I've Been Loving You / Organ Solo / Thank You / What Is And What Should Never Be / Moby Dick / How Many More Times (including The Hunter, Boogie Chillun', High Flyin Mama, Down By The River, Travelling Riverside Blues, Long Distance Call, The Lemon Song) / Whole Lotta Love

Plant teases the crowd with "Living Loving Maid" lyrics "With a purple umbrella" after "Heartbreaker," just as the song does on the *Led Zeppelin II* album. Led Zeppelin never played "Living Loving Maid" live, and when Plant was in a good mood, he would occasionally throw in the first few words of the song as a tease. He really did not like the song, which would explain why it was never performed live.

11 March 1970, Musikhalle, Hamburg, Germany (8:00 p.m.)

SETLIST: We're Gonna Groove / I Can't Quit You Baby / Dazed And Confused / Heartbreaker / White Summer / Black Mountain Side / Since I've Been Loving You / Organ Solo / Thank You / What Is And What Should Never Be / Moby Dick / How Many More Times (including Bolero, The Hunter, Think You Need A Shot [The Needle]), Boogie Chillun', Move On Down The Line, Bottle It Up And Go, They're Red Hot, Cumberland Gap, Long Distance Call, The Lemon Song) / Whole Lotta Love

12 March 1970, Rheinehalle, Dusseldorf, Germany (8:00 p.m.)

SETLIST: Communication Breakdown / I Can't Quit You Baby / Dazed And Confused / Heartbreaker / White Summer / Black Mountain Side / Since I've Been Loving You / Organ Solo / Thank You / Moby Dick / How Many More Times (including Bolero, The Hunter, Boogie Chillun', Move On Down The Line, Hideaway, Bottle It Up And Go, Cumberland Gap, They're Red Hot, The Lemon Song) / Whole Lotta Love

The usual opener, "We're Gonna Groove," is replaced with "Communication Breakdown." A good show, but you can feel the band are happy that it is the last night of the tour and looking forward to a few days rest before starting their North American tour on 21 March 1970.

LED ZEPPELIN FIFTH US TOUR

21 MARCH 1970–19 APRIL 1970

21 March 1970, Pacific Coliseum, Vancouver, British Columbia, Canada (8:00 p.m.)

SETLIST: We're Gonna Groove / I Can't Quit You Baby / Dazed And Confused / Heartbreaker / White Summer / Black Mountain Side / Since I've Been Loving You / Organ Solo / Thank You / What Is And What Should Never Be / Moby Dick / How Many More Times / Whole Lotta Love / Communication Breakdown (including Ramble On)

❝ As the concert drew to a close during the fever pitch of 'Whole Lotta Love,' the massive crowd surged forward and about 50 senseless fans spoiled it for the group and the audience by vaulting up onto the 15-foot high stage. 'Never before in the history of Led Zeppelin has this happened,' Plant shouted mock-serious into the microphone, not knowing whether to be offended or flattered. When the stage was finally cleared, Led Zeppelin came back for two encores and a standing ovation that was a fitting tribute to one of the most talented rock groups in the business today. ❞

—*EXPRESS* (Review from 24 March 1970)

Press advert for Led Zeppelin's appearance at the Vancouver Coliseum on 21 March 1970.

22 March 1970, Seattle Arena, Seattle, Washington (8:00 p.m.)

SETLIST NOT KNOWN BUT WOULD PROBABLY HAVE CONSISTED OF: We're Gonna Groove / I Can't Quit You Baby / Dazed And Confused / Heartbreaker / White Summer / Black Mountain Side / Since I've Been Loving You / Organ Solo / Thank You / Moby Dick / How Many More Times / Whole Lotta Love / Communication Breakdown

23 March 1970, Portland Memorial Coliseum, Portland, Oregon (8:00 p.m.)

SETLIST NOT KNOWN BUT WOULD PROBABLY HAVE CONSISTED OF: We're Gonna Groove / I Can't Quit You Baby / Dazed And Confused / Heartbreaker / White Summer / Black Mountain Side / Since I've Been Loving You / Organ Solo / Thank You / Moby Dick / How Many More Times / Whole Lotta Love / Communication Breakdown

25 March 1970, Denver Coliseum, Denver, Colorado (8:00 p.m.)

SETLIST: We're Gonna Groove / I Can't Quit You Baby / Dazed And Confused / Heartbreaker / Since I've Been Loving You / Organ Solo / Thank You / Moby Dick / How Many More Times (including Ramble On, Bolero, The Hunter, Think You Need A Shot [The Needle], Boogie Chillun', Move On Down The Line, I Can't Be Satisfied, The Lemon Song) / Whole Lotta Love

66 Rock has many facets these days and Led Zeppelin is among the best in its particular area. They aren't especially inventive; their lyrics, for instance, range from banal sexual innuendos to tired 'you cheated, you lied' laments. But they are skillful enough to overpower friends and foes alike with good, solid rock 'n' roll music. Eleven thousand heads bobbing in unison is proof of Led Zeppelin's worth to the world of electric music. When you turn on a discriminating audience, you know you're doing something right. 99

—*DENVER POST* (Review from 26 March 1970)

26 March 1970, Salt Palace, Salt Lake City, Utah (8:00 p.m.)

SETLIST NOT KNOWN BUT WOULD PROBABLY HAVE CONSISTED OF: We're Gonna Groove / I Can't Quit You Baby / Dazed And Confused / Heartbreaker / White Summer / Black Mountain Side / Since I've Been Loving You / Organ Solo / Thank You / Moby Dick / How Many More Times / Whole Lotta Love / Communication Breakdown

27 March 1970, the Forum, Inglewood, Los Angeles, California (8:30 p.m. A rowdy audience interrupt the concert. This happened quite often at shows at this time as unrest between police and concert-goers intensified.)

SETLIST: We're Gonna Groove / Dazed And Confused / Heartbreaker / Bring It On Home / White Summer / Black Mountain Side / Since I've Been Loving You / Organ Solo / Thank You / What Is And What Should Never Be / Moby Dick / How Many More Times (including Bolero, The Hunter, Think You Need A Shot [The Needle], I'm A Man, Boogie Chillun', High Flying Mama, The Lemon Song) / Whole Lotta Love / Communication Breakdown (including Down By The River)

There must have been something in the water in California as Los Angeles and Led Zeppelin just loved each other. This was their hometown in many ways and when they played here something magical always happened. Tonight was no exception as the band put on one of their best all-time performances. The whole band is "on" from the word go. You just knew it was going to be one of those shows when Plant announced, "Good evening. Everybody feel alright? Tonight we intend to get everybody looser than anybody's ever been loose . . . even with cod liver oil!" The band plays

a powerful "We're Gonna Groove" as opener followed by "Dazed And Confused" with some intuitive soloing from the band members. A spectacular "Heartbreaker" with Jimmy in top form followed this.

The crowd understandably goes wild and Plant tries to calm things down a bit: "The people who are standing in the aisles, can they sit on the floor or whatever. There's some people behind can't see. So if anybody knows they are obstructing somebody else's view, can they respect that fact or move, then everybody can see!" Tension was in the air and before they played "Since I've Been Loving You," Plant dedicated the song to "the little men with the suits on who keep pushing everybody back down the aisle. It's their big day, y'see. They can't understand it." Perhaps the biggest highlight was the wild encore version of "Whole Lotta Love," which featured a musical duel between Jimmy Page on the theremin and John Paul Jones on a heavily distorted Hammond organ.

66 At the end of the evening, hundreds had pushed their way into the aisles near the stage and thousands of others were standing in rhythm to the music. The concert, which had been sold out for weeks, showed that Led Zeppelin is largely trying to recreate the sounds that have dominated English blues-rock in recent years. Appearing without any support act, the group was onstage from 8:45 to 11:15 p.m. Like the Stones, they have a gyrating lead singer in Robert Plant and their best received songs have bawdy, under-the-counter lyrics. 99

—*LOS ANGELES TIMES* (Review from March 1970)

28 March 1970, Dallas Memorial Auditorium, Dallas, Texas (8:00 p.m.)

SETLIST (INCOMPLETE): We're Gonna Groove / Dazed And Confused / Heartbreaker / Bring It On Home / White Summer / Black Mountain Side / Since I've Been Loving You / Organ Solo / Thank You / What Is And What Should Never Be / Moby Dick / How Many More Times / Whole Lotta Love

29 March 1970, Hofheinz Pavilion, University of Houston, Houston, Texas (8:30 p.m.)

SETLIST (INCOMPLETE): We're Gonna Groove / Dazed And Confused / Heartbreaker / Bring It On Home / White Summer / Black Mountain Side / Since I've Been Loving You / Organ Solo / Thank You / What Is And What Should Never Be / Moby Dick / How Many More Times (including Bolero, Lickin' Stick, Think You Need A Shot [The Needle], For What It's Worth, Tobacco Road) / Whole Lotta Love

30 March 1970, Civic Arena, Pittsburgh, Pennsylvania (8:00 p.m. The concert was cut short when the band walked offstage to stop police from using batons on the rioting audience members.)

SETLIST NOT KNOWN BUT WOULD PROBABLY HAVE CONSISTED OF: We're Gonna Groove / I Can't Quit You Baby / Dazed And Confused / Heartbreaker / White Summer / Black Mountain Side / Since I've Been Loving You / Organ Solo / Thank You / Moby Dick / How Many More Times / Whole Lotta Love / Communication Breakdown

31 March 1970, the Spectrum, Philadelphia, Pennsylvania (8:30 p.m.)

SETLIST NOT KNOWN BUT WOULD PROBABLY HAVE CONSISTED OF: We're Gonna Groove / I Can't Quit You Baby / Dazed And Confused / Heartbreaker / White Summer / Black Mountain Side / Since I've Been Loving You / Organ Solo / Thank You / Moby Dick / How Many More Times / Whole Lotta Love / Communication Breakdown

APRIL 1970

2 April 1970, Charleston Civic Center Coliseum, Charleston, West Virginia (8:00 p.m.)

SETLIST NOT KNOWN BUT WOULD PROBABLY HAVE CONSISTED OF: We're Gonna Groove / I Can't Quit You Baby / Dazed And Confused / Heartbreaker / White Summer / Black Mountain Side / Since I've Been Loving You / Organ Solo / Thank You / Moby Dick / How Many More Times / Whole Lotta Love / Communication Breakdown

66 Zeppelin is not thin on material. They dip liberally into their two millionseller albums and have been previewing—on this, their fifth U.S. tour—a sure hit from *Led Zeppelin III*, a blues called 'Since I've Been Loving You.' . . . Robert Plant deserves his growing reputation as the most sexually exciting personality in rock. But he deserves more. Plant is more musician than he is pretty goldilocks rock and roll star. He has the guts to get into a blues like 'Bring It on Home' and the range and musical sense to do something with it. 99

—RAY BRACK

(Review in unknown Charleston newspaper, 3 April 1970)

3 April 1970, Macon Coliseum, Macon, Georgia

SETLIST NOT KNOWN BUT WOULD PROBABLY HAVE CONSISTED OF: We're Gonna Groove / I Can't Quit You Baby / Dazed And Confused / Heartbreaker / White Summer / Black Mountain Side / Since I've Been Loving You / Organ Solo / Thank You / Moby Dick / How Many More Times / Whole Lotta Love

Press advert for Led Zeppelin's appearance at the Civic Center in Charleston, West Virginia.

4 April 1970, Indiana State Fairgrounds Coliseum, Indianapolis, Indiana (8:00 p.m.)

SETLIST NOT KNOWN BUT WOULD PROBABLY HAVE CONSISTED OF: We're Gonna Groove / I Can't Quit You Baby / Dazed And Confused / Heartbreaker / White Summer / Black Mountain Side / Since I've Been Loving You / Organ Solo / Thank You / Moby Dick / How Many More Times / Whole Lotta Love

5 April 1970, Baltimore Civic Center, Baltimore, Maryland (8:00 p.m. Not a particularly good show. The boisterous crowd doesn't help and Robert Plant's microphone cuts out at regular intervals.)

SETLIST: We're Gonna Groove / Dazed And Confused / Heartbreaker / Bring It On Home / White Summer / Black Mountain Side / Organ Solo / Thank You / What Is and What Should Never Be / Moby Dick / How Many More Times (including Bolero, The Hunter, Think You Need A Shot [The Needle]), Boogie Chillun', Move On Down The Line, That's Alright Mama, My Baby Left Me, Honey Bee, The Lemon Song) / Whole Lotta Love

Press advert for Led Zeppelin's appearance at the Charlotte Coliseum, Charlotte, North Carolina.

7 April 1970, Charlotte Coliseum, Charlotte, North Carolina (8:00 p.m.)

SETLIST: We're Gonna Groove / Dazed And Confused / Heartbreaker / Bring It On Home / White Summer / Black Mountain Side / Since I've Been Loving You / Organ Solo / Thank You / What Is And What Should Never Be / Moby Dick / Whole Lotta Love

8 April 1970, J. S. Dorton Arena, Raleigh, Morth Carolina (8:00 p.m.)

SETLIST: We're Gonna Groove / Dazed And Confused / Heartbreaker/ Bring It On Home / White Summer / Black Mountain Side / Since I've Been Loving You / Organ Solo / Thank You / What Is And What Should Never Be / Moby Dick / How Many More Times / Whole Lotta Love

66 After waiting more than 45 minutes for the show to begin, the patient audience was rewarded with five minutes of ear-splitting feedback. In order to avoid the echo within the arena, which Jimi Hendrix encountered recently, the performers had to present their music at their maximum volume. Because of this, the audience had to adjust to the powerful beat of sound. Unlike most rock concerts, the audience spent a great portion of the show saluting the solos in standing ovations. 99

—*RALEIGH NEWS AND OBSERVER* (Review from 9 April 1970)

9 April 1970, Curtis Hixon Hall, Tampa, Florida (8:30 p.m.)

SETLIST: We're Gonna Groove / Dazed And Confused / Heartbreaker / Bring It On Home / White Summer / Black Mountain Side / Since I've Been Loving You / Organ Solo / Thank You / What Is And What Should Never Be / Moby Dick / How Many More Times (including Bolero, The Hunter, Think You Need A Shot [The Needle]), Boogie Chillun', High Flyin' Mama, Mess O' Blues, My Baby, The Lemon Song) / Whole Lotta Love

66 Zeppelin turned in one of the truly great performances in this area. Some of the biggest names in rock have been at Curtis Hixon but few—besides B.B. King—have received the welcome afforded these slender English boys. And more amazing than the group's ability to perform is the fact they came on the stage and started their first number four minutes before show time. This was promised by the promoter, National Shows Inc., but few hardened rock fans believed it. Led Zeppelin is one group that would be welcome back. 99

—*THE INDEPENDENT* (Review from 10 April 1970)

10 April 1970, Miami Beach Convention Center, Miami, Florida (8:30 p.m.)

SETLIST NOT KNOWN BUT WOULD PROBABLY HAVE CONSISTED OF: We're Gonna Groove / I Can't Quit You Baby / Dazed And Confused / Heartbreaker / White Summer / Black Mountain Side / Since I've Been Loving You / Organ Solo / Thank You / Moby Dick / How Many More Times / Whole Lotta Love

The concert adverts had promised a two-and-a-half-hour show from Led Zeppelin. Unfortunately, this was yet another show that was marred by problems caused by an overexcited crowd and a large police presence whose sole purpose was to keep them calm. The show was soldout, with many people being unable to get tickets for this major concert event in Miami. Those unlucky ones tried to push their way in but were greeted by the full force of the Miami Beach Police, who showed no restraint in stopping the crowd by any means necessary. Surprisingly, the concert itself was great, but Robert Plant kept having to plead with audience members to stay calm and sit back down in their seats. The end result was that the band had to curtail their set by forty-five minutes.

11 April 1970, Kiel Auditorium, St. Louis, Missouri (8:00 p.m.)

SETLIST: We're Gonna Groove / Dazed And Confused / Heartbreaker / Bring It On Home / White Summer / Black Mountain Side / Since I've Been Loving You / Organ Solo / Thank You / What Is And What Should Never Be / Moby Dick / How Many More Times / Whole Lotta Love

A review in a local paper shows that not everyone understands the power and glory of Led Zeppelin:

66 Much of their music goes in the direction of egoistic excess that makes so much of contemporary jazz essentially boring music. At one point in the concert, they even resorted to that hoary jazz trick of leaving the drummer onstage alone for a 15-minute solo. The things Page can do with a guitar are astounding. . . . But his music like that of the rest of the group, is a series of crescendos with no build-up, no sense of space. . . . One longs for a BB King or an Eric Clapton to break through the mass of noise and play some music.

—*POST-DISPATCH* (Review from 13 April 1970)

12 April 1970, Metropolitan Sports Center, Bloomingdale, Minnesota (7:30 p.m.)

SETLIST NOT KNOWN BUT WOULD PROBABLY HAVE CONSISTED OF: We're Gonna Groove / I Can't Quit You Baby / Dazed And Confused / Heartbreaker / White Summer / Black Mountain Side / Since I've Been Loving You / Organ Solo / Thank You / Moby Dick / How Many More Times / Whole Lotta Love

13 April 1970, Montreal Forum, Montreal, Quebec (8:00 p.m.)

SETLIST NOT KNOWN BUT WOULD PROBABLY HAVE CONSISTED OF: We're Gonna Groove / I Can't Quit You Baby / Dazed And Confused / Heartbreaker / White Summer / Black Mountain Side / Since I've Been Loving You / Organ Solo / Thank You / Moby Dick / How Many More Times / Whole Lotta Love

14 April 1970, Ottawa Civic Centre Arena, Ottawa, Alberta, Canada (8:30 p.m.)

SETLIST: We're Gonna Groove / Dazed And Confused / Heartbreaker / Bring It On Home / White Summer / Black Mountain Side / Since I've Been Loving You / Organ Solo / Thank You / Moby Dick / How Many More Times / Whole Lotta Love

66 The Zeppelin presented themselves not only as splendid musicians but as true showmen. Although the group arrived late, they performed a thrilling show with a highlight of John Bonham's drum solo without drum sticks. Bonham formed such a rapport with the audience it seemed that you and he were alone. Everyone was aware of this and it gave added reason for the standing ovation given him. 99

—*THE JOURNAL* (Review from 15 April 1970)

16 April 1970, Roberts Municipal Stadium, Evansville, Indiana (7:30 p.m. The band come on thirty minutes late and their equipment fails early on in the set before resuming.)

SETLIST NOT KNOWN BUT WOULD PROBABLY HAVE CONSISTED OF: We're Gonna Groove / I Can't Quit You Baby / Dazed And Confused / Heartbreaker / White Summer / Black Mountain Side / Since I've Been Loving You / Organ Solo / Thank You / Moby Dick / How Many More Times / Whole Lotta Love

17 April 1970, Mid-South Coliseum, Memphis, Tennessee (8:00 p.m. Once again there are problems between the audience and the local police, who are determined to keep fans seated at all times. Upon arrival at their Holiday Inn motel before the show, the band were awarded with "The Key to the City of Memphis" in front of a huge crowd of reporters in the lobby. Afterward, both Jimmy Page and Robert Plant take the opportunity to visit the famous Sun Studios, only to find that they were shut.)

SETLIST: We're Gonna Groove / Dazed And Confused / Heartbreaker / Bring It On Home / White Summer / Black Mountain Side / Since I've Been Loving You / Organ Solo / Thank You / What Is And What Should Never Be / Moby Dick / How Many More Times (including Bolero, The Hunter, Think You Need A Shot [The Needle], Boogie Mama, High Flying Mama, Memphis Tennessee, For What It's Worth, Ramble On, Tobacco Road, Honey Bee, Long Distance Call, The Lemon Song, That's Alright Mama) / Whole Lotta Love

Dynamic show. Plant gets many cheers when he states, "We've waited for a long time to come to Memphis, in fact, ever since we were born, I think!" The audience recording available from this show reveals how tight the bass/drum/guitar interplay was. Page is breathtaking during "Heartbreaker" and he achieves what can only be described as crackling sounds with the theremin. It sounds like he is starting to come up with the "Kashmir" riff during "Black Mountain Side." By the time the band hit "How Many More Times," things were getting out of control, so Plant tried to diffuse the situation: "I want the policemen to put their hands together. Put those lights down! You're beautiful—even with the light on!" Yet another wonderful show.

18 April 1970, Arizona Veterans Memorial Coliseum, Phoenix, Arizona (6:30 p.m. The show had to be cut short due to Robert Plant feeling ill from exhaustion.)

Jimmy Page on the Julie Felix Show at BBC Television Studios. (Rex)

SETLIST: We're Gonna Groove / Dazed And Confused / Heartbreaker / Bring It On Home / White Summer / Black Mountain Side / Organ Solo / Thank You / Moby Dick / Whole Lotta Love / Jimmy Page Announcements

The show is cut shortly after "Whole Lotta Love" when Jimmy Page explains that Robert Plant is ill: "You've been a fantastic audience, but there's been something happening tonight. . . . Robert's been very ill and as he came off he's just collapsed and we've just called for a doctor. We'd really like to do more, but obviously it's impossible." Plant was having problems with his voice tonight and had to sing for most of the time in a much lower scale. This was also the last time that "White Summer" / "Black Mountain Side" would be played until the 1977 tour.

19 April 1970, Las Vegas Convention Center, Las Vegas, Nevada (8:00 p.m. The show was canceled due to Robert Plant's exhaustion.)

JIMMY PAGE BBC TELEVISON APPEARANCE

23 APRIL 1970

23 April 1970, *Julie Felix Show*, Studio D, BBC Television Studios, Lime Grove, Shepherds Bush, London (Jimmy Page appears as a guest on the *Julie Felix Show*. He plays "White Summer" / "Black Mountain Side." The recording session

takes place on 23 April and is broadcast at 11:10 p.m. on BBC1, 26 April 1970. Julie Felix's introduction of Jimmy Page: "My next guest this evening is a member of certainly the most successful group to come out of Britain in the last couple of years. Led Zeppelin LPs top both the British and American charts and the lead guitarist in that group is definitely a very talented and a special musician. Ladies and gentlemen . . . Jimmy Page!" Color footage of the show survives in the BBC archives.)

MAY 1970

24 May 1970, Mothers Club, Erdington, Birmingham, West Midlands (Robert Plant and John Bonham have a jam with Cochise this evening.)

JUNE 1970

ICELAND / EUROPEAN TOUR

22 JUNE 1970–19 JULY 1970

22 June 1970, Laugardalsholl Sports Arena, Reykjavik, Iceland (Led Zeppelin make their first appearance in Iceland to represent the UK's pop industry as part of a cultural exchange program organized by the UK government. Around 5,000 people attended the concert, which ran over two hours. Some black-and-white footage exists of the band arriving at the airport and a small portion of "Dazed And Confused" from the evening show are available on the Led Zeppelin DVD that was released in 2003. In the 6 June 1970 issue of Disc and Music Echo, manager Peter Grant confirms that Led Zeppelin will be releasing a film and stated: "A camera team will be travelling with them to Iceland on 22 June and the whole thing should be tied up within a couple of months." Footage from the January Royal Albert Hall concert would have been the main focus, as would some "on the road" footage from the American tour. The film was never released in its intended form.)

27 June 1970, Madison Square Garden, New York City, New York (An afternoon and evening show are scheduled, but were canceled due to the band's appearance at the Bath Festival. Both shows are rescheduled to 19 September 1970.)

28 June 1970, Second Bath Festival of Blues and Progressive Music, Royal Bath and West Showground, Somerset (Festival starts at midday and Led Zeppelin come on around 8:30 p.m. Also on the bill are Canned Heat, John Mayall and the Bluesbreakers, Steppenwolf, Pink Floyd, It's a Beautiful Day, Fairport Convention, Donovan, Frank Zappa and the Mothers of Invention, the Flock, Hot Tuna, and many others. One of Led Zeppelin's greatest shows

ever in the UK. Sadly it was not one that was preserved other than on an average audience recording. It could have been different, though. Their performance was officially filmed by Peter Whitehead, but poor lighting at the festival coupled with the fact that the daylight film in the cameras could not cope with the night filming meant that most of the footage was unusable. Led Zeppelin previewed some new songs at the show to gage audience response to new material for their third album, which was being recorded at the time. The first was the powerful opener at the concert, "Immigrant Song," which had only recently been written and had a completely different vocal arrangement to the later album version. The second new song was "That's The

Press advert for Led Zeppelin's appearance at the Laugardalsholl Sports Center, Reykjavik, Iceland, on 22 June 1970.

Obscure advert for *Led Zeppelin III*.

Way," which was introduced under its working title "The Boy Next Door." The third new number for the UK was "Since I've Been Loving You," which had been played in a very embryonic form at the Albert Hall show on 9 January 1970. Now it was complete and would go on to be a fan favorite both on Led Zeppelin III and in concert. The band were clearly happy to be away from the hassles with police and crowd control in the US, as Robert Plant mentions, "We've been playing America a lot recently and we really thought that coming back here we might have a dodgy time. There's a lot of things going wrong in America at the moment that are getting a bit sticky. It's really nice to come to an open-air festival where there are no bad things happening and everything's turned out beautiful.")

SETLIST: Immigrant Song / Heartbreaker / Dazed And Confused / Bring It On Home / Since I've Been Loving You / Organ Solo / Thank You / That's The Way / What Is And What Should Never Be / Moby Dick / How Many More Times (including The Hunter, Think You Need A Shot [The Needle], Boogie Chillun', The Lemon Song, Need Your Love Tonight, That's Alright Mama) / Whole Lotta Love / Communication Breakdown / Rock 'n' Roll Medley (Long Tall Sally, Say Mama, Johnny B. Goode, That's Alright Mama)

66 They kicked off with a new riff from their next album called 'Immigrant Song.' They actually took some time to warm up the crowd, but this may have been intentional as they built up to a fantastic climax with an act lasting over three hours. Jimmy produced his violin bow to attack the guitar strings, and John Paul was featured on Hammond organ on 'Since I've Been Loving You.' It was after John Bonham's phenomenal drum solo—violent, aggressive and furiously fast—had brought the crowd permanently to their feet that the real fun began! They had contrasted their rock style with the beautiful 'The First Time' (later called 'That's the Way') featuring John Paul Jones on mandolin and Jim on six-string acoustic with Robert singing in the most attractive restrained style. Now it was time for the other extreme. A wild rock medley—'How Many More Times.' As dusk fell and the lights flickered on, the band roared into 'Communication Breakdown.' In their final minutes, they paid tribute to the masters of Rock and Roll with the songs of Little Richard, Elvis Presley and Chuck Berry. 99

—*MELODY MAKER* (Review from 4 July 1970)

Alternate artwork for the Bath Festival on 28 June 1970.

Bath Festival of Blues and Progressive Music poster with Led Zeppelin on 28 June 1970.

Led Zeppelin onstage at the Bath Festival of Blues and Progressive Music 28 June 1970. (Rex)

JULY 1970

LED ZEPPELIN GERMAN TOUR

16 JULY 1970–19 JULY 1970

A short tour of Germany was very successful. The band played well and received positive reviews, both in the press and among the fans. Like a lot of other countries at the time, there was always a heavy police presence at rock concerts to prevent any trouble with over-excitable fans. Luckily, everybody behaved and there was no major trouble, except for a few broken windows at the Sporthalle in Cologne when disgruntled ticketless concertgoers were refused entry. More and more portable tape recorders were being made available on the market, which meant that many fans wanted to record concerts for a souvenir of the evening. Others wanted to share that souvenir with other fans and pressed the shows on vinyl to sell in shops. Peter Grant was very aware of the situation and made it his business to stop people recording the shows for fear of bootlegs being made. He did not

differentiate between fan and bootleg recordings. He would frequently be seen getting in among the crowd destroying tapes and equipment, much to the dismay of the tapers. That would explain why there are no good recordings from this tour!

16 July 1970, Sporthalle, Cologne, Germany (8:00 p.m.)

SETLIST NOT KNOWN BUT WOULD PROBABLY HAVE CONSISTED OF: Immigrant Song / Heartbreaker / Dazed And Confused / Bring It On Home / That's Way / Bron-Yr-Aur / Since I've Been Loving You / Organ Solo / Thank You / What Is And What Should Never Be / Moby Dick / Whole Lotta Love / Communication Breakdown

17 July 1970, Grugahalle, Essen, Germany (8:00 p.m.)

SETLIST NOT KNOWN BUT WOULD PROBABLY HAVE CONSISTED OF: Immigrant Song / Heartbreaker / Dazed And Confused / Bring It On Home / That's Way / Bron-Yr-Aur / Since I've Been Loving You / Organ Solo / Thank You / What Is And What Should Never Be / Moby Dick / Whole Lotta Love / Communication Breakdown

18 July 1970, Festhalle, Frankfurt, Germany (8:00 p.m. *Melody Maker*'s Chris Welch joins the band onstage for "Whole Lotta Love" on timbales.)

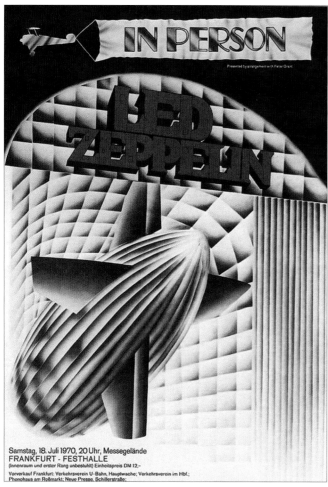

Poster advertising Led Zeppelin's appearance at the Festhalle in Frankfurt on 18 July 1970.

SETLIST: Immigrant Song / Heartbreaker / Dazed And Confused / Bring It On Home / That's The Way / Bron-Yr-Aur / Since I've Been Loving You / Organ Solo / Thank You / What Is And What Should Never Be / Moby Dick / Whole Lotta Love / Communication Breakdown / Rock 'n' Roll Medley.

19 July 1970, Deutschlandhalle, Berlin, Germany (8:00 p.m.)

SETLIST: Immigrant Song / Heartbreaker / Dazed And Confused / Bring It On Home / Since I've Been Loving You / Organ Solo / Thank You / That's The Way / Bron-Yr-Aur / What Is And What Should Never Be / Moby Dick / Whole Lotta Love (including Boogie Chillun', Red House, The Lemon Song, Down In Virginia, Hoochie Coochie Man, Honey Bee, Long Distance Call, Think You Need A Shot [The Needle]) / Communication Breakdown

LED ZEPPELIN SIXTH US TOUR

5 AUGUST 1970–19 SEPTEMBER 1970

Led Zeppelin's stature was getting greater by the day, especially in America. Peter Grant negotiated what would end up being their biggest grossing tour to date by playing in larger venues holding up to 18,000 people. They would soon be the biggest rock band in the world.

The tour should have started in Cincinnati on 5 August, but a week's worth of shows had to be canceled due to John Paul Jones having to stay in England because his father was very ill.

5 August 1970, Cincinnati, Ohio (Canceled due to John Paul Jones's father being very ill.)

6 August 1970, Olympia Stadium, Detroit, Michigan (Canceled due to John Paul Jones's father being very ill. Rescheduled for 28 August 1970.)

7 August 1970, Cleveland Public Auditorium, Ohio (Canceled due to John Paul Jones's father being very ill. Rescheduled for 26 August 1970.)

8 August 1970, Pittsburgh, Pennsylvania (Canceled due to John Paul Jones's father being very ill. The band was also erroneously billed to appear at the Strawberry Fields Festival at Strawberry Fields, Mosport Park, Bowmanville, Ontario, Canada. The festival took place between 7 August and 9 August 1970 and consisted of the following acts: Delaney and Bonnie and Friends, Cactus, Leonard Cohen, Eric Burdon and War, Grand Funk Railroad, Fat, Hog Heaven, Jethro Tull, King Biscuit Boy and Crowbar, Luke and the Apostles and More!, Melanie, Mountain, Procol Harum, Sly and the Family Stone, Ten Years After, and the Youngbloods.)

9 August 1970, Boston Garden, Boston, Massachusetts (Canceled due to John Paul Jones's father being very ill. Rescheduled to 9 September 1970.)

10 August 1970, Hampton Coliseum, Hampton Beach, Virginia (Canceled due to John Paul Jones's father being very ill. Rescheduled to 17 August 1970.)

11 August 1970, Charlotte, North Carolina (Canceled due to John Paul Jones's father being very ill.)

12 August 1970, Jacksonville, Florida (Canceled due to John Paul Jones' father being very ill.)

13 August 1970, Tallahassee, Florida (Canceled due to John Paul Jones's father being very ill.)

14 August 1970, Boston College Stadium, Chestnut Hill, Massachusetts (The show was canceled due to pressure from local affluent residents, who objected to the festival taking place fearing public order problems, as well as noise issues. The mayor, who obviously needed to keep his wealthy residents happy, withdrew the college's license. Led Zeppelin were rebooked for a show at the Boston Gardens on 8 September 1970, which was later changed to 9 September 1970. Led Zeppelin had originally been scheduled to headline the festival with the following support acts: Junior Wells, Buddy Guy Blues Band, Amboy Dukes, Big Brother and the Holding Company, American Dream, Stark Forest Group, Cactus, Swallow, Lighthouse, MC5, the Stooges, the Allman Brothers Band, and Catfish.)

15 August 1970, Yale Bowl, New Haven, Connecticut (8:15 p.m.)

SETLIST: Immigrant Song / Heartbreaker / Dazed And Confused / Bring It On Home / That's The Way / Bron-Yr-Aur / Since I've Been Loving You / Organ Solo / Thank You / What Is And What Should Never Be / Moby Dick / Whole Lotta Love (including Boogie Chillun' / Hi-Heel Sneakers, High Flying Mama, Shake, Move On Down The Line, I'm Moving On, Honey Bee, The Lemon Song, Think You Need A Shot [The Needle]) / Communication Breakdown (including Good Times Bad Times)

17 August 1970, Hampton Coliseum, Hampton Beach, Virginia (The show was rescheduled from 10 August 1970.)

SETLIST: Immigrant Song / Heartbreaker / Dazed And Confused / Bring It On Home / That's The Way / Bron-Yr-Aur / Since I've Been Loving You / Organ Solo / Thank You / What Is And What Should Never Be / Moby Dick / Whole Lotta Love (including Back In The USA, Boogie Chillun', I'm Moving On) / Communication Breakdown (including Good Times Bad Times)

19 August 1970, Municipal Auditorium, Kansas City, Kansas, Missouri

SETLIST NOT KNOWN BUT WOULD PROBABLY HAVE CONSISTED OF: Immigrant Song / Heartbreaker / Dazed And Confused / Bring It On Home / That's Way / Bron-Yr-Aur / Since I've Been Loving You / Organ Solo / Thank You / What Is And What Should Never Be / Moby Dick / Whole Lotta Love / Communication Breakdown

20 August 1970, Oklahoma State Fair, Oklahoma City, Oklahoma

SETLIST NOT KNOWN BUT WOULD PROBABLY HAVE CONSISTED OF: Immigrant Song / Heartbreaker / Dazed And Confused / Bring It On Home / That's Way / Bron-Yr-Aur / Since I've Been Loving You / Organ Solo / Thank You / What Is And What Should Never Be / Moby Dick / Whole Lotta Love / Communication Breakdown

Led Zeppelin were erroneously billed to appear at the Strawberry Fields Festival in Moncton, New Brunswick, on this newspaper advert.

Jimmy Page onstage at the Oklahoma City Fairgrounds Arena. (Photo by Carl Dunn)

Led Zeppelin onstage at the Oklahoma City Fairgrounds Arena. (Photo by Carl Dunn)

SETLIST: Immigrant Song / Heartbreaker / Dazed And Confused (including White Summer) / Bring It On Home / That's The Way / Bron-Yr-Aur / Since I've Been Loving You / Organ Solo / Thank You / What Is And What Should Never Be / Moby Dick / Whole Lotta Love (including Boogie Chillun', High Flyin' Mama, Matchbox, That's Alright, Heartbeat, The Lemon Song, My Baby Left Me, That's Alright Mama) / Communication Breakdown

22 August 1970, Tarrant County Arena, Fort Worth, Texas (8:00 p.m.)

SETLIST NOT KNOWN BUT WOULD PROBABLY HAVE CONSISTED OF: Immigrant Song / Heartbreaker / Dazed And Confused / Bring It On Home / That's Way / Bron-Yr-Aur / Since I've Been Loving You / Organ Solo / Thank You / What Is And What Should Never Be / Moby Dick / Whole Lotta Love / Communication Breakdown

23 August 1970, Hemisfair Arena, San Antonio, Texas (Canceled due to local juvenile diphtheria outbreak.)

25 August 1970, Municipal Auditorium, Nashville, Tennessee (8:00 p.m.)

SETLIST NOT KNOWN BUT WOULD PROBABLY HAVE CONSISTED OF: Immigrant Song / Heartbreaker / Dazed And Confused / Bring It On Home / That's Way / Bron-Yr-Aur / Since I've Been Loving You / Organ Solo / Thank You / What Is And What Should Never Be / Moby Dick / Whole Lotta Love

21 August 1970, Tulsa Assembly Center, Tulsa, Oklahoma (There is some unrest at the show, with authorities putting on the house lights halfway through "Heartbreaker" due to fans getting out of their seats. At that point the band stop playing and Plant tells the audience, "Actually you can turn down the house lights now. Turn the lights off! Everybody sit still. Before we carry on, the lights go down. No, listen, if we're gonna have a good time and you are, we're gonna have to work hand in glove with the so-called authorities. So, you sit down and they'll be cool and turn the lights off. So let's wait for them to turn off the lights." The audience calmed down and the house lights went down to massive cheers. Plant goes on to state, "That's not a victory—that's common sense, so don't take it as a victory!" Page then carried on with his guitar solo. The show is truncated, and then stopped due to riotous audience.)

Fans await Led Zeppelin at the Oklahoma City Fairgrounds Arena in Oklahoma City. (Photo by Carl Dunn)

Robert Plant and Jimmy Page at the Tarrant County Convention Center, Fort Worth, Texas. (Photo by Carl Dunn)

26 August 1970, Public Hall, Cleveland, Ohio (5:30 p.m. The concert was rescheduled from 7 August 1970. The show time was brought forward to 5:30 p.m. from 8:30 p.m. so that John Paul Jones could leave early to fly back to England due to the death of his father. He leaves before the encore, and when the band return to the stage an unknown female bass player wearing a "Belkin Productions" T-shirt on joins the band for the last encore.)

SETLIST NOT KNOWN BUT WOULD PROBABLY HAVE CONSISTED OF: Immigrant Song / Heartbreaker / Dazed And Confused / Bring It On Home / That's Way / Bron-Yr-Aur / Since I've Been Loving You / Organ Solo / Thank You / Whole Lotta Love / Moby Dick / What Is And What Should Never Be

66 When the remaining group members returned to the stage, Jones had split to England for family reasons and Plant said that was it, but as the audience pressed to the stage, they agreed to continue. As they got set to do more, Page popped a string. To fill the gap Plant started to play his harp while Bonham started in on the tabla drums. When Page fixed his guitar, he joined in on the jam. They were then joined by a girl in a Belkin Production tee shirt who played bass to finish the night. 99

—*CLEVELAND TELEGRAM* (Review from August 1970)

Robert Plant onstage at the Tarrant County Convention Center, Fort Worth, Texas. (Photo by Carl Dunn)

SETLIST NOT KNOWN BUT WOULD PROBABLY HAVE CONSISTED OF: Immigrant Song / Heartbreaker / Dazed And Confused / Bring It On Home / That's Way / Bron-Yr-Aur / Since I've Been Loving You / Organ Solo / Thank You / What Is And What Should Never Be / Moby Dick / Whole Lotta Love / Communication Breakdown

31 August 1970, Milwaukee Arena, Milwaukee, Wisconsin (8:00 p.m. Rescheduled from August 27, 1970.)

SETLIST: Immigrant Song / Heartbreaker / Dazed And Confused / Bring It On Home / That's The Way / Bron-Yr-Aur / Since I've Been Loving You / Organ Solo / Thank You / What Is And What Should Never Be / Moby Dick / Whole Lotta Love

SEPTEMBER 1970

1 September 1970, Seattle Center Coliseum, Seattle, Washington (8:00 p.m. Once again a rowdy crowd spoilt the show. A clearly annoyed Page tries to calm the audience down in the acoustic set. The band do not return for an encore.)

SETLIST NOT KNOWN BUT WOULD PROBABLY HAVE CONSISTED OF: Immigrant Song / Heartbreaker / Dazed And Confused / Bring It On Home / That's Way / Bron-Yr-Aur / Since I've Been Loving You / Organ Solo / Thank You / What Is And What Should Never Be / Moby Dick / Whole Lotta Love

27 August 1970, Milwaukee Arena, Milwaukee, Wisconsin (Canceled due to the death of John Paul Jones's father and rescheduled to August 31, 1970.)

28 August 1970, Olympia Stadium, Detroit, Michigan (8:00 p.m. The show was rescheduled from 6 August 1970 and started a couple hours late.)

SETLIST: Immigrant Song / Heartbreaker / Dazed And Confused / Bring It On Home / That's The Way / Bron-Yr-Aur / Since I've Been Loving You / Organ Solo / Thank You / What Is And What Is Should Never Be / Moby Dick / Whole Lotta Love

29 August 1970, "Man-Pop" Festival, Winnipeg Arena, Winnipeg, Manitoba (The venue was originally going to be at the Winnipeg Stadium but is moved to the indoor Winnipeg Arena due to rain. Some of Led Zeppelin's equipment does not arrive in Winnipeg, so they borrowed from other bands on the bill. According to the Guess Who's Randy Bachman, he loans Jimmy Page his Les Paul that was used on the classic "American Woman" for the show.)

Jimmy Page onstage at the Tarrant County Convention Center, Fort Worth, Texas. (Photo by Carl Dunn)

Jimmy Page onstage at the Tarrant County Convention Center, Fort Worth, Texas. (Photo by Carl Dunn)

TIME CHANGE — Due to a death in the family of one of the stars, the Led Zeppelin concert — originally scheduled for 8:30 tomorrow night in Public Hall — has been changed to 5:30 p.m. tomorrow in Public Hall. If this new time is inconvenient for advance ticket holders, they can get refunds before 3 p.m. tomorrow from the locations where they purchased the tickets. Tickets at the door will be $6.50. The Led Zeppelin will fly to England immediately after the show for the funeral in the family of John Paul Jones.

Press announcement warning ticket holders that the show would start three hours earlier than advertised, allowing John Paul Jones time to catch a flight home to England to attend his father's funeral.

2 September 1970, Oakland Coliseum, Oakland, California (8:00 p.m. The setlist says it all, really. Led Zeppelin are in top form and the playing is simply amazing. The whole show is a highlight, but the "Whole Lotta Love" medley is something else! On top of that, we get "Train Kept A Rollin'" in the encores. The whole of the West Coast shows are magical.)

SETLIST: Immigrant Song / Heartbreaker / Dazed And Confused / Bring It On Home / That's The Way / Bron-Yr-Aur / Since I've Been Loving You / Organ Solo / Thank You / What Is And What Should Never Be / Moby Dick / Whole Lotta Love (including Boogie Chillun', Boppin' The Blues, Lawdy Miss Clawdy, For What It's Worth, Honey Bee, Long Distance Call, I'm Moving On, Fortune Teller, That's Alright Mama) / Communication Breakdown (including Good Times Bad Times) / The Train Kept A Rollin' / Blueberry Hill / Long Tall Sally

3 September 1970, Sports Arena, San Diego, California (Another rowdy crowd tonight. Jimmy has equipment problems during the acoustic set and they abandon "Bron-Yr-Aur" and went straight into "Since I've Been Loving You")

SETLIST: Immigrant Song / Heartbreaker / Dazed And Confused / Bring It On Home / That's The Way / Since I've Been Loving You / Organ Solo / Thank You / What Is And What Should Never Be / Moby Dick / Whole Lotta Love (including Boogie Chillun', Roberta, Crosscut Saw Blues, I've Got To Find My Baby, Honey Bee, The Lemon Song, Think You Need A Shot [The Needle], Lawdy Miss Clawdy) / Communication Breakdown

4 September 1970, the Forum, Inglewood, Los Angeles, California (8:30 p.m. DJ J. J. Jackson introduced the band this evening.)

What a night. The band are at their best, fun and dynamic. Surely a strong contender for the best-ever Led Zeppelin concert. Luckily there were at least six tapers this evening who were recording the event for posterity. This show became one of the first-ever Led Zeppelin bootlegs and has become a fan favorite. The double vinyl bootleg was called *Live On Blueberry Hill* as the band played it as a final encore. It has been re-released countless times on CD in the digital age. No Led Zeppelin collection is complete without a copy of this show! Several gems tonight, such as the rarely played "Out On The Tiles" from *Led Zeppelin III* and a killer "Communication Breakdown," which included "Good Times Bad Times," "For What It's Worth," and "I Saw Her Standing There." The band were particularly pleased at the positive response to the sit-down acoustic section, which had caused problems at some gigs prior to Los Angeles. Plant goes into detail about the origins of their second acoustic number this evening, "This is a thing called 'Bron-Yr-Aur.' This is the name of a little cottage in the mountains of Snowdonia in Wales, and 'Bron-Yr-Aur' is the Welsh equivalent of the phrase 'Golden Breast.' This is so, because of its position every morning as the sun rises

and it's a really remarkable place and so after staying there for a while and deciding it was time to leave for various reasons, we couldn't really just leave it and forget about it. You've probably all been to a place like that, only we can tell about it and you can't tell us."

SETLIST: Immigrant Song / Heartbreaker / Dazed And Confused / Bring It On Home / That's Way / Bron-Yr-Aur / Since I've Been Loving You / Organ Solo / Thank You / What Is And What Should Never Be / Moby Dick / Whole Lotta Love (including Boogie Chillun', I'm Movin' On, Red House, Some Other Guy, Think It Over) / Communication Breakdown (including Good Times Bad Times, For What It's Worth, I Saw Her Standing There) / Out On The Tiles / Blueberry Hill

JAM WITH FAIRPORT CONVENTION

4 September 1970, Troubadour, Santa Monica Blvd., West Hollywood, California (After their LA Forum gig, all four members of Led Zeppelin head down to the Troubadour in Los Angeles and join Fairport Convention for their second set. Fairport Convention were there for three nights, all of which were professionally recorded by the Wally Heider mobile truck. An album, *House Full: Fairport Convention Live at the LA Troubadour*, was later released, but without any of the Led Zeppelin tracks. The tapes from all three nights reside in Universal Records' tape archive.)

Advert celebrating Led Zeppelin's huge success.

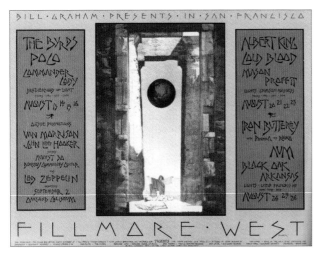

Poster for Led Zeppelin's appearance at the Oakland Coliseum on 2 September 1970.

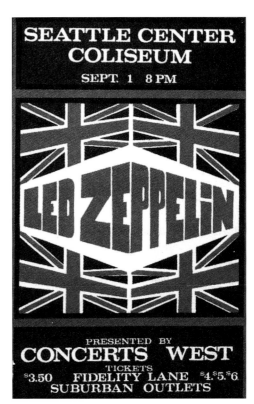

Press advert for Led Zeppelin's appearance at the Seattle Centre Coliseum on 1 September 1970.

Press advert for Led Zeppelin's appearance at the Forum in Los Angeles on 4 September 1970. The concert was immortalized on the *Blueberry Hill* bootleg.

6 September 1970, Honolulu International Center Arena, Honolulu, Hawaii (Two shows at 7:00 p.m. and 10:30 p.m.)

SETLIST: Immigrant Song / Dazed And Confused / Heartbreaker / Since I've Been Loving You / What Is And What Should Never Be / Moby Dick / Whole Lotta Love (including Boogie Chillun', Stop Messing Round, I'm Moving On, Shake Your Moneymaker, Some Other Guy, I've Got To Find My Baby) / Communication Breakdown (including American Woman)

66 Times have been good to Led Zeppelin. They are making both good money and good music. . . . They did some material from the third album which has for or five acoustical numbers. Both Jimmy Page and Robert Plant are more relaxed and human now. The first concert had them being pretty much concerned with being rock stars, but that is over now. Plant seemed especially perceptive about what was going on around him. He stopped the show twice for emergencies, something which they probably would not have done the first time they were here (last year).99

—*HONOLULU ADVERTISER* (Review from 7 September 1970)

9 September 1970, Boston Garden, Boston, Massachusetts (Two shows at 5:15 p.m. and 8:45 p.m. were scheduled. However, as the first house had only sold around 1,200 tickets, the band canceled the early show and only played the evening show. Peter Grant did not want to admit to canceling the early show for that reason and told the *Boston Globe*, "[The group] didn't complete their Sunday night concert until well into early Monday morning. In addition, being English, we were not aware of the Labor Day holiday which did not allow for air freight shipments and also our sound system had to come from Dallas, Texas." However, American Airlines confirmed to the promoter that they delivered 365 days a year. But Grant stuck to his

story and the band did not play the 5:15 p.m. show. DJ J. J. Jackson introduced the band: "They haven't been here since last November, so can we have a big hand for Led Zeppelin." The band is in good form, despite yet another rowdy crowd. Robert Plant tried to appeal to them to be calm, "Can you move back and clear the aisles for a while so we can get a good thing going." He tried several more times throughout the show. These problems really hindered the band during this period.)

SETLIST: Immigrant Song / Heartbreaker / Dazed And Confused / Bring It On Home / That's Way / Bron-Yr-Aur / Since I've Been Loving You / Organ Solo / Thank You / What Is And What Should Never Be / Moby Dick / Whole Lotta Love (including Boogie Chillun', Stop Messing Round, Ramble On, For What It's Worth, Some Other Guy, Honey Bee, The Lemon Song) / Communication Breakdown

16 September 1970, *Melody Maker* Poll Awards, the Savoy Hotel, Strand, London WC2 (Led Zeppelin returned to England for a short break and attend the *Melody Maker* Awards at the Savoy in London, where they knock the Beatles off the "Top Group" section in both the British and International categories.)

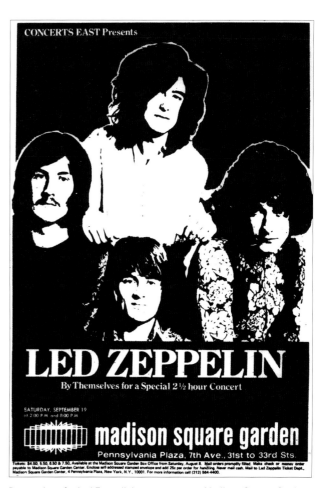

Press advert for Led Zeppelin's appearance at Madison Square Garden, New York City, on 19 September 1970.

19 September 1970, Madison Square Garden, New York City, New York (Two shows at 2:00 p.m. and 8:00 p.m. These shows were originally slated for 27 June, but their summer US tour had to be rescheduled when the band decided to headline the Bath Festival in the UK, despite being offered $200,000. The first show at Madison Square Garden is tinged with some sadness as Jimi Hendrix had just died. Robert Plant tells the crowd just before "What Is And What Should Never Be," "I think it's really hard ever having to say something about something that's quite a delicate point. But yesterday something happened—Jimi Hendrix died and we're all very sorry because he contributed a lot to the current music thing, and we'd like to just hope that everybody thinks it's a real shame . . . Jimi Hendrix!" Their performance is solid, but you can tell they are reserving energy levels for the evening show performance. Not surprisingly, the evening show is spectacular. Knowing that they are heading back home the following day inspires the band even more. The audience is very noisy, and Plant has to calm them down at times. The rock 'n' roll numbers are the icing on the cake, with the band clearly enjoying themselves playing some more obscure gems from their youth.)

SETLIST (AFTERNOON SHOW): Immigrant Song / Heartbreaker / Dazed And Confused / Bring It On Home / That's Way / Bron-Yr-Aur / Since I've Been Loving You / Organ Solo / Thank You / What Is And What Should Never Be / Moby Dick / Whole Lotta Love (including Boogie Chillun', High Flyin' Mama, For What It's Worth, Honey Bee, The Lemon Song) / Communication Breakdown (including American Woman).

SETLIST (EVENING SHOW): Immigrant Song / Heartbreaker / Dazed And Confused / Bring It On Home / That's Way / Bron-Yr-Aur / Since I've Been Loving You / Organ Solo / Thank You / What Is And What Should Never Be / Moby Dick / Whole Lotta Love (including Boogie Chillun', Dust My Broom, Bottle Up and Go, Lawdy Miss Clawdy, For What It's Worth, Cinnamon Girl, Some Other Guy, The Train Kept A Rollin', I'm A King Bee,

El Paso Blues, CC Rider, Baby What You Want Me To Do, Honey Bee, The Lemon Song) / Out On The Tiles / Communication Breakdown (including Gallows Pole) / The Girl Can't Help It (including Talking 'Bout You, Twenty Flight Rock) / How Many More Times (including The Hunter, Cadillac, Blueberry Hill)

66 Led Zeppelin finished their American tour with around 200,000 dollars worth of business at the big Madison Square Garden, where they nearly filled the first concert and completely packed the second. They were the only act on the bill and so each member earned himself around 30,000 dollars (after deductions) for just under six hours work. But work it was—second show received such audience reaction, comparable with the Stones at their Madison date, that several long encores were done by the group. 99

—***RECORD MIRROR*** (Review from October 1970)

20 September 1970, Cole Field House, University of Maryland, Maryland (The show was canceled after university officials said it violated university rules to have only five major concert programs being held in Cole Field House per year and also cited concerns over the logistics of the concert.)

OCTOBER 1970

5 October 1970, Town Hall, Birmingham, Midlands (Eric Clapton's new group, Derek and the Dominos, with Bronco as support, play at the Town Hall as part of their UK tour. Robert Plant is in the audience tonight to see his old mates in Bronco. He was backstage with them after their set and as he went out to see the set by Derek and the Dominos, he walked through a door that led him straight onto the stage. Unnoticed by the band who were already playing away, he was quickly escorted away by a couple of roadies. Members of the audience clearly thought that this was going to be the jam of the year. It was more than likely a mistake by Plant rather than a planned jam session.)

1969–1970
Recording Sessions

6

LED ZEPPELIN III SESSIONS

DECEMBER 1969

OLYMPIC SOUND STUDIOS
117 Church Road, Barnes, London, SW13

13 DECEMBER 1969

JENNINGS FARM BLUES (Jimmy Page / Robert Plant / John Paul Jones) (Also titled "Bron-Yr-Aur Stomp" on tape box. Several takes are attempted before a master is made.) Available on bonus CD in the deluxe edition of *Led Zeppelin III* released June 2014.

66 This is a chord sequence and structure for an electric version for a song I wrote on acoustic guitar termed 'Bar III.' The title by Robert Plant, 'Jennings Farm Blues,' was named after his house at the time. There were a number of alternative versions attempted during the session, the one I settled for acquired a number of quickfire overdubs. Although it was recorded at Olympic Studios in London with engineer Andy Johns, it was to be recorded acoustically some six months later and became 'Bron-Yr-Aur Stomp.' 99

—**JIMMY PAGE** (From his website)

PRODUCER: JIMMY PAGE
ENGINEER: ANDY JOHNS

MAY 1970–JUNE 1970

OLYMPIC SOUND STUDIOS
Studio 2, 117 Church Road, Barnes, London, SW13

6 MAY 1970

POOR TOM (Jimmy Page / Robert Plant) (Various takes made, including a basic instrumental and a final master with vocal overdubs.) Available on *Coda* on vinyl US Swan Song 90051-1 released 19 November 1982, Swan Song UK A 0051 released 22 November 1982 / on remastered CD Swan Song 7567-92444-2 released 1994 / Also available on the remastered edition of *Coda* released July 2015.

29 MAY 1970

SONG IN F (Overlord) (Jimmy Page / Robert Plant) (Later retitled "Immigrant Song.") Available on *Led Zeppelin III* vinyl Atlantic 2401002 released October 1970 / CD Atlantic released June 2014, remastered along with deluxe edition bonus CD.

HEY HEY WHAT CAN I DO (Jimmy Page / Robert Plant) Available as B-side of "Immigrant Song" single Atlantic 45-2777 released November 1970 / also included exclusively on the expanded version of *Coda* found in the *Complete Studio Recordings* box set Atlantic label 7 82526-2 released September 1993. (Worth noting that the regular version of *Coda* sold independently of the box does not have any bonus tracks. Later available on the companion disc of the super-deluxe-edition box set of *Coda* released July 2015.)

30 MAY 1970

THE BOY NEXT DOOR (Jimmy Page / Robert Plant) (Later retitled "That's The Way.") Available on *Led Zeppelin III* vinyl Atlantic 2401002 released October 1970 / CD Atlantic released June 2014, remastered along with deluxe edition bonus CD.

3 JUNE 1970

MY MY OH MY (Jimmy Page / Robert Plant) (Later retitled "Friends.") Available on *Led Zeppelin III* vinyl Atlantic 2401002 released October 1970 / CD Atlantic released June 2014, remastered along with deluxe edition bonus CD.

CELEBRATION DAY (Jimmy Page / Robert Plant / John Paul Jones) Available on *Led Zeppelin III* vinyl Atlantic 2401002 released October 1970 / CD Atlantic released June 2014, remastered along with deluxe edition bonus CD.

BATHROOM SOUND (Jimmy Page / Robert Plant / John Bonham) (Later retitled "Out On The Tiles.") Available on *Led Zeppelin III* vinyl Atlantic 2401002 released October 1970 / CD Atlantic released June 2014, remastered along with deluxe edition bonus CD.

5 JUNE 1970

SINCE I'VE BEEN LOVING YOU (Jimmy Page / Robert Plant / John Paul Jones) Available on *Led Zeppelin III* vinyl Atlantic 2401002 released October 1970 / CD Atlantic released June 2014, remastered along with deluxe edition bonus CD.

POOR TOM (Jimmy Page / Robert Plant) Instrumental mix, available on the companion disc of the super-deluxe-edition box set of *Coda* released July 2015.)

10 JUNE 1970

KEY TO THE HIGHWAY / TROUBLE IN MIND (Big Bill Broonzy / Charlie Seager / Richard M. Jones) Available on bonus CD of *Led Zeppelin III* deluxe edition on Atlantic released June 2014 remastered.

HATS OFF TO ROY HARPER (Traditional, arranged by Charles Obscure) Available on *Led Zeppelin III* vinyl Atlantic 2401002 released October 1970 / CD Atlantic released June 2014, remastered along with deluxe edition bonus CD.

JULY 1970

ISLAND STUDIOS
Studio 1, Basing Street, London W11

5 JULY 1970

GALLOWS POLE (Traditional arranged by Jimmy Page and Robert Plant) Available on *Led Zeppelin III* vinyl Atlantic 2401002 released October 1970 / CD Atlantic released June 2014, remastered along with deluxe edition bonus CD.

ST. TRISTAN'S SWORD (Page) Available on the companion disc of the super-deluxe-edition box set of *Coda* released July 2015.

6 JULY 1970

BRON-YR-AUR STOMP (Jimmy Page / Robert Plant / John Paul Jones) Available on *Led Zeppelin III* vinyl Atlantic 2401002 released October 1970 / CD Atlantic released June 2014, remastered along with deluxe edition bonus CD.

TANGERINE (Jimmy Page) Available on *Led Zeppelin III* vinyl Atlantic 2401002 released October 1970 / CD Atlantic released June 2014, remastered along with deluxe edition bonus CD.

PRODUCER: JIMMY PAGE
ENGINEER: ANDY JOHNS

AUGUST 1970

ARDENT STUDIOS
1457 National Street, Memphis, Tennessee

The band were under pressure to finish the album and were forced to do it while on the road in America, just as they had done for *Led Zeppelin II*. The studio of choice was Ardent Studios in Memphis, with Terry Manning as the engineer of choice. Overdubs, editing, tracking, and mixing were all done here on and off throughout August with Jimmy, and whoever else was required, flying to and from Memphis in between tour dates. The final masters were finished on 23 August, and Terry Manning flew to Nashville on 24 August to hand the finished tapes over to Peter Grant.

GUEST RECORDING SESSIONS

Guest Session for Mike Heron

ISLAND STUDIOS
8-10 Basing Street, London W11

OCTOBER 1970

LADY WONDER (Mike Heron) Available on B-side of "Call Me Diamond" single Island WIP 6101 released April 1971 / also available as a bonus track on *Smiling Men with Bad Reputations* CD Fledg'ling Records FLED 3041 released October 2003.

MIKE HERON: VOCALS, ACOUSTIC GUITAR
JIMMY PAGE: ELECTRIC GUITAR, SLIDE GUITAR

DAVE PEGG: BASS
DAVE MATTOCKS: DRUMS
PRODUCER: JOE BOYD
ENGINEER: ROGER MAYER

OCTOBER 1970

Guest Session for Roy Harper
ABBEY ROAD STUDIOS, STUDIO 3

3 Abbey Road, London NW8

THE SAME OLD ROCK (Roy Harper) Available on Stormcock album *Harvest* SHVL789 released 1971.

ROY HARPER: VOCALS, ACOUSTIC GUITAR
JIMMY PAGE: ACOUSTIC GUITAR
PRODUCER: PETER JENNER
ENGINEER: PHIL MACDONALD

1971:
7 Breaking Ground in the UK

In November 1970, Page and Plant had returned to the seclusion of Bron-Yr-Aur, the small cottage in the Welsh valleys, to write some new material for the next album. In December 1970, the band started recording at Olympic Studios in Barnes, but Jimmy Page felt he wanted to record in a more conducive environment that would allow the band more freedom away from the restrictions of a studio. Jimmy had heard of an old manor house for rent in Hampshire that had been used by Fleetwood Mac for rehearsals. Headley Grange was a three-story manor house located in Headley, East Hampshire, that was originally built in 1795 as a poor house for the local infirm and orphaned folk. By the early 1970s, it became available for rent and was used by several bands for rehearsals and recording, despite the fact that it hadn't been converted into a proper studio. The rooms were pretty much empty with plenty of ambient sound and only the odd acoustic screen being used to add some separation and acoustic control. Led Zeppelin were the first band to use the place for recording, hiring the Rolling Stones mobile with Andy Johns doing the engineering. They had six days of rehearsal and then hired the truck for six days to record the album.

In an interview with Caroline Boucher for *Disc and Music Echo* (13 February 1971), Robert Plant ran through some of the material the band had recorded for the new album, as well as letting readers know what it won't be known as:

> This next album will not be called *Led Zeppelin 4*. We'll think of something else. So far we've got 14 tracks down and we did quite a bit with a mobile truck down in Hampshire. At times it sounds like early Presley records drumming. Then

we've got Stu who plays piano for the Stones sometimes, on a couple of tracks, really earthy rock. John Paul's done a couple of things using recorders and he's been using the synthesizer very tastefully. Then there's a nice ten minute thing, "Stairway To Heaven," which starts off acoustically and just builds up. In my opinion it's one of the nicest things we've done. Then there's "Sloppy Drunk" on which I play guitar and Jimmy plays mandolin, you can imagine it being played as people dive round the maypole. With 14 tracks we have enough for two albums, but we won't put out a double album. People can appreciate a single album more because there's only eight tracks as opposed to 16.

A lot of unsubstantiated rumors of Led Zeppelin splitting were reported in many of the music papers in the early part of the year. The reports carried on to say that individual members would be pursuing solo projects. A spokesperson for the band had to repeatedly deny that the band were splitting up. Nobody seemed to know how or why such rumors started as the band had just completed their new album and were about to go on tour. Splitting up was the last thing on their mind.

Early in the year, the band decided to undertake a tour of England playing small venues and clubs as a way of reconnecting with their roots and try out some of their newly recorded material. Jimmy Page also felt that by playing the smaller clubs where they had originally started playing, that it would give a boost to the venues. *Melody Maker* announced the tour in their issue dated 6 February 1971. Tickets sold out the instant they went on sale at the various venues, and many people complained that the band should have played bigger venues to cope with the overwhelming demand. As a way of getting the people who missed out on tickets to hear what they were like in concert, the band organized to play their second live BBC concert, which would be broadcast nationally.

LED ZEPPELIN SIXTH UK TOUR— BACK TO THE CLUBS

5 MARCH 1971–1 APRIL 1971

5 March 1971, Ulster Hall, Belfast, Northern Ireland (8:30 p.m. Belfast is treated to debut of songs from Led Zeppelin's fourth studio album, "Black Dog," "Stairway To Heaven," "Going To California," and "Rock And Roll.")

SETLIST: Immigrant Song / Heartbreaker / Since I've Been Loving You / Out On The Tiles Intro / Black Dog / Dazed And Confused / Stairway To Heaven / Going To California / What Is And What Should Never Be / Moby Dick / Whole Lotta Love (including Boogie Chillun', Bottle Up And Go, They're Red Hot, Cumberland Gap, Honey Bee, Think You Need A Shot [The Needle], The Lemon Song) / Communication Breakdown / Rock And Roll

The band are excited at being able to play some new material and the energy levels are high. The setlist is just right, flooring the audience with two classics as their opening salvo, "Immigrant Song" and "Heartbreaker," before cooling them down with the bluesy "Since I've Been Loving You." A small mistake in "Black Dog" was probably not even noticed on the night as it was the first time played in public. This show is pretty historic in that it features the first-ever performance of what would soon take over "Whole Lotta Love" as their all-time classic song, "Stairway To Heaven."

6 March 1971, National Boxing Stadium, Dublin, Ireland (8:30 p.m. Phil Carson, from Atlantic Records, joins the band on bass for a version of Eddie Cochran's "C'mon Everybody.")

SETLIST: Immigrant Song / Heartbreaker / Since I've Been Loving You / Out On The Tiles Intro / Black Dog / Stairway To Heaven / Dazed And Confused / Going To California / What Is And What Should Never Be / Moby Dick / Whole Lotta Love (including Boogie Chillun', Suzie Q, Some Other Guy, Honey Bee, Sugar Mama Blues, Think You Need A Shot [The Needle], The Lemon Song, That's Alright Mama) / Communication Breakdown / C'mon Everybody

> 66 Led Zeppelin were playing the second concert of their current British tour after a three-month layoff for recording work, and having played a sensational concert the night before in Belfast, came south and proceeded to whip up the Dublin fans into a cheering, stamping, throbbing mass. The standing ovation started long before the show was over, and at the end the Zeppelin had to come back for several encores before they could get away. Their performance comprised of material from their previous three albums and a preview of some of the tracks from the forthcoming album. 99
>
> **—TONY WILSON**
> (Review in *Disc and Music Echo*, 13 March 1971)

9 March 1971, the Refectory, Leeds University, Leeds, West Yorkshire

SETLIST UNKNOWN BUT PROBABLY CONSISTED OF THE FOLLOWING: Immigrant Song / Heartbreaker / Since I've Been Loving You / Out On The Tiles Intro / Black Dog / Stairway To Heaven / Dazed And Confused / Going To California / What Is And What Should Never Be / Moby Dick / Whole Lotta Love (including Boogie Chillun', Suzie Q, Some Other Guy, Honey Bee, Sugar Mama Blues, Think You Need A Shot [The Needle], The Lemon Song, That's Alright Mama) / Communication Breakdown

Press advert for Led Zeppelin's appearance at Southampton University, Southampton, on 11 March 1971.

Led Zeppelin go back to the clubs in England, March 1971.
(Michael Putland/Getty Images)

66 During their long three-hour set, they performed three new numbers, which were previously unrecorded and this might possibly be on their fourth album. They were: 'Going to California,' 'Black Dog,' and 'Stairway to Heaven,' the latter being exceptional. A number which I didn't really expect was a slow 12-bar blues with John Paul Jones providing an organ backing for some really beautiful guitar from Jimmy Page. After two hours without a really total response from the audience, Led Zeppelin walked off the stage only to be brought back on after a standing ovation from an ecstatic audience, to play hard rock and roll for another hour of repeated encores until Zeppelin finished an extremely satisfying set. **99**

—**DENNIS ROBBINS** (Review in *Wessex Scene*)

13 March 1971, Bath Pavilion, Bath, Somerset

SETLIST UNKNOWN BUT PROBABLY CONSISTED OF THE FOLLOWING: Immigrant Song / Heartbreaker / Since I've Been Loving You / Black Dog / Dazed And Confused / Stairway To Heaven / Going To California / That's The Way / What Is And What Should Never Be / Moby Dick / Whole Lotta Love (medley) / Communication Breakdown

10 March 1971, University of Kent, Students Union, Rutherford College, Canterbury, Kent (9:00 p.m. Led Zeppelin are a Rag Week attraction at Rutherford College. Although the band feel they have put on a good show, there is little audience reaction. Robert Plant referred to them as being frigid.)

SETLIST: Immigrant Song / Heartbreaker / Since I've Been Loving You / Out On The Tiles Intro / Black Dog / Stairway To Heaven / Dazed And Confused / Going To California / What Is And What Should Never Be / Moby Dick / Whole Lotta Love / Communication Breakdown

11 March 1971, Old Union Refectory, Southampton University, Southampton, Hampshire (8:00 p.m.)

SETLIST UNKNOWN BUT PROBABLY CONSISTED OF THE FOLLOWING: Immigrant Song / Heartbreaker / Since I've Been Loving You / Out On The Tiles Intro / Black Dog / Stairway To Heaven / Dazed And Confused / Going To California / What Is And What Should Never Be / Moby Dick / Whole Lotta Love (including Boogie Chillun', Suzie Q, Some Other Guy, Honey Bee, Sugar Mama Blues, Think You Need A Shot [The Needle], The Lemon Song, That's Alright Mama) / Communication Breakdown

Jimmy Page onstage at Trentham Gardens, Stoke on Trent, 14 March 1971. (Rex)

Led Zeppelin onstage at Trentham Gardens, Stoke on Trent, 14 March 1971. (Rex)

14 March 1971, Trentham Gardens Ballroom, Hanley, Stoke-On-Trent (8:00 p.m.)

SETLIST UNKNOWN BUT PROBABLY CONSISTED OF THE FOLLOWING: Immigrant Song / Heartbreaker / Since I've Been Loving You / Black Dog / Dazed And Confused / Stairway To Heaven / Going To California / That's The Way / What Is And What Should Never Be / Moby Dick / Whole Lotta Love (medley) / Communication Breakdown

16 March 1971, Mountford Hall, Liverpool University, Liverpool, Merseyside (The show was canceled due to Robert Plant having laryngitis. Rescheduled to May 10, 1971.)

18 March 1971, Mayfair (Fillmore North), Newcastle, Newcastle-Upon-Tyne (8:00 p.m.)

SETLIST UNKNOWN BUT PROBABLY CONSISTED OF THE FOLLOWING: Immigrant Song / Heartbreaker / Since I've Been Loving You / Black Dog / Dazed And Confused / Stairway To Heaven / Going To California / That's The Way / What Is And What Should Never Be / Moby Dick / Whole Lotta Love (medley) / Communication Breakdown

19 March 1971, Union Buildings, Manchester University, Manchester (8:30 p.m.)

SETLIST UNKNOWN BUT PROBABLY CONSISTED OF THE FOLLOWING: Immigrant Song / Heartbreaker / Since I've Been Loving You / Black Dog / Dazed And Confused / Stairway To Heaven / Going To California / That's The Way / What Is And What Should Never Be / Moby Dick / Whole Lotta Love (medley) / Communication Breakdown

20 March 1971, the Belfry, Sutton Coldfield, West Midlands (7:30 p.m.)

SETLIST UNKNOWN BUT PROBABLY CONSISTED OF THE FOLLOWING: Immigrant Song / Heartbreaker / Since I've Been Loving You / Black Dog / Dazed And Confused / Stairway To Heaven / Going To California / That's The Way / What Is And What Should Never Be / Moby Dick / Whole Lotta Love (medley) / Communication Breakdown

❝ The material battering the fans from all sides included the old favourites: 'Since I've Been Loving You,' 'Communication Breakdown,' and the immortal 'Whole Lotta Love,' with 'Black Dog,' 'Going To California,' and the aesthetic 'Stairway To Heaven' from the fourth album. Their stage show is so exciting that you have to become involved as they go from side to side. Their albums don't seem to make you realize this, but are a good second-best if you are one of those who couldn't manage the concert tour. ❞

—**T. McNALLY,** (Review in *New Musical Express*, March 1971)

21 March 1971, Nottingham Boat Club, Nottingham, East Midlands (7:30 p.m.)

SETLIST UNKNOWN BUT PROBABLY CONSISTED OF THE FOLLOWING: Immigrant Song / Heartbreaker / Since I've Been Loving You / Black Dog / Dazed And Confused / Stairway To Heaven / Going To California / That's The Way / What Is And What Should Never Be / Moby Dick / Whole Lotta Love (medley) / Communication Breakdown

23 March 1971, Marquee Club, Soho, London (7:30 p.m.)

SETLIST UNKNOWN BUT PROBABLY CONSISTED OF THE FOLLOWING: Immigrant Song / Heartbreaker / Since I've Been Loving You / Black Dog / Dazed And Confused / Stairway To Heaven / Going To California / That's The Way / What Is And What Should Never Be / Moby Dick / Whole Lotta Love (medley) / Communication Breakdown

The Marquee Club's phone line had been flooded with calls for tickets since the announcement of the "Back to the Clubs" tour. Tickets for the Marquee eventually went on sale on 1 March 1971 and were limited to one ticket per club member. People were queuing around the block. Ticket prices were low and the band were not making any money from the tour. Robert Plant told Caroline Boucher in *Disc and Music Echo,* "To go into the clubs to play and make nothing at all seems to be the only way we can go without being crucified." A heartfelt review in *Melody Maker* seems to miss the point that this was part of a "back to the clubs" tour.

❝ It was all very nostalgic for Led Zeppelin to play London's Marquee Club, but was it such a good idea really? Naturally the place was packed to overflowing. Naturally the group was pretty good, though the sound suffered from the small surroundings. But how much better it might have been if Zep had chosen the Lyceum or the Roundhouse for the only London venue on the current tour. As it was, hundreds instead of thousands were able to see the

group who a little over two years ago played here as the 'Former Yardbirds' and attracted little interest. ❞

—**CHRIS CHARLESWORTH**
(Review in *Melody Maker*, March 1971)

25 March 1971 *In Concert*, BBC Paris Theatre, Lower Regent Street, London (The show was canceled due to Robert Plant's ongoing laryngitis problems. It was rescheduled for 1 April 1971. Producer Jeff Griffin bought in Brinsley Schwarz and the Keef Hartley Band to substitute for Led Zeppelin and audience members were assured that they would be allowed to attend the rearranged date.)

APRIL 1971

After a long absence, Led Zeppelin return to the BBC and Radio One for another *In Concert* session with John Peel in front of a lucky crowd of 400 crammed into the Paris Cinema. It was probably more as producer Jeff Griffin was pretty sure that they broke all the fire regulations that night. Led Zeppelin was originally scheduled to play on 25 March 1971, but had to reschedule due to Robert Plant experiencing throat problems due to overwork on tour. Robert Plant explains what happened and apologizes to the audience for the original cancellation: "First I'd like to say sorry about last week. But we did eighteen dates in about six days or at least twenty days and my voice just gave up completely. We hope it's all in condition tonight, if not, cheer because you're on the radio." The BBC logs show that the band had a rehearsal allocated for a 3:00 p.m. start and a recording slot for the actual concert between 9:00 p.m. and 10:45 p.m. An edited edition of the concert was broadcast between 7:00 p.m. and 8:00 p.m. on John Peel's *In Concert* program on Radio One, Sunday, 4 April 1971. It was repeated between 7:00 p.m. and 8:00 p.m. on *Sound of the Seventies*, Radio One, Wednesday, 7 April 1971. The following numbers were broadcast: "Immigrant Song," "Dazed And Confused," "Stairway To Heaven," "Going To California," "That's The Way," "What Is And What Should Never Be," and "Whole Lotta Love."

Preparations for a BBC transcription disc, as well as the broadcast were made on 2 April 1971 by Jimmy Page and Robert Plant using the master tapes. They were very hands-on and suggested which edits could be made to the "Whole Lotta Love" medley so that it would fit the one-hour format needed for the BBC *In Concert* show. Transcription discs were made by the BBC so that they could license them to radio stations around the world who subscribed to the BBC transcription service. Usually they would press 100 copies of each disc with strict instructions to the overseas radio network to destroy the disc at the end of the license period. This did not always happen and original discs are worth a lot of money on the collectors market. Unfortunately, a lot of fakes were also made and were sometimes hard to differentiate from the real thing if you are not an expert. The Led Zeppelin *In Concert* transcription disc was done at the BBC's Transcription Studios located at Kensington House, Richmond Way, London W14. Interestingly, the 12-inch vinyl album featured a slightly different track selection to the broadcast. It included the following songs: John Peel Introduction, "Communication Breakdown," "Dazed And Confused," "Going To California," "Stairway To Heaven," "What Is And What Should Never Be," and "Whole Lotta Love" (edited version). Another transcription album was released by the BBC in 1983 with another track selection featuring an introduction by Richard Skinner. Side one featured "Immigrant Song," "Heartbreaker," "Out On The Tiles" (Intro) / "Black Dog," "Going To California," "That's The Way," "What Is And What Should Never Be," and side two had "Communication Breakdown," "Stairway To Heaven," "Whole Lotta Love (Medley)." It's worth noting that both of these discs had "Communication Breakdown," which was not broadcast originally.

The complete concert details and availability are listed below.

BBC PARIS CINEMA
4–12 Lower Regent Street, London W1

1 April 1971

JOHN PEEL INTRODUCTION

IMMIGRANT SONG (Jimmy Page / Robert Plant) (3:20)
Available on *BBC Sessions* CD Atlantic 7567-83061-2 released November 1997.

JIMMY PAGE: 1958 GIBSON LES PAUL GUITAR
ROBERT PLANT: LEAD VOCALS
JOHN PAUL JONES: BASS
JOHN BONHAM: DRUMS

HEARTBREAKER (Jimmy Page / Robert Plant / John Paul Jones / John Bonham) (5:16) Available on *BBC Sessions* CD Atlantic 7567-83061-2 released November 1997.

JIMMY PAGE: 1958 GIBSON LES PAUL GUITAR
ROBERT PLANT: LEAD VOCALS
JOHN PAUL JONES: BASS
JOHN BONHAM: DRUMS

SINCE I'VE BEEN LOVING YOU (Jimmy Page / Robert Plant / John Paul Jones) (6:56) Available on *BBC Sessions* CD Atlantic 7567-83061-2 released November 1997.

JIMMY PAGE: 1958 GIBSON LES PAUL GUITAR
ROBERT PLANT: LEAD VOCALS
JOHN PAUL JONES: HAMMOND ORGAN
JOHN BONHAM: DRUMS

BLACK DOG (Jimmy Page / Robert Plant / John Paul Jones) (5:17) Available on *BBC Sessions* CD Atlantic 7567-83061-2 released November 1997.

JIMMY PAGE: 1958 GIBSON LES PAUL GUITAR
ROBERT PLANT: LEAD VOCALS
JOHN PAUL JONES: BASS
JOHN BONHAM: DRUMS

DAZED AND CONFUSED (Jimmy Page) (18:36) Available on *BBC Sessions* CD Atlantic 7567-83061-2 released November 1997.

JIMMY PAGE: 1958 GIBSON LES PAUL GUITAR
ROBERT PLANT: LEAD VOCALS
JOHN PAUL JONES: BASS
JOHN BONHAM: DRUMS

STAIRWAY TO HEAVEN (Jimmy Page / Robert Plant) (8:49) Available on *BBC Sessions* CD Atlantic 7567-83061-2 released November 1997.

JIMMY PAGE: GIBSON EDS-1275 DOUBLE-NECK GUITAR
ROBERT PLANT: LEAD VOCALS
JOHN PAUL JONES: BASS
JOHN BONHAM: DRUMS

GOING TO CALIFORNIA (Jimmy Page / Robert Plant) (3:54) Available on *BBC Sessions* CD Atlantic 7567-83061-2 released November 1997.

JIMMY PAGE: ACOUSTIC GUITAR
ROBERT PLANT: LEAD VOCALS
JOHN PAUL JONES: MANDOLIN

THAT'S THE WAY (Jimmy Page / Robert Plant) (5:43) Available on *BBC Sessions* CD Atlantic 7567-83061-2 released November 1997.

JIMMY PAGE: ACOUSTIC GUITAR
ROBERT PLANT: LEAD VOCALS, TAMBOURINE
JOHN PAUL JONES: MANDOLIN

WHAT IS AND WHAT SHOULD NEVER BE (Jimmy Page / Robert Plant) (4:15) unreleased

> JIMMY PAGE: 1958 GIBSON LES PAUL GUITAR
> ROBERT PLANT: LEAD VOCALS
> JOHN PAUL JONES: BASS
> JOHN BONHAM: DRUMS

WHOLE LOTTA LOVE (Jimmy Page / Robert Plant / John Paul Jones / John Bonham / Willie Dixon) (Medley including "Boogie Chillun'," "Trucking Little Mama," "Fixin' to Die," "That's Alright Mama," "For What It's Worth," "Mess Of Blues," "Honey Bee," "The Lemon Song") Several cuts have been made on the *BBC Sessions* CD version of "Whole Lotta Love," reducing the length by around seven minutes. At the 6:00-minute mark, 90 seconds of the guitar solo has been excised as has "Trucking Little Mama"; at the 9:15 mark, "For What It's Worth" has been excised; and at the 11:29 mark, both "Honey Bee" and "The Lemon Song" are also gone. Jon Astley, the engineer on the *BBC Sessions* CD release, has stated that these were cut due to space restrictions. Available on *BBC Sessions* CD Atlantic 7567-83061-2 released November 1997.

> JIMMY PAGE: 1958 GIBSON LES PAUL GUITAR
> ROBERT PLANT: LEAD VOCALS
> JOHN PAUL JONES: BASS
> JOHN BONHAM: DRUMS

THANK YOU (Jimmy Page / Robert Plant) (6:37) Available on *BBC Sessions* CD Atlantic 7567-83061-2 released November 1997.

> JIMMY PAGE: 1958 GIBSON LES PAUL GUITAR
> ROBERT PLANT: LEAD VOCALS
> JOHN PAUL JONES: HAMMOND ORGAN
> JOHN BONHAM: DRUMS

COMMUNICATION BREAKDOWN (including "Feel So Bad") (Jimmy Page / John Paul Jones / John Bonham) (5:35) unreleased

> JIMMY PAGE: 1958 GIBSON LES PAUL GUITAR
> ROBERT PLANT: LEAD VOCALS
> JOHN PAUL JONES: BASS
> JOHN BONHAM: DRUMS
> PRODUCER FOR ORIGINAL BBC SHOW: JEFF GRIFFIN

The BBC 1971 concert epitomized the whole "Back to the Clubs" tour ethos. You could not get a much smaller space than the Paris Cinema with room for only 400 people. As many people were unable to get tickets for this smaller venue tour, this was Led Zeppelin's way of making sure that fans did not miss out. The performance was truly inspired, even with Robert Plant's voice not fully recovered, he and the band put in a tremendous performance. It was a show of many firsts, including the first broadcast of "Stairway To Heaven." Surprisingly there is a little nervousness that can be detected, but that only gives the concert an edge not always found at other shows. Over and above everything else, tonight showed how well the band's style shifts had become effortless and seamless. The opening numbers are hard and heavy. "Immigrant Song" is especially powerful with Page unleashing a fluent solo. Before you get a chance to catch your breath, the band hit you with "Heartbreaker," always a live favorite from *Led Zeppelin II*. The intensity continues with the smoking blues vibes of "Since I've Been Loving You," which is probably one of their best-ever performances of it. The acoustic segment worked extremely well in the small clubs, and the BBC set is no exception.

The terminally laid-back John Peel came back onstage before "Whole Lotta Love" for a quick intro: "I'm going to sing on the next one." Luckily he was joking! The band finish with a lengthy version with the usual rock 'n' roll medley before encoring with "Thank You" and "Communication Breakdown." The concert broadcast ended up as one of the most bootlegged shows by the band. Multiple vinyl editions were released as were CDs in the digital age. Somehow, the complete unedited concert escaped from the BBC vaults in the late '90s and made its way into bootleggers hands, which gave fans a chance to hear the whole show for the first time.

LED ZEPPELIN SCANDINAVIAN / EUROPEAN TOUR

3 MAY 1971–5 JULY 1971

MAY 1971

> 3 May 1971, K. B. Hallen, Copenhagen, Denmark (Tonight's show is best known for the first live performances of "Four Sticks" and "Gallows Pole." Also features the debuts of "Celebration Day" and "Misty Mountain Hop.")

SETLIST: Immigrant Song / Heartbreaker / Since I've Been Loving You / Dazed And Confused / Out On The Tiles Intro / Black Dog / Stairway To Heaven / Going To California / That's The Way / What Is And What Should Never Be / Four Sticks / Gallows Pole / Whole Lotta Love (including Boogie Chillun', Bottle Up And Go, They're Red Hot, That's Alright Mama, Mess O' Blues, Honey Bee, Sugar Mama Blues, The Lemon Song) / Communication Breakdown (including Celebration Day) / Misty Mountain Hop / Rock And Roll

A stunning experimental show that pretty much previews all of the forthcoming *Led Zeppelin IV* album. Despite a boisterous crowd, the band are clearly enjoying themselves and are very relaxed. Plant did have to ask the audience to calm down after a wild version of "Heartbreaker": "Whoa, stop! You stop! Tell him to stop—because any trouble and we go off! We can't play if there's gonna be this going on through every number, so somebody had better tell him in Danish what the score is! We cannot play if there's gonna be a constant passage of people moving. We'd rather people sit on the floor, sit down! We wanna give you a concert of music and we cannot do that if there's a lot of people running around." One of the big surprises tonight is the performance of "Four Sticks," which is introduced by Plant: "We're gonna try something that we have never ever tried before and there's every chance it'll fall apart. If it does, we'll stop and start again. This hasn't even got a title yet but we'll think of one as the night goes on!" It worked well considering this was the first-ever live performance of it. Surprisingly they rarely played it again. Another surprise was a rocking version of "Gallows Pole" with Page using his 12-string electric guitar. After tying it a few more times the band dropped it permanently from the set.

66 Zeppelin played material from their three LPs and presented a few new songs, which we were told appear on their next album. The best one's title was drowned by the applauding and cheering audience, but is called something like 'Stairways To Heaven,' a beautiful number, starting softly with Jimmy Page on guitar and a silent Robert Plant, joined by John Paul Jones on organ and then building and building in force and speed into a breathtaking climax, where everybody went wild, a real inferno of sound. 99

—GEORGE SORENSEN
(Review in *New Musical Express*, May 1971)

10 May 1971, Mountford Hall, University of Liverpool, Liverpool, England (7:30 p.m. The show was rescheduled from 16 March 1971.)

SETLIST NOT KNOWN BUT WOULD PROBABLY HAVE CONSISTED OF THE FOLLOWING: Immigrant Song / Heartbreaker / Since I've Been Loving You / Black Dog / Dazed And Confused / Stairway To Heaven / Going To California / That's The Way / Celebration Day / What Is And What Should Never Be / Moby Dick / Whole Lotta Love (medley)

JUNE 1971

29 June 1971, Elbow Room, 146 High Street, Birmingham, West Midlands (John Bonham jams with Roy Wood, Dave Pegg, Jeff Lynne, and Bev Bevan, among others for a Rock Revival night. Bonham had played at the venue with some of his other bands in the mid-'60s.)

JULY 1971

5 July 1971, Velodromo Vigorelli, Milan, Italy (9:00 p.m. The concert is part of a government-sponsored day-long music festival that included a variety of Italian acts. In all, 15,000 fans packed into the outdoor Vigorelli Velodromo stadium in Milan, with Led Zeppelin headlining that evening. The show ended abruptly as riots broke out and the venue filled with tear gas and some of the band's PA was damaged. The police had blocked off the whole area around the arena, and the band members had to stay locked in their dressing rooms to wait until the situation was contained. It was a complete fiasco. The band never returned to Italy.)

SETLIST: Immigrant Song / Heartbreaker / Since I've Been Loving You / Out On The Tiles Intro / Black Dog / Dazed And Confused / Whole Lotta Love

LED ZEPPELIN SWISS TOUR
7 AUGUST 1971–8 AUGUST 1971

7 August 1971, Montreux Casino Hall, Montreux, Switzerland (6:00 p.m.)

SETLIST: Immigrant Song / Heartbreaker / Since I've Been Loving You / Out On The Tiles Intro / Black Dog / Dazed And Confused / Stairway To Heaven / Going To California / That's The Way / Celebration Day / What Is And What Should Never Be / Whole Lotta Love (including Boogie Chillun', That's Alright Mama, Ramble On, Gambler's Blues, I'm A Man, Honey Bee, Sugar Mama Blues, Gee Baby Ain't I Good To You, Kind Hearted Woman Blues) / Weekend

Due to the number of people unable to get tickets for the shows, Peter Grant and promoter Claude Nobs came up with an idea of putting a PA system outside the venue that would relay the sound of the concert for the unlucky fans who could not get in. The band are in a relaxed mood and put in a fine performance. The setlist was the same that would be played on their forthcoming US tour at the end of the month.

Led Zeppelin onstage at the Tarrant County Convention Center, Fort Worth, Texas, on 23 August 1971. (Photo by Carl Dunn)

8 August 1971, Montreux Casino Hall, Montreux, Switzerland (6:00 p.m.)

SETLIST NOT KNOWN BUT WOULD PROBABLY HAVE CONSISTED OF THE FOLLOWING: Immigrant Song / Heartbreaker / Since I've Been Loving You / Black Dog / Dazed And Confused / Stairway To Heaven / Going To California / That's The Way / Celebration Day / What Is And What Should Never Be / Moby Dick / Whole Lotta Love (medley) / Organ Solo / Thank You

LED ZEPPELIN SEVENTH US TOUR
19 AUGUST 1971–17 SEPTEMBER 1971

19 August 1971, Pacific Coliseum, Vancouver, British Columbia, Canada (8:30 p.m.)

SETLIST NOT KNOWN BUT WOULD PROBABLY HAVE CONSISTED OF THE FOLLOWING: Immigrant Song / Heartbreaker / Since I've Been Loving You / Out On The Tiles Intro / Black Dog / Dazed And Confused / Stairway To Heaven / Celebration Day / That's The Way / What Is And What Should Never Be / Moby Dick / Whole Lotta Love (including Boogie Chillun', My Baby Left Me, Mess O' Blues, You Shook Me) / Communication Breakdown / Organ Solo / Thank You

This show is best remembered as the one where Peter Grant smashed up a Canadian official's noise measuring equipment thinking it was a bootlegger taping the show. The *New Musical Express* in England reported, "Led Zeppelin cause plenty of action in the audience as well as on stage! Zeppelin is in the middle of an American tour. Last weekend in Vancouver the band played in a hockey arena which houses over 13,000 people but it wasn't enough and nearly

3,000 didn't get in. Inevitably the police clashed with the punters outside. During the show a group of government scientists were checking sound levels but their equipment was mistaken for bootlegging gear. Their equipment was summarily destroyed. The local police are looking for the band's manager for questioning."

21 August 1971, the Forum, Inglewood, Los Angeles, California (8:30 p.m.)

SETLIST: Immigrant Song / Heartbreaker / Since I've Been Loving You / Out On The Tiles Intro / Black Dog / Dazed And Confused / Stairway To Heaven / That's The Way / Going To California / What Is And What Should Never Be / Whole Lotta Love (including Boogie Chillun', I'm Moving On, That's Alright Mama, Dr. Kitch, Mess O' Blues, Got A Lot O'Livin' To Do, Honey Bee, Sugar Mama Blues, Gee, Baby Ain't I Good To You, Kind Hearted Woman Blues) / Weekend / Rock And Roll / Communication Breakdown / Organ Solo / Thank You

Once again, the band play amazingly for the Los Angeles crowd, which is rewarded with a lengthy version of "Whole Lotta Love" with many covers in the medley. The night ends with a beautiful "Thank You," which sums up the band's feeling toward the audience.

22 August 1971, the Forum, Inglewood, Los Angeles, California (8:30 p.m.)

SETLIST: Walk Don't Run / Immigrant Song / Heartbreaker / Since I've Been Loving You / Out On The Tiles Intro / Black Dog / Dazed And Confused / Stairway To Heaven / Celebration Day / That's The Way / What Is And What Should Never Be / Moby Dick / Whole Lotta Love (including Boogie Chillun', My Baby Left Me, Mess O' Blues, You Shook Me) / Communication Breakdown / Organ Solo / Thank You

Just when you think the previous night's performance could not be bettered, Led Zeppelin put in another killer performance, opening up with a surprise cover of the Venture's "Walk Don't Run" hit single before pulverizing the crowd with "Immigrant Song." Plant is not taking any chances with his voice, though, as he went all out at the previous show and has to warn the audience that "tonight my voice is really fucked, so I don't think we're gonna do much harmonizing. But we're gonna try—so, vibe on!" It was true that at some points his voice sounded a little worn, particularly on "Stairway To Heaven," but to be honest this was in no way going to ruin what was otherwise an impeccable and dynamic concert.

23 August 1971, Tarrant County Arena, Fort Worth, Texas (8:00 p.m.)

SETLIST: Immigrant Song / Heartbreaker / Since I've Been Loving You / Out On The Tiles Intro / Black Dog / Dazed And Confused / Stairway To Heaven / Celebration Day / That's The Way / Going To California / What Is And What Should Never Be / Moby Dick / Whole Lotta Love (including Boogie Chillun', Bottle Up And Go, Cumberland Gap, They're Red Hot, She's A Truckin' Little Baby, Mess O' Blues, You Shook Me) / Communication Breakdown / Organ Solo / Thank You

24 August 1971, Dallas Memorial Auditorium, Dallas, Texas

SETLIST NOT KNOWN BUT WOULD PROBABLY HAVE CONSISTED OF THE FOLLOWING: Immigrant Song / Heartbreaker / Since I've Been Loving You / Out On The Tiles Intro / Black Dog / Dazed And Confused / Stairway To Heaven / Celebration Day / That's The Way / What Is And What Should Never Be / Moby Dick / Whole Lotta Love (including Boogie Chillun', My Baby Left Me, Mess O' Blues, You Shook Me) / Communication Breakdown / Organ Solo / Thank You

25 August 1971, Hofheinz Pavilion, Houston, Texas (The show was rescheduled for 26 August 1971 at the Sam Houston Coliseum.)

26 August 1971, Sam Houston Coliseum, Houston, Texas (The show was switched from the Hofheinz Pavilion, Houston, Texas, and rescheduled from 25 August 1971.)

SETLIST NOT KNOWN BUT WOULD PROBABLY HAVE CONSISTED OF THE FOLLOWING: Immigrant Song / Heartbreaker / Since I've Been Loving You / Out On The Tiles Intro / Black Dog / Dazed And Confused / Stairway To Heaven / Celebration Day / That's The Way / What Is And What Should Never Be / Moby Dick / Whole Lotta Love (including Boogie Chillun', My Baby Left Me, Mess O' Blues, You Shook Me) / Communication Breakdown / Organ Solo / Thank You

26 August 1971, San Antonio Hemisfair Arena, San Antonio, Texas (The show was rescheduled for 27 August 1971 at the Municipal Auditorium.)

27 August 1971, San Antonio Municipal Auditorium, San Antonio, Texas (8:00 p.m. Rescheduled from 26 August 1971.)

SETLIST NOT KNOWN BUT WOULD PROBABLY HAVE CONSISTED OF THE FOLLOWING: Immigrant Song / Heartbreaker / Since I've Been Loving You / Out On The Tiles Intro / Black Dog / Dazed And Confused / Stairway To Heaven / Celebration Day / That's The Way / What Is And What Should Never Be / Moby Dick / Whole Lotta Love (including Boogie Chillun', My Baby Left Me, Mess O' Blues, You Shook Me) / Communication Breakdown / Organ Solo / Thank You

28 August 1971, St. Louis Arena, St. Louis, Missouri

SETLIST NOT KNOWN BUT WOULD PROBABLY HAVE CONSISTED OF THE FOLLOWING: Immigrant Song / Heartbreaker / Since I've Been Loving You / Out On The Tiles Intro / Black Dog / Dazed And Confused / Stairway To Heaven / Celebration Day / That's The Way / What Is And What Should Never Be / Moby Dick / Whole Lotta Love (including Boogie Chillun', My Baby Left Me, Mess O' Blues, You Shook Me) / Communication Breakdown / Organ Solo / Thank You

Press advert for Led Zeppelin's appearance at the Municipal Auditorium in New Orleans on 29 August 1971.

29 August 1971, New Orleans Municipal Auditorium, New Orleans, Louisiana (8:00 p.m.)

SETLIST NOT KNOWN BUT WOULD PROBABLY HAVE CONSISTED OF THE FOLLOWING: Immigrant Song / Heartbreaker / Since I've Been Loving You / Out On The Tiles Intro / Black Dog / Dazed And Confused / Stairway To Heaven / Celebration Day / That's The Way / What Is And What Should Never Be / Moby Dick / Whole Lotta Love (including Boogie Chillun', My Baby Left Me, Mess O' Blues, You Shook Me) / Communication Breakdown / Organ Solo / Thank You

31 August 1971, Orlando Sports Stadium, Orlando, Florida (8:00 p.m.)

SETLIST: Immigrant Song / Heartbreaker / Since I've Been Loving You / Dazed And Confused / Out On The Tiles Intro / Black Dog / Stairway To Heaven / Celebration Day / That's The Way / Going To California / What Is And What Should Never Be / Moby Dick Whole Lotta Love (including Boogie Chillun', My Baby Left Me, Mess O' Blues) / Organ Solo / Thank You

SEPTEMBER 1971

1 September 1971, Sportatorium, Hollywood, Florida (8:00 p.m. The concert was moved from Miami Jai Alai Fronton, Miami, Florida.)

SETLIST NOT KNOWN BUT WOULD PROBABLY HAVE CONSISTED OF THE FOLLOWING: Immigrant Song / Heartbreaker / Since I've Been Loving You / Out On The Tiles Intro / Black Dog / Dazed And Confused / Stairway To Heaven / Celebration Day / That's The Way / What Is And What Should Never Be / Moby Dick / Whole Lotta Love (including Boogie Chillun', My Baby Left Me, Mess O' Blues, You Shook Me) / Communication Breakdown / Organ Solo / Thank You

3 September 1971, Madison Square Garden, New York City, New York (8:00 p.m. Scott Muni introduced the band.)

SETLIST: Immigrant Song / Heartbreaker / Since I've Been Loving You / Out On The Tiles Intro / Black Dog / Dazed And Confused / Stairway To Heaven / Celebration Day / That's The Way / Going To California / What Is And What Should Never Be / Moby Dick / Whole Lotta Love (including Boogie Chillun', My Baby Left Me, Mess O' Blues, You Shook Me) / Communication Breakdown / Organ Solo / Thank You / Rock And Roll

A fabulous show for a very appreciative New York crowd. The band are totally together and on fire tonight driving the crowd wild. Robert Plant greets them by saying, "Good evening. How have you been? I think we're gonna get a bit warm tonight!" And warm they get with some truly inspired improvisations. This is why every show is different musically speaking and why there is such a frenzied collecting market for any live recordings of the band. Mistakes here and there

Press advert for Led Zeppelin's appearance at the Orlando Sports Stadium, Florida, on 31 August 1971.

are totally acceptable. It's live, for goodness sakes. It's all about the vibe and tonight it was exceptional. It did get scary toward the end when the adoring crowd pushed forward and charged the stage. A shaken Plant pleads for the crowd to move back: "You've gotta move back. Move back. Move back or we can't go on! Move right back! It's not fair to everybody else. Besides I'm scared of heights!" Plant's words calmed the situation as the band stopped playing and the crowd slowly moved back and the band carried on with "Thank You" before a final kick-ass version of "Rock And Roll," which was still unreleased at the time of the performance and was still being referred to as "It's Been A long Time." It was getting a bit scary again and Plant leaves the crowd with some final words, "I gotta tell you, I can't hear a thing I'm saying. All the equipment's fallen out!" And then they were gone.

4 September 1971, Maple Leaf Gardens, Toronto, Ontario, Canada (8:00 p.m.)

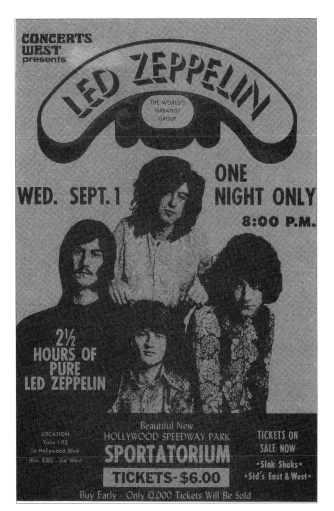

Press advert for Led Zeppelin's appearance at the Hollywood Speedway Park Sportatorium in Florida on 1 September 1971

Press advert for Led Zeppelin's concert at Madison Square Garden, New York City, on 3 September 1971.

SETLIST: Immigrant Song / Heartbreaker / Since I've Been Loving You / Out On The Tiles Intro / Black Dog / Dazed And Confused / Stairway To Heaven / Celebration Day / That's The Way / Going To California / What Is And What Should Never Be / Moby Dick / Whole Lotta Love (including Boogie Chillun', My Baby Left Me, Mess O' Blues, You Shook Me, Gee, Baby Ain't I Good To You, Kind Hearted Woman Blues) / Communication Breakdown / Organ Solo / Thank You

The amazing Madison Square Garden show must have tired the band as Toronto fans have to make do with a slightly more sluggish set. The crowd are very noisy, causing Plant to tell them, "Listen. It really amazes me, because anybody who's been to England knows that when you go to a concert, there's such a thing as listening to what's going on! Unfortunately, we're faced with the problem in our free society where a lot of people come to listen, and there's a lot of people who are making a racket so nobody hears what's going on. We've got some things to say but every time I go to open my mouth, there's another spokesman. . . . If the guy next to you is trying to listen, you've got to respect that and be quiet. So the whole thing's a bit circular respect thing. So many of those big festivals fell apart because the respect wasn't a uniform one, and the thing with these concerts is that they normally are!"

5 September 1971, International Amphitheatre, Chicago, Illinois (7:00 p.m.)

Rare handbill advertising Led Zeppelin's charity appearance in Hiroshima's Municipal Gymnasium, Japan, on 27 September 1971.

SETLIST NOT KNOWN BUT WOULD PROBABLY HAVE CONSISTED OF THE FOLLOWING: Immigrant Song / Heartbreaker / Since I've Been Loving You / Out On The Tiles Intro / Black Dog / Dazed And Confused / Stairway To Heaven / Celebration Day / That's The Way / What Is And What Should Never Be / Moby Dick / Whole Lotta Love (including Boogie Chillun', My Baby Left Me, Mess O' Blues, You Shook Me) / Communication Breakdown / Organ Solo / Thank You

7 September 1971, Boston Garden, Boston, Massachusetts (8:00 p.m.)

SETLIST: Immigrant Song / Heartbreaker / Since I've Been Loving You / Out On The Tiles Intro / Black Dog / Dazed And Confused / Celebration Day / That's The Way / Going To California / What Is And What Should Never Be / Moby Dick / Stairway To Heaven / Whole Lotta Love / Communication Breakdown / Organ Solo / Thank You / Rock And Roll

Dynamic show with many highlights. "Heartbreaker," "Black Dog," "Dazed And Confused" are just some of the crowd pleasers that drive the crowd wild. So much so that Robert Plant has to try and calm them down, "No! No! You gotta cool it! Listen, I gotta put things straight. We had a bit of trouble in New York the other day, when so many people got onstage that it fell apart. Listen! Listen! Listen to me! . . . If everybody gets on the stage, then the police will stop the thing. So what we wanna do is play as much of the new stuff and old stuff as we can without it falling apart!" The adrenaline-charged version of "Rock And Roll" is the final encore and then they were gone. Another incredible evening for the band and fans alike.

66 Thudding along, some of the hundredweight tunes they did were (staged to a throbbing bass line) 'Heartbreaker' and 'Since I've Been Loving You,' (enter from stage right a thumping drumbeat) 'Black Dog' and 'Dazed and Confused,' (enter a few hundred people to rush the stage) 'Whole Lotta Love,' (mix with a few monstrous electric guitar chords) 'I Can't Quit You,' (a long long, piercing scream) and a symbolic 'Communication Breakdown.' 99

—REVIEW FROM THE BOSTON GLOBE

9 September 1971, Hampton Roads Coliseum, Hampton Beach, Virginia

SETLIST (INCOMPLETE): Immigrant Song / Heartbreaker / Since I've Been Loving You / Out On The Tiles Intro / Black Dog / Dazed And Confused / Stairway To Heaven / Celebration Day / That's The Way / Going To California / What Is And What Should Never Be / Moby Dick / Whole Lotta Love (medley)

10 September 1971, Onondaga County War Memorial Auditorium, Syracuse, New York (8:00 p.m. Support from Black Sabbath.)

SETLIST NOT KNOWN BUT WOULD PROBABLY HAVE CONSISTED OF THE FOLLOWING: Immigrant Song / Heartbreaker / Since I've Been Loving You / Out On The Tiles Intro / Black Dog / Dazed And Confused / Stairway To Heaven / Celebration Day / That's The Way / What Is And What Should Never Be / Moby Dick / Whole Lotta Love (including Boogie Chillun', My Baby Left Me, Mess O' Blues, You Shook Me) / Communication Breakdown / Organ Solo / Thank You

11 September 1971, Rochester Community War Memorial, Rochester, New York (Support from Black Sabbath)

SETLIST: Immigrant Song / Heartbreaker / Since I've Been Loving You / Out On The Tiles Intro / Black Dog / Dazed And Confused / Stairway To Heaven / Celebration Day / That's The Way / Going To California / What Is And What Should Never Be / Moby Dick / Whole Lotta Love (including Boogie Chillun', Hello Mary Lou, Mess O' Blues, You Shook Me) / Organ Solo / Thank You

13 September 1971, Berkeley Community Theatre, Berkeley, California (8:00 p.m.)

SETLIST: Immigrant Song / Heartbreaker / Since I've Been Loving You / Out On The Tiles Intro / Black Dog / Dazed And Confused / Stairway To Heaven / Celebration Day / That's The Way / Going To California / What Is And What Should Never Be / Moby Dick / Whole Lotta Love (including Boogie Chillun', Hello Mary Lou, Mess O' Blues, You Shook Me, Gee, Baby Ain't I Good To You, Kind Hearted Woman Blues) / Communication Breakdown / Rock And Roll

66 The concert, which started 20 minutes late, began with the barely recognizable 'Immigrant Song,' with Page improvising to the hilt throughout the number and Plant dancing around onstage spastically to the tune. 'Since I've Been Loving You,' was moving, dramatic and gutsy, but absolutely too loud and so was 'Black Dog,' from the newest album. Zeppelin's 'Celebration Day,' a hard, driving number that was unbelievably loud, shook the auditorium and the people in it. A quiet and peaceful interlude where the group sat down and performed a couple of tunes including the lyrical and soothing (to the ear) 'Going to California' almost saved the evening. 99

—REVIEW FROM *OAKLAND TRIBUNE*

14 September 1971, Berkeley Community Theatre, Berkeley, California (8:00 p.m.)

SETLIST: Immigrant Song / Heartbreaker / Since I've Been Loving You / Out On The Tiles Intro / Black Dog / Dazed And Confused / Stairway To Heaven / Celebration Day / That's The Way / Going To California / What Is And What Should Never Be / Moby Dick / Whole Lotta Love (including Just A Little Bit, Boogie Chillun', Hello Mary Lou, My Baby Left Me, Mess O' Blues, You Shook Me, The Lemon Song) / Rock And Roll

A great show, as was the first night. The whole band is playing incredibly well and Page is in particularly sparkling form, and his solo on "Heartbreaker" is spectacular. Plant is in a great mood, talking with the crowd at several intervals: "You should have come last night. Last night there were several bowler-hatted beatniks. There was a pollution alert today and I lost my voice. This is one from millions and millions of years ago, just when the good things were checking themselves out." The band then play an epic "Dazed And Confused," which tonight included a bit of the MC5's "Back In The USA." When Page was tuning up for "Going To California," Plant talks to the audience about the song: "This is quite a moving night for me. This is a thing that got together . . . I was going to say in the Scottish Highlands, or the Welsh mountains, but I think it was something like the Gotham Hotel, West 37th Street. Here's to the days when things were really nice and simple and everything was far out, all the time. On that theme, it's not a very good cup of tea you get over here!" This show also had the distinction of being released as one of the first vinyl bootlegs of the band as *Going To California*, which had remarkable sound quality for an audience recording.

16 September 1971, Civic Auditorium, Honolulu, Hawaii (8:00 p.m.)

SETLIST NOT KNOWN BUT WOULD PROBABLY HAVE CONSISTED OF THE FOLLOWING: Immigrant Song / Heartbreaker / Since I've Been Loving You / Out On The Tiles Intro / Black Dog / Dazed And Confused / Stairway To Heaven / Celebration Day / That's The Way / What Is And What Should Never Be / Moby Dick / Whole Lotta Love (medley) / Communication Breakdown

> 66 The real irony of Led Zeppelin's two hour performance last night was that they played their own review in their last number, Communication Breakdown. The show itself was marred by a generally sloppy performance on the part of the group, rather noisy behaviour on the part of some of the 4,000 people in attendance, and a hot and sweaty atmosphere on the part of the good old poorly ventilated Civic Auditorium. The music was limp and uneven during all but a small part of the evening. They started with Immigrant Song and from the first note it was obvious that these guys were not into what they were doing.
>
> —*HONOLULU STAR BULLETIN* (Review dated 17 September 1971)

17 September 1971, Civic Auditorium, Honolulu, Hawaii (8:00 p.m.)

SETLIST NOT KNOWN BUT WOULD PROBABLY HAVE CONSISTED OF THE FOLLOWING: Immigrant Song / Heartbreaker / Since I've Been Loving You / Out On The Tiles Intro / Black Dog / Dazed And Confused / Stairway To Heaven / Celebration Day / That's The Way / What Is And What Should Never Be / Moby Dick / Whole Lotta Love medley / Communication Breakdown

Several fan reports from tonight's show were as equally bad as the first night reviews.

LED ZEPPELIN FIRST JAPANESE TOUR
23 SEPTEMBER 1971–29 SEPTEMBER 1971

Although reports from Hawaii were not exactly glowing, by the time they arrived in Japan the band were in great form. They enjoyed being in Japan and loved the appreciative fans who were nothing but respectful. It was a complete culture change from the US audiences. There were no firecrackers and no boisterous rioting crowds here, only enthusiastic fans who occasionally got overexcited at seeing the band for the first time. The Japanese tour was recorded by Warner-Pioneer, except the show in Hiroshima. New to the setlist in the acoustic section was "Tangerine" from *Led Zeppelin III* on which Page played a 1970 Giannini GWSCRA12-P Craviola 12-string acoustic. He used it onstage from 24 September 1971 to 28 June 1972.

On the way back from Japan, the band stopped off in Hong Kong, Thailand, and India for a short vacation. Lots of footage was taken with their newly acquired cine cameras.

23 September 1971, Budokan, Tokyo, Japan (6:30 p.m. Warner-Pioneer Japan recorded the show on 8-track tape. Portions of this show were considered for release as *How the East Was Won* as a companion piece to *How the West Was Won* but remains unreleased.)

SETLIST: Immigrant Song / Heartbreaker / Since I've Been Loving You / Out On The Tiles Intro / Black Dog / Dazed And Confused / Stairway To Heaven / Celebration Day / Bron-Yr-Aur Stomp Intro / That's The Way / Going To California / What Is And What Should Never Be / Moby Dick / Whole Lotta Love (including Hello Mary Lou, Mess O' Blues, Evil Woman, Tobacco Road, Good Times Bad Times, For What It's Worth, How Many More Times, The Hunter, You Shook Me, Gee Baby Ain't I Good To You, Kind Hearted Woman Blues) / Communication Breakdown

The band are energized for the opening date of their first Japanese tour. Aware that English is not that well understood, Plant tells the crowd, "I understand that in Japan not many people speak English. Anyway, every day it's getting better. We'd like to say that so far we've had an incredible time, a wonderful time. We haven't even played a concert yet and we've all really been having a ball. I'm gonna do my best to make this the best time we've ever had, because it seems to be such a difference to America. America doesn't seem to be so good anymore, unfortunately. Maybe it'll get better." The Japanese crowds appreciated the acoustic set and generally sat quietly and listened. Plant spoke at length to explain the background to "Going To California": "A long time ago in 1967, there was a place called San Francisco, and San Francisco was responsible for many good things, including everybody's head. Right on, man! I dunno what happened after 1967, maybe it was the truck drivers. Anyway. It's still there and it's in California." A lengthy "Whole Lotta Love" medley was absolutely insane and drove the crowd wild. A handful of fans could not contain their excitement and attempted to clamber up onstage during the final encore, "Communication Breakdown." This was unusual behaviour at shows in Japan and showed what an impact the band must have had to overexcite the fans so much.

24 September 1971, Budokan, Tokyo, Japan (2:00 p.m. Warner-Pioneer Japan recorded the show on 8-track tape. Portions of this show were considered for release as *How the East Was Won* as a companion piece but remains unreleased.)

SETLIST: Immigrant Song / Heartbreaker / Since I've Been Loving You / Out On The Tiles Intro / Black Dog / Dazed And Confused / Celebration Day / That's The Way / Going To California / Tangerine / What Is And What Should Never Be / Moby Dick / Whole Lotta Love (including Boogie Chillun', Cocaine, Rave On, Your Time Is Gonna Come, I'm A Man, The Hunter, Hello Mary Lou, Pretty Woman, How Many More Times) / Organ Solo / Thank You / Communication Breakdown

The second Budokan show is every bit as good as the previous night's show. The show today was an afternoon show, which prompted Plant to introduce John Bonham as "The only person who could do it. The only person who was in his pyjamas ten minutes before the show. The right honorable John Bonham!" The band are clearly having a ball and Plant dedicates all the new numbers to Cliff Richard, who at the time happened to be bigger in Japan than Led Zeppelin! At least he had several "Live in Japan" albums released! Still, Japan being the land of technology allowed many local fans to have good recording equipment and all of the band's shows have been released on bootleg over the years. The highlight of the concert has to be the first-ever performance of "Tangerine" during the acoustic section to the delight of the audience. The "Whole Lotta Love" medley contained several surprises, including several lines from the never performed "Your Time Is Gonna Come" from *Led Zeppelin I.*

27 September 1971, Hiroshima-ken Taiikukan, Hiroshima, Japan (Led Zeppelin play a charity concert for the benefit of victims of the atom bomb. The show was not professionally recorded.)

SETLIST: Immigrant Song / Heartbreaker / Since I've Been Loving You / Out On The Tiles Intro / Black Dog / Dazed And Confused / Stairway To Heaven / Celebration Day / That's The Way / Going To California / Tangerine / What Is And What Should Never Be / Moby Dick / Whole Lotta Love (including In The Light, Boogie Chillun', Let's Have Fun, Be-Bop-A-Lula) / Communication Breakdown

After their last Tokyo show, the band traveled to Kyoto where they spent the day sightseeing. In the evening they went to a popular nightclub, Saturday, where Jimmy Page, John Bonham, and John Paul Jones had a jam for around forty minutes, according to local reports, borrowing the nightclub band's instruments. The following day, 26 September, they made their way to Hiroshima for their next gig, which would take place on 27 September. When they arrived, they visited the Hiroshima Peace Memorial (Genbaku Dome), which sat above the only building structure that was left standing near the bomb's hypocenter. The ruin serves as a memorial to the people who were killed in the atomic bomb drop in 1945. Led Zeppelin would play their concert in Hiroshima as a benefit to aid the victims of the atom bomb, many of whom still suffered from radiation effects several decades on. The show itself was another high-energy performance by the band. A beautiful version of "Since I've Been Loving You" has to be mentioned as one of the highlights tonight. Once again fans had been driven to attempt to get onstage during the last encore, "Communication Breakdown," and Plant had to tell them, "Whoa, you must stop it! Please do not come on the stage. Stay here and be cool. Please sit down. Sit on the floor, mate!"

28 September 1971, Festival Hall, Osaka, Japan (7:00 p.m. Warner-Pioneer Japan recorded the show on 8-track tape. Portions of this show were considered for release as *How the East Was Won* as a companion piece to *How the West Was Won* but remains unreleased.)

SETLIST: Immigrant Song / Heartbreaker / Since I've Been Loving You / Out On The Tiles Intro / Black Dog / Dazed And Confused / Stairway To Heaven / Please Please Me (snippet) / From Me To You (snippet) / Celebration Day / Bron-Yr-Aur Stomp / That's The Way / Going To California / We Shall Overcome / Tangerine / Down By The Riverside / What Is And What Should Never Be / Moby Dick / Whole Lotta Love (including Boogie Chillun', D In Love, Bachelor Boy, C'mon Baby, Maybeline, Hello Mary Lou) / C'mon Everybody / Hi-Heel Sneakers / Communication Breakdown

What a show! The whole band is flying high tonight and deliver one of their best shows this year. The audience is respectfully quiet, which is something Led Zeppelin is not used to. Some great and unusual covers are played tonight, including two hits by Cliff Richard with "D In Love" and "Bachelor Boy" in the "Whole

Lotta Love" medley. Led Zeppelin crew member Clive Coulson joins in on vocals during "C'mon Everybody" and "Hi-Heel Sneakers." Phil Carson from Atlantic Records joined in and took over on bass for these two numbers as John Paul Jones played organ.

29 September 1971, Festival Hall, Osaka, Japan (7:00 p.m. Warner-Pioneer Japan recorded the show on 8-track tape. Portions of this show were considered for release as *How the East Was Won* as a companion picce to *How the West Was Won* but remains unreleased.)

SETLIST: Immigrant Song / Heartbreaker / Since I've Been Loving You / Out On The Tiles Intro / Black Dog / Dazed And Confused / Stairway To Heaven / Celebration Day / That's The Way / Going To California / Tangerine / Friends / What Is And What Should Never Be / Moby Dick / Whole Lotta Love (including Boogie Chillun', Tossin' And Turnin', Twist And Shout, Fortune Teller, Good Times Bad Times, You Shook Me) / Communication Breakdown / Organ Solo / Thank You / Rock And Roll

Tonight's show is the last in Japan and the band go all out. All members of Led Zeppelin had enjoyed their first-ever visit to Japan, and Plant tells the crowd in Osaka, "We spent two weeks in wonderful, glorious Japan, which has been incredible. Great hotels, great bars, great people, and without giving you any bullshit, this is our last night in Japan and we're gonna have a good time and I think you will!" Being the last night, there are some of the usual hijinks, such as John Bonham disappearing for most of the acoustic set, prompting Plant to get the audience to chant "Mr. Bonham." Plant jokingly tells the crowd Bonham must have gone off with a geisha. He went on to apologize, "Japan is a wonderful place and you're too much. You're putting up with a lot. We don't usually do things like this!" He may have been apologizing for the mayhem caused back at the Tokyo Hilton when John Bonham and Richard Cole destroyed two rooms and a hallway using Samurai swords. It earned the band a lifetime ban from the hotel. "Dazed And Confused" is one of the longest versions ever played to date and includes some intense improvisational jams. The polite applause after the number finished caused Plant to remark, "You're too quiet. Much too slow, too silly and fast asleep." This was a tour of many surprises, and tonight it was the only known live performance of "Friends" from *Led Zeppelin III*, and a final encore of "Rock And Roll" from the forthcoming *Led Zeppelin IV*.

LED ZEPPELIN SEVENTH UK TOUR
11 NOVEMBER 1971–21 DECEMBER 1971

After a welcome break, the band is back in the UK for their seventh tour there. The sixteen-date tour is tied in with the severely delayed but much-anticipated *Led Zeppelin IV* release in November 1971. Unlike their "Back to the Clubs" tour, which had attracted criticism for playing too many small venues preventing many fans from getting tickets, they would now play larger venues. Even so, the ticket allocation sold out within hours of going on sale, such was their popularity. The venues largely consisted of city halls, except in London where the band would play two special shows at the Empire Pool in Wembley.

11 November 1971, City Hall, Newcastle, Newcastle-Upon-Tyne (8:00 p.m.)

SETLIST: Immigrant Song / Heartbreaker / Out On The Tiles Intro / Black Dog / Since I've Been Loving You / Rock And Roll / Stairway To Heaven / That's The Way / Going To California / Tangerine / Dazed And Confused / What Is And What Should Never Be / Celebration Day / Whole Lotta Love / Communication Breakdown

Considering this is the opening night, the band are in fine shape and the crowd are very vocal in showing their appreciation. Plant introduced the new album tonight: "Now then, today's the day of the Teddy Bear's picnic, and to go with it, the new album came out. I know what they say about the length of time between the two, and I'm sure you can read all sorts of reports and toss a coin!" "Rock And Roll" is now in the main set and "Moby Dick" was not played at every show. Surprisingly, some critics were not impressed with the gig. Stu Bennett reporting for *Disc* magazine said, "The group that has brought the rock back to rock and roll were, for me at least, awful. The tragedy of it all was this band can play, and Plant can sing to rival any group in the world. They proved this with one new track, 'Stairway To Heaven.' But, alas, the mediocrity of the rest of the gig could easily be seen. Plant immediately sank to rock bottom in my estimation. True enough, Page did some amazing things with that guitar. But only spasmodically."

12 November 1971, Locarno Ballroom, Sunderland, Tyne And Wear (7:00 p.m. Some people claim to have been at the gig and others claim it was canceled and others say it was moved to the Mecca Ballroom in Newcastle. No press photos or reviews exist of either show.)

Press advert for Led Zeppelin's appearance at Caird Hall, Dundee, Scotland, on 13 November 1971.

13 November 1971, Caird Hall, Dundee, Scotland (8:15 p.m.)

SETLIST: Immigrant Song / Heartbreaker / Out On The Tiles Intro / Black Dog / Rock And Roll / Since I've Been Loving You / Stairway To Heaven / That's The Way / Bron-Yr-Aur Stomp / Tangerine / Dazed And Confused / What Is And What Should Never Be / Moby Dick / Whole Lotta Love (including Boogie Chillun', Hello Mary Lou, Mess O' Blues, Honey Bee, The Lemon Song, Gee, Baby Ain't I Good To You, Kind Hearted Woman Blues) / Communication Breakdown

16 November 1971, St. Matthews Baths Halls, Ipswich, Suffolk (8:00 p.m.)

SETLIST: Immigrant Song / Heartbreaker / Out On The Tiles Intro / Black Dog / Since I've Been Loving You / Rock And Roll / That's The Way / Tangerine / Dazed And Confused / What Is And What Should Never Be / Celebration Day / Whole Lotta Love (including Boogie Chillun', Hello Mary Lou, Mess O' Blues, Honey Bee, Going Down Slow) / Weekend / Gallows Pole

A fabulous show that is held in the local swimming baths hall. The pool had to be drained before being covered over by a wooden floor which was suspended by a wooden support structure. The unusual venue prompted Plant tell the audience, "I don't know whether the 12-foot end's this one or that one. God help us! I'm sure you must have had a Town Hall! It's gonna be a silly night tonight. We'd like you all to feel at home. Just think of the drop beneath you and the drop that might come eventually!" These smaller out-of-town gigs were very relaxed and the band were clearly more at ease than higher profile shows in London. "Dazed And Confused" is particularly good tonight with some inspired jams. At the song's

conclusion Plant proudly states, "Wonderful!" The big surprise tonight was the two unusual encores, Eddie Cochran's "Weekend" and "Gallows Pole," the latter being the first known performance of the song since the Copenhagen gig on 3 May 1971. It is amazing that so many of these smaller shows were taped by various audience members in very reasonable sound quality. Without these pioneers, the Led Zeppelin collecting community would have far less knowledge. People's memories are not reliable, but the tapes reveal the truth.

17 November 1971, Mayfair Suite, Kinetic Circus, Birmingham, West Midlands (8:00 p.m.)

SETLIST NOT KNOWN BUT WOULD PROBABLY HAVE CONSISTED OF THE FOLLOWING: Immigrant Song / Heartbreaker / Out On The Tiles Intro / Black Dog / Since I've Been Loving You / Celebration Day / Stairway To Heaven / Going To California / That's The Way / Tangerine / Bron-Y-Aur Stomp / Dazed And Confused / What Is And What Should Never Be / Rock And Roll / Whole Lotta Love

18 November 1971, Students Union, University of Sheffield, Sheffield, South Yorkshire (8:30 p.m.)

SETLIST NOT KNOWN BUT WOULD PROBABLY HAVE CONSISTED OF THE FOLLOWING: Immigrant Song / Heartbreaker / Out On The Tiles Intro / Black Dog / Since I've Been Loving You / Celebration Day / Stairway To Heaven / Going To California / That's The Way / Tangerine / Bron-Y-Aur Stomp / Dazed And Confused / What Is And What Should Never Be / Rock And Roll / Whole Lotta Love

20 November 1971, "Electric Magic," Wembley Empire Pool, Wembley, Middlesex (5:00 p.m. Support from a variety of circus acts, Bronco, and Stone the Crows)

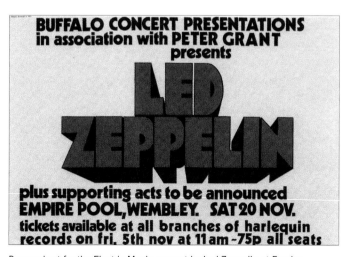

Press advert for the Electric Magic concert by Led Zeppelin at Empire Pool in Wembley on 20 November 1971.

Led Zeppelin onstage during the Electric Magic concert at Empire Pool in Wembley on 20 November 1971. (Rex)

SETLIST: Immigrant Song / Heartbreaker / Out On The Tiles Intro / Black Dog / Since I've Been Loving You / Rock And Roll / Stairway To Heaven / Going To California / That's The Way / Tangerine / Dazed And Confused / What Is And What Should Never Be / Celebration Day / Moby Dick / Whole Lotta Love (including Boogie Chillun', Hello Mary Lou, Mess O' Blues, Honey Bee, Going Down Slow)

Amazing show! Unlike the smaller out-of-town shows, the two Empire Pool shows were a five-hour visual feast featuring support bands along with plate spinners, a few acrobats, and several pigs wearing policeman hats and ruffles around their necks who just seemed to amble around onstage not doing very much. There were several merchandising stalls set up inside the arena selling T-shirts and a fabulous poster for only 30 pence that is today worth a small fortune in mint condition. It was a particularly cold winter in England and the venue was exceptionally cold inside.

However, the Empire Pool was often used for popular children's events, which meant using the arena as an ice rink. As a result, they could not turn the heating on because the arena seats were placed on planks of wood that covered the ice rink beneath them, and would have melted the ice. But Led Zeppelin soon warmed up the audience, many of them witnessing their might for the first time. The opening salvo of "Immigrant Song" and "Heartbreaker" pretty much took the heads off most people in the first few rows. The volume was ear-shattering and several people in close proximity to the PA had to leave their seats as a result. One of the first things Plant mentions is his disappointment with the pigs: "I expected a bit more from the pigs! Did you? I could have brought some goats!" This night is possibly the best night of the UK tour. The playing is intense and the band is totally together having already played six shows prior to London. "Dazed

And Confused" was again a big highlight with Page in startling form. Despite a recording doing the rounds from this show that includes a version of "Dancing Days," they categorically did not perform it and that particular number is from a different show altogether.

66 We are at home with Led Zep, comfy on a cold perishing English night. Even the elderly stewarts are enjoying it. 'I've been here years,' says one, 'And I've never known such happy, polite people. Everyone says 'please' and everyone says 'thank you.' I want to see this group Led Zeppelin!' This was an English band playing like crazy, and enjoying every minute they stood there on stage. They played non-stop for the best part of three hours. Enormous. They played about everything they've ever written. Nothing, just nothing, was spared. This was no job, this was no 'gig'. It was an event for all. So they get paid a lot of bread, well, people paid that bread, and I'll reckon they got every penny's worth. It was a great night.99

—ROY HOLLINGWORTH

(Review in *Melody Maker*, 27 November 1971)

21 November 1971, Electric Magic, Wembley Empire Pool, Wembley, Middlesex (5:00 p.m. Support from a variety of circus acts, Home, Stone the Crows, and DJ Jeff Dexter)

SETLIST: Immigrant Song / Heartbreaker / Out On The Tiles Intro / Black Dog / Since I've Been Loving You / Rock And Roll / Stairway To Heaven / Going To California / That's The Way / Tangerine / Bron-Yr-Aur Stomp / Dazed And Confused / Celebration Day / What Is And What Should Never Be / Moby Dick / Whole Lotta Love.

23 November 1971, Preston Public Hall, Preston, Lancashire (7:45 p.m. John Bonham's brother Mick makes a guest appearance on congas in "Whole Lotta Love.")

SETLIST NOT KNOWN BUT WOULD PROBABLY HAVE CONSISTED OF THE FOLLOWING: Immigrant Song / Heartbreaker / Out On The Tiles Intro / Black Dog / Since I've Been Loving You / Celebration Day / Stairway To Heaven / Going To California / That's The Way / Tangerine / Bron-Y-Aur Stomp / Dazed And Confused / What Is And What Should Never Be / Rock And Roll / Whole Lotta Love

24 November 1971, Free Trade Hall, Manchester, Greater Manchester (7:45 p.m.)

SETLIST: Immigrant Song / Heartbreaker / Out On The Tiles Intro / Black Dog / Since I've Been Loving You / Celebration Day / Stairway To Heaven / Going To California / That's The Way / Tangerine / Bron-Y-Aur Stomp / Dazed And Confused / What Is And What Should Never Be / Rock And Roll / Whole Lotta Love (including Just A Little Bit, Boogie Chillun', Rave On, Hello Mary Lou) / Thank You

Press advert for Led Zeppelin's appearance at Empire Pool in Wembley on 21 November 1971.

The band continue being on a roll with some magnificent playing. Bonham and Jones are in top form pushing Plant and Page to new highs. Plant fears he is coming down with the flu: "Gosh. I think I got that flu that's going about. I was in bed 'til half past six, and it's nice to be back. . . . I dunno, where are we? In Manchester. Manchester, right! It's good to be back." The acoustic set tonight is inspired and the band are clearly enjoying the softer numbers. An absolute killer version of "Dazed And Confused" blows the crowd away. It is very long, probably to give Plant's voice a break and has a cool and funky wah-wah "Shaft" theme segment in it.

25 November 1971, Queens Hall, Percy Gee Building, Leicester University, Leicester, East Midlands (8:00 p.m.)

SETLIST: Immigrant Song / Heartbreaker / Out On The Tiles Intro / Black Dog / Since I've Been Loving You / Celebration Day / Going To California / That's The Way / Tangerine / Bron-Yr-Aur Stomp / Dazed And Confused / Stairway To Heaven / What Is And What Should Never Be / Whole Lotta Love (including Just A Little Bit, Going Down, Boogie Chillun', Hello Mary Lou, Rave On, Mess O' Blues, So Many Roads, The Lemon Song) / Rock And Roll / Communication Breakdown

Another fabulous concert with an amazing extended "Whole Lotta Love" medley featuring the usual selection of rock 'n' roll and blues numbers. "Tangerine" had to be stopped after a minute due to a technical problem. It was restarted after the issue was sorted out. "Dazed And Confused" again features the theme from "Shaft" segment. This great show ended with a final encore from *Led Zeppelin I*, "Communication Breakdown."

29 November 1971, Liverpool Stadium, Liverpool, Merseyside (8:30 p.m.)

SETLIST NOT KNOWN BUT WOULD PROBABLY HAVE CONSISTED OF THE FOLLOWING: Immigrant Song / Heartbreaker / Out On The Tiles Intro / Black Dog / Since I've Been Loving You / Celebration Day / Stairway To Heaven / Going To California / That's The Way / Tangerine / Bron-Y-Aur Stomp / Dazed And Confused / What Is And What Should Never Be / Rock And Roll / Whole Lotta Love

30 November 1971, Kings Hall Belle Vue, Manchester, Greater Manchester (7:45 p.m. This date was added to the original itinerary after the Free Trade Hall gig on 24 November had sold out so quickly. Unfortunately, after one encore the band had to stop due to a rioting crowd invading the stage.)

SETLIST NOT KNOWN BUT WOULD PROBABLY HAVE CONSISTED OF THE FOLLOWING: Immigrant Song / Heartbreaker / Out On The Tiles Intro / Black Dog / Since I've Been Loving You / Celebration Day / Stairway To Heaven / Going To California / That's The Way / Tangerine / Bron-Y-Aur Stomp / Dazed And Confused / What Is And What Should Never Be / Rock And Roll / Whole Lotta Love

DECEMBER 1971

2 December 1971, Starkers Royal Arcade Ballroom, Bournemouth, Dorset (8:00 p.m.)

SETLIST: Immigrant Song / Heartbreaker / Out On The Tiles Intro / Black Dog / Since I've Been Loving You / Stairway To Heaven / Going To California / That's The Way / Tangerine / Bron-Y-Aur Stomp / Dazed And Confused / What Is And What Should Never Be / Rock And Roll / Whole Lotta Love (including Just A Little Bit, Gambler's Blues, Steppin' Out, Bottle Up and

Go, They're Red Hot, Cumberland Gap, She's A Truckin' Little Mama, Boogie Chillun', Heartbeat, Hello Mary Lou, Lawdy Miss Clawdy, I Can't Quit You Baby, How Many More Times, Shame Shame Shame, Let's Get Together) / Communication Breakdown / Weekend / It'll Be Me

"Dazed And Confused" continues to be the central improvisational number. Page varies his funky "Shaft" theme into something resembling "The Crunge" from *Houses of the Holy*. A lot of future Led Zeppelin songs were derived from jams and riffs developed in "Dazed And Confused" and "Whole Lotta Love." Tonight the "Whole Lotta Love" medley contains a rare, and possibly unique, version of Buddy Holly's "Heartbeat." "Weekend" and "It'll Be Me" are the final two encores and round off an incredible evening.

9 December 1971, Locarno Ballroom, Coventry, West Midlands (8:00 p.m. This date was added to the original itinerary at the last minute. The show was stopped after three songs and DJ Pete Waterman came onstage and told everyone to leave the building due to a bomb scare. As it was during the height of the IRA terror campaigns in England, the threat was taken seriously. The show restarted later after the police felt it was safe.)

SETLIST NOT KNOWN BUT WOULD PROBABLY HAVE CONSISTED OF THE FOLLOWING: Immigrant Song / Heartbreaker / Out On The Tiles Intro / Black Dog / Since I've Been Loving You / Celebration Day / Stairway To Heaven / Going To California / That's The Way / Tangerine / Bron-Y-Aur Stomp / Dazed And Confused / What Is And What Should Never Be / Rock And Roll / Whole Lotta Love

15 December 1971, City Hall, Salisbury, Wiltshire (8:30 p.m. Support bands were Jerusalem and Marble Orchard. The show was canceled at short notice due to Jimmy Page having the flu. Both support acts performed and Led Zeppelin rescheduled to play the gig on 21 December 1971.)

21 December 1971, City Hall, Salisbury, Wiltshire (8:30 p.m. Rescheduled from 15 December 1971.)

SETLIST NOT KNOWN BUT WOULD PROBABLY HAVE CONSISTED OF THE FOLLOWING: Immigrant Song / Heartbreaker / Out On The Tiles Intro / Black Dog / Since I've Been Loving You / Celebration Day / Stairway To Heaven / Going To California / That's The Way / Tangerine / Bron-Y-Aur Stomp / Dazed And Confused / What Is And What Should Never Be / Rock And Roll / Whole Lotta Love

Press advert for Led Zeppelin's appearance at Starkers, Royal Ballrooms, Bournemouth, on 2 December 1971.

8 1971 Recording Sessions

LED ZEPPELIN IV (UNTITLED) SESSIONS

NOVEMBER 1970–APRIL 1971

In many ways the new album was a continuation of where *Led Zeppelin III* left off. It would again mix riff-based numbers with more pastoral folksy songs. Recording in the informal setting of an old house took some pressure off and gave more scope for spontaneity. In fact, one of the classic Led Zeppelin songs, "Rock And Roll," is a perfect example of that. A simple jam started by John Bonham on his cymbal led into Little Richard's "Keep A Knockin'," on which he was quickly joined by Ian Stewart on barrelhouse piano, followed by Jimmy Page and John Paul Jones. Robert Plant, always a master of adlib lyrics, started singing a chorus of "It's been a long time since I rock 'n' rolled." Within fifteen minutes they had a song with a provisional title of "It's Been A Long Time." Credited to all four members of the band, the song was later retitled to the more appropriate "Rock And Roll."

66 Bonzo played that drum thing, just messing around while we were working on another song, and I joined in on a riff, and though it only lasted about quarter of a minute, we listened to the playback and heard the basis of a whole song, which we then got together . . . it took about 15 minutes. Things like that often happen.99

—JIMMY PAGE (Talking about "Rock And Roll," from an interview by Pete Frame, December 1972)

Ian Stewart, from the Rolling Stones, attended the sessions and was a good influence to have around, as well as being friends with the band. Another jam was loosely based on Richie Valens's "Ooh My Head," which again featured Ian Stewart's barellhouse piano along with added echo slap by Bonham and authentic '50s-style guitar by Page. Adding to the quirkiness of the number was the solo played by Page on mandolin. Plant's vocals also have a slight '50s echo as he sings some archetypal rockabilly lyrics. Simply titled, "Boogie With Stu," the song was left off *Led Zeppelin IV* as it did not really fit and later used more appropriately on the *Physical Graffiti* double album.

"Four Sticks" was so called because Bonham used four drum sticks to achieve the flammy sound. Unfortunately, Andy Johns made a mistake by compressing the drum sound on the basic tracks, which would later make it very difficult to mix as he could not undo the compression. He tried around seven different mixes and was never happy with any of them.

Another influence during the recording sessions was a black Labrador that would hang around at the Grange. The band were taken with him and named one of their most famous songs after him, "Black Dog." It was a collaborative effort between Page and Jones and turned out to be an archetypal Led Zeppelin heavy number with a powerful bass riff and triple tracked guitar by Jimmy Page.

Acoustic guitars and mandolins were again featured on the new album's sessions, as they had for *Led Zeppelin III*. The gorgeous Joni Mitchell–influenced

Jimmy Page onstage at Trentham Gardens during Led Zeppelin's 1971 UK tour. (Rex)

"Going To California," which despite its title was written back at Bron-Yr-Aur in the winter, was in the same vein as "That's The Way." It was very much an homage to the West Coast scene. Another number that had West Coast influences was the Neil Young–inspired "Down By The Seaside." Like "Boogie With Stu," it was decided to hold it back as it did not fit in the general style and vibe of the tracklist for the album. Luckily it did see the light of day eventually on *Physical Graffiti*.

Although at this point Led Zeppelin were still better known for being a heavy rock band, they were just as creative with their acoustic material. They were ahead of their time, and critics eventually had no choice but to catch up with them. Perhaps the album's best acoustic song is a folk song by Robert Plant, which found its influence in Celtic mythology.

The imagery of the lyrics was inspired by a book he had read about the fifteenth and sixteenth century Anglo-Scottish wars, which had mostly been fought along the border of the two countries. The song was based around call-and-answer lyrics and Plant felt strongly that the number would benefit with another voice. He chose Fairport Convention's Sandy Denny and the resulting masculine-feminine dynamic is awe-inspiring. The actual song started life almost by accident when Jimmy Page picked up John Paul Jones's mandolin and played a series of chords. It was the first time he had experimented with a mandolin and his approach was probably different from other players, but it worked and formed the basis of the song's instrumentation.

Kansas Joe McCoy and Memphis Minnie's "When The Levee Breaks" was completely reworked for the sessions by Jimmy Page. It is one of the most talked about numbers from *Led Zeppelin IV* because of the incredible drum sound achieved. The song is all about the drums and the dense layers of sound that are built around them, along with many other effects, including phased vocals and backward-echoed harmonica, all of which contributed to the song being one of Led Zeppelin's most adventurous recordings. Accounts differ about whose idea it was, but let's be generous and say it was a combination of Page and Andy Johns. Bonham's kit was moved from one of the rooms they had been recording in and into the center of the ground floor lobby, which had staircases going up to the upper-floor landings. It was basically a large hall with amazing space and natural echo. Two Beyerdynamic M160 microphones were placed on the second flight of stairs pointing toward the kit, and a couple of limiters were placed over the two mics. A Binson Echorec echo device that Jimmy Page had recently bought was also used. The unit had a steel drum instead of tape, which gave it a very unique sound. It was connected to the mixer like any other outboard echo device. When Bonham played his kit on "When The Levee Breaks," the limiters had plenty of room to breathe and thanks to the Binson Echorec, he achieved a unique sound that can be heard to great effect on the record.

Another song that started life at Headley Grange and finished at Island Studios was "Night Flight." Lyrically, it is a surprisingly depressing song about an impending threat of nuclear war. The usually upbeat Plant had been influenced by the negative newspaper headlines about the dangers of nuclear testing at the time, and wanted to reflect that in the song. This was yet another song held back and finally released on *Physical Graffiti*.

"No Quarter," which would later appear on the *Houses of the Holy* album, was started at these sessions. Here it sounded a lot more jazzier and even had a slight samba feel to it. It would have been interesting to see how it would have sounded had they finished it here. As it was, it was re-recorded with a different arrangement for their next album.

At the time of recording the now-classic Led Zeppelin anthem "Stairway To Heaven," nobody realized quite what an impact it would have. Its origins started around a wood fire at the Bron-Y-Aur cottage back in November 1970 and was eventually recorded at Headley Grange and finished at Island Studios. The basic track was recorded first with Jimmy Page on acoustic guitar, John Bonham on drums, and John Paul Jones playing an upright Hohner piano. The basic track alone sounded beautiful already. John Paul Jones then added his bass, followed by Page overdubbing electric rhythm guitar. The next step was to add the 12-string guitar, and Page used his Fender Electric XII plugged directly into the board, which gave the guitar a clean bell-like tone. John Paul Jones then mulitracked his recorder parts, and Jimmy Page was free to record the guitar solo, which he played on a Telecaster through a Supro amp. He tried various solos and was not particularly happy with any of them. Finally he played three amazing takes, all very different from each other, and he selected the one that is on the album. The idea of using the recorder was John Paul Jones's, which gave the song a slightly medieval, feel. Page's original idea was to have used an electric piano, but after hearing Jones's parts he much preferred the sound of the recorder. Robert Plant then added his vocals after a few minor changes to the lyrics. He pretty much did it in two takes and the song was finished. Jimmy Page admitted later that the song broke all the rules of studio session work by speeding up gradually. It was viewed as a no-no. "Stairway" starts to speed up at around the halfway point and leads to an incredible crescendo. The idea influenced many other bands that also found success with the same formula. A classic example would be "Freebird" by Lynyrd Skynyrd.

66 The music came first. I'd written it over a long period; the intro place in Bron-Y-Aur, in the cottage, and other parts came together piece by piece. When we came to record it, at Headley Grange, we were so inspired by how the song could come out, with the building passages and all the possibilities, that Robert came out with the lyrics just like that. . . . I'd say that he produced 40 percent of the lyrics almost immediately. We all threw in ideas, like Bonzo not coming in until the song was underway—to create a change of gear, so to speak—and the song and arrangement just came together. 99

—**JIMMY PAGE** (Talking about "Stairway To Heaven," from an interview by Pete Frame, December 1972)

With the album sessions finished, Andy Johns recommended that the album be mixed at Sunset Sound in Los Angeles as he had felt that it would provide a good sound. So Page and Johns flew out with the tapes only to find that the mixes sounded very different when played back in London at Olympic Studios on their monitor speakers. While the tapes had sounded bright and detailed at Sunset Sound, back in London they sounded as if the headroom had been squashed. As a result the album would miss its proposed April release date, which was to tie in with their "Back To The Clubs" tour. Members of the band unfairly blamed Johns and were quite vocal in their annoyance at the time. The album was finally remixed at Olympic Studios and Island Studios in April in between their UK and European tours. The only track to survive from the Sunset Sound mix was "When The Levee Breaks." In October 2014, *Led Zeppelin IV* was re-released as a deluxe edition featuring a bonus disc of different mixes and works in progress. Included was the Sunset Sound mix of "Stairway To Heaven."

The album known universally as *Led Zeppelin IV* was finally released in November 1972. The cover featured an old framed photo of an old man hunched over carrying a bale of hazel on his back. It was hung on the wall of a dilapidated house that had clearly half fallen down. Because *Led Zeppelin III* had got such a battering in the press, the band decided they wanted to underplay the whole Led Zeppelin name and let the album speak for itself and decided they wanted no mention of the band on the album sleeve whatsoever. After a long battle with Atlantic Records, the band won their argument to have absolutely no writing on the front or back cover of the album. The band were not named on the inside sleeve but were represented by four symbols, which at the time were a great source of mystery and suited the band just fine.

Musically speaking, this is Led Zeppelin's masterpiece. And although some fans would vote *Physical Graffiti* as their favorite album, the four symbols album remains a strong contender for the best rock album of all time.

ROLLING STONES MOBILE STUDIO
Headley Grange, Liphook Road, Headley, Hampshire

ROCK AND ROLL (Jimmy Page / Robert Plant / John Paul Jones / John Bonham) Available on *Led Zeppelin IV (Untitled)* vinyl Atlantic US SD7208 released 8 November 1971 / Atlantic UK 2401 012 released 12 November 1971 / released in remastered form on CD in October 2014 with bonus CD of alternate mixes and works in progress.

BOOGIE WITH STU (John Bonham / John Paul Jones / Jimmy Page / Robert Plant / Ian Stewart / Mrs. Valens) Available on *Physical Graffiti* vinyl Swan Song US SS-2-200 released 24 February November 1975 / Swan Song UK SSK 89400 released 24 February 1975. Sunset Sound mix available on the *Physical Graffiti* companion disc released February 2015.

NIGHT FLIGHT (John Paul Jones / Jimmy Page / Robert Plant) (Basic track recorded. Overdubs done at Island Studios and later released on *Physical Graffiti*.) Available on *Physical Graffiti* vinyl Swan Song US SS-2-200 released 24 February 1975 / Swan Song UK SSK 89400 released 24 February 1975.

BLACK DOG (Jimmy Page / Robert Plant / John Paul Jones) Available on *Led Zeppelin IV (Untitled)* vinyl Atlantic US SD7208 released 8 November 1971 / Atlantic UK 2401 012 released 12 November 1971 / released in remastered form on CD in October 2014 with bonus CD of alternate mixes and works in progress.

THE BATTLE OF EVERMORE (Jimmy Page / Robert Plant) (Sandy Denny's vocals were overdubbed later at Island Studios.) Available on *Led Zeppelin IV (Untitled)* vinyl Atlantic US SD7208 released 8 November 1971 / Atlantic UK 2401 012 released 12 November 1971 / released in remastered form on CD in October 2014 with bonus CD of alternate mixes and works in progress.

MISTY MOUNTAIN HOP (Jimmy Page / Robert Plant / John Paul Jones) Available on *Led Zeppelin IV (Untitled)* vinyl Atlantic US SD7208 released 8 November 1971 / Atlantic UK 2401 012 released 12 November 1971 / released in remastered form on CD in October 2014 with bonus CD of alternate mixes and works in progress.

GOING TO CALIFORNIA (Jimmy Page / Robert Plant) Available on *Led Zeppelin IV (Untitled)* vinyl Atlantic US SD7208 released 8 November 1971 / Atlantic UK 2401 012 released 12 November 1971 / released in remastered form on CD in October 2014 with bonus CD of alternate mixes and works in progress.

WHEN THE LEVEE BREAKS (Jimmy Page / Robert Plant / John Paul Jones / John Bonham / Memphis Minnie) Available on *Led Zeppelin IV (Untitled)* vinyl Atlantic US SD7208 released 8 November 1971 / Atlantic UK 2401 012 released 12 November 1971 / released in remastered form on CD in October 2014 with bonus CD of alternate mixes and works in progress.

NO QUARTER (Jimmy Page / Robert Plant / John Paul Jones) (Early version of the song was worked on but not fully developed. It was later revisited for their *Houses of the Holy* album in 1972.) Unreleased

ISLAND STUDIOS
Studio 1, Basing Street, London W11

WHEN THE LEVEE BREAKS (Jimmy Page / Robert Plant / John Paul Jones / John Bonham / Memphis Minnie) Available on the companion disc of the super-deluxe-edition box set of *Coda* released July 2015.

DOWN BY THE SEASIDE (Jimmy Page / Robert Plant) Available on *Physical Graffiti* vinyl Swan Song US SS-2-200 released 24 February 1975 / Swan Song UK SSK 89400 released 24 February 1975.

STAIRWAY TO HEAVEN (Jimmy Page / Robert Plant) Available on *Led Zeppelin IV (Untitled)* vinyl Atlantic US SD7208 released 8 November 1971 / Atlantic UK 2401 012 released 12 November 1971 / released in remastered form on CD in October 2014 with bonus CD of alternate mixes and works in progress.

FOUR STICKS (Jimmy Page / Robert Plant) Available on *Led Zeppelin IV (Untitled)* vinyl Atlantic US SD7208 released 8 November 1971 / Atlantic UK 2401 012 released 12 November 1971 / released in remastered form on cd in October 2014 with bonus CD of alternate mixes and works in progress.

THE BATTLE OF EVERMORE (Jimmy Page / Robert Plant) (Sandy Denny's vocals are overdubbed on the finished master.) Available on *Led Zeppelin IV (Untitled)* vinyl Atlantic US SD7208 released 8 November 1971 / Atlantic UK 2401 012 released 12 November 1971 / released in remastered form on CD in October 2014 with bonus CD of alternate mixes and works in progress.

NIGHT FLIGHT (John Paul Jones / Jimmy Page / Robert Plant) (Basic track recorded at Headley Grange. Overdubs done at Island Studios and later released on *Physical Graffiti*.) Available on *Physical Graffiti* vinyl Swan Song US SS-2-200 released 24 February 1975 / Swan Song UK SSK 89400 released 24 February 1975.

PRODUCER: JIMMY PAGE
ENGINEER: ANDY JOHNS

1972:
Led Zeppelin Continue Their Plan for World Domination

Yet another busy year for Led Zeppelin, which would include their first-ever tour of Australia and New Zealand. Page had of course previously visited Australia in 1967 when touring with the Yardbirds, but the political climate had changed a lot in Australia since then, especially with their involvement in the Vietnam War. A lot of young people were protesting and there was some unrest. The ultra-conservative government did not care for anything that could remotely be seen as degenerate behavior among the youth of the day. The thought of Led Zeppelin invading their country did not exactly fill them with joy and they set about making life difficult for the band. The morning after their first concert in Perth, the police raided their hotel rooms in search of drugs they were sure they would find. Much to their obvious annoyance, they found none and left in a huff with no apologies. Luckily, other than the occasional weather problems associated with playing outdoor venues, the band's tour in Australia and New Zealand can be seen as a success. However, it would seem that they were not that keen in repeating that success as they never returned as Led Zeppelin.

After the tour finished, the band concentrated their focus on the preparation and recording of a new album. Page and Jones had already recorded some demos at their respective home studios and the time came for the band to get together to rehearse some new numbers. They chose a large remote farmhouse located deep in the Dorset countryside a short distance from a place called Puddletown. The house had quite a bit of

history attached to it. Not only did people say it was haunted, but more interestingly, Thomas Hardy used this farmhouse as a basis for the farmhouse where Tess stayed for his *Tess of the d'Urbervilles* novel. In the late '60s and early '70s Ilsington Farmhouse was famously used by the Crazy World of Arthur Brown to record several albums. After Arthur Brown's departure to Kingdom Come, his ex-bandmates stayed on at the farm to play and record new music as Rustic Hinge. As a way of earning some extra money, the band hired out the farmhouse and studio. The studio itself, called Jabberwocky Studios, was basically a high-quality demo studio with two stereo Revox tape recorders going through a four-channel mixer. It was also a great space for rehearsing, which is what Led Zeppelin used it for. Yes had also used the place previously, and it was ideal for avoiding distractions and unwanted attention from the public. The sessions moved on to Mick Jagger's country mansion, Stargroves, and then to Olympic and Island Studios, before ending in New York at Electric Lady Studios for some final overdubs and mixing in June during their eighth US tour.

FEBRUARY 1972

6 February 1972, Lafayette Club, Wolverhampton, West Midlands (Robert Plant and John Bonham jam with Fairport Convention and their new guitarist, Roger Hill.)

LED ZEPPELIN AUSTRALIA– NEW ZEALAND TOUR

16 FEBRUARY 1972–3 MARCH 1972

Led Zeppelin were keen to look for other territories to play in, other than the usual places. To that end, in late 1971, Peter Grant had asked Richard Cole to go and check out potential venues for the band in Australasia. Although the band had originally wanted to play in Singapore, and possibly Hong Kong, ahead of the Australian and New Zealand dates, it proved problematic. Unfortunately strict laws banning long hair in Singapore meant that the band were unable to enter the country and potential shows were canceled as a result. Instead, the band decided to go visit Bombay in India as tourists, before heading to Australia.

16 February 1972, Subiaco Oval, Perth, Australia (8:00 p.m.)

Press advert for Led Zeppelin's 1972 Australian tour.

SETLIST NOT KNOWN BUT WOULD PROBABLY HAVE BEEN TAKEN FROM THE FOLLOWING: Immigrant Song / Heartbreaker / Out On The Tiles Intro / Black Dog / Since I've Been Loving You / Stairway To Heaven / Going To California / That's The Way / Tangerine / Dazed And Confused / What Is And What Should Never Be / Whole Lotta Love (medley)

There were troubles with the police and around 300 people ramming the entrance gates at the Subiaco Oval wanting to get in for free. Eight thousand people were already in the venue and it was filled to capacity.

Eventually police reinforcements had to be called in to manage the situation. As the band were ending their main set, crowds started surging forward and several ended up onstage with the band. Plant was able to control the situation until they played their encore, which prompted all the fans onstage to stand up and start dancing. The band needed help in getting off the stage and back to their waiting cars backstage. Plant had his shirt ripped by eager fans wanting a souvenir. The band later went to a local nightclub and ended up jamming on some classic rock 'n' roll covers to the delight of their Australian label staff who had organized the evening.

18 February 1972, Memorial Drive Park, Adelaide, Australia (Canceled due to heavy downpour of rain, which caused the stage to buckle and dampened the amplification equipment, making it unsafe. The show is rescheduled for the next day, 19 February.)

66 A buckled stage and damp amplifying equipment forced last night the postponement of the UK rock group Led Zeppelin's appearance at Memorial Drive until tonight. . . . The Led Zeppelin had brought to Adelaide about 11,800 lb of stage equipment to produce what was expected to be the loudest rock sounds heard here. 5AD, which was co-sponsoring the show with Channel 7, had continually broadcast the postponement and only about 200 of 7000 people who had booked for the show arrived at Memorial Drive. 99

—THE *ADVERTISER* (Saturday, 19 February 1972)

19 February 1972, Memorial Drive Park, Adelaide, Australia (8:15 p.m.)

SETLIST: Immigrant Song / Heartbreaker / Out On The Tiles Intro / Black Dog / Since I've Been Loving You / Stairway To Heaven / Going To California / That's The Way / Tangerine / Bron-Y-Aur Stomp / Dazed And Confused / What Is And What Should Never Be / Moby Dick / Whole Lotta Love (including Boogie Chillun', Hello Mary Lou, Let's Have A Party, That's Alright Mama, Going Down Slow, The Shape I'm In) / Communication Breakdown

66 From the start, all eyes were on brilliant lead guitarist Jimmy Page. His electric guitar work was extraordinary. At one stage, using a bow, he smashed out a string of piercing notes only to end with a run of delicate sitar-sounding music. Thunderous applause followed all his work. Drummer John Bonham's steady beat that at times sounded like a hammer striking steel. . . . Singer Robin Plant [*sic*] overcame an 'Australian bug' in his throat and broke into his own in 'Black Dog,' 'Stairway To The Stars' [*sic*] and 'Let's Have A Party.' 99

—RICHARD MITCHELL

(Review in the *Advertiser*, 21 February 1972)

Led Zeppelin onstage at the Sydney Showground, Sydney, Australia, on 27 February 1972. (Rex)

20 February 1972, Kooyong Stadium, Kooyong, Melbourne, Australia (3:00 p.m.)

SETLIST: Immigrant Song / Heartbreaker / Out On The Tiles Intro / Black Dog / Since I've Been Loving You / Stairway To Heaven / Going To California / That's The Way / Tangerine / Bron-Y-Aur Stomp / Dazed And Confused / Rock And Roll / Whole Lotta Love (including Boogie Chillun', Let's Have A Party)

A daylight show by the band. By 3:00 p.m. the venue was packed. Shortly after, the band walked on unannounced taking the crowd by surprise. Plant welcomes them with a "Good afternoon!" Not happy with their response, he tries, "I can't hear you!" and is rewarded with a loud "Good afternoon!" Page then starts "Immigrant Song" and the crowd goes wild. The band play a great set and both Plant and Page are very animated throughout the show. A little rain started to fall during "Dazed And Confused," which prompted Plant to sing, "Well, it's started to rain, I think it's time we gotta go. If we don't go now, we're gonna die, I don't wanna know!" The band went offstage promising to return when it stopped. After ten minutes they came back on and played their last two songs, "Rock And Roll" and the "Whole Lotta Love" medley, which had to be cut short due to more rain. The crowd was delirious and went home happy.

25 February 1972, Western Springs Stadium, Western Springs, Auckland, New Zealand (8:00 p.m.)

SETLIST: Immigrant Song / Heartbreaker / Out On The Tiles Intro / Black Dog / Since I've Been Loving You / Celebration Day / Stairway To Heaven / Going To California / That's The Way / Tangerine / Bron-Y-Aur Stomp / Dazed And Confused / What Is And What Should Never Be / Moby Dick / Rock And Roll / Whole Lotta Love (including Boogie Chillun', Hello Mary Lou, Let's Have A Party, Going Down Slow, The Shape I'm In) / Communication Breakdown

27 February 1972, Sydney Showground, Sydney, Australia (2:00 p.m. Parts of the show are filmed by members of the crew on amateur equipment. Fragments were used on the Whole Lotta Love promo video in 1997 and on the Led Zeppelin DVD in 2003, which used the multitrack recording of "Immigrant Song" from Long Beach Arena, 27 June 1972, dubbed over the black-and-white footage from Sydney.)

SETLIST: Immigrant Song / Heartbreaker / Out On The Tiles Intro / Black Dog / Since I've Been Loving You / Stairway To Heaven / Going To California / That's The Way / Tangerine / Bron-Y-Aur Stomp / Dazed And Confused / What Is And What

Should Never Be / Moby Dick / Rock And Roll / Whole Lotta Love (including Boogie Chillun', Hello Mary Lou, The Rover, Let's Have A Party, Lawdy Miss Clawdy, Going Down Slow) / Communication Breakdown / Organ Solo / Thank You

Another open-air show and Plant asks the crowd for their cooperation: "Now listen! We've already come across the one problem we were told about. Now, there's been a lot of mistakes about this thing, but we don't want to make any mistakes and neither do you, alright? So don't come past this barrier, otherwise there's gonna be some shit. And why don't you sit down . . . and if it rains, we're gonna have to stop. That's a fact, it'll blow up! Take a seat!" Nobody wanted a repeat of the stage invasion that had happened in Perth. The crowd for the Sydney concert was estimated at around 28,000, the largest ever for a Sydney rock concert, so it was not surprising that Plant laid down the ground rules from the start. The biggest surprise of the night was the performance of an instrumental version of "The Rover" during the "Whole Lotta Love" medley. It was originally planned for the *Houses of the Holy* album, but was finally released on *Physical Graffiti* in 1975.

Press advert for Led Zeppelin's appearance at the Oude Rai in Amsterdam on 27 May 1972.

Led Zeppelin onstage at the Oude Rai in Amsterdam on 27 May 1972. (Gijsbert Hanekroot/Getty Images)

66 Senior police officers at the concert estimated the crowd at 'at least 30,000.' According to showground officials the three stands used last Sunday have a maximum capacity of 25,000— so whatever way you look at it the ground was dangerously overcrowded. Despite the fact that there were no seats left at mid-day and no standing room by 1:30 p.m., people were still coming through the gates at 2:30 p.m. The overcrowding that existed before the fences were stormed must never be allowed to occur again because next time someone could be killed in the crush."

—**DAVID D. BRYANT** (Review in the *Sun-Herald*, 5 March 1972)

29 February 1972, Festival Hall, Brisbane, Australia
(8:00 p.m.)

SETLIST: Immigrant Song / Heartbreaker / Out On The Tiles Intro / Black Dog / Since I've Been Loving You / Celebration Day / Stairway To Heaven / Going To California / That's The Way / Tangerine / Bron-Y-Aur Stomp / Dazed And Confused / What Is And What Should Never Be / Moby Dick / Whole Lotta Love (including Bottle Up And Go, Cumberland Gap, They're Red Hot, She's A Truckin' Little Baby, The Wanderer, Hello Mary Lou, Let's Have A Party, Going Down Slow)

The band finish their successful tour with their only indoor show in Australia. A rather excitable crowd force Plant to stop "That's The Way." The song is only restarted after they listen to his instructions and sit down. The band play a one-off version of Dion's "The Wanderer" during the "Whole Lotta Love" medley.

LED ZEPPELIN EUROPEAN TOUR— WARM-UP FOR US TOUR

27 MAY 1972–28 MAY 1972

The band recorded their new album, *Houses of the Holy*, between April and May 1972, with a little additional recording and mixing in New York in June. Once again, lengthy delays with the artwork meant that the album could not be released in time for the US tour, which is what the band had hoped.

Led Zeppelin onstage at the Oude Rai in Amsterdam on 27 May 1972. (Gijsbert Hanekroot/Getty Images)

The band arrive at Oude Rai in Amsterdam early and spend most of the afternoon rehearsing and fine-tuning the set that will eventually be taken to America.

27 May 1972, Oude Rai, Amsterdam, Holland (8:30 p.m. Part of "Immigrant Song" from this concert is shown on a local Dutch television show called *Hard Rock Heaven*. Also shown is footage of the band arriving at their hotel and Richard Cole talking with the promoter.)

SETLIST: Immigrant Song / Heartbreaker / Out On The Tiles Intro / Black Dog / Since I've Been Loving You / Celebration Day / Stairway To Heaven / Bron-Y-Aur Stomp / Dazed And Confused / What Is And What Should Never Be / Moby Dick / Whole Lotta Love (including Everybody Needs Somebody To Love, Boogie Chillun', Hello Mary Lou, Running Bear, That's Alright Mama, Tobacco Road, Hoochie Coochie Man, Going Down Slow, The Shape I'm In), Rock And Roll, Communication Breakdown

"Dazed And Confused" includes a few riffs of "The Crunge," which had recently been recorded. The band play a rare version of Jiles Perry Richardson's "Running Bear" as part of the "Whole Lotta Love" medley. They would only play it another two times in their career, the next night in Brussels and in Montreal on 7 June 1972. They often played one-off rarities during this medley.

28 May 1972, Forest National, Brussels, Belgium (8:30 p.m.)

SETLIST: Immigrant Song / Heartbreaker / Out On The Tiles Intro / Black Dog / Since I've Been Loving You / Stairway To Heaven / Going To California That's The Way / Bron-Y-Aur Stomp / Dazed And Confused / What Is And What Should Never Be / Whole Lotta Love (including Everybody Needs Somebody To Love, Boogie Chillun', Hello Mary Lou, Running Bear, Lawdy Miss Clawdy, Heartbreak Hotel, Don't Be Cruel, Going Down Slow)

This was Led Zeppelin's first show in Brussels, and Belgium for that matter, and the fans are going mad with excitement. The rowdy crowd are quite a distraction for the band and Plant has to keep asking them to settle down, especially during the acoustic set. "Going To California" has to be stopped because of the crowd noise levels. Jimmy Page would have the same problem in Brussels during the 1980 tour when he had to stop "White Summer." A firecracker is thrown onstage during "Dazed And Confused" and the band decide to drop "Moby Dick" and shorten the set because of the crowd's boisterous behavior.

LED ZEPPELIN EIGHTH US TOUR
6 JUNE 1972–28 JUNE 1972

The band head off to America for their eighth tour over there. The shows would now be a minimum of three hours, giving fans great value for their money. Most bands would play around ninety minutes maximum at this time, so Zeppelin were pioneers in that respect. The reaction to their live shows was phenomenal, yet the band were disheartened at the lack of acknowledgment from their own country, who seemed to ignore their achievements at the time.

In the meantime, they were playing to sold-out arenas in the US with next to no advertising and getting incredible reactions. The band was on fire and this tour was one of their best. Luckily several shows were professionally recorded and eventually released as *How the West Was Won*, enabling people to hear just how dynamic they were during this tour. But despite the sold-out venues and universally appreciative fan reaction, it was the Rolling Stones who attracted all the press attention. They were touring America at the same time and *Rolling Stone* magazine in particular were fawning all over the Stones and ignoring Led Zeppelin.

On the *Melody Maker* cover in England, US–based Roy Hollingworth asked the million-dollar question, "Led Zeppelin—the forgotten giants?" He goes on to say, "Does anybody really know how big Led Zeppelin are? So you'll get reports of English bands doing 'well' in America and the reports will be long. You'll

hear the Stones, Elton John and the Faces before you hear Led Zeppelin. Somehow somebody forgot Led Zeppelin when they were writing home. And yet for four years they have been slaying America. For four years they have met with the dooming criticism that they could never do as well again, and yet they've come back, and done better." It would take until 1975 for everyone to wake up to the fact that Led Zeppelin were the greatest rock band in the world, especially *Rolling Stone* magazine.

6 June 1972, Cobo Arena, Detroit, Michigan

SETLIST NOT KNOWN BUT WOULD HAVE LIKELY BEEN:
Immigrant Song / Heartbreaker / Out On The Tiles Intro / Black Dog / Since I've Been Loving You / Stairway To Heaven / Going To California / That's The Way / Tangerine / Bron-Y-Aur Stomp / Dazed And Confused / What Is And What Should Never Be / Moby Dick / Whole Lotta Love / Rock And Roll / Organ Solo / Thank You

7 June 1972, Montreal Forum, Montreal, Quebec, Canada (8:00 p.m.)

SETLIST: Immigrant Song / Heartbreaker / Out On The Tiles Intro / Black Dog / Since I've Been Loving You / Stairway To Heaven / Going To California / That's The Way / Tangerine / Bron-Y-Aur Stomp / Dazed And Confused (including Walter's Walk) / What Is And What Should Never Be / Moby Dick / Whole Lotta Love (including Everybody Needs Somebody To Love, Boogie Chillun' / Hello Mary Lou, Running Bear, Money Honey, Mess O' Blues, Going Down Slow, When The Levee Breaks) / Rock And Roll / Organ Solo / Thank You

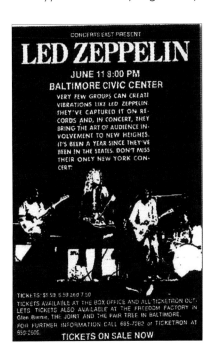

Press advert for Led Zeppelin's appearance at the Civic Center in Baltimore on 11 June 1972.

A good show but the usual firecracker and crowd problems arise, causing Plant to tell the members of the audience, "I can hear it. It really doesn't sound so good. Everywhere we go around the country, everybody wants somebody else to stand up or sit down and every time I say anything about one thing or the other, there's lots of chaos. So can you sit down?" "Dazed And Confused" included part of "Walters Walk," which had been recorded the previous month at Olympic Studios in Barnes.

8 June 1972, Boston Garden, Boston, Massachusetts (No evidence that this show took place and sources state that this was in fact a day off.)

9 June 1972, Charlotte Coliseum, Charlotte, North Carolina

SETLIST: Immigrant Song / Heartbreaker / Celebration Day / Out On The Tiles Intro / Black Dog / Since I've Been Loving You / Stairway To Heaven / Going To California / That's The Way / Tangerine / Bron-Y-Aur Stomp / Dazed And Confused (including Walter's Walk) / What Is And What Should Never Be / Moby Dick / Whole Lotta Love (including Everybody Needs Somebody To Love instrumental) / Rock And Roll / Communication Breakdown

The band are a little laid back at this show, but provide a big surprise with a rare performance of "Celebration Day." The acoustic set is particularly inspired, although the crowd is restless. "Whole Lotta Love" is without the usual medley for some unknown reason, but two high-energy encores more than make up for it.

10 June 1972 Buffalo Memorial Auditorium, Buffalo, New York (8:00 p.m.)

Press advert for Led Zeppelin's appearance at the Memorial Coliseum in Portland on 17 June 1972.

SETLIST NOT KNOWN BUT WOULD HAVE LIKELY BEEN: Immigrant Song / Heartbreaker / Out On The Tiles Intro / Black Dog / Since I've Been Loving You / Stairway To Heaven / Going To California / That's The Way / Tangerine / Bron-Y-Aur Stomp / Dazed And Confused / What Is And What Should Never Be / Moby Dick / Whole Lotta Love / Rock And Roll / Communication Breakdown

11 June 1972, Baltimore Civic Center, Baltimore, Maryland (8:30 p.m.)

SETLIST: Immigrant Song / Heartbreaker / Out On The Tiles Intro / Black Dog / Since I've Been Loving You / Stairway To Heaven / Going To California / That's The Way / Tangerine / Bron-Y-Aur Stomp / Dazed And Confused (including The Crunge, Walter's Walk, Hots On For Nowhere) / What Is And What Should Never Be / Moby Dick / Whole Lotta Love (including Everybody Needs Somebody To Love, Boogie Chillun', I Need Your Love Tonight, Hello Mary Lou, Heartbreak Hotel, Going Down, Going Down Slow) / Rock And Roll / Communication Breakdown (including It's Your Thing, Bold Soul Sister)

The band are thrilled about having seen Elvis Presley live at Madison Square Garden the previous afternoon, and Plant tells the crowd, "We went to see Elvis Presley the other day. Far out, as you would say. I tell you that that guy did so much for music a long time ago. He went in the army and never got hurt. I'll tell you what, he was really something. Now his voice has gone down about two or three tones and keys seemed to have changed a bit. His waist is a bit bigger than it was at one time." Inspired by seeing the King, the band play "I Need Your Love Tonight" and "Heartbreak Hotel" during the "Whole Lotta Love" medley.

66 Page has curbed his zeal for excessively long solos—although he uncorked one on Dazed and Confused, that was outstanding mainly for its length, in favor of more pungent statements. He also has given up fretting with the mike stand, an early device and now bows the guitar strings, brandishing the bow high in the air after sawing away at the strings to conduct the after-notes echoing through the speakers. Page and Led Zeppelin have both come a long way since their first appearance in this area at the Laurel Pop Festival in 1969. 99

—*BALTIMORE SUN* (Review in June 1972)

13 June 1972, the Spectrum, Philadelphia, Pennsylvania (8:00 p.m. Additional show added to the original 1972 US tour itinerary.)

SETLIST: Immigrant Song / Heartbreaker (including The 59th Street Bridge Song (Feelin' Groovy) / Out On The Tiles Intro / Black Dog / Bring It On Home (including The Lemon Song, Cat's Squirrel) / Since I've Been Loving You / Stairway To Heaven / Going To California / That's The Way / Tangerine / Bron-Y-Aur Stomp / Dazed And Confused (including Walter's Walk, The Crunge) / What Is And What Should Never Be / Moby Dick / Whole Lotta Love (medley) / Rock And Roll

A poor and incomplete recording made by an audience member enables the listener to realize that this was a good show with a surprise appearance of "Bring It On Home," not played since their show in Belfast on 5 March 1971.

14 June 1972, Nassau Veterans Memorial Coliseum, Uniondale, New York (8:00 p.m.)

SETLIST: Immigrant Song / Heartbreaker / Out On The Tiles Intro / Black Dog / Since I've Been Loving You / Stairway To Heaven / Going To California / That's The Way / Tangerine / Bron-Y-Aur Stomp / Dazed And Confused (including Walter's Walk, The Crunge) / What Is And What Should Never Be / Moby Dick / Whole Lotta Love (including Everybody Needs Somebody To Love, Boogie Chillun', Bottle Up And Go, Cumberland Gap, They're Red Hot, She's A Truckin' Little Baby, Hello Mary Lou, Lawdy Miss Clawdy, Going Down Slow) / Rock And Roll / Communication Breakdown (including Bold Soul Sister, The Lemon Song) / Weekend / Bring It On Home

Absolutely epic set with the band playing one of their best shows of 1972. The band sound like an unstoppable freight train that only slows down for the acoustic set before picking up speed again. Breathtaking versions of "Dazed And Confused" and "Whole Lotta Love" are just two particular highlights. The band play four encores, including a rare performance of Eddie Cochran's "Weekend."

15 June 1972, Nassau Veterans Memorial Coliseum, Uniondale, New York (8:00 p.m.)

SETLIST: Drone Intro / Immigrant Song / Heartbreaker / Out On The Tiles Intro / Black Dog / Since I've Been Loving You / Stairway To Heaven / Going To California / That's The Way / Tangerine / Bron-Y-Aur Stomp / Dazed And Confused / What Is And What Should Never Be / Moby Dick / Whole Lotta Love (including Everybody Needs Somebody To Love, Boogie Chillun', Willie And The Hand Jive, Hello Mary Lou, Money Honey, Heartbreak Hotel, Bottle Up and Go, They're Red Hot, It's Tight Like That, Going Down Slow)

The Drone intro is introduced tonight and makes for a very atmospheric start of the show. After putting in such a frenetic performance the previous night, one would imagine that the band might take it easy. But that simply was not the case and they put in another killer performance. Obvious highlight is a lengthy "Whole Lotta Love" medley featuring many rarities.

16 June 1972, War Memorial Auditorium, Rochester, New York (No evidence that this show took place and sources state that this was in fact a day off.)

17 June 1972, Portland Memorial Coliseum, Portland, Oregon (8:00 p.m.)

SETLIST: Drone Intro / Immigrant Song / Heartbreaker / Out On The Tiles Intro / Black Dog / Since I've Been Loving You / Stairway To Heaven / Going To California / That's The Way / Tangerine / Bron-Y-Aur Stomp / Dazed And Confused / What Is And What Should Never Be / Moby Dick / Whole Lotta Love (including Boogie Chillun', Boppin' The Blues, Hello Mary Lou, Going Down Slow) / Rock And Roll

18 June 1972, Pacific Coliseum, Vancouver, British Columbia, Canada (The show was canceled because 2,000 rioting fans had tried to break down the doors of the arena for a Rolling Stones concert a few weeks prior, injuring several people in the process, including over thirty policemen. Fearing a similar situation with Led Zeppelin, and despite that the show was sold-out, the authorities canceled it and the concert was swiftly moved to Seattle. Fans were given a choice of a refund or going to a replacement concert in Seattle. Special buses were hired for shipping fans to and from Vancouver to Seattle.)

18 June 1972, Seattle Center Coliseum, Seattle, Washington (8:00 p.m.)

SETLIST (INCOMPLETE): Drone Intro / Immigrant Song / Heartbreaker / Out On The Tiles Intro / Black Dog / Since I've Been Loving You / Stairway To Heaven / Going To California / That's The Way / Tangerine / Bron-Y-Aur Stomp / Dazed And Confused / What Is And What Should Never Be / Moby Dick / Whole Lotta Love (medley)

Everyone knows about the next show, but from what exists of tonight's show, it sounded like it was probably every bit as great as the next night. This show was the replacement one for fans from Vancouver who were bused in and out. Plant reminds the crowd, "Well, what can we say? Somebody tried to do a lot of damage in Vancouver, I believe; breaking doors down and all that old shit! It's pretty unfortunate, really, when we try to stand for an alternative idea to the system that goes on now, and we're talking about love and peace and somebody's smashing everything up. I don't really know the situation, but I know that we couldn't go this year. We couldn't even go across the border. So, anybody from Vancouver here? Well, that's a nice one! We've always had such a good time there." Although there were crowd problems during the acoustic set, it did not seem to affect the performance.

19 June 1972, Seattle Center Coliseum, Seattle, Washington

Press advert for Led Zeppelin's appearance at the Center Coliseum in Seattle on 19 June 1972.

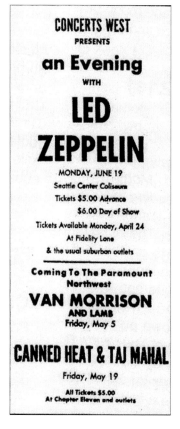

SETLIST: Drone Intro / Immigrant Song / Heartbreaker / Out On The Tiles Intro / Black Dog / The Ocean / Since I've Been Loving You / Stairway To Heaven / Going To California / Black Country Woman / That's The Way / Tangerine / Bron-Y-Aur Stomp / Dazed And Confused (including Walter's Walk, The Crunge) / What Is And What Should Never Be / Dancing Days / Moby Dick / Whole Lotta Love (including Everybody Needs Somebody To Love, Boogie Chillun', Let's Have A Party, Hello Mary Lou, Only The Lonely, Heartbreak Hotel, Going Down Slow) / Rock And Roll / Organ Solo / Thank You / Money / Over The Hills And Far Away / Dancing Days

This is one of a select number of gigs played by Led Zeppelin over their twelve-year career that is considered to be their best ever. Seattle was like LA for the band and they always enjoyed being in the city and played some incredible shows there. Tonight was no exception with a performance lasting well over three hours with five encores! There are several previews from the new album, including "Dancing Days," which was played twice tonight. Plant introduced it as, "We got another new one we want to do, off the next album. Freshly rehearsed, ah, about thirty minutes before you came here. This is a song about the summer. It's called "Dancing Days."" After the first performance, Plant tells the crowd, "Well, that's the first time. That's the first time, I believe, we've ever done that. All being well, we're gonna get this album out before the summer goes, otherwise it's like past tense. That was 'Dancing Days'." "Black Country Woman" gets it's premiere here, and it would not be played again until the 1977 US tour, albeit in a truncated version. A second version of "Dancing Days" is played as a fifth and final encore, which is introduced with humor by Plant: "This is one that you may have heard about two hours ago. We like it so much, we're gonna do it again!"

21 June 1972, Denver Coliseum, Denver, Colorado

SETLIST NOT KNOWN BUT WOULD HAVE LIKELY BEEN: Drone Intro / Immigrant Song / Heartbreaker / Out On The Tiles Intro / Black Dog / Since I've Been Loving You / Stairway To Heaven / Going To California / That's The Way / Tangerine / Bron-Y-Aur Stomp / Dazed And Confused / What Is And What Should Never Be / Moby Dick / Whole Lotta Love / Rock And Roll / Thank You / The Ocean

22 June 1972, Swing Auditorium, San Bernardino, California (8:00 p.m.)

SETLIST: Drone Intro / Immigrant Song / Heartbreaker / Out On The Tiles Intro / Black Dog / Since I've Been Loving You / Stairway To Heaven / Going To California / That's The Way / Tangerine / Bron-Y-Aur Stomp / Dazed And Confused (including Walter's Walk, The Crunge) / What Is And What Should Never Be / Moby Dick / Whole Lotta Love (including Everybody Needs Somebody To Love, Boogie Chillun', Let's Have A Party, Hello Mary Lou, Going Down Slow) / Rock And Roll

Jimmy Page during the acoustic segment of the concert at the Sports Arena in San Diego, California, on 23 June 1972. (Laurance Ratner/Getty Images)

After the Seattle extravaganzas, the setlist tonight returned to the standard format for the tour. The band was in fine form despite constant interruptions caused by firecrackers being thrown at the stage. The crowd seemed a little stoned and laid back, so Plant tries to liven them up during the funky passage in "Dazed And Confused": "C'mon, all you white folks—do the Crunge!"

23 June 1972, Sports Arena, San Diego, California (8:00 p.m.)

SETLIST NOT KNOWN BUT WOULD HAVE LIKELY BEEN:
Drone Intro / Immigrant Song / Heartbreaker / Out On The Tiles Intro / Black Dog / Since I've Been Loving You / Stairway To Heaven / Going To California / That's The Way / Tangerine / Bron-Y-Aur Stomp / Dazed And Confused / What Is And What Should Never Be / Moby Dick / Whole Lotta Love / Rock And Roll / Thank You / The Ocean

25 June 1972, the Forum, Los Angeles, California (7:30 p.m. The concert was professionally recorded on the Wally Heider Mobile Studio.)

SETLIST: Drone Intro / Immigrant Song / Heartbreaker / Over The Hills And Far Away / Out On The Tiles Intro / Black Dog / Since I've Been Loving You / Stairway To Heaven / Going To California / That's The Way / Tangerine / Bron-Y-Aur Stomp / Dazed And Confused (including Walter's Walk, The Crunge) / What Is And What Should Never Be / Dancing Days / Moby Dick / Whole Lotta Love (including Just A Little Bit, Everybody Needs Somebody To Love, Boogie Chillun', Let's Have A Party, Hello Mary Lou, Heartbreak Hotel, Slow Down, Going Down Slow, The Shape I'm In) / Rock And Roll / The Ocean / Louie Louie / Organ Solo / Thank You / Communication Breakdown / Bring It On Home

The following numbers from the LA Forum show were used on the live triple-CD *How the West Was Won* released on Atlantic Records in May 2003:

IMMIGRANT SONG (Mix of tonight with the Long Beach 27 March version)

HEARTBREAKER (Mix of tonight with the Long Beach 27 March version)

BLACK DOG (Mix of tonight with the Long Beach 27 March version)

OVER THE HILLS AND FAR AWAY (Mix of tonight with the Long Beach 27 March version)

THAT'S THE WAY

DAZED AND CONFUSED (including Walter's Walk, The Crunge)

MOBY DICK

WHOLE LOTTA LOVE (including Let's Have A Party)

THE OCEAN

BRING IT ON HOME

RECORDED BY: WALLY HEIDER MOBILE
ENGINEER: EDDIE KRAMER
PRODUCER: JIMMY PAGE

Led Zeppelin loved the West Coast. Plant tells the audience, "I think we're gonna have a good time. In fact, I can't remember coming here when it's been bad." This was one of those fabulous evenings where the stars aligned. If anyone wants to hear what Led Zeppelin were all about in concert, this is a good place to start. The band do not hold back. A surprise for the audience that night was the yet to be released "Over The Hills And Far Away," which was from the next album, *Houses of the Holy*. Plant tells the audience, "We'd like to try a number off the new album. We haven't really decided what we're gonna do at the end of it yet, so you'll have to bear with us! This is a thing called 'Over The Hills And Far Away,' which is always a good place to be." "Since I've Been Loving You" is incredible, but Page ended up picking the equally good version from Long Beach for the live CD. "Dancing Days" is clearly a number the band enjoyed playing, and tonight's version is amazing. Plant introduced it by giving fans some info on a possible title for the next Led Zeppelin album: "Here's a song off the new album, and it's not gonna be called *Led Zeppelin Five*, it's got

every possibility of being called *Burn That Candle*. This is a track from it. It's about summertime and good things." Led Zeppelin did not end up using the title, but years later bootleggers paraphrased Plant's title when they released the *Burn Like A Candle* bootleg. A near-thirty-minute version of the "Whole Lotta Love" medley floors the audience, who by now had become very animated, and it looked like problems could arise between the crowd and the police presence in the arena. Luckily the situation was calmed and the band played four encores before being called back for more by a frantic crowd. Plant jokingly remarked, "You don't even give us a chance to have a cigarette, do ya? I was thinking of the other variety actually!" They leave the crowd with "Communication Breakdown" and "Bring It On Home."

27 June 1972, Long Beach Arena, Long Beach, California (8:00 p.m. The concert was professionally recorded on the Wally Heider Mobile Studio.)

SETLIST: Drone Intro / Immigrant Song / Heartbreaker / Out On The Tiles Intro / Black Dog / Over The Hills And Far Away / Since I've Been Loving You / Stairway To Heaven / Going To California / That's The Way / Tangerine / Bron-Y-Aur Stomp / Dazed And Confused (including Walter's Walk, The Crunge) / What Is And What Should Never Be / Dancing Days / Moby Dick / Whole Lotta Love (including Just A Little Bit, Everybody Needs Somebody To Love, Boogie Chillun', Let's Have A Party, Hello Mary Lou, Blueberry Hill, Going Down Slow) / Rock And Roll

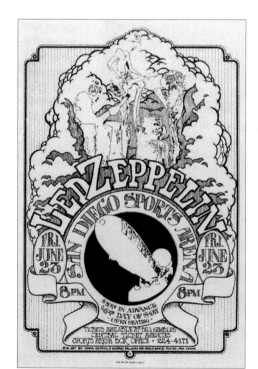

Press advert for Led Zeppelin's appearance at the Sports Arena in San Diego on 23 June 1972.

Led Zeppelin at the Forum in Los Angeles on 25 June 1972, where part of their live CD *How the West Was Won* was recorded. (Jeffrey Mayer/Getty Images)

The following numbers from the Long Beach Arena show were used on the live triple-CD *How the West Was Won* released on Atlantic Records in May 2003:

DRONE INTRO

IMMIGRANT SONG (Mix of tonight with the LA Forum 25 March version)

HEARTBREAKER (Mix of tonight with the LA Forum 25 March version)

BLACK DOG (Mix of tonight with the LA Forum 25 March version)

OVER THE HILLS AND FAR AWAY (Mix of tonight with the LA Forum 25 March version)

SINCE I'VE BEEN LOVING YOU

STAIRWAY TO HEAVEN (The Mellotron was taken from the Southampton University show on 22 January 1973.)

GOING TO CALIFORNIA

BRON-Y-AUR STOMP

WHAT IS AND WHAT SHOULD NEVER BE

BOOGIE CHILLUN', HELLO MARY LOU, GOING DOWN SLOW (from the Whole Lotta Love medley)

ROCK AND ROLL

RECORDED BY: WALLY HEIDER MOBILE
ENGINEER: EDDIE KRAMER
PRODUCER: JIMMY PAGE

Another high-energy show that was thankfully also recorded professionally. Both the Long Beach and LA shows perfectly demonstrate why Led Zeppelin were at their best live.

28 June 1972, Community Center, Tucson, Arizona

SETLIST: Drone Intro / Immigrant Song / Heartbreaker / Out On The Tiles Intro / Black Dog / Over The Hills And Far Away / Since I've Been Loving You / Stairway To Heaven / Bron-Y-Aur Stomp / Dazed And Confused (including Walter's Walk, The Crunge) / What Is And What Should Never Be / Dancing Days / Moby Dick / Whole Lotta Love (including Everybody Needs Somebody To Love, Boogie Chillun', Let's Have A Party, Stuck On You, Hello Mary Lou, Going Down Slow) / Rock And Roll

The 1972 US tour finale is just as spectacular as the others on this remarkable tour that almost went unnoticed in the music press.

LED ZEPPELIN SECOND JAPANESE TOUR

2 OCTOBER 1972–10 OCTOBER 1972

Japan is a nation of music lovers and any band that visits is warmly greeted by its people. As with the first time they went to Japan, various audience members recorded every show. In the digital age, the shows

Rare handbill for Led Zeppelin's appearance at the Budokan in Tokyo on 2 and 3 October 1972.

slowly started to come out on bootleg CD in Japan, which ultimately meant that most fans had the pleasure of hearing what they missed back in the US or Europe at the time.

Although the recently completed *Houses of the Holy* album would not be released until March 1973, the band previewed several numbers from it on tour. It is interesting to note that "The Song Remains The Same" was alternatively introduced in Japan as "Zep," "The Overture," and "The Campaign." In terms of instruments, the major change was John Paul Jones, who now used a M400 Mellotron onstage for "Stairway To Heaven," "The Rain Song," and "Thank You." The only drawback with the Mellotron was its tendency to go out of tune. Jimmy Page also started to use a Gibson EDS-1275 double-neck six and 12-string guitar for "Stairway To Heaven," "The Song Remains The Same," and "The Rain Song."

Halfway through the Japanese tour, the band took a few days off and visited Hong Kong. Arriving on 6 October, the band held a press conference to say that Peter Grant was holding talks with two local promoters with a view of playing some concerts there. Nothing came of the talks, and after doing some sightseeing, the band returned to Japan on 8 October to resume their tour.

Jimmy Page and Robert Plant decide to head off to India after the Japanese tour to do some recording with local Indian musicians. They ended up jamming with some local bands at a nightclub, as well as in the disco located in the basement of the Taj Mahal hotel in Bombay.

2 October 1972, Budokan, Tokyo, Japan (6:30 p.m.)

SETLIST: Rock And Roll / Over The Hills And Far Away / Out On The Tiles / Black Dog / Misty Mountain Hop / Since I've Been Loving You / Dancing Days / Bron-Y-Aur Stomp / The Song Remains The Same / The Rain Song / Dazed And Confused (including The Crunge) / Stairway To Heaven / Whole Lotta Love (including Just A Little Bit, Everybody Needs Somebody To Love, Boogie Chillun', My Baby Left Me, Killing Floor, I Can't Quit You Baby) / Heartbreaker / Immigrant Song / Communication Breakdown

The Japanese 1972 tour opened with two shows at Tokyo's legendary Budokan Hall that saw the band playing a new setlist, whose basic structure would form the basis for future tours by them. "Rock And Roll" from *Led Zeppelin IV* took over from "The

Rare handbill for Led Zeppelin's appearance at the Budokan in Tokyo on 2 and 3 October 1972.

Immigrant Song" as the new powerhouse opener. "The Song Remains The Same," which segued into "The Rain Song," was introduced tonight as "Zep." "Misty Mountain Top" led perfectly into "Since I've Been Loving You." Among the highlights at tonight's show are the improvisational "Dazed And Confused" and the lengthy "Whole Lotta Love" medley, which tonight included a rare outing of Howlin' Wolf's "Killing Floor." "Communication Breakdown" is the final encore tonight and is the only performance of the tour.

3 October 1972, Budokan, Tokyo, Japan (6:30 p.m.)

SETLIST: Rock And Roll / Out On The Tiles Intro / Black Dog / Over The Hills And Far Away / Misty Mountain Hop / Since I've Been Loving You / Dancing Days / Bron-Y-Aur Stomp / The Song Remains The Same / The Rain Song / Dazed And Confused (including The Crunge) / Stairway To Heaven / Whole Lotta Love (including Everybody Needs Somebody To Love, Boogie Chillun', Let's Have A Party, You Shook Me) / Immigrant Song / The Ocean

Good show, which in many ways is similar to the opening night. Plant attempts to speak to the crowd in poor English thinking that would be easier for them to understand him: "It is very good to be back. When group come to Tokyo—group have fun! We should clap you!" There are a few set changes. "Black Dog" swaps places with "Over The Hills And Far Away," and "Heartbreaker" and "Communication Breakdown" are dropped from the set. Tonight, "The Song Remains The Same" is introduced as being "The Overture." Plant informs the audience, "Last night it was called 'Zep,' tonight we'll call it—'The Overture.'"

4 October 1972, Festival Hall, Osaka, Japan (6:00 p.m.)

SETLIST: Rock And Roll / Out On The Tiles Intro / Black Dog / Over The Hills And Far Away / Misty Mountain Hop / Since I've Been Loving You / Dancing Days / Bron-Y-Aur Stomp / The Song Remains The Same / The Rain Song / Dazed And Confused (including San Francisco [instrumental], The Crunge) / Stairway To Heaven / Whole Lotta Love (including Everybody Needs Somebody To Love, Boogie Chillun', Got A Lot O' Livin' To Do, Let's Have A Party, You Shook Me, The Lemon Song) / Heartbreaker / Immigrant Song

The band are more laid-back and are perhaps starting to suffer from jetlag. Plant's voice seems to be struggling at times. Scott Mackenzie's "San Francisco (Be Sure To Wear Flowers In Your Hair)" is played instrumentally in the improv part of "Dazed And Confused" and would be developed further on later tours. Another Elvis rarity, "Got A Lot O' Livin' To Do," is played in the "Whole Lotta Love" medley tonight.

5 October 1972, Nagoya-Shi Kokaido, Nagoya, Japan (6:30 p.m.)

SETLIST: Rock And Roll / Out On The Tiles Intro / Black Dog / Misty Mountain Hop / Since I've Been Loving You / Dancing Days / Bron-Y-Aur Stomp / The Song Remains The Same / The Rain Song / Dazed And Confused (including The Crunge) / Stairway To Heaven / Whole Lotta Love (including Everybody Needs Somebody To Love, Boogie Chillun', Feel So Good, Let's Have A Party, You Shook Me) / Mellotron Solo (including Sakura Sakura) / Thank You

Another very good performance. "Over The Hills And Far Away" is dropped from the set tonight. "Thank You" is performed for the only time on this Japanese tour. It was preceded by a Mellotron solo from John Paul Jones, which included the traditional Japanese song "Sakura Sakura," which delighted the crowd.

9 October 1972, Festival Hall, Osaka, Japan (8:00 p.m.)

SETLIST: Rock And Roll / Out On The Tiles Intro / Black Dog / Over The Hills And Far Away / Misty Mountain Hop / Since I've Been Loving You / Dancing Days / The Song Remains The Same / The Rain Song / Dazed And Confused (including Down By The River, The Crunge) / Stairway To Heaven / Moby Dick / Whole Lotta Love (including Everybody Needs Somebody To Love, Something's Got A Hold On Me, Leave My Woman Alone, Lawdy Miss Clawdy, Heartbreak Hotel, Wear My Ring Around Your Neck, Going Down Slow) / Stand By Me / Immigrant Song

Robert Plant tells the crowd that they have just returned from Hong Kong. "We've just come back from Hong Kong. We went to Hong Kong for a few days and we're well knackered!" Tired or not, this is the best show of the tour, with a frenetic performance by the band, full of dynamics. Plant continues to have difficulty naming "The Song Remains The Same," which tonight he introduces by saying, "We can't find a name for it. We'll call it . . . The Campaign." A lengthy "Dazed And Confused" has snippets of Neil Young's "Down By The River" in the improvisational part of the number. One of the biggest surprises of the night was John Bonham playing "Moby Dick," the only time it was played on this Japanese tour. He was comically introduced as John "Samurai" Bonham. The other surprise was a unique stand-alone performance of Ben E King's "Stand By Me" as one of two encores.

10 October 1972, Kyoto Kaikan, Kyoto, Japan (6:30 p.m.)

SETLIST: Rock And Roll / Out On The Tiles Intro / Black Dog / Misty Mountain Hop / Since I've Been Loving You / The Song Remains The Same / The Rain Song / Dazed And Confused / Stairway To Heaven / Over The Hills And Far Away / Whole Lotta Love (including Everybody Needs Somebody To Love, Boogie Chillun', That's Alright Mama, Let's Jump The Broomstick, Going Down Slow) / Immigrant Song

The last show of their Japanese tour also turns out to be their shortest. A distinctly soulless performance by the band, who sound like they are simply going through the motions. Brenda Lee's "Let's Jump The Broomstick" makes a rare and unique appearance in the "Whole Lotta Love" medley.

16 October 1972, Slip Disc, Bombay, India (After their tour of Japan, Robert Plant and Jimmy Page decided to spend a few days in India to do some recording with local musicians. After the session, they headed off to the Slip Disc, a local music club. Western rock musicians had never visited the club, so their presence was quite unusual. They were coerced into playing a short thirty-minute set

at the Slip Disc club in Bombay backed by Jameel Shaikh from Atomic Forest on drums and Xerxes Gobhai from the Human Bondage on bass. Both these bands were hugely popular in India throughout the '70s. The Slip Disc's DJ, Arul Harris, recorded the event on a cassette direct from the in-house PA system, but the tape has sadly disappeared. Plant sang through a Fender Super-Reverb guitar amp belonging to Madhukar Dhas, lead singer with Atomic Forest. It must be said that individual memories of the event have faded over the years and everyone has slightly different recollections of the evening.)

66 Yes, I was there when Jimmy Page and Robert Plant came to Slip Disc all those years ago. Though I did only exchange a few words with them that day, I really didn't discuss what they were doing in Bombay, so am unaware of their recordings earlier that day. I do recall them mentioning that they were meeting and working with some Indian classical musicians in India. When we were able to persuade them to play a couple of tunes at the Slip Disc, I had to go home and bring my electric guitar, for there wasn't one there at the time, and I lived very close by. So Jimmy Page played on my beat-up old Hofner and I never wiped the fretboard after that! (Kidding!). The next day, the band I was playing in at the time, Atomic Forest, was setting up our gear and doing a sound-check at the Blow Up, another club close by, at the Taj Hotel, when Robert Plant walked in on us (they were staying at the Taj) and jammed on a couple of 12-bar blues patterns with us. That was exciting. I would've loved to have chatted more with them, particularly with Page because I admired him and had followed his playing from the Yardbirds days, but they were constantly mobbed by a lot of fans and I realized their manager, who was with them, was anxious and protective. Didn't realize then how much ink (and interest) would be spent on that incident so many years later. 99

—**FRED MANRICKS** (Guitarist with Atomic Forest)

66 Before we knew where we were, we were playing, and I was singing though a Fender amplifier about 15' x 12' and Page was playing on a Fujiyama guitar with piano strings on it, and we were playing 'Whole Lotta Love' but like the bass and the drummer fell apart and they just kept me and Page on stage blowing up with this whole club full of elated people who have never seen Western rock musicians, let alone heard them squawk though a 12" x 15" amplifier which must have come over with the Nazi infiltration or whatever it was. 99

—**ROBERT PLANT** (*Zigzag*, August 1973, number 33)

17 October 1972, Blow Up Club, Taj Hotel, Bombay, India (Plant and Page have an early hours jam with various local musicians.)

66 There was some kind of collaboration between the Human Bondage and Page and Plant. At the Slip Disc, they used Suresh's guitar. He said he was using piano strings. Ramzan, the boss at the Slip Disc, had a party for them and the Bondage. Some girls too— no names. We all jammed later at the Blow Up at about 4:30 a.m. Mainly Fred Manricks, Xerxes Gobhai, Plant, myself on drums, and Page. And maybe Babu Joseph. Plant autographed my drum head, but I later had to sell it to keep the wolf from the door! 99

—STEVE SIQUEIRA (Drummer with Brief Encounter, who were one of the house bands at the Blow Up club at the Taj Mahal hotel. He later joined Atomic Forest.)

LED ZEPPELIN SWISS TOUR

28 OCTOBER 1972–29 OCTOBER 1972

The band plays two warm-up shows in Montreux to get ready for their extensive forthcoming UK tour.

28 October 1972, Pavilion De Montreux, Montreux, Switzerland (6:30 p.m. Ray Charles and Three Dog Night share the bill this evening.)

SETLIST: Rock And Roll / Over The Hills And Far Away / Out On The Tiles Intro / Black Dog / Misty Mountain Hop / Since I've Been Loving You / Dancing Days / Bron-Y-Aur Stomp / The Song Remains The Same / The Rain Song / Dazed And Confused / Stairway To Heaven / Whole Lotta Love (including Let's Have A Party, I Need Your Love Tonight, Heartbreak Hotel) / Heartbreaker

29 October 1972, Pavilion De Montreux, Montreux, Switzerland (5:00 p.m. Ray Charles and Three Dog Night share the bill this evening.)

SETLIST NOT KNOWN BUT WOULD HAVE LIKELY BEEN: Rock And Roll / Over The Hills And Far Away / Out On The Tiles Intro / Black Dog / Misty Mountain Hop / Since I've Been Loving You / Dancing Days / Bron-Y-Aur Stomp / The Song Remains The Same / The Rain Song / Dazed And Confused / Stairway To Heaven / Whole Lotta Love / Heartbreaker

Melody Maker's Chris Charlesworth had this to say about the two Montreux shows: "The decision to play these 'warm-up' gigs augurs well for some Zep shows here soon. If they do come off, take my advice, go and see them. They will reshape your values about what is genuine and what is not. They just have to be the best heavy band this country has produced."

LED ZEPPELIN EIGHTH UK TOUR

30 NOVEMBER 1972–23 DECEMBER 1972

At the end of November 1972, the band embarked on their longest UK tour to date, consolidating their massive popularity throughout the country. Sadly, it would also be the last time to catch the band in small-to-medium venues in the UK as the era of large arenas loomed closer. The highly anticipated tour sold out in hours, with 110,000 tickets being snapped up by eager fans. In London, many keen fans spent a cold winter night queuing outside the Harlequin record shop in Oxford Street to buy their tickets for the two Alexandra Palace shows. The big change this time was a new policy welcoming the UK press to attend the shows, as they now realized that the lack in reports on the band may have been partially due to their previous anti-press attitude. The band rehearsed at the Rainbow Theatre in Finsbury Park before playing their first gig in Newcastle at the City Hall.

NOVEMBER 1972

30 November 1972, City Hall, Newcastle, Newcastle-Upon-Tyne (7:30 p.m.)

SETLIST: Rock And Roll / Over The Hills And Far Away / Out On The Tiles Intro / Black Dog / Misty Mountain Hop / Since I've Been Loving You / Dancing Days / Bron-Y-Aur Stomp / The Song Remains The Same / The Rain Song / Dazed And Confused / Stairway To Heaven / Whole Lotta Love (including Everybody Needs Somebody To Love, Boogie Chillun', Let's Have A Party, Going Down Slow) / Immigrant Song / Heartbreaker / Mellotron Solo / Thank You

The band is clearly nervous and as a result the performance is a little ragged in places. But the crowd seemed oblivious to that fact and cheered their heroes on. An uninspired "Dazed And Confused" is disappointing and shorter than later performances and probably sums up the overall show tonight. "Immigrant Song" and "Heartbreaker," both of which had previously opened their shows in past years, were performed as encores.

DECEMBER 1972

1 December 1972, City Hall, Newcastle, Tyne And Wear
(7:30 p.m.)

SETLIST (NOT COMPLETE): Rock And Roll / Over The Hills And Far Away / Out On The Tiles Intro / Black Dog / Misty Mountain Hop / Since I've Been Loving You / Dancing Days / Bron-Y-Aur Stomp / The Song Remains The Same / The Rain Song / Dazed And Confused / Stairway To Heaven / Whole Lotta Love (including Everybody Needs Somebody To Love, Boogie Chillun', I Need Your Love Tonight, For What It's Worth, Heartbreak Hotel)

A much better performance as first-night nerves had clearly dissipated. "Dazed And Confused" is back to its former glory and Page is in fine form.

3 December 1972, Greens Playhouse, Glasgow, Scotland
(8:00 p.m.)

SETLIST NOT KNOWN BUT WOULD HAVE LIKELY BEEN: Rock And Roll / Over The Hills And Far Away / Out On The Tiles Intro / Black Dog / Misty Mountain Hop / Since I've Been Loving You / Dancing Days / Bron-Yr-Aur Stomp / The Song Remains The Same / The Rain Song / Dazed And Confused / Stairway To Heaven / Whole Lotta Love / Heartbreaker

4 December 1972, Greens Playhouse, Glasgow, Scotland
(8:00 p.m.)

SETLIST: Rock And Roll / Over The Hills And Far Away / Out On The Tiles Intro / Black Dog / Misty Mountain Hop / Since I've Been Loving You / Dancing Days / Bron-Y-Aur Stomp / The Song Remains The Same / The Rain Song / Dazed And Confused (including Cowgirl In The Sand, The Crunge) / Stairway To Heaven / Whole Lotta Love (including Everybody Needs Somebody To Love, Boogie Chillun', Let's Have A Party, Stuck On You, I Can't Quit You Baby) / Heartbreaker / Mellotron Solo / Thank You

By the fourth night, the band are more comfortable and relaxed, playing to an exuberant Glasgow crowd who nearly bring the house down. "Dazed And Confused" was the key number at each show, in as much as it was the number allowing Page almost a free reign in which direction the jam section would head off in. Tonight was a good example of that, very inspired and improvisational.

7 December 1972, Hardrock Concert Theatre, Manchester, Greater Manchester (8:30 p.m.)

SETLIST NOT KNOWN BUT WOULD HAVE LIKELY BEEN: Rock And Roll / Over The Hills And Far Away / Out On The Tiles Intro / Black Dog / Misty Mountain Hop / Since I've Been Loving You / Dancing Days / Bron-Yr-Aur Stomp / The Song Remains The Same / The Rain Song / Dazed And Confused / Stairway To Heaven / Whole Lotta Love / Heartbreaker

8 December 1972, Hardrock Concert Theatre, Manchester, Greater Manchester (8:30 p.m.)

SETLIST: Rock And Roll / Over The Hills And Far Away / Out On The Tiles Intro / Black Dog / Misty Mountain Hop / Since I've Been Loving You / Dancing Days / Bron-Y-Aur Stomp / The Song Remains The Same / The Rain Song / Dazed And Confused / Stairway To Heaven / Whole Lotta Love (including Everybody Needs Somebody To Love, It's Your Thing, High Flyin' Mama, Boogie Chillun', Say Mama, Let's Have A Party, I Can't Quit You Baby, Going Down Slow, The Shape I'm In) / Heartbreaker / Immigrant Song / Communication Breakdown

11 December 1972, Capitol Theatre, Cardiff, Wales

SETLIST: Rock And Roll / Over The Hills And Far Away / Out On The Tiles Intro / Black Dog / Misty Mountain Hop / Since I've Been Loving You / Dancing Days / Bron-Y-Aur Stomp / The Song Remains The Same / The Rain Song / Dazed And Confused / Stairway To Heaven / Whole Lotta Love (including Blue Suede Shoes, Let's Have A Party, Boogie Chillun', Be-Bop-A-Lula) / Heartbreaker / The Ocean / Mellotron Solo / Thank You

Along with "Dazed And Confused," the "Whole Lotta Love" medley was the other constantly changing piece where the band would play any given rock 'n' roll or blues number that they felt like at the time. This is what makes bootleg recordings so enjoyable and help build up a picture of what Led Zeppelin were like in concert throughout the years. The *New Musical Express*'s Nick Kent attends the show in Cardiff and he files a good review: "The big surprise of the tour is Page, who's up

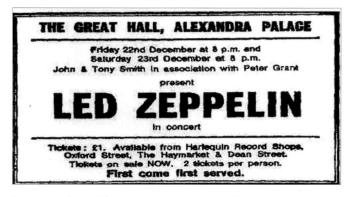

Press advert for Led Zeppelin's appearances at the Great Hall at Alexandra Palace in London on 22 and 23 December 1972.

and rockin' alongside the Lemon Squeeze Kid. While Plant tends to move in curves with the emphasis on the hips, Page seems more deranged, doing knee-bends, thrusting out and using the guitar neck as a bayonet. He even moves like a demon when playing his weighty twin-neck guitar. Flashing weird evil grins when the mood takes him."

12 December 1972, Capitol Theatre, Cardiff, Wales

SETLIST: Rock And Roll / Over The Hills And Far Away / Out On The Tiles Intro / Black Dog / Misty Mountain Hop / Since I've Been Loving You / Dancing Days / Bron-Y-Aur Stomp / The Song Remains The Same / The Rain Song / Dazed And Confused / Stairway To Heaven / Whole Lotta Love (including Let's Have A Party, Heartbreak Hotel, I Can't Quit You Baby, Going Down Slow, The Shape I'm In) / Old MacDonald Had A Farm (snippet) / Immigrant Song / Heartbreaker / Mellotron Solo / Thank You

16 December 1972, Birmingham Odeon, Birmingham, West Midlands (7:30 p.m.)

SETLIST: Rock And Roll / Over The Hills And Far Away / Out On The Tiles Intro / Black Dog / Misty Mountain Hop / Since I've Been Loving You / Dancing Days / Bron-Y-Aur Stomp / The Song Remains The Same / The Rain Song / Dazed And Confused / Stairway To Heaven / Whole Lotta Love (including Everybody Needs Somebody To Love, Boogie Chillun', Let's Have A Party, Heartbreak Hotel, I Can't Quit You Baby, The Shape I'm In) / Heartbreaker

17 December 1972, Birmingham Odeon, Birmingham, West Midlands (7:30 p.m.)

SETLIST NOT KNOWN BUT WOULD HAVE LIKELY BEEN:
Rock And Roll / Over The Hills And Far Away / Out On The Tiles Intro / Black Dog / Misty Mountain Hop / Since I've Been Loving You / Dancing Days / Bron-Yr-Aur Stomp / The Song Remains The Same / The Rain Song / Dazed And Confused / Stairway To Heaven / Whole Lotta Love / Heartbreaker

20 December 1972, Brighton Dome, Brighton, Sussex (7:30 p.m.)

SETLIST: Rock And Roll / Over The Hills And Far Away / Out On The Tiles Intro / Black Dog / Misty Mountain Hop / Since I've Been Loving You / Dancing Days / Bron-Y-Aur Stomp / The Song Remains The Same / The Rain Song / Dazed And Confused / Stairway To Heaven / Whole Lotta Love (including Just A Little Bit, Everybody Needs Somebody To Love, Boogie Chillun', Let's Have A Party, Jenny Jenny, Mystery Train, Heartbreak Hotel, Going Down Slow, I Can't Quit You Baby) / Heartbreaker / Christmas Tunes Medley

22 December 1972, the Great Hall, Alexandra Palace, London (8:00 p.m.)

SETLIST: Rock And Roll / Over The Hills And Far Away / Out On The Tiles Intro / Black Dog / Misty Mountain Hop / Since I've Been Loving You / Dancing Days / Bron-Y-Aur Stomp / The Song Remains The Same / The Rain Song / Dazed And Confused (including San Francisco) / Stairway To Heaven / Whole Lotta Love (including Everybody Needs Somebody To Love, Boogie Chillun', Let's Have A Party, Heartbreak Hotel, I Can't Quit You Baby, Going Down Slow, The Shape I'm In) / Immigrant Song / Heartbreaker / Mellotron Solo / Thank You

This was the second to last show of 1972 and what a great show it was, despite the venue's poor acoustics and soulless atmosphere. The venue could have held twice the number of people but fire regulations prevented that from happening. It was also a typical English winter night and the crowd took time to warm up, especially as they had queued in the cold waiting to enter the venue. The band does their best to warm up the crowd, who are sitting on a cold floor but are a little quiet. It had nothing to do with Led Zeppelin and their playing, which was nothing but joyous and tight. Plant remarked, "It's a bit warmer than the last gig we managed to pull off—that was at that notorious Wembley place. Well, I think we must install the warmth of our bodies into this place very quickly, before we all freeze! It's always the same—freezing!" Clearly the Christmas spirit was in the air and Plant commented before launching into "Dazed And Confused," "You lucky people. It's getting very close to Christmas and if we were all as straight as we used to be, we should be at the office party now." Page and Jones are in top form, as is Bonham, who thunders away on drums. The crowd eventually rose to their feet for "Stairway" and the remainder of the set. Their reward was the suitably titled "Thank You," which featured a longer than usual intro from John Paul Jones on organ.

23 December 1972, the Great Hall, Alexandra Palace, London (8:00 p.m.)

SETLIST: Rock And Roll / Over The Hills And Far Away / Out On The Tiles Intro / Black Dog / Misty Mountain Hop / Since I've Been Loving You / Dancing Days / Bron-Y-Aur Stomp / The Song Remains The Same / The Rain Song / Dazed And Confused (including San Francisco) / Stairway To Heaven / Whole Lotta Love (including The Crunge, Everybody Needs Somebody To Love, Boogie Chillun, Let's Have A Party, Heartbreak Hotel, I Can't Quit You Baby, Going Down Slow, The Shape I'm In) / Heartbreaker

The final show of 1972 and once again the crowd is low-key for the same reasons as the previous night. Led Zeppelin are not quite as on form as they were on 22 December, but nevertheless put on an exciting show. Plant is again feeling the Christmas spirit: "Good evening! A merry 23rd of December! Tonight we've got Father Christmas himself with us—John Bonham! Tin Pan Alley's answer to Father Christmas!" By "Stairway To Heaven," the crowd had warmed up and went crazy. So much so that Plant had to stop the song after a minute and tell the crowd, "Listen, I gotta tell you something before you all start shrieking about. First, it is the 23rd December and it is supposed to be the season of goodwill. So, if you all sit down, there's people at the back who prefer to sit, 'cos really it's one of the hardest numbers to do without a monkey house going crazy!" Once the crowd settled down, the band re-started the number. A persistent heckler who kept shouting out for Bonham to play "Moby Dick" had Plant answering him in his usual humorous way, "He doesn't do 'Moby Dick' anymore. He's writing a new one. It's called 'The Titanic.'" The evening ended with a heavy version of "Heartbreaker," which Plant dedicated to their friend Roy Harper. Chris Charlesworth reviewed the show for *Melody Maker* and confirmed what everyone already knew:

Alexandra Palace was never built to rock. The atmosphere inside this giant hall seemed cold and forbidding. It would have been possible to fit twice as many fans inside but fire regulations don't permit that so there was an abundance of space around the throng who crowded into the centre. And for those who didn't get a chance to get into the centre, seeing and hearing Zep was a chancy business. If you were tall you could probably see over a sea of heads, but even then there was a diminishing sound that flew up into the rafters and returned as a disjointed series of echoes. My guess is that only half of the fans heard the music as it should have been heard.

LED ZEPPELIN
HOUSES OF THE HOLY SESSIONS

MARCH 1972–JUNE 1972

JABBERWOCKY STUDIOS
Ilsington Farmhouse, Ilsington Road, Puddletown, Dorset

INITIAL REHEARSALS AND DEMO RECORDINGS

66 During the routining of 'The Song Remains the Same,' (then titled 'The Plumpton and Worcester Races'), the half-time vocal section was born and 'The Overture' shaped into a song. These rehearsals were done in Puddletown, on the River Piddle in Dorset. When we came to record this on 18th May 1972 on the Rolling Stones' mobile truck at Stargroves, the backing track of 'The Song Remains the Same' was played on a Fender electric 12-string, with Les Paul overdubs and standard tuning. 'The Rain Song' was in an unorthodox tuning on the six-string. 9

       —JIMMY PAGE (Recalling the rehearsals and later recording sessions on his website)

ROLLING STONES MOBILE STUDIO
Stargroves, East End, Newbury, Berkshire

THE SONG REMAINS THE SAME
THE RAIN SONG
OVER THE HILLS AND FAR AWAY
THE CRUNGE
D'YER MAK'ER

THE ROVER
BLACK COUNTRY WOMAN
WALTER'S WALK

THE EFFECT IS SHATTERING...

Press advert for the forthcoming *Houses of the Holy* album.

OLYMPIC SOUND STUDIOS
Studio 1, 117 Church Road,
Barnes, London, SW13

HOUSES OF THE HOLY, NO QUARTER, THE ROVER (mixing)

ISLAND STUDIOS
Studio 1, Basing Street, London W11

DANCING DAYS (overdubs)

ELECTRIC LADY STUDIOS
52 West Eighth Street, New York

FINAL MIXING AND OVERDUBS

Before making formal recordings, several of the songs proposed for the *Houses of the Holy* album had already been done as demos at Jimmy Page's and John Paul

Press advert for the forthcoming *Houses of the Holy* album.

Jones's respective home studios. The band then got together at an isolated farmhouse in Puddletown, Dorset, for album rehearsals. The farmhouse also had a studio, called Jabberwocky, which enabled them to do some group demos. Eddie Kramer and Led Zeppelin had had a falling out at Electric Lady Studios during the mixing of *Led Zeppelin III* after a row broke out over a Zeppelin roadie's dumping of food on the studio floor. It was all pretty silly, but tempers got frayed and the end result was that Eddie was not invited to work with the band on *Led Zeppelin IV* and Andy Johns got the job. However, when the time came to record *Houses of the Holy*, Page again asked Kramer to fly over to England and engineer the new sessions. He knew him well and liked his work. They were comfortable with each other. It must be said that at the time Page had been unhappy with Andy Johns due to the problems with the mixing of *Led Zeppelin IV* at Sunset Sound Studios.

Page had wanted to book Headley Grange again for *Houses of the Holy*, but it was not available. Instead, Mick Jagger's country mansion, Stargroves, was booked along with the Rolling Stones Mobile Studio truck. Eddie recalled that they were able to get several tracks down, which ended up being split between the *Houses of the Holy* and *Physical Graffiti* albums. One of the first tracks recorded was the epic "The Song Remains The Same" and when they had finished the complex session at around 5 a.m., the band wanted some fun. Plant suggested they record something in the vein of Ral Donner and Ricky Nelson. Jimmy started a chord sequence quickly followed by John Paul Jones, who laid down a solid blue-beat style bass line followed by Bonham on drums. They knew straight away that they had a new number here and that is how "D'yer Mak'er" was born. It was a great time for the band and that joy was reflected in the way they approached the sessions for numbers such as "D'yer Mak'er" and "The Crunge." "Black Country Woman" was recorded on the lawn outside the mansion, and as Robert Plant was singing, a jet plane passed overhead and can clearly be heard in the final recording. Plant wanted it left in. Overall, though, the band were not too happy with the acoustics at Stargroves compared with what they achieved at Headley Grange, and after a week or so relocated to Olympic Studios for further sessions and overdubs.

Some older songs, like "No Quarter," which had started as a very jazzy number during the rehearsals for the fourth album, was now more formalized over various takes. Dominated by John Paul Jones's keyboards, this would later go on to become a hugely popular live number, where it was expanded into a lengthy improvisational piece showcasing Page and Jones's instrumental skills. Each performance would be unique.

THE SONG REMAINS THE SAME (Jimmy Page / Robert Plant) Available on *Houses of the Holy* vinyl Atlantic US SD7255 released 18 March 1973 / Atlantic UK K 50014 released 26 March 1973 / released in remastered form on CD in October 2014 with bonus CD of alternate mixes and works in progress.

THE RAIN SONG (Jimmy Page / Robert Plant) Available on *Houses of the Holy* vinyl Atlantic US SD7255 released 18 March 1973 / Atlantic UK K 50014 released 26 March 1973 / released in remastered form on CD in October 2014 with bonus CD of alternate mixes and works in progress.

DANCING DAYS (Jimmy Page / Robert Plant) Available on *Houses of the Holy* vinyl Atlantic US SD7255 released 18 March 1973 / Atlantic UK K 50014 released 26 March 1973 / released in remastered form on CD in October 2014 with bonus CD of alternate mixes and works in progress.

BLACK COUNTRY WOMAN (Jimmy Page / Robert Plant) Available on *Physical Graffiti* vinyl Swan Song US SS-2-200 released 24 February November 1975 / Swan Song UK SSK 89400 released 24 February 1975.

THE ROVER (Jimmy Page / Robert Plant) Available on *Physical Graffiti* vinyl Swan Song US SS-2-200 released 24 February November 1975 / Swan Song UK SSK 89400 released 24 February 1975

D'YER MAK'ER (John Bonham / John Paul Jones / Jimmy Page / Robert Plant) Available on *Houses of the Holy* vinyl Atlantic US SD7255 released 18 March 1973 / Atlantic UK K 50014 released 26 March 1973 / released in remastered form on CD in October 2014 with bonus CD of alternate mixes and works in progress.

HOUSES OF THE HOLY (Jimmy Page / Robert Plant) Available on *Physical Graffiti* vinyl Swan Song US SS-2-200 released 24 February November 1975 / Swan Song UK SSK 89400 released 24 February 1975

WALTER'S WALK (Jimmy Page / Robert Plant) Available on *Coda* on vinyl US Swan Song 90051-1 released 19 November 1982 / Swan Song UK A 0051 released 22 November 1982 / on remastered CD Swan Song 7567-92444-2 released 1994.

THE OCEAN (John Bonham / John Paul Jones / Jimmy Page / Robert Plant) Available on *Houses of the Holy* vinyl Atlantic US SD7255 released 18 March 1973 / Atlantic UK K 50014 released 26 March 1973 / released in remastered form on CD in October 2014 with bonus CD of alternate mixes and works in progress.

THE CRUNGE (John Bonham / John Paul Jones / Jimmy Page / Robert Plant) Available on *Houses of the Holy* vinyl Atlantic US SD7255 released 18 March 1973 / Atlantic UK K 50014 released 26 March 1973 / released in remastered form on CD in October 2014 with bonus CD of alternate mixes and works in progress.

OVER THE HILLS AND FAR AWAY (Jimmy Page / Robert Plant) Available on *Houses of the Holy* vinyl Atlantic US SD7255 released 18 March 1973 / Atlantic UK K 50014 released 26 March 1973 / released in remastered form on CD in October 2014 with bonus CD of alternate mixes and works in progress.

NO QUARTER (Jimmy Page / Robert Plant / John Paul Jones) Available on *Houses of the Holy* vinyl Atlantic US SD7255 released 18 March 1973 / Atlantic UK K 50014 released 26 March 1973 / released in remastered form on CD in October 2014 with bonus CD of alternate mixes and works in progress.

PRODUCER: JIMMY PAGE
ENGINEER: EDDIE KRAMER, ANDY JOHNS, GEORGE CHKIANTZ, ROD THEAR

1972 GUEST RECORDING SESSIONS

John Bonham Guest Session for Jimmy Stevens

MORGAN STUDIOS
169–171 High Road, Willesden Green, London NW10

APRIL 1972

John Bonham joins Jimmy Stevens for sessions for his album, which was released in 1973.

DON'T FREAK ME OUT (Jimmy Stevens) Released September 1972 in the UK on the *Don't Freak Me Out* album, Atlantic K 40414 / released January 1973 in the US on *Paid My Dues* album RSO SO 872.

JIMMY STEVENS: PIANO, VOCALS
ALAN KENDALL: GUITAR
JOHN BONHAM: DRUMS
MAURICE GIBB: ORGAN, BASS

IS IT ME BABE (Jimmy Stevens) Released September 1972 in the UK on the *Don't Freak Me Out* album, Atlantic K 40414 / released January 1973 in the US on *Paid My Dues* album RSO SO 872.

> JIMMY STEVENS: PIANO, VOCALS
> ALAN KENDALL: GUITAR
> JOHN BONHAM: DRUMS
> MAURICE GIBB: BASS
> PRODUCER: MAURICE GIBB
> ENGINEER: ROBIN BLACK

Jam Session with Black Sabbath

RECORD PLANT
West Third Street, Los Angeles, California

26 JUNE 1972

Tony Iommi has mentioned in interviews that he has tapes of Led Zeppelin dropping in on Black Sabbath's *IV* album sessions. Some reports say it was just a jam, others say that a number called "Supernaut" was recorded. Either way, tapes are in existence.

JULY 1972

JIMMY PAGE GUEST SESSION FOR ROY HARPER

ABBEY ROAD STUDIOS
3 Abbey Road, London NW8

BANK OF THE DEAD (Roy Harper) Available as A-side of 7-inch single "Harvest" HAR5059 released October 1972 / album *Lifemask* Harvest SHVL808 released February 1973.

> ROY HARPER: VOCALS, ACOUSTIC GUITAR
> JIMMY PAGE: ELECTRIC GUITAR
> TONY CARR: DRUMS

THE LORD'S PRAYER (Roy Harper) album *Lifemask* Harvest SHVL808 released February 1973

> ROY HARPER: VOCALS, ACOUSTIC GUITAR, BASS, SYNTHESIZER
> JIMMY PAGE: ELECTRIC GUITAR
> TONY CARR: BONGOS
> STEVE BROUGHTON: BONGOS
> BRIAN DAVISON: DRUMS
> BRIAN ODGERS: BASS
> RAY WARLEIGH: FLUTE
> PRODUCER: PETER JENNER
> ENGINEER: JOHN LECKIE

JIMMY PAGE AND ROBERT PLANT BOMBAY SESSION

EMI RECORDING STUDIOS
Universal Insurance Building,
Sir Pherozeshah Mehta Road,
Fort, Bombay 400001, India

16 OCTOBER 1972

FRIENDS (Several takes made, but none considered good enough for a master)

FOUR STICKS (Several takes made, but none considered good enough for a master)

A fascinating session that has somehow attained legendary status over the years. On a visit to Bombay in October 1972, Jimmy Page and Robert Plant wanted to explore the possibility of recording some music with Indian musicians. Jimmy knew Ravi Shankar and asked him for some help in recruiting musicians. He suggested a former student of his, Vijay Raghav Rao, who at the time was the main composer and arranger of soundtracks for Films Division of India. He was highly respected and a multi-talented musician. Rao arranged for some of his musicians such as Sultan Khan, who played the sarangi, to come into the studio, and the result is the so called Bombay Sessions," a brave attempt to fuse together two completely different styles of music. The two songs they chose to record were "Friends" and "Four Sticks," both of which lent themselves to Indian music tunings. There were definitely some communication breakdowns between East and West at the session, both verbally and musically and nothing more developed from this one-off experimental recording. Despite what Robert Plant and Jimmy Page have said in interviews over the years, they did not record with the Bombay Symphony Orchestra. Both numbers were finally given an official release in July 2015 on the companion disc of *Coda*.

❝ I did some recording with some of the Bombay Symphony Orchestra in Bombay, and afterwards we went to this silly club. I mean Bombay, unless you have been to Bombay you can't really imagine the stink, and the wretchedness, and the impoverished state of things. The upper class Indian, and the Anglo-Indian—the people that are clamouring and grabbing the Western idea—it's going to fall right through their fingers, because it is going to collapse before they get a good grip of it; but they will grab it enough to open a discotheque in sunny Bombay where you have got six million people sleeping on the street every night, and taxis just driving over them by accident when they don't see them in the dark, and you have a disco around the corner called the Slipped-Disc [It was actually called the Slip Disc]. **"**

—**ROBERT PLANT** (Recalling the Bombay trip in an interview in *ZigZag* magazine in 1973)

" We did some recording in India . . . yes, they have got studios there just about. It turned out to be experimental recording, but it needn't have been. Unfortunately, the Indian Government have got a lot of trouble with the black market, so there is no lawful importation of modern equipment. What's left are remnants of everything that has been brought in. **"**

—**ROBERT PLANT** (Interviewed by Caroline Boucher, *Disc and Music Echo*, 21 April 1973)

1973:
The World in Their Hands

11

A very busy year promoting their *Houses of the Holy* album, which started with the second part of their eighth UK tour in Sheffield on 2 January ending in Preston on 30 January. This was followed by a Scandinavian and European tour before heading back to the US for a lengthy two-part tour.

Houses of the Holy received a mixed reception from the press at the time, with most of the criticism being aimed at "The Crunge" and "D'yer Mak'er" and "The Rain Song." Yet from *Led Zeppelin III* onward, the band had worked hard to prove to people that they had more to offer than a few heavy riffs. *Rolling Stone* magazine in particular was still keeping up their anti-Zeppelin campaign with a vitriolic review:

> "The Crunge" reproduces James Brown so faithfully that it's every bit as boring, repetitive and clichéd as "Good Foot." Yakety-yak guitar, boom-boom bass, astoundingly idiotic lyrics ("When she walks, she walks, and when she talks, she talks"). "D'yer Mak'er" is even worse, a pathetic stab at reggae that would probably get the Zep laughed off the island if they bothered playing it in Jamaica. Like every other band following rock's latest fad, Led Zeppelin shows little understanding of what reggae is about—"D'yer Mak'er" is obnoxiously heavy-handed and totally devoid of the native form's sensibilities.

Perhaps more surprisingly, back in the UK, *Melody Maker*'s Chris Welch also gave a harsh commentary in the newspaper, stating that the album had "frankly dull material like the 'Rain Song,'" which was just one of his many criticisms. The detractors kind of missed the point. It showed the lighter side of Led Zeppelin. It showed they had a sense of humor. How can you fail

to smile when you hear "D'yer Mak'er"? Neither John Paul Jones nor John Bonham were particularly keen on "D'yer Mak'er," but Plant loved it and wanted it on the album. He even pushed for it to be a single, which would have been a good idea at the time. As for "The Crunge," it was a good foot-tapping, hip-wiggling slice of funk that found its origins in the jams of "Dazed And Confused" as well as "Whole Lotta Love." It was Led Zeppelin paying homage to James Brown. When you look at the numbers found on *Houses of the Holy*, you will notice that every number was played at one time or another during the 1972 to 1975 tours. Not bad for an album that was badly criticized at the time of release.

Plant in particular took offense at the criticism as he wrote all the lyrics for the album, which he felt gave it some consistency. Page was more philosophical about the reviews as he told *NME* in April 1973, "I don't really care. It doesn't really make any difference. I'm deaf to the album now because we made it such a long time ago, but I know there's some good stuff there." People also wanted to know why it had taken so much time for their last two albums to be released. Page answered in the same *NME* interview, "I'm sure people aren't aware of this, I'm sure they think we sit on our arses all day long, but we don't. All I know is I haven't stopped for three years. . . . I haven't had a holiday since the group started. There's just so much going on as far as studio work, or rehearsing, or touring. Then again, there's songwriting as well."

By 1973 glam rock had taken over the charts in the US and UK. David Bowie had *Aladdin Sane*, Alice Cooper had *Billion Dollar Babies,* and Elton John had *Don't Shoot Me I'm Only the Piano Player.* As a result, it took slightly longer for Led Zeppelin's *Houses of the Holy* album to reach the coveted number-one position. Atlantic released "Over The Hills And Far Away" backed with "Dancing Days" as a way of promoting the album and US tour.

The 1973 US tour had the benefit of a new visually exciting light show and a more glamorous wardrobe for the band befitting their stature and the changing times in fashion. Page told *Circus* magazine in November 1973 about his feelings about the light show: "It was something new for us, we've had lighting before on other occasions when people have just turned up and done it, but we've never really planned anything. This time we routined all the lighting before we came over. It took about three or four days rehearsing to get it really tight, so that it augmented our set. It was really well-received, and sometimes you found the lighting effects getting applause on their own, which is really good. It made more of a show that way." He also went on to talk about all the preparations that went into the tour: "We rehearsed the whole show at this place called Old Street Studios in England. It's an abandoned film studio. You see, it's very difficult to get rehearsal rooms in England because of the noise. Anywhere, for any group, it's the same story. Every group is up against the same problem. But the studio we used is a nice place that nobody uses for films anymore. The film business is a bit crummy, I suppose. Everybody makes cheap budget films and they don't use those places anymore."

Peter Grant wanted this tour to show the world that Led Zeppelin were the biggest act of the day. To that end he let it be known that the US tour, their longest ever, would be grossing $5 million. The fans certainly got value for money with concerts lasting a minimum of three hours along with a new spectacular light show. Also new was the Starship, a Boeing 720B passenger jet that had been customized for private hire and used by the band to get them from city to city on the tour.

LED ZEPPELIN EIGHTH UK TOUR
2 JANUARY 1973–30 JANUARY 1973

2 January 1973, City Hall, Sheffield, Yorkshire (8:00 p.m.)

SETLIST: Rock And Roll / Over The Hills And Far Away / Black Dog / Misty Mountain Hop / Since I've Been Loving You / Dancing Days / The Song Remains The Same / Rain Song / Dazed And Confused (including San Francisco) / Stairway To Heaven / Whole Lotta Love (including Everybody Needs Someone To Love, Boogie Chillun', Let's Have A Party, Heartbreak Hotel, I Can't Quit You Baby, Going Down Slow), Heartbreaker

High-energy show that is let down by Robert Plant's voice. Let's face it, he never dressed appropriately for the winter, and seemingly was always coming down with colds or throat infections, which resulted in shows being canceled. This time he caught the flu after his car broke down on the way to the gig, and he had to hitch a ride in the cold. He really should have had his mum on tour with him to remind him to dress properly for the cold weather! Surprisingly they did not cancel the gig but dropped "Bron-Y-Aur Stomp" from the set. One advantage of poor old Planty being under the weather meant that Page and the band could extend their jams to save his vocal chords. The crowds were treated to an extended and adventurous "Dazed And Confused" with some amazing guitar work from Page. The next two shows were canceled to allow Plant some recuperation time.

66 Guitarist Jimmy Page was the best thing that ever happened to the group. The ex-Yardbird (but don't keep reminding him of that) is the jewel encrusted throne of this particular treasure. His playing is majestic and tireless, the guitar slung low at the hip. Sometimes it's a double-neck at other times he revives old memories by dragging a bow across the strings to create sounds that are a mixture of a Wurlitzer being tortured and a huge monster in extreme pain. 99

—*SHEFFIELD STAR* (Review on 3 January, 1973)

3 January 1973, Grand Hall, Preston Guildhall, Lancashire (8:00 p.m. Canceled due to Robert Plant being unwell with flu. The show is rescheduled for 30 January.)

4 January 1973, St. George's Hall, Bradford, Yorkshire (Canceled due to Robert Plant coming down with flu. The show is rescheduled for 18 January.)

7 January 1973, New Theatre, Oxford, Oxfordshire

SETLIST: Rock And Roll / Over The Hills And Far Away / Out On The Tiles Intro / Black Dog / Misty Mountain Hop / Since I've Been Loving You / Dancing Days / Bron-Y-Aur Stomp / The Song Remains The Same / The Rain Song / Dazed And Confused (including San Francisco) / Stairway To Heaven / Whole Lotta Love (including Everybody Needs Somebody To Love) / Heartbreaker

Robert Plant's voice is still suffering from the aftermath of flu. The rest of the band are in fine form and fans are happy with the show.

14 January 1973, Empire Theatre, Liverpool, Merseyside (7:00 p.m.)

SETLIST: Rock And Roll / Over The Hills And Far Away / Out On The Tiles Intro / Black Dog / Misty Mountain Hop / Since I've Been Loving You / Dancing Days / Bron Y Aur Stomp / The Song Remains The Same / The Rain Song / Dazed And Confused (including San Francisco) / Stairway To Heaven / Whole Lotta Love (including Everybody Needs Somebody To Love, Boogie Chillun', Baby I Don't Care, Let's Have A Party, I Can't Quit You Baby, Stones In My Passway, Going Down Slow, The Shape I'm In) / Heartbreaker / The Ocean

Robert Plant is struggling with his voice still. Otherwise an excellent show with the band firing on all cylinders. Page is exceptional on "Dazed And Confused."

15 January 1973, Trentham Gardens Ballroom, Stoke on Trent, Staffordshire (8:00 p.m.)

SETLIST: Rock And Roll / Over The Hills And Far Away / Out On The Tiles Intro / Black Dog / Misty Mountain Hop / Since I've Been Loving You / Dancing Days / Bron-Y-Aur Stomp / The Song Remains The Same / The Rain Song / Dazed And Confused (including San Francisco) / Stairway To Heaven / Whole Lotta Love (including Voodoo Chile [Slight Return], Just A Little Bit, Everybody Needs Somebody To Love, Boogie Chillun', Baby I Don't Care, Let's Have A Party) / Heartbreaker

Great show and Plant's voice is starting to recover. A fabulous "Whole Lotta Love" tonight with fragments of Jimi Hendrix's "Voodoo Chile" added. The year 1973 was shaping up to be one of the best for Led Zeppelin.

16 January 1973, King's Hall, Aberystwyth, Wales (7:30 p.m.)

SETLIST NOT KNOWN BUT WOULD HAVE LIKELY BEEN: Rock And Roll / Over The Hills And Far Away / Out On The Tiles Intro / Black Dog / Misty Mountain Hop / Since I've Been Loving You / Dancing Days / Bron-Y-Aur Stomp / The Song Remains The Same / The Rain Song / Dazed And Confused / Stairway To Heaven / Whole Lotta Love / Heartbreaker

18 January 1973, St. George's Hall, Bradford, Yorkshire (7:30 p.m. Rescheduled from 4 January 1973.)

SETLIST: Rock And Roll / Over The Hills And Far Away / Out On The Tiles Intro / Black Dog / Misty Mountain Hop / Since I've Been Loving You / Dancing Days / Bron-Y-Aur Stomp / The Song Remains The Same / The Rain Song / Dazed And

Confused (including San Francisco) / Stairway To Heaven / Whole Lotta Love (including Just A Little Bit, Everybody Needs Somebody To Love, Boogie Chillun', Baby I Don't Care, Blue Suede Shoes, Let's Have A Party, I Can't Quit You Baby, Stones In My Passway, Going Down Slow) / Heartbreaker / Immigrant Song

21 January 1973, Gaumont Theatre, Southampton, Hampshire (8:00 p.m.)

SETLIST NOT KNOWN BUT WOULD HAVE LIKELY BEEN: Rock And Roll / Over The Hills And Far Away / Out On The Tiles Intro / Black Dog / Misty Mountain Hop / Since I've Been Loving You / Dancing Days / Bron-Y-Aur Stomp / The Song Remains The Same / The Rain Song / Dazed And Confused / Stairway To Heaven / Whole Lotta Love / Heartbreaker

22 January 1973, the Old Refectory, Student Union Building, Southampton University, Southampton, Hampshire (8:00 p.m. This intimate concert was recorded using the Rolling Stones Mobile Studio with a view of releasing a live album later in the year. It never happened, and when various live concerts were digitized for the *How the West Was Won* release, Southampton was rejected in favor of the Los

Poster advertising Led Zeppelin's appearance at the small Old Refectory at Southampton University.

149

Angeles and Long Beach shows, although the Mellotron from "Stairway To Heaven" was used from this show as a substitute for the Hammond organ from 1972.)

SETLIST: Rock And Roll / Over The Hills And Far Away / Out On The Tiles Intro / Black Dog / Misty Mountain Hop / Since I've Been Loving You / Dancing Days / The Song Remains The Same / The Rain Song / Dazed And Confused (including San Francisco) / Stairway To Heaven / Whole Lotta Love (including Everybody Needs Somebody To Love, Boogie Chillun', Baby I Don't Care, Let's Have A Party, I Can't Quit You Baby, Stones In My Passway, Going Down Slow) / Heartbreaker / Mellotron Solo / Thank You / How Many More Times (including The Hunter) / Communication Breakdown

❝ University of Southampton: For two days, Southampton was blessed with the presence of the world's top rock band. On the first, it was the turn of the town, with Led Zeppelin blowing the minds of 2 1/2 thousand fans at the Gaumont. But the next day, our heroes came to the Union, and played to us in the Black Hole of Calcutta, or Old Refectory as it is sometimes known. The Gaumont concert had been pretty tight, but not as good as I would have expected from a band that had been on the road for the past two months. But all my doubts were dispelled the next day. I don't know if it was the atmosphere, or just being right at the front of the audience, but the Old Refectory concert was just fantastic. There's no other word for it. They enjoyed it, and we enjoyed it, and that's what matters. As usual, they were a bit slow to warm up—in fact 'Rock and Roll,' their opening number, was very rough, and the next, 'The Lady,' a track from LZ 5, wasn't much better either. 'Black Dog' followed, and the audience joined in instantly on the ah-ah, aaah chorus, whereas it took the Gaumont audience a couple of goes to get it right. LZ were beginning to cook. 'Misty Mountain Hop' and 'Since I've Been Loving You' came next, giving John Paul Jones a chance to show us his dexterity on the keyboards. Until 'Loving You' Jimmy Page had been churning out the riffs to make the numbers boogie, but on this one he gave us his first solo, very fast one second, and slow the next, getting everything out of each note. Just to watch him moving his fingers up and down the fretboard made very me very envious—he must have some natural gift. 'Dancing Days' and 'The Song Remains the Same,' two new numbers were the next, the first, a straight rocker very much in the LZ style, and the second, a longish complex number, starting and finishing with some low tempo-melodic guitar playing, and connected with a heavy rocking bit and a superb organ solo from John Paul Jones. The next number Robert Plant dedicated to the manager of the Gaumont—'Dazed and Confused.' This, a track from their first album, was used as a showpiece for Page's long guitar solo. For part of this he used a big bow, and the highlight was when he hit the strings and got the note to echo back to him. When he'd been playing for about 10

minutes, the rest of the band joined in and stretched the number out to about 25 minutes. Next was a beam of clear, white light, as Plant called 'Stairway to Heaven.' Plant's vocals, which had been a bit hidden by Page's guitar before, came through beautifully, the song gradually rising to the peak of that superb rocking ending. That got everybody on their feet, and shouting for every LZ number under the sun. But Plant asked everybody to shut up for a moment, while he told them about his visit to the toilet. On the bog wall, he saw this name—Alan Whitehead and this next number was dedicated to him. It was 'Whole Lotta Love.' The band went into a number of old rock and roll tunes, then 'I Can't Quit You Babe,' and back to 'Whole Lotta Love—for a tremendous climax to the show. A few minutes clapping, and they were back to give us 'Heartbreaker,' and then 'Thank You,' featuring John Paul Jones with a long organ intro, and back for a third time. Plant said how much they'd enjoyed the gig, and then they proceeded play 'How Many More Times,' the first time they'd done it for 2 1/2 years. But you'd never have known it, it was so tight. Straight into 'Communication Breakdown,' and then it was all over. See you again, they said, and a very knackered goodnight. This was the only gig they recorded on the whole tour because they reckon the acoustics of the old Refectory are good—and after the show Jimmy Page said there would probably be a live album later this year. Let's hope so— it'd be a great souvenir of a great show.❞

—**JOHN CLARK** (Review in the *Wessex Scene*)

25 January 1973, Music Hall, Aberdeen, Scotland (7:30 p.m.)

SETLIST: Rock And Roll / Over The Hills And Far Away / Out On The Tiles Intro / Black Dog / Misty Mountain Hop / Since I've Been Loving You / Dancing Days / Bron-Y-Aur Stomp / The Song Remains The Same / The Rain Song / Dazed And Confused (including San Francisco) / Stairway To Heaven / Whole Lotta Love (including Everybody Needs Somebody To Love, Boogie Chillun', Baby I Don't Care, Let's Have A Party, I Can't Quit You Baby, Going Down Slow, The Shape I'm In) / Heartbreaker / What Is And What Should Never Be / The Ocean

27 January 1973, Caird Hall, Dundee, Scotland (7:30 p.m.)

SETLIST: Rock And Roll / Over The Hills And Far Away / Out On The Tiles Intro / Black Dog / Misty Mountain Hop / Since I've Been Loving You / Dancing Days / Bron-Y-Aur Stomp / The Song Remains The Same / The Rain Song / Dazed And Confused / Stairway To Heaven / Whole Lotta Love (including Everybody Needs Somebody To Love, Boogie Chillun', Baby I Don't Care, Let's Have A Party, I Can't Quit You Baby, Going Down Slow, The Shape I'm In, Ramble On) / Heartbreaker / Communication Breakdown

28 January 1973, King's Theatre, Edinburgh, Scotland

SETLIST: Rock And Roll / Over The Hills And Far Away / Out On The Tiles Intro / Black Dog / Misty Mountain Hop / Since I've Been Loving You / Dancing Days / Bron-Y-Aur Stomp / The Song Remains The Same / The Rain Song / Dazed And Confused (including San Francisco) / Stairway To Heaven / Whole Lotta Love (medley) / Heartbreaker / Mellotron Solo / Thank You

❝ Any thoughts of Led Zeppelin's stamina giving out at the King's Theatre Edinburgh, on Sunday, on what was the second to last gig of their exhausting two month British tour, were promptly dispelled before a full and running-over fanatical crowd of 1,472. The band flexed their muscles with 'Black Dog' and two and a half hours later were still bombarding their audience with 'Heartbreaker' and 'Thank You' for encores. Most of the stuff was familiar. Nothing from Jimmy Page was more dynamic than 'Dazed And Confused' where his bowed work held the faithful spellbound. ❞

　　—JOHN ANDERSON (Review in *Sounds*, 3 February 1973)

30 January 1973, Grand Hall, Preston Guildhall, Preston, Lancashire (Rescheduled from 3 January 1973)

SETLIST: Rock And Roll / Over The Hills And Far Away / Out On The Tiles Intro / Black Dog / Misty Mountain Hop / Since I've Been Loving You / Dancing Days / Bron-Y-Aur Stomp / The Song Remains The Same / The Rain Song / Dazed And Confused (including San Francisco) / Stairway To Heaven / Whole Lotta Love (including Everybody Needs Somebody To Love, Boogie Chillun', Baby I Don't Care, Let's Have A Party, I Can't Quit You Baby, Going Down Slow) / Heartbreaker

LED ZEPPELIN SCANDINAVIAN TOUR
2 MARCH 1973–6 MARCH 1972

2 March 1973, K. B. Hallen, Copenhagen, Denmark (8:00 p.m.)

SETLIST NOT KNOWN BUT WOULD HAVE LIKELY BEEN: Rock And Roll / Over The Hills And Far Away / Out On The Tiles Intro / Black Dog / Misty Mountain Hop / Since I've Been Loving You / Dancing Days / Bron-Y-Aur Stomp / The Song Remains The Same / The Rain Song / Dazed And Confused / Stairway To Heaven / Whole Lotta Love / Heartbreaker

4 March 1973, Scandinavium Arena, Gothenburg, Sweden (7:30 p.m.)

SETLIST NOT KNOWN BUT WOULD HAVE LIKELY BEEN: Rock And Roll / Over The Hills And Far Away / Out On The Tiles Intro / Black Dog / Misty Mountain Hop / Since I've Been Loving You / Dancing Days / Bron-Y-Aur Stomp / The Song Remains The Same / The Rain Song / Dazed And Confused / Stairway To Heaven / Whole Lotta Love / Heartbreaker

6 March 1973, Kungliga Tennishallen, Stockholm, Sweden (8:00 p.m.)

SETLIST: Rock And Roll / Over The Hills And Far Away / Out On The Tiles Intro / Black Dog / Misty Mountain Hop / Since I've Been Loving You / Dancing Days / Bron-Y-Aur Stomp / The Song Remains The Same / The Rain Song / Dazed And Confused (including San Francisco) / Stairway To Heaven / Whole Lotta Love (including Everybody Needs Somebody To Love, In The Light, Boogie Woogie, Baby I Don't Care, Let's Have A Party, I Can't Quit You Baby, Going Down Slow) / Heartbreaker / The Ocean

LED ZEPPELIN THIRD EUROPEAN TOUR
14 MARCH 1973–2 APRIL 1973

14 March 1973, Messehalle, Nuremberg, Germany (8:00 p.m.)

SETLIST: Rock And Roll / Over The Hills And Far Away / Out On The Tiles Intro / Black Dog / Misty Mountain Hop / Since I've Been Loving You / Dancing Days / Bron-Y-Aur Stomp / The Song Remains The Same / The Rain Song / Dazed And Confused (including San Francisco) / Stairway To Heaven / Whole Lotta Love (including Everybody Needs Somebody To Love, Boogie Chillun', Baby I Don't Care, Let's Have A Party, I Can't Quit You Baby, The Lemon Song) / Heartbreaker

16 March 1973, Stadhalle, Vienna, Austria (7:00 p.m.)

SETLIST: Rock And Roll / Over The Hills And Far Away / Out On The Tiles Intro / Black Dog / Misty Mountain Hop / Since I've Been Loving You / Dancing Days / Bron-Y-Aur Stomp / The Song Remains The Same / The Rain Song / Dazed And Confused (including San Francisco) / Stairway To Heaven / Whole Lotta Love (including Boogie Chillun', Baby I Don't Care, Let's Have A Party, I Can't Quit You Baby, Killing Floor) / Heartbreaker

Judging from the tapes that have circulated from the various shows, the band were clearly on form for the 1973 concerts and Vienna stands out as one of the

Poster advertising Led Zeppelin's 1973 German tour.

Press advert for Led Zeppelin's 1973 German tour.

best. Everyone is in top form and Page once again shows he is a masterful player. The band are also in good humor as Plant shows sympathy for an ailing John Paul Jones: "Mr. Jones has colic—must be careful! So all your spiritual feelings must go straight to Mr. Jones's stomach." Plant also mischievously announces "Dancing Days" as a song "about little schoolgirls, not too young mind you, and my love for them. . . . Remember what happened to Jerry Lee Lewis, I think I'll take it easy!"

17 March 1973, Olympiahalle, Munich, Germany (8:00 p.m.)

SETLIST: Rock And Roll / Over The Hills And Far Away / Out On The Tiles Intro / Black Dog / Misty Mountain Hop / Since I've Been Loving You / Dancing Days / Bron-Y-Aur Stomp / The Song Remains The Same / The Rain Song / Dazed And Confused (including San Francisco) / Stairway To Heaven / Whole Lotta Love (including Everybody Needs Somebody To Love, Boogie Chillun', Baby I Don't Care, Let's Have A Party, I Can't Quit You Baby, The Lemon Song, Going Down Slow) / Heartbreaker

Two amazing shows, one after the other, perfectly exemplified the consistency of the band's performances at this time. Munich was every bit as exciting as the Vienna concert and there is no reason to doubt that other shows were of a similar standard. The group dynamics are simply exceptional and the performances are stunning. "Dazed And Confused" and "Whole Lotta Love" are epic. Page's playing is phenomenal and Plant's vocals are really strong. As always the bottom end provided by the impeccable rhythm section are rock solid. They could do no wrong at this period.

19 March 1973, Deutschlandhalle, Berlin, Germany (8:00 p.m.)

SETLIST: Rock And Roll / Over The Hills And Far Away / Out On The Tiles Intro / Black Dog / Misty Mountain Hop / Since I've Been Loving You / Dancing Days / Bron-Y-Aur Stomp / The Song Remains The Same / The Rain Song / Dazed And Confused (including San Francisco, Superstition) / Stairway To Heaven / Whole Lotta Love (including Everybody Needs Somebody To Love, Boogie Chillun', Baby I Don't Care, Let's Have A Party, I Can't Quit You Baby, The Lemon Song)

Plant's vocals are starting to show signs of strain, which is not surprising, but does not detract from yet another incredible performance by a band who are on top of their game. The acoustic section is also well received by fans and allows everyone to have a breather. Plant is in a playful mood and adds a few lines from the Beatles "Please Please Me" after a perfect "Stairway To Heaven." Nice to hear him enjoying singing "Stairway" at this period, when he still put in a lot of feeling into the song. When you compare the late '70s and 1980 renditions, you can tell he'd had enough of singing it and had no passion left for it. "Whole Lotta Love" is introduced as "a song that really invokes the finest physical feelings for a person, without violence, it's usually called sex. Tomorrow we go to Hamburg … to the Reeperbahn where things are beautiful all the time. This one is for the Eros Centre."

21 March 1973, Musikhalle, Hamburg, Germany (8:00 p.m.)

SETLIST: Rock And Roll / Over The Hills And Far Away / Out On The Tiles Intro / Black Dog / Misty Mountain Hop / Since I've Been Loving You / Dancing Days / Bron-Y-Aur Stomp / The Song Remains The Same / The Rain Song / Dazed And Confused (including San Francisco) / Stairway To Heaven / Whole Lotta Love (including The Crunge, Everybody Needs Somebody To Love, D'yer Mak'er, Boogie Chillun', Baby I Don't Care, Let's Have A Party, I Can't Quit You Baby, The Lemon Song) / The Ocean

As you would have imagined, the show is yet another incredible performance culminating in one of the best "Whole Lotta Love" medleys from the tour. Bonham has been driving Page along for most of the show. Page reciprocates and the intuitive playing between the two musicians is a joy to hear. All in all, a classic performance.

22 March 1973, Grugahalle, Essen, Germany (8:00 p.m.)

SETLIST: Rock And Roll / Over The Hills And Far Away / Out On The Tiles Intro / Black Dog / Misty Mountain Hop / Since I've Been Loving You / Dancing Days / Bron-Y-Aur Stomp / The Song Remains The Same / The Rain Song / Dazed And Confused (including San Francisco, snippets of Walter's Walk) / Stairway To Heaven / Whole Lotta Love (including Everybody Needs Somebody To Love, Turn On Your Love Light, Boogie Chillun', Baby I Don't Care, Let's Have A Party, I Can't Quit You Baby, The Lemon Song) / Heartbreaker

Better known as a venue for the Rockpalast television shows, Led Zeppelin invade the Grugahalle in Essen for a heavy and dynamic concert. Despite Page having technical issues with his Les Paul guitar, his playing is simply out of this world on "Since I've Been Loving You" and "Dazed And Confused." Plant continues to make humorous inappropriate claims about "Dancing Days" by announcing that the song is about "the innocent love of little schoolgirls and my perversion toward it. We love little schoolgirls, fourteen . . . or fifteen!" The "Whole Lotta Love" medley is always inspired due to the improvisational nature of the number, and tonight's version is full of endlessly flowing solos. The passion emanating from the stage is breathtaking.

24 March 1973, Ortenauhalle, Offenburg, Germany (8:00 p.m.)

SETLIST: Rock And Roll / Over The Hills And Far Away / Out On The Tiles Intro / Black Dog / Misty Mountain Hop / Since I've Been Loving You / Bron-Y-Aur Stomp / The Song Remains The Same / The Rain Song / Dazed And Confused (including San Francisco) / Stairway To Heaven / Whole Lotta Love (including Cold Sweat, Everybody Needs Somebody To Love, Boogie Chillun', Baby I Don't Care, Let's Have A Party, I Can't Quit You Baby, The Lemon Song) / Heartbreaker

Several fans say that the last date of the German tour was the best. In truth, it is very subjective as pretty much every date up to this point has been spectacular for one reason or another. So it comes down to personal choice really. Either way, tonight's show is yet another incredible concert with some amazing solos by Page. The whole concert performance is slick and polished, but still kept fresh by new improvisations. The good vibes that had been felt up to this point would soon disappear on their next venue in France.

26 March 1973, Palais Des Sports, Lyon, France (8:30 p.m. An eventful show, and not for the right reasons. A member of the public managed to run onstage before being unceremoniously thrown back into the crowd, and the power cut off during "Stairway To Heaven." They resumed as soon as the power was restored, but unbeknownst to the band, who were onstage at the time, several hundred people broke down the venue doors, resulting in many fights breaking out, and several people having to be taken to hospital as a result.)

SETLIST: Rock And Roll / Over The Hills And Far Away / Out On The Tiles Intro / Black Dog / Misty Mountain Hop / Since I've Been Loving You / Dancing Days / Bron-Y-Aur Stomp / The Song Remains The Same / The Rain Song / Dazed And Confused (including San Francisco) / Stairway To Heaven / Whole Lotta Love (including Everybody Needs Somebody To Love, Boogie Chillun', Baby I Don't Care, Let's Have A Party, I Can't Quit You Baby, The Lemon Song) / Heartbreaker

27 March 1973, Parc Des Expositions, Nancy, France (8:00 p.m.)

SETLIST: Rock And Roll / Over The Hills And Far Away / Out On The Tiles Intro / Black Dog / Misty Mountain Hop / Since I've Been Loving You / The Song Remains The Same / The Rain Song / Dazed And Confused (including San Francisco) / Stairway To Heaven / Whole Lotta Love (including Everybody Needs Somebody To Love, Boogie Chillun', Baby I Don't Care, Let's Have A Party, I Can't Quit You Baby)

The band are unable to enter the venue and cannot even get a message to the promoter. Eventually Richard Cole and Peter Grant have to break the backstage doors down to gain access. The band have a major falling out with the promoter over the incident. On top of that, the backstage area had no facilities to speak of, and worse, their security was not guaranteed. As a result the concert this evening is cut short and the next two shows are canceled. Given the circumstances, the show is not particularly good, but John Bonham is ferocious on drums.

The following morning, Robert Plant gives his view to *Best* magazine about the Nancy concert and the cancellation of the next two shows, and possibly the whole French tour:

We are leaving this morning and heading back to England. We are sincerely sorry to have to cancel the rest of our French tour, but after the serious incidents over the last two days it would be impossible for us to continue. In Lyon there were fights, several thousand people broke down the doors of the venue when we were playing, causing several injuries. On the other hand, in Nancy we had to break down the doors because nobody wanted to open the backstage area to us. The whole organization of these shows was appalling. At this stage we do not even know if we will play the Paris show. We will come back on Saturday to check everything out ourselves and make sure everything is in order with good security for the public and us. We feel sorry to let down our fans in Lille and Marseille, but it would be impossible to play in such circumstances.

29 March 1973, Palais Des Sports, Marseilles, France (Canceled due to problems with local promoters.)

31 March 1973, Palais Des Sports, Lilles, France (Canceled due to problems with local promoters.)

APRIL 1973

1 April 1973, Centre Sportif, Ile Des Vannes, Saint-Ouen, Paris, France (6:00 p.m.)

SETLIST: Rock And Roll / Over The Hills And Far Away / Out On The Tiles Intro / Black Dog / Misty Mountain Hop / Since I've Been Loving You / Dancing Days / Bron-Y-Aur Stomp / The Song Remains The Same / The Rain Song / Dazed And Confused (including San Francisco) / Stairway To Heaven / Whole Lotta Love (including Everybody Needs Somebody To Love, Boogie Chillun', Baby I Don't Care, Let's Have A Party, I Can't Quit You Baby, The Lemon Song)

It seems that all the problems that had occurred at the earlier French shows had now been resolved and Led Zeppelin are welcomed to the stage with wild applause. The band are in great form with playing that is tight and concise in its execution. Both Jimmy Page and John Bonham, who were a little laid-back at the previous French shows, were now in full swing in Paris and put in a spectacular performance.

2 April 1973, Centre Sportif, Ile Des Vannes, Saint-Ouen, Paris, France (9:00 p.m.)

SETLIST: Rock And Roll / Over The Hills And Far Away / Out On The Tiles Intro / Black Dog / Misty Mountain Hop / Since I've Been Loving You / Dancing Days / Bron-Yr-Aur Stomp / That's The Way / The Song Remains The Same / The Rain Song / Dazed And Confused (including San Francisco) / Stairway To Heaven / Whole Lotta Love (including Everybody Needs Somebody To Love, Going Down, Boogie Chillun', Baby I Don't Care) / Heartbreaker

Another great show. In fact, aside from the early French shows, the 1973 European tour saw the band playing at the height of their powers. At this show Plant has some monitor problems, but it does not prevent this from being another stellar performance by the whole band. The common thread throughout this tour is how much Page and Bonham were so locked into each other musically, and it is a joy to hear that on the recordings that circulate from these shows.

Led Zeppelin live on
their 1973 US tour.
(Jeffrey Mayer/Getty Images)

LED ZEPPELIN
NINTH US TOUR

4 MAY 1973–29 JULY 1973

After a month away from the road, the band are a little
loose despite rehearsing and it will take them a few
shows before they are back to top form again.

4 May 1973, Atlanta Stadium, Atlanta, Georgia (8:00 p.m.)

SETLIST NOT KNOWN BUT WOULD LIKELY HAVE INCLUDED:
Rock And Roll / Celebration Day / Bring It On Home Intro /
Black Dog / Over The Hills And Far Away / Misty Mountain
Hop / Since I've Been Loving You / No Quarter / The Song
Remains The Same / The Rain Song / Dazed And Confused
(including San Francisco) / Stairway To Heaven / Moby Dick /
Heartbreaker / Whole Lotta Love (including Boogie Chillun') /
The Ocean / Communication Breakdown

¡ ONLY GEORGIA APPEARANCE !

CONCERTS WEST
PRESENTS

LED
ZEPPELIN

FRI. MAY 4-8 P.M.
ATLANTA STADIUM

FESTIVAL SEATING — ON THE GRASS!!!
IN THE STANDS!!!

ADVANCE $5.00; DOOR $6.00 Tickets now on sale at the Atlanta
Stadium and all Ticketron Locations: (Rich's, Sears, Jim Salle's,
Mother's, Eller's, Trust Co. of Ga.)

GET YOUR TICKETS NOW!

Poster advertising
Led Zeppelin's 1973
German tour.

Press advert for Led Zeppelin's 1973 US tour.

Led Zeppelin start their US tour in style by setting a record for the largest concert crowd in Georgia's history, drawing nearly 40,000 fans to the Fulton County Stadium, earning them a reported $246,000 in ticket sales

5 May 1973, Tampa Stadium, Tampa, Florida (8:00 p.m.)

SETLIST: Rock And Roll / Celebration Day / Bring It On Home Intro / Black Dog / Over The Hills And Far Away / Misty Mountain Hop / Since I've Been Loving You / No Quarter / The Song Remains The Same / The Rain Song / Dazed And Confused (including San Francisco) / Stairway To Heaven / Moby Dick / Heartbreaker / Whole Lotta Love (including Boogie Chillun') / The Ocean / Communication Breakdown

Only the second date of the tour and another record-breaking evening. They broke the attendance record with a crowd numbering 56,800, earning the band an estimated $309,000 gross. Adverts were placed in several newspapers throughout the US the following day proudly declaring that Led Zeppelin's Tampa

concert was the largest audience for a single artist performance in history. Plant triumphantly welcomes the massive crowd by telling them, "Hello. It seems between us we've done something nobody's ever done before . . . and that's fantastic!" The setlist was changed from the European tour, but the overall performance varied between good and sloppy. The band are struggling to get back into the groove they had found back on the European tour.

7 May 1973, Memorial Coliseum, Jacksonville, Florida (8:00 p.m.)

SETLIST NOT KNOWN BUT WOULD HAVE INCLUDED: Rock And Roll / Celebration Day / Bring It On Home Intro / Black Dog / Over The Hills And Far Away / Misty Mountain Hop / Since I've Been Loving You / No Quarter / The Song Remains The Same / The Rain Song / Dazed And Confused (including San Francisco) / Stairway To Heaven / Moby Dick / Heartbreaker / Whole Lotta Love (including Boogie Chillun')

66 There were no intermissions, no waiting, no tuning up, no bullshit. Just music. Just gorgeous Rock 'n' Roll music at its most desperate. The performance was so incredibly timed that you never were completely aware of just exactly when one number started and another began, and the acoustic numbers and the ballads blended in perfectly with the rockers. You couldn't help but beg for more. It was impossible to be a part of that experience and not watch, and listen with a total awe. We don't have bands like this, you know. YOU don't have bands like this . . . but you do have Led Zeppelin. And they know what they have. They know the high they can achieve, and they're here again—their album is number one in the country and they're going to go and play everywhere and celebrate Rock 'n' Roll. God bless them! 99

—**LISA ROBINSON** (Review in *Disc*, May 1973)

Press advert celebrating the largest ever audience to attend a concert, Led Zeppelin's concert at Tampa Stadium, Florida, on 5 May 1973.

10 May 1973, Memorial Coliseum, University of Alabama, Tuscaloosa, Alabama (8:00 p.m.)

SETLIST NOT KNOWN BUT WOULD HAVE INCLUDED:
Rock And Roll / Celebration Day / Bring It On Home Intro / Black Dog / Over The Hills And Far Away / Misty Mountain Hop / Since I've Been Loving You / No Quarter / The Song Remains The Same / The Rain Song / Dazed And Confused (including San Francisco) / Stairway To Heaven / Moby Dick / Heartbreaker / Whole Lotta Love (including Boogie Chillun')

11 May 1973, St. Louis Arena, St. Louis, Missouri (8:00 p.m.)

SETLIST NOT KNOWN BUT WOULD HAVE INCLUDED:
Rock And Roll / Celebration Day / Bring It On Home Intro / Black Dog / Over The Hills And Far Away / Misty Mountain Hop / Since I've Been Loving You / No Quarter / The Song Remains The Same / The Rain Song / Dazed And Confused (including San Francisco) / Stairway To Heaven / Moby Dick / Heartbreaker / Whole Lotta Love (including Boogie Chillun')

13 May 1973, Municipal Auditorium, Mobile, Alabama (8:00 p.m.)

SETLIST: Rock And Roll / Celebration Day / Bring It On Home Intro / Black Dog / Over The Hills And Far Away / Misty Mountain Hop / Since I've Been Loving You / No Quarter / The Song Remains The Same / The Rain Song / Dazed And Confused (including San Francisco) / Stairway To Heaven / Moby Dick / Heartbreaker / Whole Lotta Love (including Boogie Chillun')

The band have got their mojo back and the performance tonight has all the fluidity and dynamics found on the European tour. The beauty of Page's playing, especially

Press advert for Led Zeppelin's appearance at Memorial Coliseum, Tuscaloosa, Alabama.

at this time, was the different approaches he made to his playing every night. His solos and passages would vary from song to song at every show, which is why so many fans are desperate to collect as many live concerts by the band as they can. The problem with going into the unknown like that meant that you opened yourself up to making mistakes, especially if the rest of the band are not tuned in to what you are doing. It kept the band on its toes and the music fresh and vibrant on a daily basis. The particular highlights tonight were a beautifully arranged "Over The Hills And Far Away," a mighty version of "Misty Mountain Hop," which led into "Since I've Been Loving You" with a superb solo by Page. "Dazed And Confused" was especially epic and the final encore, "Whole Lotta Love," had the crowd screaming for more.

14 May 1973, Municipal Auditorium, New Orleans, Louisiana (8:00 p.m.)

SETLIST: Rock And Roll / Celebration Day / Bring It On Home Intro / Black Dog / Over The Hills And Far Away / Misty Mountain Hop / Since I've Been Loving You / No Quarter / The Song Remains The Same / The Rain Song / Dazed And Confused (including San Francisco, Crossroads) / Stairway To Heaven / Moby Dick / Heartbreaker / Whole Lotta Love (including The Crunge, Boogie Chillun') / Communication Breakdown (including Cold Sweat)

A fun night with Plant in humorous mood. The house lights were turned on at regular intervals as the authorities wanted to monitor the crowds. Plant tells them, "We've got to get these house lights down. It's pretty pointless us bringing our own lights, if we've got these things going on. Mr. Cole, can you take your dress off and get these lights turned down please?" The best line of the evening, though, has to be reserved for the introduction to "Moby Dick": "I once heard a song called 'The Witch Queen Of New Orleans.' Well, tonight, I'm pleased to announce that John Bonham is 'The Drag Queen Of New Orleans!'" Page was momentarily caught out and missed his cue because he was laughing so much. Musically the show is stunning with heavy versions of "Dazed And Confused" along with "Heartbreaker" and "Whole Lotta Love." The crowd was treated to an extra encore of "Communication Breakdown."

16 May 1973, Sam Houston Coliseum, Houston, Texas (8:00 p.m.)

Jimmy Page onstage at Memorial Auditorium in Dallas, Texas, on 18 May 1973. (Photo by Carl Dunn)

SETLIST: Rock And Roll / Celebration Day / Bring It On Home Intro / Black Dog / Over The Hills And Far Away / Misty Mountain Hop / Since I've Been Loving You / No Quarter / The Song Remains The Same / The Rain Song / Dazed And Confused (including San Francisco) / Stairway To Heaven / Moby Dick / Heartbreaker / Whole Lotta Love (including Boogie Chillun')

Sound issues cause several problems tonight and the playing suffers as a result. John Paul Jones supposedly has two broken ribs as Plant informed the crowd, "John Paul Jones has got two fractured ribs and he's still managing to stand. I think that's fantastic! That's not really fun at all . . . we thought he'd got the clap."

19 May 1973, Tarrant County Arena, Fort Worth, Texas (8:00 p.m.)

SETLIST: Rock And Roll / Celebration Day / Bring It On Home Intro / Black Dog / Over The Hills And Far Away / Misty Mountain Hop / Since I've Been Loving You / No Quarter / The Song Remains The Same / The Rain Song / Dazed And Confused (including San Francisco) / Stairway To Heaven / Moby Dick / Heartbreaker / Whole Lotta Love (including Boogie Chillun')

Another fab show, although Plant is irked that the audience did not join in on "Black Dog," "What happened to you on the Ah!—Ah!? You were jerking off. What happened?" "Dazed And Confused" is dedicated to a groupie friend of the band's, "The Butter Queen—Fantastic! Do you know what it's like? Far out . . . she is too much really."

SETLIST: Rock And Roll / Celebration Day / Bring It On Home Intro / Black Dog / Over The Hills And Far Away / Misty Mountain Hop / Since I've Been Loving You / No Quarter / The Song Remains The Same / The Rain Song / Dazed And Confused (including San Francisco) / Stairway To Heaven / Moby Dick / Heartbreaker / Whole Lotta Love (including Going Down, Boogie Chillun') / Communication Breakdown

One of those tight but loose shows. Plant introduces "Misty Mountain Hop" as a song "about what happens when you take a stroll on a Sunday afternoon with a packet of cigarette papers and some good grass and . . . I'm not advocating it . . . just telling the story!"

18 May 1973, Memorial Auditorium, Dallas, Texas (8:00 p.m.)

John Paul Jones proudly wears his Alabama State Troupers T-shirt during Led Zeppelin's concert at the Tarrant County Convention Center in Fort Worth, Texas, on 19 May 1973. The Alabama State Troupers were a great band featuring Don Nix in the line-up. Clearly John Paul Jones was a fan. (Photo by Carl Dunn)

John Bonham onstage at Memorial Auditorium in Dallas, Texas, on 18 May 1973. (Photo by Carl Dunn)

22 May 1973, Hemisfair Arena, San Antonio, Texas (7:00 p.m.)

SETLIST: Rock And Roll / Celebration Day / Bring It On Home Intro / Black Dog / Over The Hills And Far Away / Misty Mountain Hop / Since I've Been Loving You / No Quarter / The Song Remains The Same / The Rain Song / Dazed And Confused (including San Francisco) / Stairway To Heaven / Moby Dick / Heartbreaker / Whole Lotta Love (including Boogie Chillun') / The Ocean

23 May 1973, University Arena, Albuquerque, New Mexico

SETLIST: Rock And Roll / Celebration Day / Bring It On Home Intro / Black Dog / Over The Hills And Far Away / Misty Mountain Hop / Since I've Been Loving You / No Quarter / The Song Remains The Same / The Rain Song / Dazed And Confused (including San Francisco) / Stairway To Heaven / Moby Dick / Heartbreaker / Whole Lotta Love (including Boogie Chillun')

66 There was nothing intellectual or sophisticated about the music the group played. It was just heavy, make-your-adrenalin-start-pumping rhythm mixed with familiar Zeppelin style vocal. And as the crowd's reaction attested, there is nothing wrong with that. The feeling one got was that the group pounded their instruments for all they were worth. And if the lead singer's dance-like gyrations were a bit too slick and the drummer a bit too uncontrolled, the concert proved for the umpteenth time that Jimmy knows his guitar. 99
—*ALBUQUERQUE JOURNAL* (Review on 24 May 1973)

25 May 1973, Denver Coliseum, Denver, Colorado (8:00 p.m.)

SETLIST: Rock And Roll / Celebration Day / Bring It On Home Intro / Black Dog / Over The Hills And Far Away / Misty Mountain Hop / Since I've Been Loving You / No Quarter / The Song Remains The Same / The Rain Song / Dazed And Confused (including San Francisco) / Stairway To Heaven / Moby Dick / Heartbreaker / Whole Lotta Love (including Boogie Chillun') / Communication Breakdown

Jimmy Page onstage at Hemisfair Arena in San Antonio, Texas, on 22 May 1973. (Photo by Carl Dunn)

26 May 1973, the Salt Palace, Salt Lake City, Utah (8:00 p.m.)

SETLIST: Rock And Roll / Celebration Day / Bring It On Home Intro / Black Dog / Over The Hills And Far Away / Misty Mountain Hop / Since I've Been Loving You / No Quarter / The Song Remains The Same / The Rain Song / Dazed And Confused / Stairway To Heaven / Moby Dick / Heartbreaker / Whole Lotta Love / Communication Breakdown

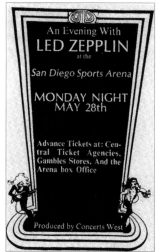

An Evening With
LED ZEPPLIN
at the
San Diego Sports Arena

MONDAY NIGHT
MAY 28th

Advance Tickets at: Central Ticket Agencies, Gambles Stores, And the Arena box Office

Produced by Concerts West

Press advert for Led Zeppelin's appearance at San Diego Sports Arena on 28 May 1973.

Page is having a slightly off night, but the show as a whole is still great. After a string break in "Over The Hills And Far Away," John Paul Jones starts playing "Georgia On My Mind" while the guitar is restrung. Sadly, it only lasted for a few verses before Page is ready to continue with the regular set. Plant informs the crowd that "The night club is now closed down and we can get on with the concert...."

28 May 1973, Sports Arena, San Diego, California (8:00 p.m.)

SETLIST: Rock And Roll / Celebration Day / Bring It On Home Intro / Black Dog / Over The Hills And Far Away / Misty Mountain Hop / Since I've Been Loving You / No Quarter / The Song Remains The Same / The Rain Song / Dazed And Confused / Moby Dick / Stairway To Heaven / Heartbreaker / Whole Lotta Love (including The Crunge, Honey Bee, Boogie Chillun', Going Down) / The Ocean

66 Accompanied by John Bonham, John Paul Jones and Robert Plant in combinations on vocals, guitar, drums and keyboards, Page shone as the supreme master of the heavy fuzz box guitar riff. His evolution from the early days of British rock with the Yardbirds appears complete. Nobody, but nobody plays guitar like Page. His is the final force, the power of a riff. A few solos Monday night were too excessive, but the sheer driving power of most over-shadowed any inadequacies. 99

—CAROL OLTEN (Review in San Diego Union, May 1973)

"Moby Dick" is played after "Dazed And Confused" tonight, and the highlight is a raunchy version of the "Whole Lotta Love" medley, which in parts is reminiscent of versions from 1970. California loved Led Zeppelin and vice versa.

30 May 1973, the Forum, Los Angeles, California (8:00 p.m. The show had to be canceled as a result of Jimmy Page spraining his hand on a wire fence at Los Angeles Airport when signing autographs the day before. He needed a few days to recuperate. The show was rescheduled to 3 June 1973.)

31 May 1973, the Forum, Los Angeles, California (8:00 p.m.)

SETLIST: Rock And Roll / Celebration Day / Bring It On Home Intro / Black Dog / Over The Hills And Far Away / Misty Mountain Hop / Since I've Been Loving You / No Quarter / The Song Remains The Same / The Rain Song / Dazed And Confused (including San Francisco) / Stairway To Heaven / Moby Dick / Heartbreaker / Whole Lotta Love (including The Crunge, Honey Bee, Just A Little Bit, Boogie Chillun') / The Ocean / Communication Breakdown

Page recovered sufficiently to play tonight's show, which also happened to be John Bonham's birthday. It has gone on to become a legendary bootleg called, not surprisingly, "Bonzo's Birthday Party." Plant informs the crowd, "Today, John Bonham is twenty-one!—he's always twenty-one! I've known the birthday baby for about fifteen years . . . and he's been a regular bastard all the time!" Plant then leads the crowd through a few verses of "Happy Birthday" for Bonzo! The energy levels are high and the band put in a super-charged performance. Page was having to put ice on his sprained left finger at regular intervals during the show, but when listening to the concert, it is not obvious as his playing is spectacular.

JUNE 1973

2 June 1973, Kezar Stadium, San Francisco, California (Doors open at 10:00 a.m. and the band take the stage at 3:30 p.m. introduced by Bill Graham. Support from Roy Harper, the Tubes, and Lee Michaels.)

Led Zeppelin onstage at the Forum in Los Angeles on 31 May 1973. (Rex)

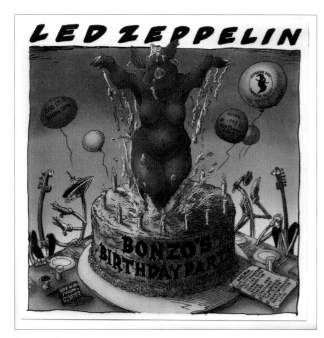

Cover art for *Bonzo's Birthday Party*, one of the most famous bootleg covers in Led Zeppelin bootleg history. Recorded at the LA Forum on 31 May 1973 on the occasion of Jon Bonham's 25th birthday.

Front cover of a bootleg album recording of Led Zeppelin at Kezar Stadium in San Francisco on 2 June 1973.

SETLIST: Rock And Roll / Celebration Day / Bring It On Home Intro / Black Dog / Over The Hills And Far Away / Misty Mountain Hop / Since I've Been Loving You / No Quarter / The Song Remains The Same / The Rain Song / Dazed And Confused (including San Francisco) / Stairway To Heaven / Moby Dick / Heartbreaker / Whole Lotta Love (including The Crunge, Just A Little Bit, Boogie Chillun') / Communication Breakdown / The Ocean

Jimmy Page's injury has now completely healed and the band put in a great performance in front of a huge open-air crowd. Fans rank this as one of their all-time favorite shows. Plant is finding it strange playing so early in the day and in daylight: "As we've been awake for a total of about two and a half hours, it doesn't really seem that we should be doing what we're doing right now, but I believe there's something to do with lightness and darkness, so we'll try a bit of lightness! Actually, I feel quite healthy. It's quite an amazing feat to be awake in the daylight. . . . Now, if I was cool I should put the mike in the stand and clear off until everything works right. Well, thank you very much for a great show, we'll see you in five minutes." The last comment was due to a technical fault that was soon sorted and the band continued without further interruptions. When Led Zeppelin are on form the highlights are often "Dazed And Confused" and "No Quarter," due to the improvisational nature of the

songs, and this show is no exception. Bonham, Jones, and Page are so locked-in with each other on these two numbers and they are strong contenders for the best versions of the 1973 tour. "Dazed And Confused" is especially spectacular tonight, full of complex rhythms laid down by John Bonham and John Paul Jones. Before playing their first encore, "Communication Breakdown," Plant announces, "We've just had a bit of water confrontation with a few people round the back, which keeps our name alive. We'd like to thank Bill Graham for getting it all together. That man has given you more music in eight years than anybody else has ever given music anywhere else in the world. I'm glad you realize it. . . . I hope he pays for us to get home now . . . he never pays us any money!"

3 June 1973, the Forum, Los Angeles, California (8:00 p.m. Rescheduled from 30 May 1973.)

SETLIST: Rock And Roll / Celebration Day / Bring It On Home Intro / Black Dog / Over The Hills And Far Away / Misty Mountain Hop / Since I've Been Loving You / No Quarter / The Song Remains The Same / The Rain Song / Dazed And Confused (including San Francisco) / Stairway To Heaven / Moby Dick / Heartbreaker / Whole Lotta Love (including The Crunge, Going Down, I'm A Man, The Hunter, Boogie Chillun') / The Ocean / Communication Breakdown / Organ Solo / Thank You

The first leg of the tour ends on a high note with possibly the best show of 1973. The band are on fire, as they usually were in Los Angeles. Robert Plant reminds the crowd about Page's injury: "You shouldn't have been here tonight and we should have been in England! As you know, the concert you originally had to come to was canceled because of Jimmy's finger. Now, this finger is very susceptible to strain and ligament pulling. Jimmy's had his finger in a bucket of cold water offstage, completely, the whole of the time since the concert was canceled. I think he's doing really well and that's a fact. It's no fun." If his finger was hurting, you certainly cannot tell from this spectacular performance, which is highlighted by Page's extraordinary playing on a thirty-minute version of "Dazed And Confused." The band had such a great time and were so pleased with the reception they received that they play a rare third encore, "Thank You." They closed the first part of the tour in style. Unfortunately, their behavior after the gig at the hotel was less stylish.

66 Not too long after the group got settled in a ninth floor suite at the Continental Hyatt House, a table came sailing out their window. . . . Then it was off to a theater to attend a party for Jo Jo Gunne. There members of the group were accused of smashing up the rest rooms and defacing paintings in the lobby. Back to their hotel they went to spread a four-foot cake around the swimming pool. It happened to be Zeppelin drummer John Bonham's 25th birthday. When George Harrison and wife Patti dropped by. Bonham threw both of them, fully clothed, into the swimming pool. 99

**—THE JUNE 1973 NEWSWIRE REPORTS ON
INCIDENTS NOT RELATED TO THE MUSIC**

JULY 1973

6 July 1973, Chicago Stadium, Chicago, Illinois (8:30 p.m.)

SETLIST: Rock And Roll / Celebration Day / Bring It On Home Intro / Black Dog / Over The Hills And Far Away / Misty Mountain Hop / Since I've Been Loving You / No Quarter / The Song Remains The Same / The Rain Song / Dazed And Confused (including San Francisco) / Stairway To Heaven / Moby Dick / Heartbreaker / Whole Lotta Love (including The Crunge, Boogie Chillun') / Communication Breakdown

Led Zeppelin onstage at Kezar Stadium in San Francisco on 2 June 1973. (Rex)

Oh dear, what a difference a month makes! Having ended the first leg with possibly the best show of the tour, the second leg gets off to a bad start in Chicago with Plant losing his voice. He tries his best and there are signs of slight improvement during the show. Crowd control once again became an issue as it often did at Led Zeppelin shows. Plant attempts to calm things down: "I'd really be obliged if you could cool all that! There's no need to be fighting. I'm sure there's plenty of fights to catch outside. . . . There is some sensible reason why these people are doing this. . . . I have never seen so much leeriness and violence, so cool it! Can you dig that?" The rest of the band are in fine form, but are let down by the PA system that occasionally fails during the course of the show. All in all a very uneven performance that is best forgotten.

66 A stage setting with complete lighting system, mirrored panels and silver balls, plus puffs of smoke and enveloping fogs, represents some borrowings from Pink Floyd, though it works well with Zeppelin's style too. So does the weird electronic music of the Theremin which guitarist Jimmy Page doubled on during Whole Lotta Love. Page took a couple of solos with some flashy guitar work, and drummer John Bonham managed to make a 15 minute or so drum solo in Moby Dick, not only powerful but incredibly engrossing.99

—*CHICAGO TRIBUNE* (Review from July 1973)

7 July 1973, Chicago Stadium, Chicago, Illinois (8:30 p.m.)

SETLIST: Rock And Roll / Celebration Day / Bring It On Home Intro / Black Dog / Over The Hills And Far Away / Misty Mountain Hop / Since I've Been Loving You / No Quarter / The Song Remains The Same / The Rain Song / Dazed And Confused (including San Francisco) / Stairway To Heaven / Moby Dick / Heartbreaker / Whole Lotta Love (including The Crunge, Boogie Chillun') / Communication Breakdown

Another mixed performance. Plant's voice is still in a bad way and the band appear sluggish at times. Plant recuperates in "Dazed And Confused" and it is a great performance, as is the remainder of the gig.

8 July 1973, the Burning Spear, Chicago, Illinois (Robert Plant jams with Bobby Bland and Otis Clay at this West Side club.)

9 July 1973, Civic Center Arena, St. Paul, Minnesota (8:00 p.m.)

SETLIST: Rock And Roll / Celebration Day / Bring It On Home Intro / Black Dog / Over The Hills And Far Away / Misty Mountain Hop / Since I've Been Loving You / No Quarter / The Song Remains The Same / The Rain Song / Dazed And Confused (including San Francisco) / Stairway To Heaven / Moby Dick / Heartbreaker / Whole Lotta Love (including The Crunge, Boogie Chillun') / Communication Breakdown

The show was marred by many firecracker incidents and the band's performance is off and sluggish as a result. All the reviews for the show are positive, though, so clearly they were not hearing what most people heard.

10 July 1973, Milwaukee Arena, Milwaukee, Wisconsin

SETLIST: Rock And Roll / Celebration Day / Bring It On Home Intro / Black Dog / Over The Hills And Far Away / Misty Mountain Hop / Since I've Been Loving You / No Quarter / The Song Remains The Same / The Rain Song / Dazed And Confused (including San Francisco) / Stairway To Heaven / Moby Dick / Heartbreaker / Whole Lotta Love (including Boogie Chillun)

Robert Plant is very welcoming and personable: "Good evening! It's very nice to be back. When did we come here last? 1969, was it? Do you remember that festival where it rained all day? Well, anyway, a lot of things changed since then, and we've had a few experiences as well." Not a bad show, but clearly the band are not as on form as they had been on the European tour. The shows on the US tour have more ups and downs.

66 Led Zep did almost all of its fans' favorites, including its only pop single hit, Whole Lotta Love. The quartet receives a lot of airplay on FM rock stations, but has not sought the AM top 40 market. The group is on one of those monster concert tours that reportedly has them carting the money away by the carload. The four musicians supposedly are drawing better crowds and making more money than the Beatles, Rolling Stones or Alice Cooper ever did. Milwaukee fans should be happy that the Arena was included in the bonanza.99

—DAMIEN JAQUES

(Review in the *Milwaukee Journal*, 11 July 1973)

12 July 1973, Cobo Arena, Detroit, Michigan

SETLIST: Rock And Roll / Celebration Day / Bring It On Home Intro / Black Dog / Over The Hills And Far Away / Misty Mountain Hop / Since I've Been Loving You / No Quarter / The Song Remains The Same / The Rain Song / Dazed And Confused (including San Francisco) / Stairway To Heaven / Moby Dick / Heartbreaker / Whole Lotta Love (including The Crunge, Going Down, Boogie Chillun) / Communication Breakdown / The Ocean

The almost forty-eight-hour break have done the band a lot of good and they play a highly energized show tonight. Although firecrackers continue to blight all the shows, Plant addresses the problem directly with the crowd in a telling way: "Don't throw any more firecrackers, 'cos that's silly! It breaks the concentration, of which we've got very little left." Well, that may have been true in Milwaukee, but tonight the performance is incredible. Plant does a good job of being the band's promotion man by informing the crowd that the band's new album, *Houses of the Holy*, "can be found on the shelves of your local record shop—rush out and buy a copy." "Whole Lotta Love" is exceptionally funky tonight and Page has fun with the theremin. Don Nix's "Going Down" is played tonight in the medley.

13 July 1973, Cobo Arena, Detroit, Michigan

SETLIST: Rock And Roll / Celebration Day / Bring It On Home Intro / Black Dog / Over The Hills And Far Away / Misty Mountain Hop / Since I've Been Loving You / No Quarter / The Song Remains The Same / The Rain Song / Dazed And Confused (including San Francisco) / Stairway To Heaven / Moby Dick / Heartbreaker / Whole Lotta Love (including The Crunge, Boogie Chillun') / Dancing Days

Another great show in Motor City. Although Plant's voice is hoarse, the band are in top form. A major surprise tonight is the final encore, "Dancing Days," which was the only time they played it on this tour, and an electric version at that. It was played again on the 1977 US tour, but as an acoustic version.

15 July 1973, Buffalo Memorial Auditorium, Buffalo, New York (8:00 p.m.)

SETLIST: Rock And Roll / Celebration Day / Bring It On Home Intro / Black Dog / Over The Hills And Far Away / Misty Mountain Hop / Since I've Been Loving You / No Quarter / The Song Remains The Same / The Rain Song / Dazed And Confused (including San Francisco) / Stairway To Heaven / Moby Dick / Heartbreaker / Whole Lotta Love (including The Crunge, Boogie Chillun') / The Ocean

The show is marred by somebody letting off flash bombs in the auditorium at several intervals. Despite this, the band are again in good form.

66 The sheer enormity of the sound did it (though the full moon may have helped), an enormity that resonates into your paleolithic pith, the cry of the dinosaur summoning out that primitive quickening in the face of monstrosity. Whatever isn't touched by the earthquake rumble of John Paul Jones' bass, John Bonham's gunshot cracks on the drums or Robert Plant's echoey heart-of-darkness voice is left quivering by the swooping electronic slices of guitarist Jimmy Page, especially his solo on the theremin. 99
—*BUFFALO EVENING NEWS* (Review on 16 July 1973)

17 July 1973, Seattle Center Coliseum, Seattle, Washington

SETLIST: Rock And Roll / Celebration Day / Bring It On Home Intro / Black Dog / Over The Hills And Far Away / Misty Mountain Hop / Since I've Been Loving You / No Quarter / The Song Remains The Same / The Rain Song / Dazed And Confused (including San Francisco) / Stairway To Heaven / Moby Dick / Heartbreaker / Whole Lotta Love (including The Crunge, Boogie Chillun') / The Ocean

The scene is set from the start with a house announcement stating, "Led Zeppelin has asked if we can get a few things straight tonight. Nobody around here digs any fireworks—please cool the fireworks. Please also, we have an area right here in front of the stage where we have many optic effects that we need to get off tonight, that we can't have any chance of anybody bumping the stage 'cos it'll completely ruin them. Their show usually runs about one hour and forty-five minutes. If you can keep the fireworks down and keep everything off the front, Led Zeppelin would like to thank you and do about three hours tonight! So, sit back and stay cool and we'll have a long great show this evening!" A wonderful show with the whole band in top form. As with most nights, the improvisational numbers, "No Quarter" and "Dazed And Confused," are particularly worthy of a mention as they have some unique arrangements tonight. Yet another reason why fans fervently collect as many shows by the band as possible.

66 Page is one of the finest electric guitarists in the world. He's done session work for everybody from Donovan to Tony Bennett and like Hendrix, has helped expand the definitions of rock by his innovations. Robert Plant is the greatest singer in rock, next to Little Richard, and that's no mean feat. . . . John Bonham, the drummer, displayed superhuman strength by lasting the full three hours without a rest, even after an energetic drum solo that must have lasted 20 minutes. John Paul Jones, an arranger and conductor before joining the group, played bass guitar, electric organ and mellotron. 99
—**PATRICK MACDONALD** (Review in *Seattle Times*, 18 July 1973)

18 July 1973 Pacific Coliseum, Vancouver, British Columbia

SETLIST: Rock And Roll / Celebration Day / Bring It On Home Intro / Black Dog / Over the Hills And Far Away / Misty Mountain Hop / Since I've Been Loving You / No Quarter / The Song Remains The Same / Rain Song / Dazed And Confused (including San Francisco) / Stairway To Heaven

An average show, which is stopped early after a performance of "Stairway To Heaven." Robert Plant had said, "Vancouver, good night" after the song and all seemed normal as the crowd stomped for the encores. Instead of the band returning to the stage, an announcer comes to the microphone to say that "Led Zeppelin has left the building. . . . Please stop for just a moment. They're trying to get Robert Plant to a hospital. Please very orderly try to cool it with the traffic while we try to get the limos through the traffic. We have to get Robert Plant to the hospital in the next few minutes. They said to thank you, you've been an unbelievable audience . . . we apologize. . . . Thank you, Vancouver!" It appears that Plant was given a "spiked" drink backstage that caused him to be ill. Don Stanley, reporting for the *Vancouver Sun*, was not impressed: "It was unfortunate for Plant (if the report was true) but fortunate for the band that they left the stage early. Their concert was terrible, unbelievably inept for the top draw in contemporary rock."

20 July 1973, Boston Garden, Boston, Massachusetts (8:00 p.m. The show is shorter than usual due to a rowdy audience.)

SETLIST: Rock And Roll / Celebration Day / Bring It On Home Intro / Black Dog / Over The Hills And Far Away / No Quarter / The Song Remains The Same / The Rain Song / Dazed And Confused (including San Francisco) / Stairway To Heaven / Heartbreaker / Whole Lotta Love (including The Crunge, Boogie Chillun')

The crowd appears to be uncontrollable and the band wisely drop "Misty Mountain Hop," "Since I've Been Loving You," and "Moby Dick" from the main set in order to attempt to calm them down. The crowd kept pushing forward and ran a constant serious risk of injury. To his credit, Robert Plant tried at several intervals during the show to calm the situation, but failed. As a result, the crowd had to miss out on the encores. A final announcement is made, "Thank you and good night! Led Zeppelin are gone!"

21 July 1973, Civic Center, Providence, Rhode Island (8:00 p.m.)

SETLIST: Rock And Roll / Celebration Day / Bring It On Home Intro / Black Dog / Over The Hills And Far Away / Misty Mountain Hop / Since I've Been Loving You / No Quarter / The Song Remains The Same / The Rain Song / Dazed And Confused (including San Francisco) / Stairway To Heaven / Moby Dick / Heartbreaker / Whole Lotta Love (including The Crunge, Boogie Chillun') / The Ocean

With the problems in Boston behind them, Led Zeppelin put in a fantastic show in Providence. The highlight has to be an outstanding performance of "No Quarter," which is introduced by an immodest Plant: "Here's something that we really like to play and we're gonna play it really fantastically."

23 July 1973, Civic Center, Baltimore, Maryland (8:00 p.m.)

SETLIST: Rock And Roll / Celebration Day / Bring It On Home Intro / Black Dog / Over The Hills And Far Away / Misty Mountain Hop / Since I've Been Loving You / No Quarter / The Song Remains The Same / The Rain Song / Dazed And Confused (including San Francisco) / Stairway To Heaven / Moby Dick / Heartbreaker / Whole Lotta Love (including Boogie Chillun') / The Ocean

Joe Massot and his crew are at the show to film as a rehearsal for the forthcoming Madison Square Garden shows in New York. They also shoot incidental footage here, such as the backstage scene in *The Song Remains the Same* film with Peter Grant bawling out the promoter over the sale of pirate posters at the gig. The show itself is truly outstanding.

24 July 1973, Three Rivers Stadium, Pittsburgh, Pennsylvania (8:00 p.m.)

SETLIST: Rock And Roll / Celebration Day / Bring It On Home Intro / Black Dog / Over The Hills And Far Away / Misty Mountain Hop / Since I've Been Loving You / No Quarter / The Song Remains The Same / The Rain Song / Dazed And Confused (including San Francisco) / Stairway To Heaven / Moby Dick / Heartbreaker / Whole Lotta Love (including The Crunge, Boogie Chillun') / The Ocean

An incredible 40,000 fans attended the show, with the band earning a reported $120,000. Joe Massot's film crew again capture some 16mm footage of the event, in readiness for the three-night finale at Madison Square Garden in New York that will eventually be released as *The Song Remains the Same* in 1976. The band are in fine form performing a dynamic heavy set. A playful Plant was in especially fine form vocally, considering he had been performing almost nightly, and threw in an ad-lib "Don't send me to the heartbreak hotel!" during "Since I've Been Loving You." Behind the scenes, there had been a bit of trouble with some people attempting to gate-crash the concert, but they were subdued by guards using water hoses. Others had made a brave, but ultimately in vain, attempt to scale the walls with ladders and were arrested. Never a dull moment at a Led Zeppelin concert!

27 July 1973 Madison Square Garden, New York, New York City (8:00 p.m. Whole concert was professionally recorded by the Bearsville Sound Studio Mobile unit and filmed.)

SETLIST: Rock And Roll / Celebration Day / Bring It On Home Intro / Black Dog / Over The Hills And Far Away / Misty Mountain Hop / Since I've Been Loving You / No Quarter / The Song Remains The Same / The Rain Song / Dazed And Confused (including San Francisco) / Stairway To Heaven / Moby Dick / Heartbreaker / Whole Lotta Love (including The Crunge, Boogie Chillun') / The Ocean

The first of three shows in New York, where the band played to 60,000 people over three nights at Madison Square Garden. The New York crowd gave the band a rapturous welcome and the band repaid them with a stunning performance. At times the crowd are a little too wild, and Plant has to calm them down: "Let's get one thing straight—stop acting like kids! Cool it a little bit!" "Dazed And Confused" is super-tight and perhaps not as improvisational as earlier performances as a result. These are the last three shows of the US tour and the band are in good form, despite the presence of film cameras. Some newspaper reviews are indifferent, largely due to the fact that the person reviewing the show does not have much knowledge of the band. This happened quite a lot, and while it is true to say that the band were not on top form on some nights, the majority of shows were worthy of praise.

❝ The film director for the project was Joe Massot who, with his film crew, had been to Baltimore and Pittsburgh two dates before New York and I hoped that they had become familiar with our shows rather than experience a baptism by fire at the run of shows at this wonderful concert arena. The sound recording was done with a mobile recording studio, courtesy of Bearsville Sound and Eddie Kramer handled the engineering on this and subsequent evenings. I knew this was going to be an epic over the next few days. ❞

—JIMMY PAGE (From his website)

28 July 1973, Madison Square Garden, New York, New York City (8:00 p.m. Whole concert was professionally recorded by the Bearsville Sound Studio Mobile unit and filmed.)

SETLIST: Rock And Roll / Celebration Day / Bring It On Home Intro / Black Dog / Over The Hills And Far Away / Misty Mountain Hop / Since I've Been Loving You / No Quarter / The Song Remains The Same / The Rain Song / Dazed And Confused (including San Francisco) / Heartbreaker / Whole Lotta Love (including The Crunge, Boogie Chillun') / The Ocean

One of those tight but loose shows. One would think that this being the middle night might result in slightly lower energy levels. But this was not the case and the band puts in another special evening. Several numbers from this show will be used in the film and accompanying soundtrack in 1976. "Since I've Been Loving You" is especially strong tonight as is "Dazed And Confused," both amazing showcases for Jimmy Page's playing.

29 July 1973, Madison Square Garden, New York, New York City (8:00 p.m. Whole concert was professionally recorded by the Bearsville Sound Studio Mobile unit and filmed. Mike Quashie, a West Indian fire-eater, made an appearance setting a gong and drum stick on fire while John Bonham was playing his drums at the end of "Whole Lotta Love.")

SETLIST: Rock And Roll / Celebration Day / Bring It On Home Intro / Black Dog / Over The Hills And Far Away / Misty Mountain Hop / Since I've Been Loving You / No Quarter / The Song Remains The Same / The Rain Song / Dazed And Confused (including San Francisco) / Stairway To Heaven / Moby Dick / Heartbreaker / Whole Lotta Love (including The Crunge, Boogie Chillun') / The Ocean / Organ Solo / Thank You

Not only the final show of the US tour, it was also their last show of 1973. The band is playing hard and loud, and knowing it was the last show, they probably put in extra energy to finish on a high. Page is in spectacular form and the improvisations in "No Quarter" are inspirational. Other highlights are "Dazed And Confused" and the now classic "Stairway To Heaven." John Bonham excels in a longer than usual "Moby Dick," which is followed by "Heartbreaker," which drove the crowd wild. The final salvo of "Whole Lotta Love," "The Ocean," and a surprise second encore, "Thank You," was off the scale.

Joe Massot filmed the three shows at Madison Square Garden. Joe was an American-born British film director and writer, who is best remembered for the 1968 film *Wonderwall,* which featured George Harrison's first soundtrack. He was a friend of Page's girlfriend, Charlotte Martin, and had been introduced to Page at dinner at their home. They became friends and Page invited him to see Led Zeppelin live at the Bath Festival in 1970, which is where he first got the idea of directing a film on them. That was also the place he first caught Peter Grant in action when he saw him throw buckets of water over some film equipment to prevent unauthorized filming of the band. Joe lost touch with Page in the ensuing couple of years, but when he noticed in the music press that Led Zeppelin were going to be touring the US in huge arenas he decided to track Page down for a talk. He pitched an idea to him about making a film on Led Zeppelin, which would include both concert and behind-the-scenes footage. Page seemed to like the idea as long as it was not just a concert film and referred him to Richard Cole, who also seemed to be in favor but explained that it was Peter Grant who would make the final decision as the band's manager. When Grant heard about the film, he initially turned it down because he wanted a better-known director for such a potentially important film, but Massot persevered and eventually was given the OK by Grant on 14 July 1973. He quickly assembled a camera crew and flew out to Boston on 19 July 1973, where he would meet Grant in person for the first time. The deal was that Led Zeppelin would pay all the bills as well as finance the project but would retain ownership of all the footage made. Their lawyer, Steve Weiss, would be handling the money side of things on behalf of Grant and the band.

Massot was told he could use gigs in Baltimore and Pittsburgh as a rehearsal for the main event in New York, three nights at Madison Square Garden, which would be the final shows of the year. He was also told to make sure he filmed some incidental footage for potential use in the film, such as the band being escorted to the gig by a police motorcycle escort. He also filmed Grant backstage chewing out some hapless bootleg T-shirt seller. This was all done using 16mm film and the concert footage would be made on 35mm film. The idea of filming the last three shows of the tour at Madison Square Garden was that it would give ample opportunity for the producer to choose the best performances from each night provided that all band members wore the same clothes over the period. Massot had supposedly asked members to be aware of

this important fact, although John Paul Jones claims not to have known about this and wore different clothes on each night. This would cause all sorts of continuity issues later on.

Eddie Kramer handled the sound in the Bearsville Sound Studio Mobile unit using 24-track tape. There were never any issues with the sound, so it is surprising that Page butchered a new version of the soundtrack in 2008 for a remastered expanded edition to tie in with a remastered version of the original film. So now fans had to put up with a poorly edited soundtrack to match the poorly edited film. It must be noted that due to legal technicalities, the film could not be changed. So, one can forgive Page for allowing it to be re-released in it's original form, albeit in a slightly more tidied edition. The fact is, even the original soundtrack had little in common with the film, so artistically speaking it would have made far more sense to pick out the best numbers from each of the three nights, and make a complete show available spread over three discs as they did for *How the West Was Won.* This was truly a missed opportunity, especially as the new version sounds, frankly, amateurish due to the way some key moments have been viciously edited out to tie in with the visuals of the DVD.

A major incident happened during the run at Madison Square Garden. $186,700 was stolen from the band's safe deposit box at the Drake Hotel. The authorities were convinced it was an inside job, but were never able to prove anything. Some people even speculated it was done for publicity. It was front-page news in the US and also made the film somewhat more dramatic by including news footage from the ensuing events surrounding the robbery. The mystery was never solved.

Massot filmed all three shows at Madison Square Garden using 35mm film on 400-foot reels, which would only give each camera about three and a half minutes worth of footage. His methods were amateurish and not planned out very well, and so much stage action was missed when the cameras needed reloading every few minutes. Incredibly, over the three-night run he and his team had not even managed to capture a complete version of "Whole Lotta Love"! There were several other missed opportunities, but not capturing the song that was the most synonymous with Led Zeppelin fans was unforgivable. He should have been better prepared, and all three shows should have been filmed in their entirety. Even Ringo Starr had been able to capture the two complete T. Rex concerts at the Empire Pool in Wembley in 1972 using five cameras with no issues. The biggest error in judgment that Massot made was hiring cameramen who had experience in regular filmmaking, but none in the filming of live concerts. As a result, nobody on the team or the band knew what was going on. Grant has to take his share of responsibility as well, as he could see that Massot was out of his depth, and should have brought in an experienced producer to help out.

In October, Massot went to England to look into filming some individual fantasy sequences of each member, which would help cover up his live concert mistakes. Page's segment was shot in Scotland near his recently bought Boleskin House on Loch Ness, which had previously been owned by Aleister Crowley. Page had insisted it be shot on a night of the full moon as he climbed up a hill where he is met by a mysterious hooded figure who turns out to be his older self. It was shot on a very wintry night in late 1973, which made it difficult to light for film. Plant was filmed on his farm in Wales, and is seen as an Arthurian knight looking for a fair maiden. John Bonham's segments were a lot easier to shoot, as well as being a lot more down to earth in nature compared to Page and Plant. He was filmed briefly on his Worcestershire farm dressed as a teddy boy, and can be seen dancing with his wife, playing pool, and teaching his young son, Jason, how to play the drums. He was also filmed drag-racing at the Santa Pod Raceway in Bedfordshire. Jones was filmed at his home in Crowborough in Sussex. In his segment he is dressed as the leader of a band of men who terrorize a village. Afterward Jones heads home to his family and can be seen leading a normal peaceful life. Clearly an analogy for his life with Led Zeppelin. Peter Grant also had a fantasy segment. He chose a 1930s gangster fashion style. Dressed as an Al Capone character, he can be seen driving a beautiful vintage car with his wife, Gloria. Also with them is Richard Cole holding a machine gun. They pull up outside a house and proceed to riddle the place with bullets. Grant was not that comfortable doing his scenes and was starting to lose interest in the whole fantasy idea.

By the end of 1973 all the footage was ready to be edited down into a film. Massot bought an expensive editing console, which took three months to be delivered. When it arrived it was set up at his

London home, and he set about trying to put together something to show Grant and the band. They had grown impatient and refused to pay for the editing machine, or any more of Massot's time, until they could start seeing results. After several months of work, Massot arranged for an initial viewing with the band at a preview theater. It was not pretty. Although the fantasy footage was okay, the concert footage left a lot to be desired in terms of synching and continuity, and there were plenty of anomalies. Grant and the band held a meeting and it was decided to bring in a new producer to finish the project. In reality everyone around the table knew it was going to be more of a salvage job.

Peter Clifton, an Australian film director and producer, was being considered to take over. He had experience filming live concerts as well as producing promotional films for various artists, such as Cat Stevens and Jimi Hendrix. He was already known to both Grant and Page as he had asked them to a screening cinema in Soho to view a film he was working on called *Sound of the City*. His idea had been to include Led Zeppelin playing "Whole Lotta Love" from the Royal Albert Hall in 1970 in the film. In fact he'd sold his film on the premise that Led Zeppelin would be in it. But Grant and Page did not give their permission as they did not like the guitar sound. Although he was pissed off at the rejection and embarrassment it caused, he did continue to chase them with a view of reviving the Royal Albert Hall film, but Led Zeppelin had moved on so much sound-wise that it was not viable. Grant had learned his lesson from hiring Massot without references and the massive cock-up that resulted because of that decision. This time he asked around about Clifton, and when he got positive feedback from people he respected, he offered him the role of producing the new film. After years of pursuing them to do a film, it seemed too good an opportunity for him to turn down.

His first job was to put together a script for the project. After three weeks, he had completed it and arranged for a meeting to see Peter Grant and Jimmy Page at Grant's home in Sussex to see if they would approve it. The response was positive and Clifton now went about discussing the tricky subject of a fee. Grant told him that it would not be a fee-based role, but that he would be on wages and made a sixth member of Led Zeppelin with equal share to the group profits from the film. He realized that was a good deal, because it was highly unlikely that such a project would fail. This would be the first-ever Led Zeppelin film and they were the biggest band on the planet at the time. However, what he had not taken into account was how long and how difficult it would be, not to mention future difficulties of having to deal with Grant and the band.

By March 1974, it fell on Peter Clifton to go and see Joe Massot and tell him the band had sacked him, and that he would now be taking over from here on in.

DECEMBER 1973

3 December 1973, Royal Albert Hall, London (Jimmy Page joins Roy Harper for a version of "Male Chauvinist Pig Blues," a number from Roy's next album called *Valentine*. Page also played on the studio version. The concert was filmed and recorded but to date has not been released.)

12 December 1973, BBC Television Centre, Shepherds Bush, London (John Paul Jones, playing bass, joins his old friend Madeline Bell for a performance on the popular *Colour My Soul* show. He also played and produced her recent *Comin' Atcha* album, which was partially recorded at his home studio).

12 1973 Recording Sessions

LED ZEPPELIN
INITIAL SESSIONS FOR
PHYSICAL GRAFFITI

OCTOBER 1973

Initial sessions for *Physical Graffiti* were due to start in October 1973 at Headley Grange. John Paul Jones in particular felt he needed to spend more time with his family, and rather than quit the band, he took a break and the band would resume sessions for their next album early in 1974. As was often the case with the Led Zeppelin, they warmed up with some rock 'n' roll standards and the following are known to have been recorded in October 1973, before the sessions were stopped. Interestingly, multiple takes exist and may have been considered for release at some stage.

RONNIE LANE MOBILE STUDIO
Headley Grange, Liphook Road, Headley, Hampshire

SICK AGAIN (Jimmy Page / Robert Plant) Early version available on companion disc of *Physical Graffiti* released February 2015.

DRIVING THROUGH KASHMIR (Later shortened to "Kashmir") (Jimmy Page / Robert Plant) Early version available on companion disc of *Physical Graffiti* released February 2015.

(YOU'RE SO SQUARE) BABY I DON'T CARE (Jerry Leiber / Mike Stoller) unreleased

JAILHOUSE ROCK (Jerry Leiber / Mike Stoller) unreleased

ONE NIGHT (Dave Bartholomew / Earl King / Anita Steinman) unreleased

DON'T BE CRUEL (Otis Blackwell) unreleased

THE GIRL OF MY BEST FRIEND (Sam Bobrick / Beverly Ross) unreleased

JAILHOUSE ROCK (Jerry Leiber / Mike Stoller) unreleased

MONEY HONEY (Jesse Stone) unreleased

SUMMERTIME BLUES (Eddie Cochran / Jerry Capehart) unreleased

PRODUCER: JIMMY PAGE
ENGINEER: RON NEVISON

GUEST RECORDING SESSIONS

Guest Session for Madeline Bell

John Paul Jones teams up with Madeline Bell for her *Comin' Atcha* album on RCA, which was released in December 1973. The album was a blend of funk, jazz, R&B, and soul, and John Paul Jones co-wrote, arranged, and produced all ten tracks and performs on all of them. The album was largely recorded at his home studio in Sussex with a further four tracks being recorded at Morgan Studios in London. John Paul Jones's wife, Mo, also contributes backing vocals to several tracks.

Jimmy Page onstage in California during the 1973 US tour. (Rex)

DORMOUSE STUDIOS
Warren House, Warren Road, Crowborough, East Sussex

FEBRUARY 1973

MAKE A MOVE (Madeline Bell / John Paul Jones) Available on *Comin' Atcha* released on RCA Records SF 8393 December 1973.

MADELINE BELL: VOCALS, BACKING VOCALS
JOHN PAUL JONES: KEYBOARDS, SYNTHESIZER, BASS GUITAR, GUITARS, BACKING VOCALS
BARRY DE SOUZA: DRUMS

MO JONES: BACKING VOCALS
JACQUES PLOQUIN: BACKING VOCALS

WITHOUT YOU (I KNOW WHAT I'LL DO) (Madeline Bell / John Paul Jones) Available on *Comin' Atcha* released on RCA Records SF 8393 December 1973.

MADELINE BELL: VOCALS, BACKING VOCALS
JOHN PAUL JONES: KEYBOARDS, SYNTHESIZER, BASS GUITAR, GUITARS, BACKING VOCALS
MO JONES: BACKING VOCALS
JACQUES PLOQUIN: BACKING VOCALS

I'M SO GLAD (Madeline Bell / John Paul Jones) Available on *Comin' Atcha* released on RCA Records SF 8393 December 1973.

MADELINE BELL: VOCALS, BACKING VOCALS
JOHN PAUL JONES: KEYBOARDS, SYNTHESIZER, BASS GUITAR,
GUITARS, BACKING VOCALS
MO JONES: BACKING VOCALS
JACQUES PLOQUIN: BACKING VOCALS

COMIN' ATCHA (Madeline Bell / John Paul Jones) Available on *Comin' Atcha* released on RCA Records SF 8393 December 1973.

MADELINE BELL: VOCALS, BACKING VOCALS
JOHN PAUL JONES: KEYBOARDS, SYNTHESIZER, BASS GUITAR,
GUITARS, BACKING VOCALS
MO JONES: BACKING VOCALS
JACQUES PLOQUIN: BACKING VOCALS

I WANNA BE AROUND (YOU!) (Madeline Bell / John Paul Jones) Available on *Comin' Atcha* released on RCA Records SF 8393 December 1973.

MADELINE BELL: VOCALS, BACKING VOCALS
JOHN PAUL JONES: KEYBOARDS, SYNTHESIZER, BASS GUITAR,
GUITARS, BACKING VOCALS
MO JONES: BACKING VOCALS
JACQUES PLOQUIN: BACKING VOCALS

THAT'S WHAT IT'S ALL ABOUT (Madeline Bell / John Paul Jones) Available on *Comin' Atcha* released on RCA Records SF 8393 December 1973.

MADELINE BELL: VOCALS, BACKING VOCALS
JOHN PAUL JONES: KEYBOARDS, SYNTHESIZER, BASS GUITAR,
GUITARS, BACKING VOCALS
MO JONES: BACKING VOCALS
JACQUES PLOQUIN: BACKING VOCALS
PRODUCER: JOHN PAUL JONES
ENGINEER: JOHN PAUL JONES

MORGAN STUDIOS
169-171 High Street, Willesdon Green, London NW10

GRAM (Madeline Bell / John Paul Jones) Available on *Comin' Atcha* released on RCA Records SF 8393 December 1973.

MADELINE BELL: VOCALS
JOHN PAUL JONES: KEYBOARDS
JEAN PIERRE AZOULAY: GUITAR
TONY NEWMAN: DRUMS
JIM LAWLESS: PERCUSSION
BARRIE ST. JOHN: BACKING VOCALS
DORIS TROY: BACKING VOCALS
JACQUES PLOQUIN: BACKING VOCALS
LIZA STRIKE: BACKING VOCALS
DAVID KATZ: ORCHESTRA

ANOTHER GIRL (Madeline Bell / John Paul Jones) Available on *Comin' Atcha* released on RCA Records SF 8393 December 1973.

MADELINE BELL: VOCALS
JOHN PAUL JONES: KEYBOARDS
JEAN PIERRE AZOULAY: GUITAR
TONY NEWMAN: DRUMS
JIM LAWLESS: PERCUSSION
BARRIE ST. JOHN: BACKING VOCALS
DORIS TROY: BACKING VOCALS
JACQUES PLOQUIN: BACKING VOCALS
LIZA STRIKE: BACKING VOCALS
DAVID KATZ: ORCHESTRA

LITTLE ONES (Madeline Bell / John Paul Jones) Available on *Comin' Atcha* released on RCA Records SF 8393 December 1973.

MADELINE BELL: VOCALS
JOHN PAUL JONES: KEYBOARDS
JEAN PIERRE AZOULAY: GUITAR
TONY NEWMAN: DRUMS
JIM LAWLESS: PERCUSSION
BARRIE ST. JOHN: BACKING VOCALS
DORIS TROY: BACKING VOCALS
JACQUES PLOQUIN: BACKING VOCALS
LIZA STRIKE: BACKING VOCALS
DAVID KATZ: ORCHESTRA

THINGS (Madeline Bell / John Paul Jones) Available on *Comin' Atcha* released on RCA Records SF 8393 December 1973.

MADELINE BELL: VOCALS
JOHN PAUL JONES: KEYBOARDS
JEAN PIERRE AZOULAY: GUITAR
TONY NEWMAN: DRUMS
JIM LAWLESS: PERCUSSION
BARRIE ST. JOHN: BACKING VOCALS
DORIS TROY: BACKING VOCALS
JACQUES PLOQUIN: BACKING VOCALS
LIZA STRIKE: BACKING VOCALS
DAVID KATZ: ORCHESTRA
PRODUCER: JOHN PAUL JONES
ENGINEER: PAUL TREGURTHA

NOVEMBER 1973

Guest Session for Jobriath's 2nd Album, *Creatures of the Street*

OLYMPIC SOUND STUDIOS
Studio 2, 117 Church Road, Barnes, London, SW13

John Paul Jones is credited on the sleeve but gives no more details as to his participation and on which track(s). Session produced by Eddie Kramer.

Guest Session for Roy Harper

ABBEY ROAD STUDIOS
3 Abbey Rd, London NW8

MALE CHAUVINIST PIG BLUES (Roy Harper) Available on
Valentine album, Harvest SHSP 4027 released February 1974.

ROY HARPER: VOCALS, GUITAR
JIMMY PAGE: ELECTRIC GUITAR
KEITH MOON: PERCUSSION
MARTY SIMON: DRUMS
PETE SEARS: BASS
MIKE GIBBS: BRASS
PRODUCED BY: PETER JENNER, ROY HARPER
ENGINEER: JOHN LECKIE

13 1974: Taking Stock

On the face of it, 1974 may have seemed a quiet year for the band, but in reality three important things happened: Led Zeppelin formed their own record label, recorded new songs for their next album, and they continued work on their concert film.

Led Zeppelin's contract with Atlantic Records came to an end in December 1973. Peter Grant and the band wanted to be more artistically and financially independent and promote themselves, as well as signing other bands that perhaps had been given a raw deal by some of the big corporate labels. After weeks of heated negotiations between Peter Grant and Atlantic's Ahmet Ertegun, an agreement was reached between the two men, and a joint statement was released to the press in January 1974. It confirmed that Led Zeppelin would be forming their own label with exclusive worldwide distribution through Atlantic Records. Their label was still unnamed at this point and during the coming months suitable premises would be found in New York and London to house label staff. New York was set up fairly quickly at 444 Madison Avenue with the band's former US publicist, Danny Goldberg, as vice president. London took a little longer as Grant had to dissolve his partnership with Mickie Most, which meant moving out of the old Oxford Street address they had shared since the '60s. Mark London, who had co-managed Stone the Crows with Grant, found new premises for the label at 484 Kings Road, in the not-so-trendy part of Chelsea. After some weeks it was decided that Abe Hoch, an executive for Atlantic and Motown Records, should run the UK operation, but after six months he was replaced by an old friend of Page's, Alan Callan.

The label seemed to start well with their first signing, Bad Company, topping the US charts. Grant was involved at every step with them, from rehearsals to recording to touring. It was something he could not maintain, though, as first and foremost he needed to look after his main charges, Led Zeppelin. They would always have to be his first priority. And there was the problem. Neither Grant, or the band, fully realized what running a label would entail. It was never going to be the altruistic vision they had hoped for. The Beatles Apple fiasco should perhaps have given them some warning signs. But no, Swan Song ended up a vanity project that was destined for failure in terms of nurturing new acts. Their friend Roy Harper was offered a deal with Swan Song, but it was not exactly in his best interests to sign with them. Roy's manager, Peter Jenner, recalled that the contract was very much in favor of Swan Song rather than Roy. He felt that they did not really know what to do with Roy, as he seemed to be a tough sell, and they could not devote the time required to make him a huge success. So Roy declined the offer and carried on with EMI and the friendship with the band remained intact. Bad Company were lucky to have had some of Grant's time, but other signings such as the Pretty Things, Dave Edmunds, Detective, and Maggie Bell, to name a few, were constantly frustrated at not being able to get hold of him, not to mention the amount of time it took to get all five owners (Peter Grant, Jimmy Page, Robert Plant, John Paul Jones, and John Bonham) of the label to reach a decision. And that was assuming you could get through to them at all, as they were scattered around the country.

Ultimately, it was Grant that suffered the most. He was being pulled in different directions and was desperately trying to hold everything together. During the following three years, his wife left him, which hit him particularly badly. His mental and physical health suffered as he turned to cocaine as a way of keeping himself going. As with all heavy users over time, he became paranoid and obnoxious, which inevitably lead to a disastrously violent encounter at the end of the 1977 US tour that would severely dent Led Zeppelin's reputation.

Back in 1973, Jimmy Page had dug out some tapes recorded over the last few years and listened to material that was left over from previous album sessions to see if some of it could be combined with newer numbers and make the next release a double album. All the other big bands had already released critically acclaimed double albums, the Beatles, the Rolling Stones, the Who, Jimi Hendrix, etc. It made sense that Led Zeppelin should release one also, especially considering their stature in the world of rock music. In November 1973, the band headed down to Headley Grange in Hampshire for rehearsals and hopefully record some new material for their next studio album. The sessions were cut short due to John Paul Jones wanting to spend more time with his family. It was not quite a crisis, but he had expressed his unhappiness at being away from home so much.

In order to prevent the situation from getting to the point where Jones would have had no choice but to quit the band, it was decided to stop the sessions and start again in early 1974. The time was not wasted, though, as Bad Company came in and recorded their first album there in place of Led Zeppelin, using the Ronnie Lane Mobile and engineer Ron Nevison. Despite the business of starting their own label and working on their film, the band were determined to record new material and were very focused on the task at hand. The band returned to Headley Grange in mid-January and stayed there until the end of February to record their next album with Jones happily back in the fold. The Ronnie Lane Mobile was already in place, as was recording engineer Ron Nevison, who had just completed work on Bad Company's first album there. The sessions with Led Zeppelin were productive and fast. They recorded nine numbers that would be considered for the next album. Nobody liked the idea of staying overnight in the damp and cold house, so

the band stayed in the more comfortable surroundings of the nearby Frensham Pond Hotel. Jimmy Page, on the other hand, was happy to lodge at Headley Grange, which enabled him to carry on working on songs and ideas during the night if he chose to.

One of the more ambitious songs was a piece that had its origins going back to 1971. It was a long song that was derived from the same well as "White Summer," a number that he had originally recorded with the Yardbirds for their *Little Games* album and later for *Led Zeppelin I*. After several takes, the song was titled "Swan Song," which was also suggested as a title for the new album. In the end, the song was shelved, but Jimmy Page would later revive it in 1984 for the Firm's first album as "Midnight Moonlight." Jimmy Page told *Hit Parade* magazine about the song and how they named their new label in January 1975:

I had this long acoustic guitar instrumental with just sparse vocal sections—the song was about 20 minutes and the vocal was about 6 minutes, and the whole thing was quite epic really. Almost semi-classical I suppose, and I did have bits of it and we were recording with the truck and there was no title for it and someone shouted out 'what's it going to be called?" and I shouted out "Swan Song!" and the whole thing stopped and we said what a great name for the LP, and all the vibes started and suddenly it was out of the LP and onto the record label.

From an artistic and creative point of view, the band were again at their peak at Headley Grange. The other core numbers recorded as basic tracks were "Custard Pie," a joyful rocker, the Stevie Wonder clavinet influenced "Trampled Underfoot," which would go on to become a live favorite, the Blind Willie Johnson derived "In My Time Of Dying," which showed they had not completely abandoned their blues roots, the exotic and mystical "In The Light," featuring some wonderful synthesizer by John Paul Jones, the beautifully melodic "Ten Years Gone," "The Wanton Song," another riff-driven diamond, the obligatory heavy rocker "Sick Again," which would also become a live favorite on the 1975 and 1977 tours, and possibly the best song on the album, the Middle Eastern tinged "Kashmir," influenced by Page and Plant's travels to Morocco and India in 1972. In April and May, overdubs and mixing were done at Olympic Studios in Barnes and the album was finished. The same cannot be said about the sleeve, which took over six months to complete satisfactorily.

By May and June of 1974, Peter Clifton had viewed all of the concert footage and realized that there was a big problem. The continuity was nonexistent and there were no cutaways. He patiently explained this to Grant and the band, none of whom had any idea about the filmmaking process. There were other problems. Although Massot had used 35mm film, he had also used 16mm film at Madison Square Garden. Clifton explained to the band and Grant that when 16mm was blown up to 35mm, it noticeably lost quality. The only way to solve the problem was to reshoot the live sequences and match up the sound to the new images. Unfortunately, this would bring its own set of new problems. Nevertheless, a soundstage was booked at Shepperton Film Studios, where the whole concert would be filmed again over several weeks in utmost secrecy. He managed to persuade the band to wear the same outfits that they had worn at Madison Square Garden to keep the continuity. Unfortunately John Paul Jones's hair was shorter than it was at the shows and he had to wear a wig to match his hair length from 1973 for the reshoot.

FEBRUARY 1974

14 February 1974, Rainbow Theatre, Finsbury, London (Robert Plant, Jimmy Page, and John Bonham take a break from recording their next album to attend a gig by Roy Harper. Roy brought on a superstar band during the second half of the show comprising Keith Moon on drums, Ronnie Lane on bass, Max Middleton on keyboards, and Jimmy Page on his Gibson Les Paul guitar. They called themselves the Intergalactic Elephant Band and they played "Male Chauvinist Pig Blues," "Same Old Rock," "Too Many Movies," and "Home." Jimmy Page played a Martin acoustic on "Same Old Rock." The show was recorded and "Too Many Movies" and "Home" appear on the double album *Flashes from the Archives of Oblivion*. John Bonham made an appearance onstage strumming an acoustic guitar, and Robert Plant came on at the end of the show telling the crowd, "Ladies and Gentlemen, Roy Harper!" The superstar band had only one rehearsal, which took place that afternoon at the venue.)

AUGUST 1974

AUGUST Shepperton Film Studios, Shepperton, Middlesex (Peter Clifton, who had taken over the direction of the Led Zeppelin movie, arranges for a soundstage for Led Zeppelin to be filmed with footage of Madison Square Garden in the background.)

31 August 1974, Free concert, Hyde Park, London (The second free concert in Hyde Park this year. The bill that day consisted of Roy Harper, Roger McGuinn, Julie Felix [another friend of John Paul Jones], Chilli Willi and the Red Hot Peppers, Kokomo, and the Maytals. John Paul Jones played bass with Roy Harper alongside David Gilmour and Steve Brougton. They would all appear on Harper's *HQ* album in 1975.)

SEPTEMBER 1974

1 September 1974, ZZ Top's "First Annual Rompin' Stompin' Barn Dance and Bar BQ," University of Texas Memorial Stadium, Austin, Texas (Massive event in front of 90,000 people headlined by ZZ Top with support from Santana, Joe Cocker and Bad Company. Jimmy Page joins Bad Company for their encore of "Rock Me Baby." They may have been bottom of the bill on this day, but Page's appearance with Bad Company made sure that they were the band people would be talking about for many weeks after the show. Jimmy Page recalls the day on his website: "Bad Company were a newly signed band on the Swan Song Label. Peter Grant and I went to see them at the Austin Pop Festival and I duly got up and had a play. I became quite pally with the members of Bad Company and in fact, teamed up with the legendary Paul Rogers to make some music in the 80's")

4 September 1974, Schaefer Music Festival, Wollman Rink, Central Park, New York (Jimmy Page joins Bad Company for their encore of "Rock Me Baby.")

14 September 1974, Quaglino's, St. James Place, London (Jimmy Page joins Crosby, Stills, Nash and Young on a small stage in the restaurant. The event was a party for the post-Wembley Stadium show headlined by CSNY earlier that day. Page plays on Neil Young's "Vampire Blues" and "On The Beach.")

DECEMBER 1974

5 December 1974, Hammersmith Odeon, Hammersmith, London (Jimmy Page and Robert Plant attend Eric Clapton's second show of his comeback tour in London.)

19 December 1974, Rainbow Theatre, Finsbury, London (Jimmy Page and John Paul Jones along with Duster Bennett, who was the support on the tour, join Bad Company for their encore of "Rock Me Baby.")

LED ZEPPELIN SESSIONS FOR *PHYSICAL GRAFFITI*

Bootleg tapes of the band rehearsing at Headley Grange have offered hardcore fans the opportunity to hear how the band rehearsed and developed songs before recording them. Among the familiar songs are embryonic versions of "In The Light," which at this stage was still called "In The Morning." "Trampled Underfoot," "The Rover," and "The Wanton Song" are all fascinating to listen to. But even better are the various versions of "In My Time Of Dying," featuring just Page and Bonham working out the correct rhythms. This is a true "fly on the wall" audio documentary about the making of their *Physical Graffiti* album.

The last few takes of "In My Time Of Dying" include some fascinating dialogue between Bonham, Page, and Plant. Bonham states, "You've got to have a count. There's got to be a count. It would be easy but the way Rob . . ." Page interrupts and tells him to "just do it again and see." Page then plays the riff and Bonham answers with some marching patterns on the drums before coming to an abrupt ending, causing Bonham to repeat, "We gotta have a count. We'll give Robert his freedom there and it doesn't matter what Rob does, we can still do it." Plant then chips in, "But where are you counting from now?" Bonham responds, "Well, I can't count where he stops because your vocals might be different. I mean, your voice might go half a beat and we're gonna be fucked." Plant in turn responds, "Ah, but if you do that it will be like 'Black Dog,' it gives me time to move." A now agitated Bonham shouts back, "But the reason we did 'Black Dog' is because we counted and you did it afterwards."

Unfortunately, the tape cuts out and we will never know how that rehearsal ended. Perhaps the most interesting song at these early rehearsals is a version of a number called "Take Me Home," which had a similar groove to "The Wanton Song." And perhaps that is why the band never got round to perfecting "Take Me Home" or indeed recording it properly. Yet another fascinating document.

14   1974 Recording Sessions

FEBRUARY 1974

RONNIE LANE MOBILE STUDIO
Headley Grange, Liphook Road,
Headley, Hampshire

DRIVING TO KASHMIR (Later shortened to "Kashmir") (Jimmy Page / Robert Plant / John Bonham) Available on *Physical Graffiti* vinyl Swan Song US SS-2-200 released 24 February November 1975 / Swan Song UK SSK 89400 released 24 February 1975.

BRANDY AND COKE (Later retitled "Trampled Underfoot") (Jimmy Page / Robert Plant / John Paul Jones) Available on *Physical Graffiti* vinyl Swan Song US SS-2-200 released 24 February November 1975 / Swan Song UK SSK 89400 released 24 February 1975.

DROP DOWN MAMA (Later retitled "Custard Pie") (Jimmy Page / Robert Plant) Available on *Physical Graffiti* vinyl Swan Song US SS-2-200 released 24 February November 1975 / Swan Song UK SSK 89400 released 24 February 1975.

EVERYONE MAKES IT THROUGH (Later retitled "In The Light") (Jimmy Page / Robert Plant / John Paul Jones) Available on *Physical Graffiti* vinyl Swan Song US SS-2-200 released 24 February November 1975 / Swan Song UK SSK 89400 released 24 February 1975.

SWAN SONG PART 1 (Jimmy Page) unreleased

SWAN SONG PART 2 (Jimmy Page) unreleased

IN MY TIME OF DYING (Jimmy Page / Robert Plant / John Paul Jones / John Bonham) Available on *Physical Graffiti* vinyl Swan Song US SS-2-200 released 24 February November 1975 / Swan Song UK SSK 89400 released 24 February 1975.

SICK AGAIN (Jimmy Page / Robert Plant) Available on *Physical Graffiti* vinyl Swan Song US SS-2-200 released 24 February November 1975 / Swan Song UK SSK 89400 released 24 February 1975.

The Ronnie Lane Mobile Studio was used to record *Physical Graffiti* (taken from an advertising brochure for the studio).

The Ronnie Lane Mobile Studio (photo from rare advertising brochure).

DESIRE (Later retitled "The Wanton Song") (Jimmy Page / Robert Plant) Available on *Physical Graffiti* vinyl Swan Song US SS-2-200 released 24 February November 1975 / Swan Song UK SSK 89400 released 24 February 1975.

TEN YEARS GONE (Jimmy Page / Robert Plant) Available on *Physical Graffiti* vinyl Swan Song US SS-2-200 released 24 February November 1975 / Swan Song UK SSK 89400 released 24 February 1975.

PRODUCER: JIMMY PAGE
ENGINEER: RON NEVISON

66 On 20 February in 1974, we recorded 'Ten Years Gone'—a song that I had brought to the party at Headley Grange. I'd already worked out the guitar orchestration for this at my home studio in Plumpton. Robert caught the mood immediately and wrote timeless lyrics to this timeless song. We also began the recording of 'Trampled Under Foot' on this day, with the working title 'Brandy and Coke.' 'Trampled Under Foot' developed in situ and was kicked off by John Paul Jones. 99

—**JIMMY PAGE** (From his website)

66 On 27 February in 1974 at Headley Grange with Led Zeppelin, I had recorded 'Drop Down Mama' (which became 'Custard Pie'), 'Everybody Makes It Through' ('In the Light') and 'Swan Song,' parts 1 and 2. 'Swan Song' was an ambitious piece that I had prepared in my home studio with a number of sections and orchestrated overdubs and we laid down two contrasting sections of it. It never made it any further than this at the time, but the song title was chosen as the name for the forthcoming label that would see the release of *Physical Graffiti*. 'Swan Song' was to be reworked, some years later, with Paul Rodgers who supplied some inspired lyrics and it became 'Midnight Moonlight.' 99

—**JIMMY PAGE** (From his website)

GUEST RECORDING SESSIONS

RECORDING SESSIONS

ABBEY ROAD STUDIOS
3 Abbey Road, London NW8

AUGUST 1974
John Paul Jones Guest Session for Roy Harper

THE GAME (Roy Harper) Available on *HQ* Harvest SHSP 4046 released June 1975.

ROY HARPER: VOCALS, GUITAR
JOHN PAUL JONES: BASS
DAVID GILMOUR: GUITAR
STEVE BROUGHTON: DRUMS
PRODUCER: PETER JENNER
ENGINEER: JOHN LECKIE

66 Dave Gilmour, John Paul Jones, and Steve Broughton were the band that played together at a Hyde Park Free Concert and then recorded the backing track for 'The Game'.99

—ROY HARPER

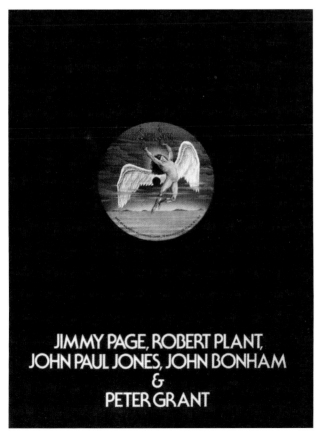

Swan Song promotional advert.

SEPTEMBER 1974

STARTLING STUDIOS
Tittenhurst Park, Ascot, Berkshire

Jimmy Page Guest Session for Maggie Bell

Jimmy Page overdubs guitar on two numbers from Maggie Bell's first Swan Song album, *Suicide Sal.* Although the album came out on the Swan Song label in the US, it was released on Polydor in the UK.

Jimmy Page and Keith Moon onstage at Roy Harper's Valentine Day concert at the Rainbow theatre in Finsbury Park, London. (Dick Barnatt/Getty Images)

181

Promotional poster advertising Led Zeppelin's double album, *Physical Graffiti*.

IF YOU DON'T KNOW (Pete Wingfield) Available on *Suicide Sal* album USA Swan Song SS 8412 released April 1975 / UK Polydor 2383-313 released April 1975 / CD Angel Air SJPCD201 released 2006.

> MAGGIE BELL: VOCALS
> JIMMY PAGE: GUITAR SOLO
> CLARK TERRY: GUITAR
> PAUL FRANCIS: DRUMS
> DELISLE HARPER: BASS
> PETE WINGFIELD: KEYBOARDS

COMIN' ON STRONG (Zoot Money / Colin Allen) Available on *Suicide Sal* album USA Swan Song SS 8412 released April 1975 / UK Polydor 2383-313 released April 1975 / CD Angel Air SJPCD201 released 2006.

> MAGGIE BELL: VOCALS
> JIMMY PAGE: GUITAR SOLO
> BRIAN BREEZE: GUITAR
> PAUL FRANCIS: DRUMS
> DELISLE HARPER: BASS
> PETE WINGFIELD: KEYBOARDS
> PRODUCER: MARK LONDON
> ENGINEER: MARTIN RUSHENT

The Ronnie Lane Mobile Studio was used to record *Physical Graffiti* (taken from an advertising brochure for the studio).

66 This album was recorded in the studio at Tittenhurst Park, which was John Lennon's house in Surrey. The house was then in the ownership of Ringo Starr. I overdubbed on the track 'If You Don't Know,' which had a solo in shades of blue, and a jaunty solo on 'Coming On Strong.' Maggie Bell was one of the signings to the Swan Song label. I'd always considered it to be a pretty good solo on 'If You Don't Know.' 99

—JIMMY PAGE (From his website)

15 1975: Welcome Home

Led Zeppelin return to the live arena this year, which would also see them releasing what many fans and critics consider to be their best album, *Physical Graffiti* The tour was announced after a much-needed eighteen-month sabbatical. Of course it was not all rest for the band during that period. Page and Plant had gone on their travels and found inspiration for some new songs, such as "Driving To Kashmir," which would later be shortened to "Kashmir" and became a massive hit in concert. The two-part 1975 US tour sold out in twenty-four hours with an estimated gross of around $5 million, a huge amount of money at the time. Stadium rock had arrived and Zeppelin were only too pleased to satisfy the fans' appetite to see and hear the band in concert.

But before the tour had even started, disaster struck. Page had sprained his finger in a hinge of a door when alighting from a train at Victoria Station, and Plant had a bad flu. The band quickly arranged a rehearsal in Minneapolis on 17 January 1975 to rearrange the setlist to suit Page's injury. Surprisingly, the now handicapped band managed to play reasonably well during the early gigs on their tenth US tour, although on some nights they were noticeably under par by their usual high standard, much to Jimmy Page's frustration. Page's playing was obviously restricted due to his injury with his third finger on the left hand and the set was adjusted accordingly to make life a little easier. This meant that "Dazed And Confused" had to be dropped because that required a lot of pressure on the injured finger. The substitute number was "How Many More Times," a song they had not played in a few years. As a result he used a two-and-three finger fretboard technique, which allowed him

to rest the sprained finger. Page told the *New Musical Express* about his injury: "It's the finger that does all the leverage and most of the work, and it really came as a blow because I just couldn't play with it." As for the equally incapacitated Plant, he dosed himself up every day and took the necessary medication for his throat, which enabled him to hold up remarkably well during the early shows.

At long last *Rolling Stone* magazine in the US finally decided to take a positive interest in the band after years of negative reviews. Maybe there was more to this band than they had previously thought? The young reporter they sent to cover the band was a guy by the name of Cameron Crowe, who accompanied a group of music magazine reporters from around the world. The resulting article was very positive and earned the band their first ever prized front cover shot in March 1975, just in time for the release of their *Physical Graffiti* double album.

Page admitted to *Rolling Stone* that he was starting to have problems with the whole touring process, but ultimately was happy with the trade-off he needed to make: "I love playing. If it was down to just that, it would be utopia. But it's not. It's aeroplanes, hotel rooms, limousines, and armed guards standing outside rooms. I don't get off on that part of it at all. But it's the price I'm willing to pay to get out and play. I was very restless over the last 18 months where we laid off and worked on the album."

Meanwhile, back in England, the BBC had some new sounds from Led Zeppelin, with some exclusive previews from the forthcoming *Physical Graffiti* double album. On 21 February, Bob Harris, presenter of the popular *Old Grey Whistle Test* television show, played

"Houses Of The Holy" and "Trampled Under Foot" against a backdrop of vintage black-and-white footage from the '20s, which was the norm when playing album tracks on the program. It was required viewing for any self-respecting UK music fan at the time. The following day, Alan "Fluff" Freeman, who hosted the *Rock Show* radio show, played "Custard Pie."

The album offered many different palettes of Led Zeppelin, all of which worked rather well in the double-album format. There was not a single sniff of filler, which was arguably the usual problem with double albums. *Physical Graffiti* took the listener on a great journey that was full of color, dynamics, drama, and character. Led Zeppelin were unlikely to better it.

After the first half of the US tour, Bonham and Jones went home to the UK for two weeks and Page and Plant went off to Dominica in the Caribbean. The second part of the US tour would be mainly in the southern states before heading to the West Coast. After the US tour, Jimmy Page headed to Electric Lady Studios in New York to continue dubbing the live music for *The Song Remains the Same* film. He would also return to New York during the Christmas holidays for more work on the project, as well as a proposed soundtrack album to tie in with the film.

LED ZEPPELIN

NOVEMBER 1974–JANUARY 1975

The band rehearse at Livewire Theater in Ealing.

EUROPEAN WARM-UPS FOR TENTH US TOUR

11 JANUARY 1975–12 JANUARY 1975

11 January 1975, Sportpaleis Ahoy, Rotterdam, Holland

SETLIST: Rock And Roll / Sick Again / Over The Hills And Far Away / When The Levee Breaks / The Song Remains The Same / The Rain Song / Kashmir / The Wanton Song / No Quarter / Trampled Underfoot / In My Time Of Dying / Stairway To Heaven / Whole Lotta Love / Out On The Tiles Intro / Black Dog / Communication Breakdown

12 January 1975, Forest National, Brussels, Belgium (8:15 p.m. Bob Harris interviews Robert Plant backstage for the *Old Grey Whistle Test* program. It is available on the 2003 *Led Zeppelin* DVD.)

SETLIST: Rock And Roll / Sick Again / Over The Hills And Far Away / When The Levee Breaks / The Song Remains The Same / The Rain Song / Kashmir / The Wanton Song / No Quarter / Trampled Underfoot / In My Time Of Dying / Stairway To Heaven / Whole Lotta Love / Out On The Tiles Intro / Black Dog / Communication Breakdown

The warm-up shows for the US tour were a little uneven, as would be expected after such a long layoff from live playing. Robert Plant even mucked up the lyrics to "Stairway To Heaven" on the first night in Rotterdam. Among new songs performed for the first time was "When The Levee Breaks," which was played at both shows and worked really well in the live arena, but surprisingly would be dropped after

Press advert for Led Zeppelin's appearance at the Ahoy in Rotterdam on 11 January 1975.

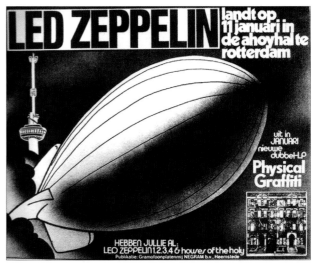

Press advert for Led Zeppelin's appearance at the Ahoy in Rotterdam on 11 January 1975.

only a few shows in the US. "The Wanton Song" was also played and was a perfect vehicle for the band to rock out. Again, it was dropped after a few dates, sadly. But what these uneven warm-ups demonstrate to the listener is how much the band are trying to find their musicality with a new setlist that would show growth, and newfound maturity, over the course of the tour that eventually led to the Earls Court dates in the summer of 1975.

LED ZEPPELIN TENTH US TOUR PART 1

18 JANUARY 1975–16 FEBRUARY 1975

18 January 1975, Metropolitan Sports Center, Bloomington, Minnesota (8:00 p.m.)

Setlist not known but would probably have contained the following: Rock And Roll / Sick Again / Over the Hills And Far Away / In My Time of Dying / The Song Remains The Same / Rain Song / Kashmir / The Wanton Song / No Quarter / When The Levee Breaks / Trampled Underfoot / Moby Dick / How Many More Times / Stairway To Heaven / Whole Lotta Love / Black Dog

20 January 1975, Chicago Stadium, Chicago, Illinois (8:00 p.m.)

SETLIST: Rock And Roll / Sick Again / Over The Hills And Far Away / When The Levee Breaks / The Song Remains The Same / The Rain Song / Kashmir / The Wanton Song / No Quarter / Trampled Underfoot / Moby Dick / In My Time Of Dying / Stairway To Heaven / Whole Lotta Love / Out On The Tiles Intro / Black Dog / Communication Breakdown

Robert Plant was thrilled to have seen Buddy Guy and Hound Dog Taylor the night before in a small Chicago club. He told *Rolling Stone* magazine: "I've already had the biggest turn-on I could imagine, and that was going to watch Buddy Guy and Hound Dog Taylor last night. I mean really: the blues isn't dead. Al Green is great, but underneath all the shim-sham, there's a town called Chicago." Unfortunately going out in the cold of a wintry Chicago night did nothing for his flu, and his voice suffered as a consequence and limits his range.

21 January 1975, Chicago Stadium, Chicago, Illinois (8:00 p.m.)

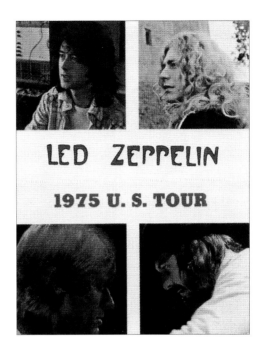

Cover of 1975 US tour program.

SETLIST: Rock And Roll / Sick Again / Over the Hills And Far Away / In My Time of Dying / The Song Remains The Same / The Rain Song / Kashmir / The Wanton Song / No Quarter / When The Levee Breaks / Trampled Underfoot / Moby Dick / How Many More Times / Stairway To Heaven / Whole Lotta Love / Black Dog

22 January 1975, Chicago Stadium, Chicago, Illinois (8:00 p.m.)

SETLIST: Rock And Roll / Sick Again / Over the Hills And Far Away / In My Time Of Dying / The Song Remains The Same / The Rain Song / Kashmir / The Wanton Song / No Quarter / Trampled Underfoot / Moby Dick / How Many More Times / Stairway To Heaven / Whole Lotta Love / Out On The Tiles Intro / Black Dog / Communication Breakdown

It is clear from the opening songs that tonight is going to be special and by far the best of the three Chicago shows. Page is clearly concentrating on his playing due to his injury and is therefore less improvisational than he would be later own the tour. His playing is clean, sharp, and concise and very enjoyable. "No Quarter" is a perfect example of this. The performances of "The Wanton Song" along with the hardly played 1975 rendition of "How Many More Times" are the highlights of the show, and it is surprising that the band chose to drop them shortly afterward.

Led Zeppelin on their
1975 US tour. (Rex)

24 January 1975, Richfield Coliseum, Cleveland, Ohio
(8:00 p.m.)

SETLIST: Rock And Roll / Sick Again / Over the Hills And Far Away / In My Time Of Dying / The Song Remains The Same / The Rain Song / Kashmir / The Wanton Song / No Quarter / Trampled Underfoot / Moby Dick / How Many More Times / Stairway To Heaven / Whole Lotta Love / Out On The Tiles Intro / Black Dog / Communication Breakdown

❝ Led Zeppelin spent their first hour on stage at the Coliseum Friday night playing music that was howlingly loud, but soggy and spiritless. It may have been the effects of guitarist Jimmy Page's intermittent slugs on a Jack Daniel's whisky bottle, or they might just have needed to get some adrenalin moving, but after that first hour the band caught fire and soared through the rest of the concert. ❞
—***BEACON JOURNAL*** (Review from January 1975)

25 January 1975, Market Square Arena, Indianapolis, Indiana
(8:00 p.m.)

SETLIST: Rock And Roll / Sick Again / Over the Hills And Far Away / In My Time Of Dying / The Song Remains The Same / The Rain Song / Kashmir / The Wanton Song / No Quarter / Trampled Underfoot / Moby Dick / How Many More Times / Stairway To Heaven / Whole Lotta Love / Out On The Tiles Intro / Black Dog

Both Page and Plant are struggling with their ailments, which seem to have come to a head at this rather under par concert, resulting in a shorter show than usual. Plant in particular was suffering as his flu was getting worse. Rather than risk any damage, it was decided to cancel the next show and have a break and resume the tour on 29 January.

27 January 1975, St. Louis Arena, St. Louis, Missouri
(Canceled due to Robert Plant's flu and was rescheduled for 16 February 1975. With Plant recuperating by himself at Led Zeppelin base camp in a Chicago hotel for four days, the rest of the band leave their bandmate behind and flew out using their jet to the warmer climes of Los Angeles, where they stayed at their favorite haunt, the Hyatt House, and partied like there was no tomorrow!)

29 January 1975, Greensboro Coliseum, Greensboro, North Carolina (8:00 p.m.)

SETLIST: Rock And Roll / Sick Again / Over the Hills And Far Away / In My Time Of Dying / The Song Remains The Same / The Rain Song / Kashmir / No Quarter / Trampled Underfoot / Moby Dick / How Many More Times / Stairway To Heaven / Whole Lotta Love / Out On The Tiles Intro / Black Dog / Communication Breakdown

The break only made the band tired after partying too much in Los Angeles. Not surprisingly this is another below par show due to Plant's and Page's ailments. In fact, some fans go so far as to say it was their worst performance ever!

31 January 1975 Olympia Stadium, Detroit, Michigan
(8:00 p.m.)

SETLIST: Rock And Roll / Sick Again / Over the Hills And Far Away / In My Time Of Dying / The Song Remains The Same / The Rain Song / Kashmir / No Quarter / Trampled Underfoot / Moby Dick / How Many More Times / Stairway To Heaven / Whole Lotta Love / Out On The Tiles Intro / Black Dog

FEBRUARY 1975

1 February 1975, Civic Arena, Pittsburgh, Pennsylvania

SETLIST NOT KNOWN BUT WOULD PROBABLY CONSISTED OF: Rock And Roll / Sick Again / Over the Hills And Far Away / In My Time Of Dying / The Song Remains The Same / The Rain Song / Kashmir / No Quarter / Trampled Underfoot / Moby Dick / How Many More Times / Stairway To Heaven / Whole Lotta Love / Out On The Tiles Intro / Black Dog

3 February 1975, Madison Square Garden, New York City, New York (8:00 p.m.)

SETLIST: Rock And Roll / Sick Again / Over The Hills And Far Away / In My Time Of Dying / The Song Remains The Same / The Rain Song / Kashmir / No Quarter / Trampled Underfoot / Moby Dick / Dazed And Confused (including San Francisco) / Stairway To Heaven / Whole Lotta Love / Out On The Tiles Intro / Black Dog / Jam / Communication Breakdown (including The Lemon Song)

The first appearance in New York on the 1975 tour and the first 1975 performance of "Dazed And Confused," which had not been played since 29 July 1973, which incidentally was at the same venue. Page is in good form and the finger is healing well despite the touring. Plant, on the other hand, is still suffering and his vocals are strained at times.

4 February 1975, Boston Gardens, Boston, Massachusetts (The show was canceled by the mayor of Boston after $30,000 worth of damage was caused to the arena by 3,000 rioting fans during ticket sales. The show was moved to the Nassau Veterans Memorial Coliseum, Uniondale, New York, on the same date.)

4 February 1975, Nassau Coliseum, Uniondale, New York (8:00 p.m.)

SETLIST: Rock And Roll / Sick Again / Over The Hills And Far Away / In My Time Of Dying / The Song Remains The Same / The Rain Song / Kashmir / No Quarter / Trampled Underfoot / Moby Dick / Dazed And Confused (including San Francisco) / Stairway To Heaven / Whole Lotta Love / Out On The Tiles Intro / Black Dog

6 February 1975, Forum, Montreal, Quebec, Canada (7:30 p.m.)

SETLIST: Rock And Roll / Sick Again / Over The Hills And Far Away / In My Time Of Dying / The Song Remains The Same / The Rain Song / Kashmir / No Quarter / Trampled Underfoot / Moby Dick / Dazed And Confused (including San Francisco) / Stairway To Heaven / Whole Lotta Love / Out On The Tiles Intro / Black Dog / Heartbreaker

7 February 1975, Madison Square Garden, New York City, New York (8:00 p.m.)

SETLIST: Rock And Roll / Sick Again / Over The Hills And Far Away / In My Time Of Dying / The Song Remains The Same / The Rain Song / Kashmir / No Quarter / Trampled Underfoot / Moby Dick / Dazed And Confused (including San Francisco) / Stairway To Heaven / Whole Lotta Love / Out On The Tiles Intro / Black Dog / Heartbreaker

8 February 1975, the Spectrum, Philadelphia, Pennsylvania (Show scheduled for 8:00 p.m. but started an hour late. Great performance with Page and Plant back in good health. A rowdy crowd spoilt what would have otherwise been a great evening.)

SETLIST: Rock And Roll / Sick Again / Over The Hills And Far Away / In My Time Of Dying / The Song Remains The Same / The Rain Song / Kashmir / No Quarter / Trampled Underfoot / Moby Dick / Dazed And Confused (including San Francisco) / Stairway To Heaven / Whole Lotta Love / Out On The Tiles Intro / Black Dog / Heartbreaker

10 February 1975, Capital Centre, Landover, Maryland (8:00 p.m.)

SETLIST: Rock And Roll / Sick Again / Over The Hills And Far Away / In My Time Of Dying / The Song Remains The Same / The Rain Song / Kashmir / No Quarter / Trampled Underfoot / Moby Dick / Dazed And Confused (including San Francisco) / Stairway To Heaven / Whole Lotta Love / Out On The Tiles Intro / Black Dog / Heartbreaker

12 February 1975, Madison Square Garden, New York City, New York (8:00 p.m. Certainly up there with the best shows of 1975. It was a typical wintry New York night with snow blizzards. Did not seem to bother Robert Plant, who tells the audience, "We came four blocks in the snow to get here . . . you realize that? People were calling me on the telephone today and saying, 'Is it gonna be on?' For a minute I was wondering about my anatomy, then I realized there was some discrepancy about the weather. Isn't it good, though, that it snows? Doesn't it change the vibe of the city? I think it's great!")

SETLIST: Rock And Roll / Sick Again / Over The Hills And Far Away / In My Time Of Dying / The Song Remains The Same / The Rain Song / Kashmir / No Quarter / Trampled Underfoot / Moby Dick / Dazed And Confused (including San Francisco) / Stairway To Heaven / Whole Lotta Love / Out On The Tiles Intro / Black Dog / Heartbreaker (including That's Alright Mama)

13 February 1975, Nassau Coliseum, Uniondale, New York (8:00 p.m.)

SETLIST: Rock And Roll / Sick Again / Over The Hills And Far Away / In My Time Of Dying / The Song Remains The Same / The Rain Song / Kashmir / No Quarter / Trampled Underfoot / Moby Dick / Dazed And Confused (including San Francisco) / Stairway To Heaven / Whole Lotta Love / Out On The Tiles Intro / Black Dog / Communication Breakdown (with Ronnie Wood)

Led Zeppelin were not known for having people jam with them. This night was one of the few exceptions, with Ronnie Wood joining the band on guitar for the final encore of "Communication Breakdown." Surprisingly, he does a good job on his solo and trading licks with Page, which can't have been easy with no rehearsal.

14 February 1975, Nassau Coliseum, Uniondale, New York (8:00 p.m.)

SETLIST: Rock And Roll / Sick Again / Over The Hills And Far Away / In My Time Of Dying / Since I've Been Loving You / The Song Remains The Same / The Rain Song / Kashmir / No Quarter / Trampled Underfoot / Moby Dick / Dazed And Confused (including San Francisco) / Stairway To Heaven / Whole Lotta Love / Out On The Tiles Intro / Black Dog / Heartbreaker

Great show for Valentine's night. Possible contender for best show of the tour with a rare outing of "Since I've Been Loving You" from *Led Zeppelin III*. Plant, who is clearly in a good mood, enlightens the audience with some Pagan facts: "Today is one of the last of the pagan traditions that is carried on into the twentieth century. It's the day for sowing the wild seeds. In fact, now they call it St. Valentine's Day . . . so, happy St. Valentine's Day. I think we should dedicate this show to St. Valentine."

Jimmy Page onstage at Tarrant County Convention Center in Fort Worth, Texas, on 3 March 1975. (Photo by Carl Dunn)

16 February 1975, the Arena, St. Louis, Missouri (The show was rescheduled from January 27, 1975. The band close out the first half of the tour in style with another outstanding show. The band take a ten-day break before resuming the tour in Houston on 27 February.)

SETLIST: Rock And Roll / Sick Again / Over The Hills And Far Away / In My Time Of Dying / The Song Remains The Same / The Rain Song / Kashmir / No Quarter / Trampled Underfoot / Moby Dick / Dazed And Confused (including a few seconds of Train Kept A Rollin', San Francisco) / Stairway To Heaven / Whole Lotta Love / Out On The Tiles Intro / Black Dog / Heartbreaker

LED ZEPPELIN TENTH US TOUR PART 2
27 FEBRUARY 1975 – 27 MARCH 1975

27 February 1975, Sam Houston Coliseum, Houston, Texas (8:00 p.m.)

SETLIST: Rock And Roll / Sick Again / Over The Hills And Far Away / In My Time Of Dying / The Song Remains The Same / The Rain Song / Kashmir / No Quarter / Trampled Underfoot / Moby Dick / Dazed And Confused (including Woodstock) / Stairway To Heaven / Whole Lotta Love (including The Crunge) / Out On The Tiles Intro / Black Dog

The "San Francisco" section in "Dazed And Confused" has now been replaced with Joni Mitchell's "Woodstock."

28 February 1975, Louisiana State University Assembly Center, Baton Rouge, Louisiana (8:00 p.m.)

SETLIST: Rock And Roll / Sick Again / Over The Hills And Far Away / In My Time Of Dying / The Song Remains The Same / The Rain Song / Kashmir / No Quarter / Trampled Underfoot / Moby Dick / Dazed And Confused (including Woodstock) / Stairway To Heaven / Whole Lotta Love (including The Crunge) / Out On The Tiles Intro / Black Dog

Another fabulous show from 1975. As you would expect, "No Quarter" and "Dazed And Confused" are spectacular with Page and Jones at their experimental best. Both songs are lengthy and the improvisations are truly jaw-dropping at times. The band are in good humor with Bonham being introduced as "the man with a bicycle clip caught in his sock . . .

Robert Plant and Jimmy Page onstage at Tarrant County Convention Center in Fort Worth, Texas, on 3 March 1975. (Photo by Carl Dunn)

the greatest percussionist since Big Ben!" As today's date was also the date of the US release for *Physical Graffiti*, Plant tells the audience, "The egg has been laid . . . or is it the guy who got laid?" Plant is very chatty this evening and ends the show with, "Baton Rouge—a really good audience . . . and Led Zeppelin, just a fun-loving bunch of boys. It's been more than our pleasure!"

MARCH 1975

3 March 1975, Tarrant County Convention Center, Fort Worth, Texas (8:00 p.m.)

Robert Plant and Jimmy Page onstage at Tarrant County Convention Center in Fort Worth, Texas, on 3 March 1975. (Photo by Carl Dunn)

Robert Plant and Jimmy Page onstage at Tarrant County Convention Center in Fort Worth, Texas, on 3 March 1975. (Photo by Carl Dunn)

SETLIST: Rock And Roll / Sick Again / Over The Hills And Far Away / In My Time Of Dying / The Song Remains The Same / The Rain Song / Kashmir / No Quarter / Trampled Underfoot / Moby Dick / Dazed And Confused (including Woodstock) / Stairway To Heaven / Whole Lotta Love (including The Crunge) / Out On The Tiles Intro / Black Dog

4 March 1975, Dallas Memorial Auditorium, Dallas, Texas (8:00 p.m.)

SETLIST: Rock And Roll / Sick Again / Over The Hills And Far Away / In My Time Of Dying / The Song Remains The Same / The Rain Song / Kashmir / No Quarter / Trampled Underfoot / Moby Dick / Dazed And Confused (including Woodstock) / Stairway To Heaven / Whole Lotta Love (including The Crunge) / Out On The Tiles Intro / Black Dog / Heartbreaker

The crowd just don't seem to be in the right mood tonight, and the band appear to be apathetic and their playing is lackadaisical. All these factors lead to a very average show. Plant had done his best to liven everybody up by interjecting humorous asides at every opportunity, but it did nothing to improve spirits. When humor failed, his ego got the better of him and sarcasm took over.

5 March 1975, Dallas Memorial Auditorium, Dallas, Texas (8:00 p.m.)

SETLIST: Rock And Roll / Sick Again / Over The Hills And Far Away / In My Time Of Dying / The Song Remains The Same / The Rain Song / Kashmir / No Quarter / Trampled Underfoot / Moby Dick / Dazed And Confused (including Woodstock) / Stairway To Heaven / Whole Lotta Love (including The Crunge) / Out On The Tiles Intro / Black Dog

After the minor disaster the previous night, the band are in a better place and play well. They are musically tighter and the improvisations in the lengthy versions of "No Quarter" and "Dazed And Confused" are highlights of the evening, as is a particularly heavy rendition of "Trampled Underfoot." "Whole Lotta Love" includes a very funky version of "The Crunge," which is followed by an encore of "Black Dog."

8 March 1975, Florida Rock Festival, West Palm Beach International Raceway, West Palm Beach, Florida (The festival was canceled by the owner of the racetrack because the promoters did not make essential improvements to the property, which would have needed to be done if the festival was to have gone ahead.)

10 March 1975, Sports Arena, San Diego, California (8:00 p.m.)

SETLIST: Rock And Roll / Sick Again / Over The Hills And Far Away / In My Time Of Dying / The Song Remains The Same / The Rain Song / Kashmir / No Quarter / Trampled Underfoot / Moby Dick / Dazed And Confused (including Woodstock) / Stairway To Heaven / Whole Lotta Love (including The Crunge) / Out On The Tiles Intro / Black Dog

11 March 1975, Long Beach Arena, Long Beach, California (8:00 p.m.)

SETLIST: Rock And Roll / Sick Again / Over The Hills And Far Away / In My Time Of Dying / The Song Remains The Same / The Rain Song / Kashmir / No Quarter / Trampled Underfoot / Moby Dick / Dazed And Confused (including Woodstock) / Stairway To Heaven / Whole Lotta Love (including The Crunge) / Out On The Tiles Intro / Black Dog

Another good show with the band clearly happy to be back in California. The band were a little late, for which Robert Plant apologizes after performing "Sick Again." "We must apologize for the slight delay, but we couldn't get into the building and we hadn't got any tickets! It's a fact. We saw a well-known scalper, but we blew it . . . and it was blown!" The audience seem a little too calm for a Led Zeppelin concert and there were the odd equipment problems, but despite these hiccups, the band play well. Plant also manages to joke about the bootleggers after "The Song Remains The Same": "For the benefit of anyone who was making a bootleg then—the 12-string was out of tune!" A near thirty-minute version of "Dazed And Confused" is one of several highlights tonight. After "Black Dog," the last encore, Robert Plant tells the audience, "Ladies and gentlemen of Long Beach . . . sleep well! Half a Quaalude with water."

12 March 1975, Long Beach Arena, Long Beach, California (8:00 p.m.)

SETLIST: Rock And Roll / Sick Again / Over The Hills And Far Away / In My Time Of Dying / The Song Remains The Same / The Rain Song / Kashmir / No Quarter / Trampled Underfoot / Moby Dick / Dazed And Confused (including Woodstock) / Stairway To Heaven / Whole Lotta Love (including The Crunge) / Out On The Tiles Intro / Black Dog / Heartbreaker (including I'm A Man)

Well, this is one of those shows that simply takes your breath away. The band are in top form and put in a very energetic set that is both dynamic and visceral in equal measure. Dylan gets a name check before "In My Time Of Dying," when it is described by Plant as, "An old work song. A long time before Mr. Zimmerman listened to it in the Village back in the '60s." Page is playing so hard that he breaks a string during "The Song Remains The Same," which was then halted by Plant: "Hang on! Hold it a minute! They didn't tell me it was like this in Valhalla! Yes, it happened for the first time in six and a half years! Does anyone remember laughter?" The song was started again as soon as Page's guitar was restrung. An incredible version of "Dazed And Confused" is dedicated to Roy Harper. "Wherever you are, Roy, don't stay in that state too long!" Another surprise this evening was the inclusion of "I'm A Man" during the final encore of "Heartbreaker."

14 March 1975, San Diego Sports Arena, San Diego, California (8:00 p.m. Date added due to the 10 March show selling out so quickly.)

SETLIST: Rock And Roll / Sick Again / Over The Hills And Far Away / In My Time Of Dying / The Song Remains The Same / The Rain Song / Kashmir / No Quarter / Trampled Underfoot / Moby Dick / Dazed And Confused (including Woodstock) / Stairway To Heaven / Whole Lotta Love (including The Crunge) / Out On The Tiles Intro / Black Dog / Heartbreaker

17 March 1975, Seattle Center Coliseum, Seattle, Washington (8:00 p.m.)

SETLIST: Rock And Roll / Sick Again / Over The Hills And Far Away / In My Time Of Dying / The Song Remains The Same / The Rain Song / Kashmir / No Quarter / Trampled Underfoot / Moby Dick / Dazed And Confused (including Woodstock) / Stairway To Heaven / Whole Lotta Love (including The Crunge) / Out On The Tiles Intro / Black Dog

Tonight's show was another amazing performance by Led Zeppelin. The whole band is in top form and playing at their best. As was often the case on the 1975 tour, the two improvisational numbers, "No Quarter" and "Dazed And Confused," are the highlights with some truly breathtaking performances by Page and Jones. The band always enjoyed playing in Seattle, and Plant tells the audience how pleased they are to be back: "As you can imagine, it's more than a pleasure to be back in this coastal town . . . a town of great fisherman, including our drummer." The joke about Bonham and fishing was of course a reference to the infamous Edgewater Inn located directly on Elliott Bay in Seattle. It was a favorite with Led Zeppelin because they could fish from their rooms and led to the notorious mud shark incident in 1969, which has been so overexaggerated over the years. Frank Zappa and the Mothers even sang a song about the incident on their live *Fillmore East June 1971* album.

19 March 1975, Pacific Coliseum, Vancouver, British Columbia, Canada (8:00 p.m.)

SETLIST: Rock And Roll / Sick Again / Over The Hills And Far Away / In My Time Of Dying / The Song Remains The Same / The Rain Song / Kashmir / No Quarter / Trampled Underfoot / Moby Dick / Dazed And Confused (including Woodstock) / Stairway To Heaven / Whole Lotta Love (including The Crunge) / Out On The Tiles Intro / Black Dog

20 March 1975, Pacific Coliseum, Vancouver, British Columbia, Canada (8:00 p.m.)

SETLIST: Rock And Roll / Sick Again / Over The Hills And Far Away / In My Time Of Dying / The Song Remains The Same / The Rain Song / Kashmir / No Quarter / Trampled Underfoot / Moby Dick / Dazed And Confused (including Woodstock) / Stairway To Heaven / Whole Lotta Love (including The Crunge) / Heartbreaker

21 March 1975, Seattle Center Coliseum, Seattle, Washington (8:00 p.m.)

SETLIST: Rock And Roll / Sick Again / Over The Hills And Far Away / In My Time Of Dying / The Song Remains The Same / The Rain Song / Kashmir / No Quarter / Since I've Been Loving You / Trampled Underfoot / Moby Dick / Dazed And Confused (including For What It's Worth, Woodstock) / Stairway To Heaven / Whole Lotta Love (including The Crunge) / Out On The Tiles Intro / Black Dog / Communication Breakdown / Heartbreaker

Epic and legendary are two words that sum up this concert, one of their very best from 1975, and a very long show. The two highlights have to be the improvisational pieces, "No Quarter," which ran to thirty minutes tonight, and "Dazed And Confused," which ran to a mind-blowing forty-five minutes. Both numbers are full of contrasts, dynamics, and superlative playing by everyone in the band. "Since I've Been Loving You" and "Communication Breakdown" make rare appearances tonight. The former was apparently unscheduled, according to Plant on the night: "There's one song that we've done twice in, in . . . I suppose since we got ripped off for all that bread in New York, ages ago. And because we really dig playing here, and for no other reason, we're gonna do it again now. I don't think anyone else in the band knows about it yet, it's a little bit of a change in the . . . sorry about that, John! You see, right on the spot! It could be "Louie Louie" but instead it's a thing from the third album . . . 'Since I've Been Loving You'."

24 March 1975, the Forum, Inglewood, Los Angeles, California (7:30 p.m.)

SETLIST: Rock And Roll / Sick Again / Over The Hills And Far Away / In My Time Of Dying / The Song Remains The Same / The Rain Song / Kashmir / No Quarter / Trampled Underfoot / Moby Dick / Dazed And Confused (including Woodstock) / Stairway To Heaven / Whole Lotta Love (including The Crunge) / Out On The Tiles Intro / Black Dog / Heartbreaker

DJ J. J. Jackson introduces the band: "Good evening! My name is J. J. Jackson of KWLOS. We're all here to welcome back to the LA area . . . Led Zeppelin!" The LA shows were always going to be good and Plant confirms that to the crowd. "This is the place, this is the one. These are the last three gigs on our American tour and so we intend them to be something of a high point for us. Obviously, we don't achieve that without a little bit of a vibe, that I can already feel, and a few smiles." Page occasionally goes out of tune, but overall this is a great LA opening.

25 March 1975, the Forum, Inglewood, Los Angeles, California (7:30 p.m.)

SETLIST: Rock And Roll / Sick Again / Over The Hills And Far Away / In My Time Of Dying / The Song Remains The Same / The Rain Song / Kashmir / No Quarter / Trampled Underfoot / Moby Dick / Dazed And Confused (including Spanish Eyes, Woodstock) / Stairway To Heaven / Whole Lotta Love (including Lickin' Stick, Sex Machine, The Crunge) / Out On The Tiles Intro / Black Dog

A warm welcome greets the band as they come onstage. Plant tells the enthusiastic LA crowd, "Last night we had a really good time. We had a great concert. It was one of the finest we've had in California for a long time!" In reality, tonight's show is even better than the opening night. It is a great night for improvisation and "Dazed And Confused" along with "No Quarter" are spectacular. The latter has a smoky jazz club feel in the middle when Page and Jones are jamming. A glorious "Trampled Underfoot" is dedicated to "all the good ladies of America who've helped us get rid of the blues from time to time on the road."

27 March 1975, the Forum, Inglewood, Los Angeles, California (7:30 p.m. DJ J. J. Jackson and *Deep Throat* star Linda Lovelace introduce the band.)

SETLIST: Rock And Roll / Sick Again / Over The Hills And Far Away / In My Time Of Dying / The Song Remains The Same / The Rain Song / Kashmir / Since I've Been Loving You / No Quarter / Trampled Underfoot / Moby Dick / Dazed And Confused / Stairway To Heaven / Whole Lotta Love (including The Crunge, Lickin' Stick) / Out On The Tiles Intro / Black Dog

The third and final night at the Forum ends their 1975 US tour on a high. In typical Led Zeppelin fashion, they surprise the audience by having infamous *Deep Throat* star Linda Lovelace introduce the band this evening. "Dazed and Confused" is the highlight tonight, clocking in at nearly fifty minutes, and features some intricate improvisation from Page expertly backed by Jones and Bonham. "No Quarter" is no slouch either tonight. An extra musical surprise came in the form of an exquisite version of "Since I've Been Loving You," one of only three versions performed on the 1975 tour. Next stop would be the welcome return of the band in their homeland of the United Kingdom.

LED ZEPPELIN UK DATES

EARLS COURT SHOWS

17 MAY 1975–25 MAY 1975

Led Zeppelin return to the UK in style. As much as they would have liked to do a tour of the whole country, it was impossible, as there were no venues big enough to accommodate their entire US stage set. So it was

EARLS COURT ARENA
(OPPOSITE WARWICK ROAD EXIT EARLS COURT TUBE STATION)

MEL BUSH by arrangement with PETER GRANT presents

LED ZEPPELIN

Saturday, May 17th, 1975
at 8-0 p.m. (Doors open 6-0)

3rd Tier Stalls £2·50

FOR CONDITIONS OF SALE SEE OVER

BLOCK 7

ROW SEAT

B 64

TO BE RETAINED

Ticket for the opening night of Led Zeppelin's return to the UK at Earls Court Arena on 17 May 1975.

decided to book the massive Earls Court Exhibition Centre in London, and organize special trains from major cities to various London rail stations for fans to get to the show. Three shows were announced initially with a further two being added shortly after due to phenomenal ticket demand. Even with the additional shows, over 100,000 mail-order ticket applications had to be returned due to the overwhelming demand. These shows were the most anticipated concerts of 1975 in the UK by far. The band had set themselves up at Shepperton Studios with their full US sound and light show for several weeks' worth of rehearsals, to ensure they were in perfect shape for their all-important homecoming shows. *Melody Maker* reported that the band setup for the five shows would include a 340,000-watt light show, a 24 by 30 foot video screen, and a 24,000-watt PA.

A different popular UK disc jockey introduced the band at each show. All five shows were recorded on 16-track tape by the Rolling Stones Mobile recording truck, just in case a live album would be considered at some point in the future. Despite rumors to the contrary, none of the shows were professionally filmed. The video cameras that were present in the hall were there simply to relay close-up images of band members, using an Eidophor projection system, to a screen located above the stage so that the crowd at the back of the hall could see what was going on. Some of the shows have survived on two-inch video, but as the images are mostly close-ups, they do not really convey any depth or atmosphere of the concerts. Also, it should be noted that the resolution of these old analog videos is limited, which means a Blu-ray would not give a quality improvement. The setlist was basically the same as the US tour, but did have the welcome return of the acoustic set in the middle.

The following Earls Court footage and audio can be found on the *Led Zeppelin* DVD from 2003:

GOING TO CALIFORNIA is largely taken from the 25 May show with some patching from the 23 May show.

THAT'S THE WAY is taken from the 25 May show.

BRON-Y-AUR STOMP is taken from the 25 May show with some patching from the 23 May show.

IN MY TIME OF DYING is taken from the 24 May show.

TRAMPLED UNDER FOOT is taken from the 25 May show with some patching from both the 23 and 24 May shows.

STAIRWAY TO HEAVEN is taken from the 25 May show with some patching from the 24 May show.

The "Earls Court" audio options menu on the *Led Zeppelin* DVD features "Bron-Y-Aur Stomp" from the 24 May show, and "Whole Lotta Love" from the 25 May show can also be found on the second disc's audio options.

Although the 23 May show was the first to be announced, the two extra shows were brought forward to 17 and 18 May. The anticipation for the opening night was incredible. As soon as the lights went down, the crowd stood up and cheered wildly to welcome Led Zeppelin back home. After a brief intro by Bob Harris—"We'd all like to welcome back to Britain . . . Led Zeppelin!"—the band launched straight into a ferocious "Rock And Roll." Unfortunately, halfway through the song, Jimmy stepped on his guitar lead and unplugged the jack plug from his Les Paul. The problem was soon fixed and the band played on. The humor was also present over the course of the shows. On the first night, "In My Time Of Dying" was dedicated to the then-Chancellor of the Exchequer, Dennis Healey, who was taxing high earners heavily at the time, causing all of the UK's talented musicians to live overseas to avoid losing 83 percent of their income over £20,000. Not surprisingly, the band did suffer from first-night nerves, and the opening night was the weakest of the five. Highlights at all the shows are dramatic versions "No Quarter" and "Dazed And Confused," with dry ice and lasers used to great effect. The crowds were completely mesmerized.

17 May 1975, Earls Court Exhibition Centre, London (8:00 p.m. *The Old Grey Whistle Test*'s Bob Harris introduced the band tonight. This show was one of two extra dates added to the original three that had been announced originally.)

SETLIST: Rock And Roll / Sick Again / Over The Hills And Far Away / In My Time Of Dying / The Song Remains The Same / The Rain Song / Kashmir / No Quarter / Tangerine / Going To California / That's The Way / Bron-Yr-Aur Stomp / Trampled Underfoot / Moby Dick / Dazed And Confused (including Woodstock) / Stairway To Heaven / Whole Lotta Love / The Crunge / Out On The Tiles Intro / Black Dog

18 May 1975, Earls Court Exhibition Centre, London (8:00 p.m. DJ Johnnie Walker introduced the band tonight. This show was the second of two extra dates added to the original three that had been announced originally.)

Press advert announcing additional dates at Earls Court Arena due to phenomenal ticket demand.

SETLIST: Rock And Roll / Sick Again / Over The Hills And Far Away / In My Time Of Dying / The Song Remains The Same / The Rain Song / Kashmir / No Quarter / Tangerine / Going To California / That's The Way / Bron-Yr-Aur Stomp / Trampled Underfoot / Moby Dick / Dazed And Confused (including Woodstock) / Stairway To Heaven / Whole Lotta Love / The Crunge / Out On The Tiles Intro / Black Dog

Led Zeppelin at Earls Court Arena during their five-night run in May 1975. (Rex)

Introduced by Johnnie Walker, the band are a lot more focused and relaxed, having got the first show under their belt. Jimmy Page is inspired tonight and it's reflected in his playing throughout the show. Highlights include a dazzling "No Quarter" and a long "Dazed And Confused." "Over The Hills And Far Away" is also worthy of praise for Page's inventive soloing.

23 May 1975, Earls Court Exhibition Centre, London (8:00 p.m. DJ David "Kid" Jensen introduced the band tonight at what was technically the first show, as remarked by Robert Plant after "Rock And Roll.")

Poster advertising concerts for Led Zeppelin at Earls Court in London for 23, 24, and 25 May 1975.

SETLIST: Rock And Roll / Sick Again / Over The Hills And Far Away / In My Time Of Dying / The Song Remains The Same / The Rain Song / Kashmir / No Quarter / Tangerine / Going To California / That's The Way / Bron-Yr-Aur Stomp / Trampled Underfoot / Moby Dick / Dazed And Confused (including San Francisco) / Stairway To Heaven / Whole Lotta Love / The Crunge / Out On The Tiles Intro / Black Dog

Tonight's show is introduced by David "Kid" Jensen: "Good evening! Welcome to the show. After an absence of something like two years, I guess we're all ready for a little *Physical Graffiti*. Please welcome to Earls Court . . . Led Zeppelin!" A very energized show. Robert Plant reminds the audience that this was really the first show. "Last weekend we did a couple of warm-up gigs for these three. We believe these were the first three gigs to be sold out, so these must be the ones with the most energy stored up." He wasn't wrong. The whole show is a highlight from beginning to end, and possibly the best of the five-night run.

24 May 1975, Earls Court Exhibition Centre, London (8:00 p.m. Capital Radio's DJ Nicky Horne introduced the band tonight.)

SETLIST: Rock And Roll / Sick Again / Over The Hills And Far Away / In My Time Of Dying / The Song Remains The Same / The Rain Song / Kashmir / No Quarter / Tangerine / Going To California / That's The Way / Bron-Yr-Aur Stomp / Trampled Underfoot / Moby Dick / Dazed And Confused (including Woodstock) / Stairway To Heaven / Whole Lotta Love / The Crunge / Out On The Tiles Intro / Black Dog

Another hot show, which was introduced by Capital Radio's Nicky Horne: "Welcome to Earls Court. For the next three hours . . . your mother wouldn't like it!" Nicky had a hugely popular radio show called *Your Mother Wouldn't Like It* at the time. This is certainly one of the best nights of the entire 1975 tour. "No Quarter" had really developed into the improvisational piece of each show and tonight's version is one of the best ever, with both Page and Jones playing at their utmost in a mesmerizing rendition that left the crown breathless. "Dazed And Confused" was equally impressive, taking the audience on a thirty-minute journey of musical bliss. Before introducing the number, Plant has a dig at Dennis Healey: "We gotta fly soon. Y'know how it goes with Dennis . . . dear Dennis. Private enterprise . . . no artists in the country anymore . . . he must be dazed and confused!" John Bonham comes up to the microphone before the

encores to give his view on the current state of UK football with a succinct "I'd like to say at this point that I think football's a load of bollocks!" which was quickly refuted by football enthusiast Plant, "I'd like to say that soccer's a wonderful sport, the best sport."

25 May 1975 Earls Court Exhibition Centre, London (8:00 p.m. DJ Alan "Fluff" Freeman introduced the band tonight.)

SETLIST: Rock And Roll / Sick Again / Over The Hills And Far Away / In My Time Of Dying / The Song Remains The Same / The Rain Song / Kashmir / No Quarter / Tangerine / Going To California / That's The Way / Bron-Yr-Aur Stomp / Trampled Underfoot / Moby Dick / Dazed And Confused (including San Francisco) / Stairway To Heaven / Whole Lotta Love / The Crunge / Out On The Tiles Intro / Black Dog / Heartbreaker / Communication Breakdown (including D'yer Mak'er)

The last night and another great show, although the performance of "Dazed And Confused" was probably the least interesting of all the Earls Court nights. It also turned out to be the last time the band would perform it. Plant put in one last exasperated comment about Dennis Healey: "This is our last concert in England for some considerable time. Still, there's always the '80s. If you see Dennis Healey, tell him we've gone!" This turned out to be quite a prophetic comment, as the band would not play in England again until 1979 at Knebworth. "No Quarter" was a highlight tonight with some inspired jamming from Page and Jones. Plant dedicated "Stairway To Heaven" to his daughter, "Carmen—this song's to a little girl who sits probably wondering what it's all about . . . so, where is the bridge? Well, Carmen, here's your chance to find out where the bridge is . . . and if you know, please let me know after the show." Page's solo is exquisite and the last night fans are treated to two extra encores. When interviewed by Chris Welch for *Melody Maker* in June, John Bonham had this to say about the Earls Court shows: "I enjoyed those concerts. I thought they were the best shows that we've ever put on in England. I always get tense before a show, and we were expecting trouble with such a huge audience. But everything went really well and although we couldn't have the laser beams at full power, I thought the video screen was well worth doing. It cost a lot of bread, but you could see close-ups you'd never be able to see normally at a concert. It was worth every penny."

On the 26 May 1975, the morning after the last Earls Court show, Robert Plant and his wife, Maureen, headed off to Agadir on the Moroccan coast for a holiday. Jimmy Page had agreed to meet Robert in Marrakech a few weeks later to attend the Marrakech folk festival. In the meantime, Page flew off to New York to work on the live material from their 1973 Madison Square Garden shows that would be used as a soundtrack album for their film. In preparation for his Moroccan adventure, Plant had brought along an expensive tape recorder and wanted to look into the possibility of recording some Berber rhythms as well as the sounds of other ethnic groups from different hill tribes in Morocco. Over the years Page and Plant had often traveled far and wide in obscure places around the globe, far away from the beaten track, to find inspiration for songs and music. And so it was on this trip.

After the folk festival, Page and Plant headed off the tourist trail in a sturdy Range Rover toward Taifa, a commune in the Taza Province near the Spanish Sahara. Although there was conflict between Spain and Morocco at the time, they surprisingly successfully negotiated getting through several police and army roadblocks on their trip. In the end, it was not the police or army that prevented them from reaching their destination, but the appalling road conditions. Eventually, the time came to leave Plant's beloved Moroccan vacation and they traveled overland to Montreux in Switzerland via Casablanca, Tangier, Gibraltar, Spain, and France. Once there they had a band meeting to discuss the next tour of America due to happen later that year. Dates were agreed and rehearsals were scheduled to start in Paris, France, on 10 August 1975, and would probably include warm-up shows in Europe as well. While in Switzerland, members of the band attended various concerts at the Montreux Jazz Festival, which ran from 3 July to 20 July 1975.

With dates for the next Led Zeppelin tour set and booked, Plant was desperate to leave Switzerland and head off to find the sun and the laid-back lifestyle he had grown accustomed to in Morocco for over a month and a half. The Greek island of Rhodes was the destination picked as he knew Phil May from the Pretty Things would be there also. Page and his wife, Charlotte, and their daughter, Scarlet, accompanied Plant and his family for the vacation. On the 3 August, Page left by himself to go to Sicily and visit a farmhouse once owned by Aleister Crowley. They

were all due to meet up in Paris on the 10 August for band rehearsals. Unfortunately, on 4 August, a rented Mini being driven by Maureen Plant went off the road and hit a tree, seriously injuring her and Robert Plant. Also in the car were their children, all of whom luckily escaped with minor injuries. Maureen had a broken pelvis and fractured skull and Robert had multiple right-leg and elbow fractures. Page's wife, Charlotte, and their daughter, Scarlet, along with Maureen's sister, had been traveling in a car behind and were able to contact the emergency services.

They were all taken to a Greek hospital where Robert Plant initially had a doctor working on him nonstop for thirty-six hours. He had to share a room with a drunken Greek soldier who had injured his head after falling down. He did not speak English, but recognized Plant and started humming "The Ocean" from the *Houses of the Holy* album as a way of communicating to Plant that he knew who he was. In the meantime, Plant was in agony and attempting to remove cockroaches off his bed. Plant's wife, Maureen, was in a far worse condition and close to dying. She had a rare blood type, and although her sister was there and able to give her some of her blood, it was not enough and more would be needed if she was to survive. Communication was not as sophisticated as it is today. No mobile phones or tablets back then. However, word finally got to Richard Cole from Charlotte Page about what happened. He quickly organized a private jet to take him along with two Harley Street specialists to go and see Plant and his family. After several protestations from the local doctors and authorities, everyone was taken back to London to Guy's Hospital for care and ongoing medical treatment.

Danny Goldberg, Vice President of Led Zeppelin's Swan Song Records, issued the following press statement on 8 August 1975 about Plant's accident:

The August–September tour of English supergroup, Led Zeppelin, has been postponed following an auto accident on the small Greek Island of Rhodes in which Led Zeppelin lead singer Robert Plant and members of his family were injured. The accident took place on Monday afternoon, August 4th. Due to the nature and extent of the injuries sustained by Plant and his family, and the inadequate medical facilities in Rhodes, a member of the London staff of Swan Song, Led Zeppelin's record company, flew to

Rhodes in a chartered jet equipped with stretchers, blood plasma, and two doctors from Harley Street, England's finest medical center. Plant and his family are currently under intensive care in a London hospital. Earlier today, physicians there diagnosed his injuries as multiple fractures of ankle, bones supporting the foot, and elbow. Following this diagnosis, it was announced by Led Zeppelin manager, Peter Grant, and Zeppelin attorney, Steve Weiss, that the August–September tour was postponed, as was the October tour that had been scheduled for the Far East. Additionally, there is the possibility that the scheduled November tour of Europe and December tour of Japan may also have to be postponed. Within the next couple of weeks, doctors expect to have a better idea of when Plant will be recovered and able to perform again. Plant's wife, Maureen, also in the car, suffered a lengthy period of concussions, and has broken her leg in several places. She has four fractures of the pelvis and facial lacerations. Plant's son, Karac, 4, suffered a fractured leg and multiple cuts and bruises. His daughter, Carmen 7, has a broken wrist, cuts and bruises.

The band was due to begin rehearsals for their forthcoming U.S. tour, in Paris on August 14. 110,000 tickets to two shows at the Oakland Stadium were completely sold out at $10 apiece. Among the other concerts which were postponed were those in Los Angeles at the Rose Bowl, Kansas City, Louisville, New Orleans, Tempe, Arizona, Denver, and Atlanta.

Danny Goldberg, Vice-President of Swan Song in the U.S.A., said that any fans or well wishers who wish to write to Plant or his family can write care of Swan Song, 484 Kings Road, London S.W. 10 OLF, England.

Led Zeppelin has been called the biggest group in rock and roll. They hold the record for the largest attendance ever drawn by a single act: 56,800 who paid to see them at Tampa Stadium in Florida on May 5, 1973, toppling a seven year old Beatles record. Their six albums have sold in excess of 15 million copies world-wide, and their most recent tour of America last winter broke records all over the country. Besides Plant, the group consists of Jimmy Page, Lead guitar, John Paul Jones, bass and keyboards, and John Bonham, drummer. Their manager is Peter Grant who is also president of Swan Song.

As a tax-exile, Robert Plant could not stay in England any longer than he already had if he was to avoid a huge tax bill. The rest of the band were already in the offshore tax haven of Jersey in the Channel Isles, and he was quickly moved there as well, where he underwent a strict regime of physical therapy. It was a very depressing time for him as Maureen was too ill to be moved and had to stay in a London hospital. The band obviously couldn't tour with Robert in the condition he was in, so it was decided to make plans to record a new Led Zeppelin studio album. It made perfect sense and would keep Plant's mind on being creative rather than pondering on his injuries more than he had to.

In September Robert Plant, along with the rest of the band and Peter Grant, relocated to the Malibu Colony on the Californian coast in five separate houses. Plant would be driven to Los Angeles every day by Benji Lefevre for physiotherapy on his arm and ankle, which was a real strain on him. In between trips to the hospital, Plant and Page would attempt to come up with some new material for the next album. Plant certainly had plenty of material for lyrics, but most of the songs were only properly developed during later rehearsals at S.I.R. (Studio Instrument Rehearsals) in Los Angeles. One song, "Achilles Last Stand," had already been started when the pair were in Morocco during the summer. Plant's depression about the seedy LA drug scene was the main inspiration behind "For Your Life," and his frustration with Grant and Page's perceived insensitivity about his incapacitated situation led to "Hots On For Nowhere." It was not a fun time for the band and the air was thick with tension. John Bonham hated the isolation of being in his house so much that he moved himself into the Hyatt House.

Before long the band started proper rehearsals for their new album at Studio Instrument Rehearsals in Los Angeles. Things did not go particularly smoothly as everyone seemed to be waiting on Jimmy Page to arrive. Often that would mean waiting until two in the morning. It was around this time that Page started dabbling with heroin. Before that it had really only been cocaine. Nevertheless, by November the entire band were ready to travel to Germany and head to Musicland Studios in Munich. It was quite a shock to arrive from sunny Los Angeles to a freezing cold winter day in Germany. They had no choice, though, as staying any longer in America would also have had tax implications on their earnings from the US. The studio was located in the basement of the Arabella Hotel, which was located in a quiet part of town. The cold weather also ensured the band would stay within the hotel and studio complex. Still, it helped keep the band focused. Whatever faults Jimmy Page may have had at the time, he certainly still knew what he was doing in the studio and the album was completed in only three weeks. Quite an achievement. The tension and sense of urgency during the sessions came across loud and clear on the *Presence* album, and is now a well-loved album by many people who previously had almost written it off at the time of release.

After the album was finished, the band returned to Jersey.

JULY 1975

11 July 1975, Montreux Jazz Festival, Montreux Casino, Montreux, Switzerland (John Paul Jones, playing bass, joins Etta James.)

20 July 1975, Montreux Jazz Festival, Montreux Casino, Montreux, Switzerland (John Paul Jones, playing bass, joins Maria Muldaur, who was best known at the time for her 1974 hit single, "Midnight at the Oasis.")

LED ZEPPELIN AUGUST 1975 US TOUR CANCELED

23 AUGUST 1975–9 SEPTEMBER 1975

Before Plant's accident, Led Zeppelin had been scheduled to do another US tour, starting with two high-profile Day on the Green concerts at the Oakland Coliseum promoted by Bill Graham. After America, the band was also planning shows in South America for the first time before heading back to the UK and Europe into early 1976. Obviously with Robert incapacitated, the whole schedule had to be canceled and Led Zeppelin would not return to the live arena until 1977.

23 August 1975, Day on the Green, Oakland Coliseum, Oakland, California (Canceled due to Robert Plant's car accident. Support would have included Joe Walsh and the Pretty Things.)

24 August 1975, Day on the Green, Oakland Coliseum, Oakland, California (Canceled due to Robert Plant's car accident. Support would have included Joe Walsh and the Pretty Things.)

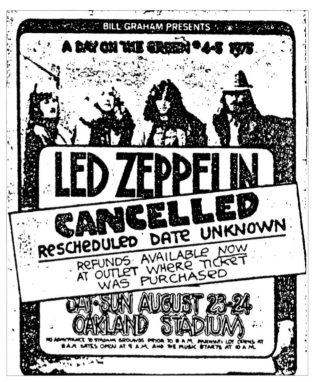

Press advert alerting the public of the cancelation of Led Zeppelin's appearance at Oakland Stadium for the Day on the Green concerts on 23 and 24 August due to Robert Plant's car accident in Greece.

27 August 1975, Tempe Stadium, Tempe, Arizona (Canceled due to Robert Plant's accident.)

29 August 1975, Arrowhead Stadium, Kansas City, Missouri (Canceled due to Robert Plant's accident.)

31 August 1975, Fulton County Stadium, Atlanta, Georgia (Canceled due to Robert Plant's accident.)

SEPTEMBER 1975

2 September 1975, Kentucky Exposition and Fairgrounds Stadium, Louisville, Kentucky (Canceled due to Robert Plant's accident.)

6 September 1975, Rose Bowl, Pasadena, California (Canceled due to Robert Plant's accident.)

9 September 1975, Lloyd Noble Center, University of Oklahoma, Norman, Oklahoma (Canceled due to Robert Plant's accident.)

All the above shows were postponed indefinitely. There were several other dates planned in America as well but not announced before the accident. They were also looking at playing in South America for the first time and looking at dates for spring 1976 in both the UK and Europe, all of which had to be canceled.

16 1975 Recording Sessions

NOVEMBER 1975

One-Off Show in Finland Canceled

5 November 1975, Uusi Messuhalli, Helsinki, Finland (The show was canceled due to Robert Plant's car accident.)

DECEMBER 1975

One-Off Appearance in Jersey

10 December 1975, Behan's, West Park, St. Helier, Jersey (After Robert Plant's car accident in Greece, the band had to become tax exiles, originally relocating to the US, and by December were in Jersey in the Channel Islands as the high-rate tax law only allowed them to be in the UK for sixty days a year. And during those sixty days they could not play in any form in the UK as it would be seen as promotional work and they would be taxed for a full tax year. Robert Plant was having to commute to Harley Street in London on a regular basis for treatment, and Jersey seemed the most convenient place. John Bonham and John Paul Jones, who were living at the Atlantic hotel in St. Brelade, had made Behan's one of their favorite watering holes. People generally left them alone and on one night, 3 December 1975, they both joined resident pianist Norman Hale for some classic rock 'n' roll numbers. A week later, they would return with Jimmy Page and Robert Plant to play a secret show. On the night, Hughie Behan, the club owner, appeared on the stage and announced that Led Zeppelin were about to do a free gig. This was probably the best kept secret in Jersey as neither the band or the owner wanted the place being inundated with vast numbers of fans. Robert Plant, who's leg was still in plaster and had to sit on a stool to sing, announced that were going to play some of the music that had influenced them when they were growing up and still loved. Rock 'n' roll. Reports about the length of the set vary from forty-five minutes to ninety minutes, depending on who you listen to. They used borrowed instruments and resident piano player Norman Hale joined the band for their set. After the concert ended, Led Zeppelin came out front and sat at some tables, which had been reserved for them and had a few drinks with some locals. The band returned to England for the Christmas holiday and returned to Jersey in the New Year. Page flew off to New York to work on the soundtrack for the band's forthcoming film, *The Song Remains the Same*.)

LED ZEPPELIN RECORDING SESSIONS FOR *PRESENCE*

REHEARSALS

STUDIO INSTRUMENT RENTALS (SIR)
6465 West Sunset Boulevard, Los Angeles, California

OCTOBER 1975

Robert Plant's car accident in August 1975 had confined him to a wheelchair for many months and resulted in the cancellation of Led Zeppelin's US tour. As the band had to be out of the UK due to the draconian tax laws at the time, it would have suited them to be on tour in the US. Instead, Jimmy Page joined a convalescing Robert Plant at his rented beach house in Malibu in September to start writing some new songs for the band's next album. One song, "Achilles Last Stand," had already been partially written in Morocco where Page and Plant had holidayed in

June and July 1975. Some rehearsal space was booked at SIR (Studio Instrument Rentals) in Los Angeles for October 1975 for the band to rehearse what would eventually become *Presence*. Some recordings leaked out from the rehearsals, and it was fascinating to hear how their creative process developed. A good example would be "Tea For One," which was played as a fast number during rehearsals. By the time they got to Munich it was transformed into a slow blues number.

MUSICLAND STUDIOS
Arabellastrasse 5, 81925
Munich, Germany

21 NOVEMBER 1975-2 DECEMBER 1975

Located in the basement of the Arabella Hotel in Munich, the band only had a couple of weeks to get their new album recorded and finished, as the Rolling Stones were booked in to finish off their *Black and Blue* album. In the end, Jimmy Page had to ask Mick Jagger if he could have an extra two days to do the final mixes. Mick agreed and Led Zeppelin completed what was probably their most focused record. They had to be focused due to the pressure of having a fixed period of time in the studio. Not only that, the area the studio was in was pretty depressing with nothing happening. Only two songs, "Nobody's Fault But Mine" and "Achilles Last Stand," would feature in the band's next tour in 1977. Both became live favorites, but several others should have been considered worthy of a live outing, such as the funky "Royal Orleans" or "For Your Life" and "Candy Store Rock." The album certainly does not have too many happy memories for Robert Plant, who was still convalescing in a wheelchair and was disappointed with his vocals at the sessions, which he has stated sounded strained and tired. Even worse was the resentment he felt toward both Jimmy Page and Peter Grant, who he felt were effectively keeping him away from his wife and children because of the commitment to the album. He was seriously starting to doubt whether it was all worth it. Jimmy Page, on the other hand, felt his guitar playing had matured to another level by that point. In fact, all the guitar overdubs were done in a single day. Quite a feat, but Page had always worked best under pressure.

The album sounds spontaneous and has a sense of urgency about it. And despite the popular view that is

Press advert for Led Zeppelin's *Presence* album.

was a dark album, there is still some humor showing through, such as in "Royal Orleans" and "Candy Store Rock." Surprisingly, though, fans of the band did not all take to *Presence*, nor did the critics. What can be said about it is that it has stood the test of time, and is more than worthy of reappraisal for the people who did not get it at the time of the original release in 1976.

While Page finished mixing the album by himself, the rest of the band relocated to Jersey as part of their tax-exile status. Jimmy flew out to join them a few days later.

10 RIBS & ALL / CARROT POD POD (John Paul Jones / Jimmy Page) Available on the *Presence* companion disc released July 2015.

TWO ONES ARE WON (Retitled "Achilles Last Stand") (Jimmy Page / Robert Plant) Available on vinyl *Presence* US Swan Song SS-8416, released 31 March 1976 / UK Swan Song SSK 59402, released 5 April 1976.

FOR YOUR LIFE (Jimmy Page / Robert Plant) Available on vinyl *Presence* US Swan Song SS-8416, released 31 March 1976 / UK Swan Song SSK 59402, released 5 April 1976.

ROYAL ORLEANS (Jimmy Page / Robert Plant / John Paul Jones / John Bonham) Available on vinyl *Presence* US Swan Song SS-8416, released 31 March 1976 / UK Swan Song SSK 59402, released 5 April 1976.

NOBODY'S FAULT BUT MINE (Jimmy Page / Robert Plant) Available on vinyl *Presence* US Swan Song SS-8416, released 31 March 1976 / UK Swan Song SSK 59402, released 5 April 1976.

CANDY STORE ROCK (Jimmy Page / Robert Plant) Available on vinyl *Presence* US Swan Song SS-8416, released 31 March 1976 / UK Swan Song SSK 59402, released 5 April 1976.

HOTS ON FOR NOWHERE (Jimmy Page / Robert Plant) Available on vinyl *Presence* US Swan Song SS-8416, released 31 March 1976 / UK Swan Song SSK 59402, released 5 April 1976.

TEA FOR ONE (9:27) (Jimmy Page / Robert Plant) Available on vinyl *Presence* US Swan Song SS-8416, released 31 March 1976 / UK Swan Song SSK 59402, released 5 April 1976.

JIMMY PAGE: ELECTRIC GUITAR, ACOUSTIC GUITAR. PEDAL STEEL GUITAR, BACKING VOCAL
ROBERT PLANT: LEAD VOCAL, HARMONICA
JOHN BONHAM: DRUMS, TYMPANI, BACKING VOCAL
JOHN PAUL JONES: BASS, MELLOTRON, SYNTHESIZER, ORGAN, PIANO, GRAND PIANO, SYNTHESIZER PIANO, SYNTHESIZED BASS, BACKING VOCAL
PRODUCED BY: JIMMY PAGE
ENGINEER: KEITH HARWOOD

GUEST RECORDING SESSIONS

John Bonham Guest Session for Paul McCartney

OLYMPIC STUDIOS
117 Church Road, Barnes, London, SW13

28 AUGUST 1975

BEWARE MY LOVE (Paul McCartney / Linda McCartney) Available as bonus track on *Wings at the Speed of Sound* deluxe-edition CD released in October 2014.

PAUL MCCARTNEY: VOCALS, PIANO
LINDA MCCARTNEY: MOOG SYNTHESIZER
DENNY LAINE: ELECTRIC GUITAR
JIMMY MCCULLOCH: BASS
JOHN BONHAM: DRUMS
PRODUCER: PAUL MCCARTNEY
ENGINEER: PHIL CHAPMAN

1976:

17 The Song Remained the Same

The early part of 1976 was all about the promotion of the all-important new studio album, which according to *Melody Maker* was going to be called *Obelisk*. They probably based their theory on the obelisk that was featured throughout the album artwork, but it ended up being called *Presence*. Recorded in only eighteen days, Plant told *Circus* magazine:

> It was really like a cry of survival. I was stuck in Malibu for a long while, and I said, 'Please, let me do something to do with music.' We already had some ammunition from our trip to Morocco—Jimmy and I had put together some epic sort of material—but every time that we started listening and thinking about the ideas that we already had put together, we shied away. We hadn't been back to England in nine or ten months, and consequently I don't think that we were in one of our more mentally stable periods, not in condition that enabled us to come to grips with what would be a huge accomplishment in our eyes. So we went to S.I.R. to work on some things. And it was hard in the beginning; I had to sit in an arm chair with my leg up in the air while the band were onstage. Slowly and painfully we began working on the album and it gradually came together. And then we went straight to Germany; that was where we did the eighteen-day shuffle. We worked pretty much straight through. We didn't—or at least I didn't—go out at all at night.

The album was released at the end of March, and some tracks were previewed on the *Old Grey Whistle Test* television show in England against a black-and-white backdrop combining a 1910 French film with an American film from the '20s. The album cover was full of the usual mystery that one came to expect from Led Zeppelin. It was left to fans to work out their own interpretation of it. A typically vague Jimmy Page gave his view on the cover to *Melody Maker* in March: "It could either be viewed as past or present. If you look at it, it could be the Forties and it could be the Seventies. It's got to be viewed in it's entirety, otherwise the whole point would be lost. I'm sorry to be elusive on it, but I don't think I should say that it's this, that and the other, because it's an ambiguous thing. Photographically it's an ambitious statement, so it's not the right thing to lay down an impression because somebody might have a more illuminating one." All the main music newspapers give the new album a unanimous thumbs-up.

As mentioned before, the tax laws in the UK were quite draconian in the mid-'70s if you were a high earner. Artists like Eric Clapton, Rod Stewart, the Rolling Stones, and others were heading to various overseas tax havens to avoid losing most of their album and touring revenue to the UK taxman. Peter Grant decided to move all of Swan Song's operations to Montreux in Switzerland for the foreseeable future. Ordinarily they would have been out on tour to solve the problem, but 1976 had to be a quiet year because of Robert Plant's incapacity after the car accident and ongoing medical treatment. It was important to keep Led Zeppelin's name alive in the music press, and it was decided to finally complete the 1973 concert film *The Song Remains the Same*. As well as promoting their new album during the early part of the year, 1976 was also about finalizing their film project and getting it in the cinemas. This was on top of releasing a live double album that would serve as a soundtrack to the film. It was not easy. Disagreements with the film director, Peter Clifton, only delayed matters further.

Among the many problems with the film were the rather pretentious symbolic fantasy sequences featuring all the individual members of the band as well as Peter Grant, all of which were inserted at the expense of live footage, which of course did not exist due to Massot's ineptitude. What was happening onstage was far more exciting. One can only imagine what Martin Scorsese would have done with the job. It is important to note that most people at that time had not had an opportunity to see Led Zeppelin up-close and personal, so sacrificing live footage was ill judged. The film simply didn't do justice to Zeppelin's legendary live prowess. Everyone knows how good Led Zeppelin were in 1973. Yet the film failed miserably in capturing the energy and dynamics of the band in full flight.

Blame cannot be solely blamed on Massot and Clifton, as dealing with Peter Grant and the band proved to be very frustrating at every turn because of their lack of understanding of the film world. In cinematic terms, it was all very amateurish. That said, it was always going to be a hit. How could it not have been? We're talking Led Zeppelin here after all. But in terms of rock 'n' roll films, it was a letdown. A junior-college film studies group could have done a better job of filming the shows and then editing the whole thing.

Interestingly, some enterprising fan(s) put together their own version of the film, which runs as a complete show from Madison Square Garden. Incredibly it is a far more satisfying experience than the official release. The other problem was that not many cinemas had a decent enough sound system that would do justice to the soundtrack. At the premiere of the film, Led Zeppelin's regular sound company, Showco, provided a stunning quadraphonic system to play back the soundtrack. Not every cinema had that luxury unfortunately. It was a painful three years in the making, but finally everyone was glad to get it out of the way and recoup their big investment. Certainly not the band's greatest moment, but it could, and should, have been.

The Song Remains the Same eventually premiered on 19 October 1976 at Cinema 1 in New York City.

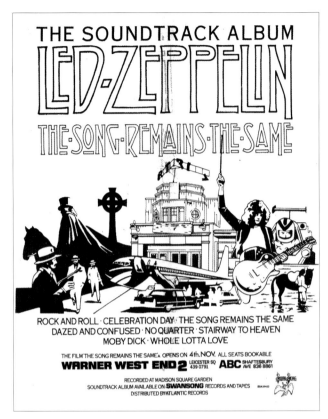

Press advert for *The Song Remains the Same* film.

SWAN SONG PRESS RELEASE FOR THE FILM:

Released on October 8, 1976—The long wait is over—Led Zeppelin comes to the cinema in THE SONG REMAINS THE SAME. A motion picture record of the group's explosive 1973 Madison Square Garden performances, THE SONG REMAINS THE SAME captures the being and essence of the four people who make Led Zeppelin the most exciting and durable of rock groups.

A film directed by Peter Clifton and Joe Massot, produced by Swan Song, Inc., with Peter Grant executive producer, the Warner Brothers movie has taken three painstakingly precise years of work to reach the cinema. Incorporating live concert footage, fantasy sequences, backstage glimpses of the band, and a personal view of them at ease at home, THE SONG REMAINS THE SAME is a rare and human look at four rock musicians: Jimmy Page, Robert Plant, John Paul Jones, and John "Bonzo" Bonham. The film was their idea, their project totally, and it is their special way of giving their millions of friends what they have been clamoring for—a personal and private tour of Led Zeppelin.

Page has been at work on the soundtrack for three years, refining and honing, matching film and sound to perfection. Released as a Swan Song album, the two record set ships platinum the second week of October.

The movie opens October 20 in New York (Cinema 1) and October 22 in Los Angeles (Fox Wilshire), San Francisco (Metro 1), Chicago (McClurg Court), Dallas (North Park 2), Toronto (Varsity 2), Boston (Cheri 1), and Atlanta (Loew's 12 Oaks 1). A limited number of tickets will be available to the public for the premieres—October 19 in New York and October 21 nationwide. All proceeds will go to the Save The Children Federation. Premiere tickets go on sale at 9:00 AM, October 16, at the respective Box Offices.

THE SONG REMAINS THE SAME reveals the members of Led Zeppelin as they really are and, for the first time, the world has a front row seat on Led Zeppelin.

The 30 October issue of *Melody Maker* has an approving cover headline, "Zeppelin Movie: honest, heavy and hot." In it their New York editor, Chris Charlesworth, praises the film: "It's been three years in the making but *The Song Remains The Same* is a classy and surely enormously successful film." On the other hand, the following month's *New Musical Express*'s Nick Kent

Poster for *The Song Remains the Same* film.

states, "This is one dumb movie." By the end of October the music press worldwide were announcing that Led Zeppelin would be back touring in 1977. So for a supposed quiet year, Led Zeppelin's name was never far away from the headlines.

MAY 1976

16 May 1976, the Forum, Los Angeles, California (Jimmy Page and Robert Plant join Bad Company for an encore of "I Just Wanna Make Love To You.")

27 May 1976, Marquee, Soho, London (Although a rumor had been circulating that Led Zeppelin would be playing on the same bill as the Pretty Things at the Marquee, only John Paul Jones turns up and joins the Pretty Things on their encore, "Route 66.")

RECORDING SESSION

MOUNTAIN RECORDING STUDIOS
Casino De Montreux, Montreux, Switzerland

12 SEPTEMBER 1976

BONZO'S MONTREUX (John Bonham) (Several takes are recorded. The 9 October 1976 issue of *Melody Maker* speculated that John Bonham was recording a solo album in Switzerland, with Jimmy Page handling production duties. In reality this was just an experimental recording with Page playing an Eventide Clock Works Harmonizer. One take was eventually mixed in 1982 at Page's home studio, Sol, in Cookham, Berkshire. It was released on *Coda*.)

PRODUCER: JIMMY PAGE
ENGINEER: JOHN TIMPERLEY

❝ I was in the studios in Montreux Casino with John Bonham and engineer John Timperley to record Bonzo's Montreux. I had recently acquired an innovative piece of equipment, the Eventide Clock Works Harmonizer and I discovered one setting where you could arrive at a steel drum sound. I wanted to employ this colour, if possible, in the palette of John Bonham's drum orchestra project. He really liked it and it's quite heavily featured in the construction of the piece. When it came to be mixed, I used the keyboard with the Harmonizer to construct the final gliss-phrases. The percussion employed on this track with John Bonham's kit were overdubbed bass drums, snare drums, tom toms, timpani, timbale, congas, backwards echo and Harmonizer. I am sure John's inspiration came from the Brazilian Samba schools. ❞

—JIMMY PAGE (From his website)

1977:
18 The Beginning of the End

Looking at it with the benefit of hindsight, it is easy to see that 1977 was the beginning of the end of Led Zeppelin. After 1975 there was nothing left to achieve. Where do you go when you have hit the very top? In Led Zeppelin's case, it was a slow decline in their creative output, both onstage and in the studio. That said, they had a very loyal fan base and their popularity had not diminished. In fact, their lack of recent concert activity actually created even more of a frenzy when tickets went on sale for their 1977 US tour. Selling tickets and albums was never going to be a problem in the short term. The 1977 US tour would gross $10 million from fifty-one dates split in three segments.

Although Led Zeppelin was all about providing great sound in concert, the visuals had to be just as spectacular. On each US tour the lights would progressively get more and more adventurous, and the 1977 US tour did not disappoint fans. One of the new visual highlights was Jimmy Page's guitar solo / theremin spot where he would be surrounded by a multicolored pyramid of laser beams. Visually it was stunning, but many people felt that the guitar piece, which could occasionally last as long as thirty minutes, was self-indulgent and boring. Although some shows were spectacular, a significant amount were average in terms of playing. A lot of that can be attributed directly to Page's health, which was starting to impact on his playing because of his heroin usage, a decision that may well have been influenced by the writings of Aleister Crowley.

In his book, *Diary of a Drug Fiend*, Crowley tells the story of a couple who enjoy the highs of heroin and cocaine until they find themselves addicted and enslaved to their habit. In the book, Crowley wrote, "The danger of the so-called habit-forming drugs is that they fool you into trying to dodge the toil essential to spiritual and intellectual development. But they are not simply man-traps. There is nothing in nature which cannot be used for our benefit, and it is up to us to use it wisely. Now, in the work you have been doing in the last week, heroin might have helped you to concentrate your mind, and cocaine to overcome the effects of fatigue."

Page had genuinely started taking heroin as a way of opening a door to new creative possibilities, and it probably did for a while. The problem is that the drug becomes addictive, which quickly removes any potential creative benefits it may have had in the first place, as Crowley found out for himself eventually.

In the meantime, John Bonham also had his demons on this tour and was often unhappy and depressed at being away from home. He turned to drink and cocaine to numb the pain and make his life on the road more bearable. It was at the expense of his health, though. On top of that the group were kept very insulated from the outside world, especially with the strict demands of insurance companies who would insure the tour against cancellation. They imposed very strict conditions on the band and their security to make sure nobody got close enough to do any harm. If these demands were not adhered to, they could loose their insurance in any potential claim that could arise, which meant that the band would be financially liable for the loss.

And then there was Peter Grant, their manager who was no longer on form due to his increasing drug problems that were in part caused by a bitter separation from his wife. This left him vulnerable, and his decision-making process was severely impaired as a result. One of the worst decisions he made was hiring John Bindon to be his right-hand man for the 1977 tour, a known criminal with a notorious thuggish reputation. This was not the kind of individual you hired to handle security at that level. It was very unprofessional, and would have repercussions that they never anticipated, but should have in the real world. If this had been the Peter Grant of 1968, he would have done things very differently. The faithful Richard Cole, who had been with the band since the early days, also had his serious drug issues now. The entourage for the new tour was simply too large to be controlled effectively with so many people who were not in good shape. Behind the scenes, the whole Led Zeppelin organization was on the road like a paranoid freak circus. It was a nightmare and the writing was on the wall for all to see.

NOVEMBER–DECEMBER 1976

E-ZEE HIRE, Market Road, London N7

Rehearsals for 1977 US Tour

JANUARY–FEBRUARY 1977

MANTICORE STUDIOS
392 North End Road, Fulham, London SW6

Rehearsals for 1977 US Tour

Led Zeppelin had started rehearsals in North London back in November 1976 for their forthcoming US tour. They continued at Manticore Studios in Fulham during January and February. Some potentially interesting, previously un-played in concert numbers were rehearsed, such as "Babe I'm Gonna Leave You," which featured Jimmy Page on pedal-steel guitar, "Custard Pie," and "Candy Store Rock." Unfortunately they never made the final selection and were dropped from the final setlist. Perhaps the most surprising element from the rehearsals was that they only included a couple of songs from their recent *Presence* album. These were "Nobody's Fault But Mine" and the powerful "Achilles Last Stand," both of which would go on to be live favorites on the tour.

There was a major change to the sound of Led Zeppelin from this point onward. John Paul Jones retired his main instrument, a 1962 Fender Jazz Bass guitar, which he felt was becoming too unreliable. He had also used a Fender V-String Bass, a fretless Fender Precision bass, and a Fender '51-style Telecaster Precision bass with the finish sanded off. By 1977 he had bought a couple of new basses from Alembic. One was an Alembic Triple Omega eight-string bass, along with an Alembic four-string bass. They were beautiful instruments and were very versatile. However, it was at the expense of the sound. The archetypal Led Zeppelin fat bottom-end had suddenly gone and changed into an unpleasant metallic sound. Sure, it could shake the foundations at any venue, but the warm sound that people had grown accustomed to with the various Fender basses was gone.

While rehearsing, some members of the band would go to London and check out the new "hip" Roxy club to hear some of the more entertaining emerging punk bands, such as the Damned and Eater. Punk fans and bands were not impressed with their presence, as Led Zeppelin and other so-called dinosaur bands were exactly the reason there was a punk movement. They wanted to sweep those bloated bands off the face of the planet. It was all a bit of a pipe dream really, and they never succeeded in getting rid of these huge rock stars, many of whom are still around today and touring successfully. The same cannot be said of those punk bands who seemed to disappear into the ether only to become a footnote in the history of punk music.

The great comeback had to be delayed unfortunately, as Robert Plant came down with laryngitis just before the tour started, severely affecting his vocal capabilities. This meant the early part of the tour had to be canceled and rescheduled. This was to prove very unsettling to Page in particular, who felt that the band had been in top form from the rehearsals and ready for the long tour. After Plant's illness he did not touch a guitar for several weeks. In a 1977 interview with Steve Rosen for *Guitar Player* magazine, Page confirmed, "We had done our rehearsals, and we were really on top, really in tip-top form. Then Robert caught laryngitis and we had to postpone a lot of dates and reshuffle them, and I didn't touch a guitar for five weeks. I got a bit panicky about that—after two years off the road that's a lot to think about."

The band now had a new plane to travel around in. Led Zeppelin's Starship jet, which they had previously used on the 1973 and 1975 tours, had been retired due to the age of the plane and associated mechanical problems. Instead they chartered Caesar's Chariot, a forty-five-seat Boeing 707 owned by the Caesars Palace Hotel in Las Vegas. Like the Starship before it, this plane also had some special features. It included large overstuffed chairs, private rooms for each member, a full bar, and a Hammond organ. On the tail was the Swan Song logo.

The first show was on 1 April 1977 in Dallas. Plant was understandably nervous, as he explained to *Melody Maker*:

> For the first one or two gigs I was really measuring every move I made, to find if I'd gone too far or whatever. . . . Ten minutes before I walked up those steps in Dallas I was cold with fright. Supposing I couldn't move around on stage properly? Because my right foot is permanently enlarged now. Well, it was killing for the first two gigs. I had to be virtually carried back on one foot. But once I'd got used to the concussive knocks of stage work it was OK, and now I've paced myself so I can work without anyone, hopefully, knowing I now have this thing to live with.

As the shows were lasting around three hours, the band wisely decided to bring back the acoustic sit-down segment, which gave them a break from the intense electric work and have a bit of intimacy with the audience. Plant was particularly good at engaging with audiences, telling them stories about the band and songs they had written, as well as occasional jokes.

Musically speaking, only two new numbers from *Presence* were played on the 1977 tour, "Achilles Last Stand" and "Nobody's Fault But Mine," both of which quickly became crowd favorites.

ORIGINAL CANCELED SHOWS

27 February 1977, Tarrant County Arena, Fort Worth, Texas (Canceled due to Robert Plant's voice being incapacitated because of a bad flu virus. Rescheduled for 22 May 1977.)

28 February 1977, the Summit, Houston, Texas (Canceled due to Robert Plant's voice being incapacitated because of a bad flu virus. Rescheduled for 21 May 1977.)

MARCH 1977

1 March 1977, Louisiana State University Assembly Center, Baton Rouge, Louisiana (Canceled due to Robert Plant's voice being incapacitated because of a bad flu virus. Rescheduled for 19 May 1977.)

3 March 1977, the Myriad, Oklahoma City, Oklahoma (Canceled due to Robert Plant's voice being incapacitated because of a bad flu virus. Rescheduled for 3 April 1977.)

4 March 1977, Memorial Auditorium, Dallas, Texas (Canceled due to Robert Plant's voice being incapacitated because of a bad flu virus. Rescheduled for 3 April 1977.)

6 March 1977, Arizona State University Activities Center Arena, Tempe, Arizona (Canceled due to Robert Plant's voice being incapacitated because of a bad flu virus. Rescheduled for 20 July 1977.)

8 March 1977, Sports Arena, San Diego, California (Canceled due to Robert Plant's voice being incapacitated because of a bad flu virus. Rescheduled for 19 June 1977.)

9 March 1977, the Forum, Los Angeles, California (Canceled due to Robert Plant's voice being incapacitated because of a bad flu virus. Rescheduled for 21 June 1977.)

12 March 1977, the Forum, Los Angeles, California (Canceled due to Robert Plant's voice being incapacitated because of a bad flu virus. Rescheduled for 22 June 1977.)

13 March 1977, the Forum, Los Angeles, California (Canceled due to Robert Plant's voice being incapacitated because of a bad flu virus. Rescheduled for 23 June 1977.)

15 March 1977, the Forum, Los Angeles, California (Canceled due to Robert Plant's voice being incapacitated because of a bad flu virus. Rescheduled for 25 June 1977.)

16 March 1977, the Forum, Los Angeles, California (Canceled due to Robert Plant's voice being incapacitated because of a bad flu virus. Rescheduled for 26 June 1977.)

APRIL 1977

1 April 1977, Maple Leaf Gardens, Toronto, Ontario, Canada (Canceled and not rescheduled.)

3 April 1977, Forum, Montreal, Quebec (Canceled and not rescheduled.)

4 April 1977, Forum, Montreal, Quebec (Canceled and not rescheduled.)

22 April 1977, University of Dayton Arena, Dayton, Ohio (Canceled and not rescheduled.)

MAY 1977

20 May 1977, Jefferson Civic Center Arena, Birmingham, Alabama (Canceled and rescheduled to 18 May 1977 to fit in with new schedule.)

21 May 1977, the Omni, Atlanta, Georgia (Canceled and rescheduled to 23 April 1977 to fit in with new schedule.)

23 May 1977, Greensboro Coliseum, North Carolina (Canceled and rescheduled to 31 May 1977.)

25 May 1977, Washington (Canceled and not rescheduled.)

APRIL 1977

LED ZEPPELIN ELEVENTH US TOUR— RESCHEDULED

1 APRIL 1977–24 JULY 1977

1 April 1977, Dallas Memorial Auditorium, Texas (The show was rescheduled from March 4, 1977.)

SETLIST: The Song Remains The Same / The Rover Intro / Sick Again / Nobody's Fault But Mine / In My Time Of Dying / Since I've Been Loving You / No Quarter / Ten Years Gone / The Battle Of Evermore / Going To California / Black Country Woman / Bron-Yr-Aur Stomp / White Summer / Black Mountain Side / Kashmir / Moby Dick / Jimmy Page Guitar Solo / Achilles Last Stand / Stairway To Heaven / Rock And Roll

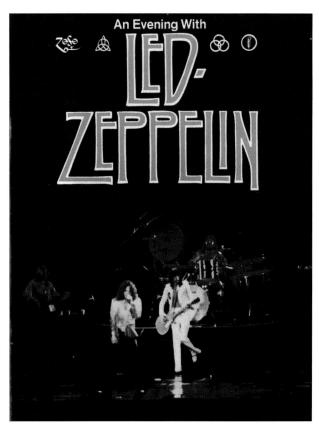

Front cover of Led Zeppelin's 1977 US tour program.

Press advert for Led Zeppelin's 1977 US tour.

The opening night was not exactly memorable. The band were very rusty after not playing live for two years. Considering this was the first gig of a major return, it was a disappointing start. Things would not improve much over the next few weeks.

3 April 1977, the Myriad, Oklahoma City, Oklahoma (The show was rescheduled from March 3, 1977.)

SETLIST: The Song Remains The Same / The Rover Intro / Sick Again / Nobody's Fault But Mine / In My Time Of Dying / Since I've Been Loving You / No Quarter / Ten Years Gone / The Battle Of Evermore / Going To California / Black Country Woman / Bron-Yr-Aur Stomp / White Summer / Black Mountain Side / Kashmir / Moby Dick / Jimmy Page Guitar Solo / Achilles Last Stand / Stairway To Heaven / Rock And Roll / Trampled Underfoot

Once again the band are clearly under-rehearsed, and PA problems just compounded the fact that the band were not in good shape. Page plays solos in the wrong key, the rhythm section is nervous, Plant's vocals are at times tentative, and there is a general feel of a band that is severely lacking in confidence, which is something that in the past could never have been said about the them.

6 April 1977, Chicago Stadium, Chicago, Illinois (8:00 p.m.)

SETLIST: The Song Remains The Same / The Rover Intro / Sick Again / Nobody's Fault But Mine / In My Time Of Dying / Since I've Been Loving You / No Quarter / Ten Years Gone / The Battle Of Evermore / Going To California / Black Country Woman / Bron-Yr-Aur Stomp / White Summer / Black Mountain Side / Kashmir / Moby Dick / Guitar Solo / Achilles Last Stand / Stairway To Heaven / Rock And Roll / Trampled Underfoot

On top of the already mentioned problems with the band, crowds were getting more unruly at shows and the big craze was throwing firecrackers at the stage. It had started back in 1975, but seemed to have gotten worse on this tour. As soon as Plant came on stage he grabbed the mic and told the crowd, "Listen! Before we start, can we ask you one thing? Can you stop throwing those firecrackers? We want to give you a lot of music, but we're not going to fight with firecrackers. Okay?! Cool it with the explosives!" Although there are moments of clarity tonight, the show overall is just not up to the usual high standards of playing that people associated with Led Zeppelin.

66 It was, in short, the usual Led Zeppelin show—a lot of music handled well, and very little bull. Plant in fact was the only member of the group who spoke at all, and then only briefly, though the group's ambience is far from aloof. But it's clear that they're there for one main purpose: to create fireworks. And speaking of that, Plant would just as soon the audience left that sort of thing to Led Zeppelin. 99

—*CHICAGO TRIBUNE* (April 1977)

7 April 1977, Chicago Stadium, Chicago, Illinois (8:00 p.m.)

SETLIST: The Song Remains The Same / The Rover Intro / Sick Again / Nobody's Fault But Mine / Since I've Been Loving You / No Quarter / Ten Years Gone / The Battle Of Evermore / Going To California / Black Country Woman / Bron-Yr-Aur Stomp / White Summer / Black Mountain Side / Kashmir / Moby Dick / Guitar Solo / Achilles Last Stand / Stairway To Heaven / Rock And Roll

The show tonight had to be shortened due to the Chicago Black Hawks hockey team having to play in the arena the following day for their all-important playoffs and it needed to be prepared for the game. The union that worked the arena demanded that Led Zeppelin finish their concert by 11:00 p.m., which would give the Showco sound team enough time to dismantle the PA system, which would then be reassembled on Saturday for that evening's show. "In

My Time Of Dying" and "Trampled Underfoot" were dropped from tonight's setlist to make sure the show ended on time.

9 April 1977, Chicago Stadium, Chicago, Illinois (8:00 p.m. The show ended abruptly when Jimmy Page collapsed onstage due to severe food poisoning. The concert was rescheduled for 2 August 1977.)

SETLIST: The Song Remains The Same / The Rover Intro / Sick Again / Nobody's Fault But Mine / Since I've Been Loving You / Ten Years Gone

It is apparent that something is wrong with Jimmy Page as his timing is really off. He starts playing the intro to "Since I've Been Loving You" only to stop after a few seconds, realizing he should have been playing "Nobody's Fault But Mine." He passed out during "Ten Years Gone" and Robert Plant makes this announcement: "Jimmy has got a bout of gastro-enteritis, which isn't helped by firecrackers, so we've gonna take a necessary five-minute break." After a few minutes it became clear that Jimmy was in no shape to go back onstage, and Richard Cole came out to tell the crowd that "Jimmy does not want to do a half-hearted show tonight. If you watch the press on Monday, this show will be rescheduled. The band feel very bad about this, but please hang on to your tickets. All tickets will be honored."

10 April 1977, Chicago Stadium, Chicago, Illinois (8:00 p.m.)

SETLIST: The Song Remains The Same / The Rover Intro / Sick Again / Nobody's Fault But Mine / In My Time Of Dying / Since I've Been Loving You / No Quarter / Ten Years Gone / The Battle Of Evermore / Going To California / Black Country Woman / Bron-Yr-Aur Stomp / Trampled Underfoot / White Summer / Black Mountain Side / Kashmir / Moby Dick / Guitar Solo / Achilles Last Stand / Stairway To Heaven / Rock And Roll

At last, the band seem to hit the ground running tonight and are in fine form and the performance is the best of the four-night Chicago run. "Ten Years Gone" has still not been perfected, though, and has several mistakes in it, as had been the case at every show so far on this tour. But overall the general performance is good, with powerful versions of "In My Time Of Dying" and "Achilles Last Stand." Plant makes light of Page's collapse the previous night: "Jimmy was feeling ill last night, but it was only a false pregnancy, so that's alright!" Plant also mentions that a local radio station had speculated on-air about the reasons for Page's collapse, saying that alcohol and substances were to blame. Plant comes to Jimmy's defense by telling the crowd, "Mr. Page neither smokes, drinks, takes women, or does anything like that, so we want an apology tomorrow and a crate of alcohol!" Bizarrely, Page comes onstage dressed in a Nazi Stormtrooper's uniform complete with cap and the obligatory black jackboots. Even more bizarrely, during "Moby Dick" he changed into his usual 1977 white satin dragon tour outfit.

12 April 1977, Metropolitan Sports Center, Bloomington, Minnesota (8:00 p.m.)

SETLIST NOT KNOWN, BUT WOULD PROBABLY HAVE CONSISTED OF THE FOLLOWING: The Song Remains The Same / The Rover Intro / Sick Again / Nobody's Fault But Mine / In My Time Of Dying / Since I've Been Loving You / No Quarter / Ten Years Gone / The Battle Of Evermore / Going To California / Black Country Woman / Bron-Yr-Aur Stomp / White Summer / Black Mountain Side / Kashmir / Moby Dick / Guitar Solo / Achilles Last Stand / Stairway To Heaven / Rock And Roll

❝ The Met's slap-happy performance can be partially attributed to their weather-delayed departure from Chicago (their permanent shuttle home-base for this part of the tour). They were detained at O'Hare Airport until 7:40; arrived in Bloomington at 8:35; made the Met at 8:50 and hit the stage at 9:10. By encore time, 12:15, their stamina reserves were obviously wasted, as evidenced by their shaky stage sauntering and pallid expressions. The tour photographer, Neal Preston, gave a succinct after-show critique, remarking: 'Well, it was probably the worst Led Zeppelin concert I'd ever seen.'❞

—**LIVE LICKS** (April 1977)

13 April 1977, St. Paul Civic Center, St. Paul, Minnesota (8:00 p.m.)

SETLIST NOT KNOWN, BUT WOULD PROBABLY HAVE CONSISTED OF THE FOLLOWING: The Song Remains The Same / The Rover Intro / Sick Again / Nobody's Fault But Mine / In My Time Of Dying / Since I've Been Loving You / No Quarter / Ten Years Gone / The Battle Of Evermore / Going To California / Black Country Woman / Bron-Yr-Aur Stomp / White Summer / Black Mountain Side / Kashmir / Moby Dick / Guitar Solo / Achilles Last Stand / Stairway To Heaven / Rock And Roll

Press advert for Led Zeppelin's appearance at Met Center in Bloomington, Minnesota, on 12 April 1977.

❝ First of all, they should drop that opening theme song (The Song Remains The Same). It's a misnomer. Any Zeppy who's held control of their ears and brain over the past seven years knows that the song hasn't been the same since Zeppelin II. Live, the British bombardiers, themselves, revealed the title to be a lie during their two vastly different performances last week in the Twin Cities. If anything, they proved that the song remains in flux, from phase to phase, album to album or even night to night.❞

—**LIVE LICKS** (April 1977)

15 April 1977 St. Louis Arena, St. Louis, Missouri (8:00 p.m.)

SETLIST NOT KNOWN, BUT WOULD PROBABLY HAVE CONSISTED OF THE FOLLOWING: The Song Remains The Same / The Rover Intro / Sick Again / Nobody's Fault But Mine / In My Time Of Dying / Since I've Been Loving You / No Quarter / Ten Years Gone / The Battle Of Evermore / Going To California / Black Country Woman / Bron-Yr-Aur Stomp / White Summer / Black Mountain Side / Kashmir / Moby Dick / Guitar Solo / Achilles Last Stand / Stairway To Heaven / Rock And Roll

17 April 1977, Market Square Arena, Indianapolis, Indiana (8:00 p.m.)

SETLIST NOT KNOWN, BUT WOULD PROBABLY HAVE CONSISTED OF THE FOLLOWING: The Song Remains The Same / The Rover Intro / Sick Again / Nobody's Fault But Mine / In My Time Of Dying / Since I've Been Loving You / No Quarter / Ten Years Gone / The Battle Of Evermore / Going To California / Black Country Woman / Bron-Yr-Aur Stomp / White Summer / Black Mountain Side / Kashmir / Moby Dick / Guitar Solo / Achilles Last Stand / Stairway To Heaven / Rock And Roll

66 Laser lights made their first appearance during John Paul Jones' relentlessly long 'No Quarter.' The lights shot to the arena ceiling (unfortunately the hall's catwalk interfered with a portion of the beams) and oscillated with Jones' keyboard frequency. The lasers reappeared again during 19-minutes [of] Achilles Last Stand, featuring lead guitarist Jimmy Page. The green beams formed a pyramid around Page as yellow beams jetted out into the arena. When the base of the pyramid rotated around the imprisoned Page, the crowd gasped in amazement. 99

—*INDIANAPOLIS NEWS* (April 1977)

19 April 1977, Riverfront Coliseum, Cincinnati, Ohio
(8:00 p.m.)

SETLIST: The Song Remains The Same / The Rover Intro / Sick Again / Nobody's Fault But Mine / Since I've Been Loving You / No Quarter / Ten Years Gone / The Battle Of Evermore / Going To California / Black Country Woman / Bron-Yr-Aur Stomp / White Summer / Black Mountain Side / Kashmir / Moby Dick / Guitar Solo / Achilles Last Stand / Stairway To Heaven / Rock And Roll

The band try and remain composed and play through what seems like a constant barrage of firecrackers and exuberant crowd noise. As usual, Robert Plant

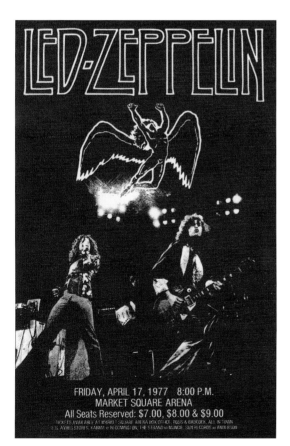

Press advert for Led Zeppelin's appearance at Market Square Arena in Indianapolis, Indiana, on 17 April 1977.

tries to calm the situation: "It's very difficult to play when you see crowds of people swaying. Keep it cool. Stand still. We don't want to see anybody get hurt." The atmosphere was tense and that is reflected in the way the band play. The local press reported that 1,000 fans tried to gate-crash the gig, which resulted in a hundred arrests when youths started fighting and throwing bottles. Only two years later there would be a similar incident when the Who played the venue. Unfortunately the rioting at that show resulted in several deaths when the crowd surged forward trying to get into the venue.

20 April 1977, Riverfront Coliseum, Cincinnati, Ohio
(8:00 p.m.)

SETLIST: The Song Remains The Same / The Rover Intro / Sick Again / Nobody's Fault But Mine / In My Time Of Dying / Since I've Been Loving You / No Quarter / Ten Years Gone / The Battle Of Evermore / Going To California / Black Country Woman / Bron-Yr-Aur Stomp / White Summer / Black Mountain Side / Kashmir / Moby Dick / Guitar Solo / The Star Spangled Banner / Achilles Last Stand / Stairway To Heaven / Rock And Roll / Trampled Underfoot

More crowd problems occurred today. A young man fell from the stadium's third level onto a ramp while he was trying to climb the wall to get into the venue. Another boisterous crowd tonight detracted the band from the job at hand.

66 For the second time in three days police had to battle fans of the British rock group 'Led Zeppelin,' but police doubled their manpower and kept trouble at a minimum here yesterday. An 18-year-old Dayton fan plunged 20 feet to a concrete ramp while trying to scale a wall, police said. Stanley Blair was reported in fair condition at Cincinnati hospital. Asst. City Manager Henry Sandman told the Cincinnati City Council that 80 police officers, paid for by the Cincinnati Coliseum, will be used hereafter to prevent outbreaks of trouble. 9

—**THE** *TELEGRAM* (21 April 1977)

23 April 1977, the Omni, Atlanta, Georgia
(8:00 p.m. Rescheduled from May 21, 1977.)

SETLIST: The Song Remains The Same / The Rover Intro / Sick Again / Nobody's Fault But Mine / In My Time Of Dying / Since I've Been Loving You / No Quarter / Ten Years Gone / The Battle Of Evermore / Going To California / Black Country Woman / Bron-Yr-Aur Stomp / White Summer / Black Mountain Side / Kashmir / Moby Dick / Guitar Solo / The Star-Spangled Banner / Achilles Last Stand / Stairway To Heaven / Rock And Roll / Trampled Underfoot

The band put on a good show with everyone in good form. The crowd go wild but are generally well behaved while showing their appreciation. "No Quarter" is getting more adventurous, with Page and Jones getting more in sync with each other during the instrumental jam section. The final encore of "Trampled Underfoot" leaves the crowd screaming for more.

25 April 1977, Freedom Hall, Louisville, Kentucky (8:00 p.m.)

SETLIST: The Song Remains The Same / The Rover Intro / Sick Again / Nobody's Fault But Mine / In My Time Of Dying / Since I've Been Loving You / No Quarter / Ten Years Gone / The Battle Of Evermore / Going To California / Black Country Woman / Bron-Yr-Aur Stomp / White Summer / Black Mountain Side / Kashmir / Moby Dick / Guitar Solo / The Star-Spangled Banner / Achilles Last Stand / Stairway To Heaven / Rock And Roll

Another good show, which is supposedly interrupted when someone in the crowd threw a full bottle toward Jimmy Page and clipped his guitar. He reportedly left the stage along with the rest of the band, and for a moment or two it looked like the show would be canceled. There is no mention of this incident in the news reports. The second half of the show has several mistakes, probably due to the intense heat in the venue.

27 April 1977, Richfield Coliseum, Cleveland, Ohio (8:00 p.m.)

SETLIST: The Song Remains The Same / The Rover Intro / Sick Again / Nobody's Fault But Mine / In My Time Of Dying / Since I've Been Loving You / No Quarter / Ten Years Gone / The Battle Of Evermore / Going To California / Black Country Woman / Bron-Yr-Aur Stomp / White Summer / Black Mountain Side / Kashmir / Moby Dick / Guitar Solo / The Star-Spangled Banner / Achilles Last Stand / Stairway To Heaven / Rock And Roll / Trampled Underfoot

This show was the first professional recording to slip into bootleggers' hands and released as a triple-vinyl set called *Destroyer*. It was sadly not one of the better shows, such as any of the later LA run, but it gave fans an opportunity to listen to a very clear live recording of the band in action. As such there are several moments that are highly enjoyable, such as "Kashmir," "Ten Years Gone," and "Achilles Last Stand." But the real highlight was the long version of "No Quarter," which always eclipsed the studio version and showed what a great improvisational band Led Zeppelin were on a good night. There are a few monitor problems during the acoustic set. As always, the crowd are wild with enthusiasm and the band are clearly feeling the vibe.

66 Led Zeppelin's show, considerably revamped since their '75 appearance in the same arena, was in general an effective mix of blues-ended structures such as In My Time of Dying, Nobody's Fault But Mine and Since I've Been Loving You. The maximum amount of instrumental stretching-out however came on No Quarter. Working from both electric and acoustic pianos, John Paul Jones again impressed with his general versatility. Jimmy Page later joined in for what to me was his apogee of an evening's worth of standout soloing. It was one of the best rock jams I've ever witnessed. 99

—*SCENE* (April 1977)

28 April 1977, Richfield Coliseum, Cleveland, Ohio (8:00 p.m.)

SETLIST: The Song Remains The Same / The Rover Intro / Sick Again / Nobody's Fault But Mine / In My Time Of Dying / Since I've Been Loving You / No Quarter / Ten Years Gone / The Battle Of Evermore / Going To California / Black Country Woman / Bron-Yr-Aur Stomp / White Summer / Black Mountain Side / Kashmir / Moby Dick / Guitar Solo (including The Star-Spangled Banner) / Achilles Last Stand / Stairway To Heaven / Rock And Roll / Trampled Underfoot

This was the night that should have been released as a professional recording. As it is, an audience recording proves to us that this was one of those magical shows where everything was right, a first on this tour. The whole band are at the height of their powers. A great show that is worthy of praise and reminded people that Led Zeppelin could still do it!

30 April 1977, Pontiac Silverdome, Pontiac, Michigan (9:30 p.m. Several video cameras feed the onstage images to large video screens placed on either side of the stage at this huge venue.)

SETLIST: The Song Remains The Same / The Rover Intro / Sick Again / Nobody's Fault But Mine / In My Time Of Dying / Since I've Been Loving You / No Quarter / Ten Years Gone / The Battle Of Evermore / Going To California / Black Country Woman / Bron-Yr-Aur Stomp / White Summer / Black Mountain Side / Kashmir / Moby Dick / Guitar Solo (including The Star-Spangled Banner) / Achilles Last Stand / Stairway To Heaven / Rock And Roll / Trampled Underfoot

The band finish the first leg with a tremendous finale at the Pontiac Silverdome. The band broke a record this night by playing in front of an audience of 77,229, the largest audience for a single-act concert. They beat their own last record of 56,800 people when they played Tampa in May 1973. The band are "on" tonight and the relatively well-behaved crowd help make this night one of the better ones on the 1977 tour. Robert Plant, John Bonham, and John Paul Jones returned home to England for a short vacation during the two-week break before the next leg was due to start. Jimmy Page decided to go to Egypt and visit one of Aleister Crowley's old haunts, Cairo.

MAY 1977

18 May 1977, Jefferson Civic Center Arena, Birmingham, Alabama (8:00 p.m. Rescheduled from May 20, 1977.)

SETLIST: The Song Remains The Same / The Rover Intro / Sick Again / Nobody's Fault But Mine / In My Time Of Dying / Since I've Been Loving You / No Quarter / Ten Years Gone / The Battle Of Evermore / Going To California / Black Country Woman / Bron-Yr-Aur Stomp / White Summer / Black Mountain Side / Kashmir / Moby Dick / Guitar Solo (including The Star-Spangled Banner) / Achilles Last Stand / Stairway To Heaven / Rock And Roll

After a short break in England, which saw the band pick up a prestigious Ivor Novello award for Outstanding Contribution to British Music," they returned to America for the second leg of their US tour. The first date was at the Jefferson Civic Center in Birmingham, Alabama, and it was a good show. The break obviously gave the band a well-earned rest and they came back energized and ready to play.

19 May 1977, Louisiana State University, Assembly Center, Baton Rouge, Louisiana (8:00 p.m.)

SETLIST: The Song Remains The Same / The Rover Intro / Sick Again / Nobody's Fault But Mine / In My Time Of Dying / Since I've Been Loving You / No Quarter / Ten Years Gone / The Battle Of Evermore / Going To California / Black Country Woman / Bron-Yr-Aur Stomp / White Summer / Black Mountain Side / Kashmir / Moby Dick / Guitar Solo (including The Star-Spangled Banner) / Achilles Last Stand / Stairway To Heaven / Rock And Roll / Trampled Underfoot

21 May 1977, the Summit, Houston, Texas (8:00 p.m.)

SETLIST: The Song Remains The Same / The Rover Intro / Sick Again / Nobody's Fault But Mine / In My Time Of Dying / Since I've Been Loving You / No Quarter / Ten Years Gone / The Battle Of Evermore / Going To California / Black Country Woman / Bron-Yr-Aur Stomp / White Summer / Black Mountain Side / Kashmir / Moby Dick / Guitar Solo (including

The Star-Spangled Banner) / Achilles Last Stand / Stairway To Heaven / Rock And Roll / Trampled Underfoot

When tickets went on sale for this gig at Warehouse Records & Tapes in Houston, the police had to get fire trucks in to hose down around 3,500 Led Zeppelin fans who were threatening to stampede the store selling tickets. This set the mood for tonight's show, which resulted in over forty arrests by police for acts of vandalism, which supposedly resulted in $500,000 worth of damages at the Summit. The band's performance turned out to be disappointing, according to local media, who viewed attending a Led Zeppelin show something akin to an endurance test. They had a point when you think about it. Dodging firecrackers and smoke bombs, getting ear bleed from the sheer volume from the massive PA, and attempting to make your way to your seat over drunk or stoned individuals who had passed out in the hallways made for an unpleasant atmosphere. Fans in the audience, though, begged to differ and enjoyed the set. John Bonham in particular was in great form this evening, especially during his solo piece, "Moby Dick."

22 May 1977, Tarrant County County Arena, Fort Worth, Texas (8:00 p.m.)

SETLIST: The Song Remains The Same / The Rover Intro / Sick Again / Nobody's Fault But Mine / In My Time Of Dying / Since I've Been Loving You / No Quarter / Ten Years Gone / The Battle Of Evermore / Going To California / Black Country Woman / Bron-Yr-Aur Stomp / White Summer / Black Mountain Side / Kashmir / Moby Dick / Guitar Solo (including The Star-Spangled Banner) / Achilles Last Stand / Stairway To Heaven / Whole Lotta Love / Rock And Roll / It'll Be Me

The hot-diggety show. Robert Plant informs the crowd that he learned that idiom today and uses it at regular intervals during the show. He had once remarked that the band's live sound was "tight but loose." Well, tonight it was one of those "more loose than tight" shows. "In My Time Of Dying" had to be restarted due to a mix-up over time signatures. Although certainly not a bad show, it was decidedly average and unremarkable in places. In a surprise move tonight, the band debut just over a minute of "Whole Lotta Love" that segues into "Rock And Roll." After "Rock And Roll," Robert Plant surprises the audience by telling them, "Well, we've had such a good time and one of our pals is here tonight, and it's not like us to normally extend the warm hand of musical friendship to anybody, but tonight we'd like to bring a friend of ours on, Mick Ralphs from Bad Company. A man who actually comes from the same part of the world as me and Bonzo, so home from home. We come from what you might call the sticks. This is an old, err . . . we gonna try something that , err . . . God knows how it's gonna sound, but I hope you all understand it's what they call a jam! It's a Jerry Lee Lewis number, it's called . . . well it's very appropriate, Mick, "It'll Be Me.'" It is a bit rough and ready but fun to hear.

25 May 1977, Capital Centre, Landover, Maryland (8:00 p.m.)

SETLIST: The Song Remains The Same / The Rover Intro / Sick Again / Nobody's Fault But Mine / In My Time Of Dying / Since I've Been Loving You / No Quarter / Ten Years Gone / The Battle Of Evermore / Going To California / Black Country Woman / Bron-Yr-Aur Stomp / White Summer / Black Mountain Side / Kashmir / Moby Dick / Guitar Solo (including The Star-Spangled Banner) / Achilles Last Stand / Stairway To Heaven / Whole Lotta Love / Rock And Roll

Having had a few days off, the band come fighting back. The Maryland run was one of the highlights of the 1977 tour. While not quite up there with the Los Angeles shows, they are still powerful and dramatic with great dynamics. The opening night offers an epic performance and the whole band is inspired.

26 May 1977, Capital Centre, Landover, Maryland (8:00 p.m.)

SETLIST: The Song Remains The Same / The Rover Intro / Sick Again / Nobody's Fault But Mine / In My Time Of Dying / Since I've Been Loving You / No Quarter / Ten Years Gone / The Battle Of Evermore / Going To California / Dancing Days / Black Country Woman / Bron-Yr-Aur Stomp / White Summer / Black Mountain Side / Kashmir / Moby Dick / Guitar Solo (including The Star-Spangled Banner) / Achilles Last Stand / Stairway To Heaven / Whole Lotta Love / Rock And Roll

Yet another great show, with a killer version of "Since I've Been Loving You." You just know the band are in a good mood at this show when they suddenly go off-piste and perform an impromptu "Dancing Days," which leads into "Black Country Woman." The version of "No Quarter" is epic, and John Bonham excels on a near-forty-minute drum solo on "Moby Dick." These are the sort of nights that Led Zeppelin collectors prize in their tape and CD collections.

28 May 1977 Capital Centre, Landover, Maryland (8:00 p.m.)

SETLIST: The Song Remains The Same / The Rover Intro / Sick Again / Nobody's Fault But Mine / In My Time Of Dying / Since I've Been Loving You / No Quarter / Ten Years Gone / The Battle Of Evermore / Going To California / Black Country Woman / Bron-Yr-Aur Stomp / White Summer / Black Mountain Side / Kashmir, Moby Dick / Guitar Solo (including The Star-Spangled Banner) / Achilles Last Stand / Stairway To Heaven / Whole Lotta Love / Rock And Roll

Another good show, with highlights being "In My Time Of Dying," which has a longer than usual pause as the band wait for Jimmy before getting into the fast boogie section, and excellent epic versions of "No Quarter" and "Kashmir." "Achilles Last Stand" is also up there despite a slightly shaky start by Page.

30 May 1977, Capital Centre, Landover, Maryland (8:00 p.m.)

SETLIST: The Song Remains The Same / The Rover Intro / Sick Again / Nobody's Fault But Mine / In My Time Of Dying / Since I've Been Loving You / No Quarter / Ten Years Gone / The Battle Of Evermore / Going To California / Black Country Woman / Bron-Yr-Aur Stomp / White Summer / Black Mountain Side / Kashmir / Moby Dick / Guitar Solo (including The Star-Spangled Banner) / Achilles Last Stand / Stairway To Heaven / Whole Lotta Love / Rock And Roll

Last night in Maryland and one of the better shows from the 1977 tour. The performance is up there with the quality of most of the Los Angeles shows. Jimmy Page is in top form, as are the rest of band, and close their four-night run on a high note.

31 May 1977 Coliseum, Greensboro, North Carolina (8:00 p.m.)

SETLIST: The Song Remains The Same / The Rover Intro / Sick Again / Nobody's Fault But Mine / In My Time Of Dying / Since I've Been Loving You / No Quarter / Ten Years Gone / The Battle Of Evermore / Going To California / Black Country Woman / Bron-Yr-Aur Stomp / White Summer / Black Mountain Side / Kashmir / Moby Dick / Guitar Solo (including The Star-Spangled Banner) / Achilles Last Stand / Stairway To Heaven / Whole Lotta Love / Rock And Roll

66 While John Paul Jones warmed up for 'No Quarter,' the fog machine covered the stage with a heavy white cloud. During his solo bit, laser beams shot upwards and bounced off the high coliseum ceiling. Jimmy Page had his moments also, performing almost non-stop with his assortment of guitars and showing off his expertise with the electric instruments. And, drummer John Bonham launched into his solo to allow the others a needed break. 99

—*THE JOURNAL* (Review on 12 June 1977)

JUNE 1977

3 June 1977, Tampa Stadium, Tampa, Florida (8:00 p.m.)

SETLIST: The Song Remains The Same / The Rover Intro / Sick Again / Nobody's Fault But Mine

The show, attended by 70,000 people, had to be stopped after about 20 minutes when there was a massive rain downpour, and there was a serious risk of electrocution threatening everyone onstage. The concert was due to be rescheduled for the next day, but had to be canceled by the authorities after a huge riot broke out soon after the show was stopped. It turns out that Peter Grant had signed the contract without realizing that it stipulated that the band would have to play in any weather conditions. Usually there would have been a rain-date clause in the contract for such an eventuality, allowing for fans to reuse their tickets for another date in better conditions. However, Grant was not in the best of shape and this was just another mistake he made by overlooking this fact before signing. He knew only too well from bitter experience about the lethal dangers of mixing water and electricity when Stone the Crows lost their guitarist, Les Harvey, to such an onstage incident when he managed the band. Someone in the organization should have gone ahead to check the site and make sure everything was in order. Grant always insisted that the open-air shows should have a metal roof; instead, there was a canvas roof that contained gallons of water from a downpour earlier in the day. Unfortunately, Grant had to meet his contractual obligations and sent the band on, only to wave them off after twenty or so minutes when the rain and wind became too dangerous.

4 June 1977, Tampa Stadium, Tampa, Florida (8:00 p.m. Canceled due to yesterdays riots and police arrests.)

7 June 1977, Madison Square Garden, New York City, New York (8:00 p.m.)

SETLIST: The Song Remains The Same / The Rover Intro / Sick Again / Nobody's Fault But Mine / In My Time Of Dying / Since I've Been Loving You / No Quarter / Ten Years Gone / The Battle Of Evermore / Going To California / Black Country Woman / Bron-Yr-Aur Stomp / White Summer / Black Mountain Side / Kashmir / Moby Dick / Guitar Solo (including The Star-Spangled Banner) / Achilles Last Stand / Stairway To Heaven / Whole Lotta Love / Rock And Roll

Led Zeppelin return to New York with a six-night run at Madison Square Garden. Plant dedicates "In My Time Of Dying" to England's Queen Elizabeth: "Tonight is the beginning of the celebration of Queen Elizabeth II's Silver Jubilee, and that's a heavy thing for us, so we'll do this one for Liz!" Overall not a brilliant show with some sloppy playing by all. The final encore, "Rock And Roll," is particularly bad, and the whole show had the usual noisy and rowdy New York crowd, who seemed to love throwing firecrackers at the stage.

66 The audience displayed restraint that bordered on saintliness during the one-hour delay before the concert started. No announcement or explanation was offered. But a substantial number of people did show stupidity bordering on sadism in greeting the band with an assault of fireworks that made the Garden seem like Da Nang. The explosions faded after a few songs when singer Robert Plant exerted his moral authority by requesting that those offenders 'cool the firecrackers—no more of those exploding things.' 99

—*NEWSDAY* (Review on June 1977)

8 June 1977, Madison Square Garden, New York City, New York (8:00 p.m.)

SETLIST: The Song Remains The Same / The Rover Intro / Sick Again / Nobody's Fault But Mine / In My Time Of Dying / Since I've Been Loving You / No Quarter / Ten Years Gone / The Battle Of Evermore / Going To California / Black Country Woman / Bron-Yr-Aur Stomp / White Summer / Black Mountain Side / Kashmir / Moby Dick / Guitar Solo / Achilles Last Stand / Stairway To Heaven / Whole Lotta Love / Rock And Roll

Another average show that is marred by a boisterous New York audience, as well as several firecrackers being let off. The whole band are sluggish.

10 June 1977, Madison Square Garden, New York City, New York (8:00 p.m.)

SETLIST: The Song Remains The Same / The Rover Intro / Sick Again / Nobody's Fault But Mine / Over The Hills And Far Away / Since I've Been Loving You / No Quarter / Ten Years Gone / The Battle Of Evermore / Going To California / Black Country Woman / Bron-Yr-Aur Stomp / White Summer / Black Mountain Side / Kashmir / Moby Dick / Heartbreaker / Guitar Solo (including The Star-Spangled Banner) / Achilles Last Stand / Stairway To Heaven / Whole Lotta Love / Rock And Roll

After a two-day break, the band come back energized and play a great show. This gig is notable as the first performance of "Over The Hills And Far Away" on this tour, which replaced "In My Time Of Dying." Another first tonight is a lively version of "Heartbreaker," which drives the crowd crazy. "No Quarter" is particularly good tonight with some excellent improvisation by Jones and Page. Possibly the best night of the six.

11 June 1977, Madison Square Garden, New York City, New York (8:00 p.m.)

SETLIST: The Song Remains The Same / The Rover Intro / Sick Again / Nobody's Fault But Mine / In My Time Of Dying / Since I've Been Loving You / No Quarter / Ten Years Gone / The Battle Of Evermore / Going To California / Black Country Woman / Bron-Yr-Aur Stomp / White Summer / Black Mountain Side / Kashmir / Moby Dick / Guitar Solo (including The Star-Spangled Banner) / Achilles Last Stand / Stairway To Heaven / Heartbreaker

The crowd is absolutely manic and the band play another good show, albeit a tad more low-key than the previous night. "Heartbreaker" is the encore tonight, and it was like 1970 all over again with Page in top shape.

13 June 1977, Madison Square Garden, New York City, New York (8:00 p.m.)

SETLIST: The Song Remains The Same / The Rover Intro / Sick Again / Nobody's Fault But Mine / Over The Hills And Far Away / Since I've Been Loving You / No Quarter / Ten Years Gone / The Battle Of Evermore / Going To California / Black Country Woman / Bron-Yr-Aur Stomp / White Summer / Black Mountain Side / Kashmir / Moby Dick / Heartbreaker / Guitar Solo (including The Star-Spangled Banner) / Achilles Last Stand / Stairway To Heaven / Whole Lotta Love / Black Dog

"Black Dog" came as a surprise to fans in attendance tonight, and was the last setlist change during this New York run. The band play a powerful high-energy show with everyone in good form.

14 June 1977, Madison Square Garden, New York City, New York (8:00 p.m.)

SETLIST: The Song Remains The Same / The Rover Intro / Sick Again / Nobody's Fault But Mine / Over The Hills And Far Away / Since I've Been Loving You / No Quarter / Ten Years Gone / The Battle Of Evermore / Going To California / Black Country Woman / Bron-Yr-Aur Stomp / White Summer / Black Mountain Side / Kashmir / Moby Dick / Guitar Solo (including The Star-Spangled Banner) / Achilles Last Stand / Stairway To Heaven / Whole Lotta Love / Rock And Roll

Final show ever in New York and it was a good one. The band continue to please the crowd with some enthusiastic playing. "Since I've Been Loving You" is one of the best versions on the whole 1977 tour, with a staggering Page solo. The band are clearly in good shape and looking forward to sunny California.

19 June 1977, Sports Arena, San Diego, California (8:00 p.m. Rescheduled from 8 March 1977.)

SETLIST: The Song Remains The Same / The Rover Intro / Sick Again / Nobody's Fault But Mine / In My Time Of Dying / Since I've Been Loving You / No Quarter / Ten Years Gone / The Battle Of Evermore / Going To California / Mystery Train / Black Country Woman / Bron-Yr-Aur Stomp / White Summer / Black Mountain Side / Kashmir / Guitar Solo (including The Star-Spangled Banner) / Achilles Last Stand / Stairway To Heaven / Whole Lotta Love / Rock And Roll

John Paul Jones has back-pain problems tonight, but they do not hamper his playing, which is impeccable like most nights, but prompts Plant to say, "He's got trouble with his back. He's been lying in bed all day. It's about time he had some sordid press. It should be noted that he doesn't just play backgammon!" Plant and Page are in good form, but John Bonham is the weak link tonight with some erratic playing throughout the show. They wisely drop "Moby Dick" from the setlist tonight.

21 June 1977, the Forum, Los Angeles, California (7:30 p.m. Rescheduled from 9 March 1977.)

SETLIST: The Song Remains The Same / The Rover Intro / Sick Again / Nobody's Fault But Mine / Over The Hills And Far Away / Since I've Been Loving You / No Quarter / Ten Years Gone / The Battle Of Evermore / Going To California / Black Country Woman / Bron-Yr-Aur Stomp / White Summer / Black Mountain Side / Kashmir / Moby Dick / Heartbreaker / Guitar Solo (including The Star-Spangled Banner) / Achilles Last Stand / Stairway To Heaven / Whole Lotta Love / Rock And Roll

As mentioned before, Los Angeles was Led Zeppelin's town, a home away from home. A lot of energy was always reserved for LA and the 1977 run was no exception. Luckily for fans, a famous taper in the area recorded all these shows. His name was Mike Millard, and at the LA Forum he used a wheelchair as a way of getting to the handicapped platform, which was situated near the side of the stage facing the massive PA speakers. He used a Nakamichi stereo cassette deck hidden under a blanket and plugged in

Jimmy Page gets his Danelectro guitar plugged in for "Kashmir" on the 1977 US tour. (Rex)

a set of AKG microphones. For the era, these were state of the art and would result in some of the best audience recordings of the band ever captured. Over the years his recordings have become legendary, and the opening night of the LA run has become one of the best known Led Zeppelin bootlegs of all time, called *Listen to This Eddie*. It has been re-issued a countless number of times by various labels since the digital age in the '90s. It can also be downloaded for free on specialist Led Zeppelin fan sites. Jimmy Page was impressed enough to use the audio of "The Song Remains The Same" from this recording in the extras footage on the *Led Zeppelin* DVD in 2003.

This show is probably their best performance from the 1977 tour, and one of their best ever for that matter. It was just one of those magical nights where everything felt right and the band played as one. On a tour that had many ups and downs, this show stands out by far as the benchmark show to beat. Hard to pick any individual highlights as the whole show is a highlight, but fans agree that the version of "No Quarter" is the most spectacular ever played.

66 Lead guitarist Jimmy Page sizzled. He moved as if he were a puppet on a string, egging the audience on as he wound around the stage like a rubber snake held up by strings. The versatile Page

223

was bathed in laser lights during a rendition of the 'Star Spangled Banner,' a la Jimi Hendrix, but with the staccato phrasing that typifies the Zeppelin style. **"**

—**THE *TELEGRAM*** (Review on June 1977)

22 June 1977, the Forum, Los Angeles, California
    (7:30 p.m. Rescheduled from 12 March 1977.)

SETLIST: The Song Remains The Same / The Rover Intro / Sick Again / Nobody's Fault But Mine / In My Time Of Dying / Since I've Been Loving You / No Quarter / Ten Years Gone / The Battle Of Evermore / Going To California / Black Country Woman / Bron-Yr-Aur Stomp / White Summer / Black Mountain Side / Kashmir / Moby Dick / Guitar Solo (including The Star-Spangled Banner) / Achilles Last Stand / Stairway To Heaven / Whole Lotta Love / Rock And Roll

After the incredible opening night, it was clear that the second show would be unlikely to top it, let alone match it. Sure enough, Jimmy Page in particular is tired and messes up several guitar parts. That said, this is still a good show overall with some great playing on "Sick Again," "Since I've Been Loving You," and "No Quarter." On the other hand, "Achilles Last Stand" is rushed and Jimmy throws everybody's timing off by almost forgetting the solo. He quickly redeems himself with a stellar solo on "Stairway To Heaven." This is the weakest night out of the six in terms of Page's playing.

23 June 1977, the Forum, Los Angeles, California (7:30 p.m.)

SETLIST: The Song Remains The Same / The Rover Intro / Sick Again / Nobody's Fault But Mine / Over The Hills And Far Away / Since I've Been Loving You / No Quarter / Ten Years Gone / The Battle Of Evermore / Going To California / Black Country Woman / Bron-Yr-Aur Stomp / White Summer / Black Mountain Side / Kashmir / Trampled Underfoot / Moby Dick / Guitar Solo (including The Star-Spangled Banner) / Achilles Last Stand / Stairway To Heaven / Whole Lotta Love / Rock And Roll

Another legendary show that came out on two double-vinyl bootlegs in the '70s called *For Badge Holders Only* parts 1 and 2. Almost as good as the opening night, Plant makes his intentions very clear from the get-go: "Good evening! Welcome to three hours of lunacy!" He was not lying. If you are wondering why this show got the nickname "Badge Holders," it is because Plant makes many references and dedications to people who are badge holders throughout the concert. Jimmy Page plays like a man possessed at this show, and the band

are not far behind him. Another highlight for LA is the return of "Trampled Underfoot" after going MIA a month before. What makes this show even more legendary is the surprise appearance of the Who's Keith Moon, who joins the band for "Moby Dick" and medley of "Whole Lotta Love" and "Rock And Roll." One can only imagine the backstage scene after the gig! Luckily there was a well-earned day off before the next show.

25 June 1977, the Forum, Los Angeles, California
    (7:30 p.m. Rescheduled from 14 March 1977.)

SETLIST: The Song Remains The Same / The Rover Intro / Sick Again / Nobody's Fault But Mine / In My Time Of Dying (including Rip It Up) / Since I've Been Loving You / No Quarter / Ten Years Gone / The Battle Of Evermore / Going To California / Black Country Woman / Bron-Yr-Aur Stomp / White Summer / Black Mountain Side / Kashmir / Trampled Underfoot / Moby Dick / Guitar Solo (including The Star-Spangled Banner) / Achilles Last Stand / Stairway To Heaven / Whole Lotta Love / Communication Breakdown

Another night in Los Angeles and it's a mesmerizing evening with Led Zeppelin. Plant keeps going with the badge holder theme he first initiated at the 23 June: "Tonight we are celebrating the Annual General Meeting of all LA Badge Holders." Clearly everyone is in a good and humorous mood. The band are tight and waste no time in getting down to business. The whole concert is one big highlight, and the crowd is treated to a surprise version of "Communication Breakdown" as a final encore.

26 June 1977, the Forum, Los Angeles, California (7:30 p.m. Rescheduled from 15 March 1977.)

SETLIST: The Song Remains The Same / The Rover Intro / Sick Again / Nobody's Fault But Mine / Over The Hills And Far Away / Since I've Been Loving You / No Quarter / Ten Years Gone / The Battle Of Evermore / Going To California / That's Alright Mama / Black Country Woman / Bron-Yr-Aur Stomp / White Summer / Black Mountain Side / Kashmir / Moby Dick / Guitar Solo (including Take The High Road) / Achilles Last Stand / Stairway To Heaven / It'll Be Me

Once again the band are in great form, and mix things up a little at this show by adding an ad hoc version on Elvis Presley's "That's Alright Mama" in their sit-down acoustic section. Led Zeppelin also demonstrate why they were an inventive improvisational band in a lengthy "No Quarter," which was really a good vehicle for John Paul Jones's and Jimmy Page's soloing skills. Very rarely did any version of "No Quarter" disappoint, and each one could be very different from the others. Another surprise was Jimmy Page dropping in "Take The High Road," a traditional Scottish ballad, in his guitar instrumental piece before "Achilles Last Stand." And closing the evening was yet another surprise in the form of a rocking version of Jerry Lee Lewis's "It'll Be Me." This is certainly in the top five best shows from the 1977 tour.

27 June 1977, the Forum, Los Angeles, California (7:30 p.m. Rescheduled from 16 March 1977.)

SETLIST: The Song Remains The Same / The Rover Intro / Sick Again / Nobody's Fault But Mine / Over The Hills And Far Away / Since I've Been Loving You / No Quarter / Ten Years Gone / The Battle Of Evermore / Going To California / I Can't Be Satisfied / Black Country Woman / Bron-Yr-Aur Stomp / Dancing Days / White Summer / Black Mountain Side / Kashmir / Trampled Underfoot / Moby Dick / Guitar Solo (including America The Beautiful, The Star-Spangled Banner) / Achilles Last Stand / Stairway To Heaven / Whole Lotta Love / Rock And Roll

All good things invariably have to come to an end, and so it was with Led Zeppelin at the LA Forum. They start slow, pacing themselves for another epic three-and-a-half-hour show. The acoustic section includes a part cover of Muddy Water's "I Can't Be Satisfied," which features Page playing some tasty slide reminiscent of the "Hats Off To Roy Harper" session on *Led Zeppelin III*. Another nice surprise in the acoustic set was the inclusion of "Dancing Days" from the *Houses of the Holy* album. Plant declares that they had not played the song in five years and they would be unlikely to play it again. It is a bit sloppy at times because they had not rehearsed it. Nevertheless, it is a nice addition to the last-night setlist, no matter what Plant says. "No Quarter" is stretched to forty minutes, giving Page and Jones ample space to improvise. It is quite majestic in its execution. If there is any disappointment at tonight's show, it is Page's solo spot, which meanders a little too long, clocking in at thirty minutes.

JULY 1977

17 July 1977, the Kingdome, Seattle, Washington (8:00 p.m.)

SETLIST: The Song Remains The Same / The Rover Intro / Sick Again / Nobody's Fault But Mine / Over The Hills And Far Away / Since I've Been Loving You / No Quarter / Ten Years Gone / The Battle Of Evermore / Going To California / Black Country Woman / Bron-Yr-Aur Stomp / White Summer / Black Mountain Side / Kashmir / Moby Dick / Guitar Solo (including America, The Star-Spangled Banner) / Achilles Last Stand / Stairway To Heaven / Whole Lotta Love / Rock And Roll

Seattle was another favorite city for the band. They had played some of their best shows here in the past, so expectations were high. A bootleg video, which was taken from the in-house feed to the huge screens on either side of the stage, has been doing the rounds in collectors' circles for years. Sadly, tonight's show is only average, but it does give the viewer an opportunity to see a Led Zeppelin show from the US 1977 tour. After a well-deserved two-week break the band should have been chomping at the bit to come out and play. Not an awful show, but when comparing it to the amazing LA run, it does pale in comparison. Some technical issues also help ruin the flow and concentration this evening. In basic terms, the band failed to take off.

> 66 It was a night of pot, pills and popcorn with the popcorn coming in a close third to the other two. But overall, the Led Zeppelin concert at the Kingdome came off without too much trouble. There were several arrests, lots of dope and booze smuggled in—either under coats or inside bodies—and some very sick kids from drinking too much. Plant promised that the 1977 tour would be 'blood, thunder and the hammer of the gods.' A squad of paramedics was geared up for the blood and everybody else was geared up for the thunder and hammer part. 9
>
> —*SEATTLE POST-INTELLIGENCER* ("62,000 Led Zeppelin Fans Jam Kingdome," Review from July 1977)

20 July 1977, Arizona State University Activities Center Arena, Tempe, Arizona (8:00 p.m. Rescheduled from 6 March 1977.)

SETLIST: The Song Remains The Same / The Rover Intro / Sick Again / Nobody's Fault But Mine / Over The Hills And Far Away / Since I've Been Loving You / No Quarter / Ten Years Gone / The Battle Of Evermore / Going To California / Black Country Woman / Bron-Yr-Aur Stomp / Dancing Days / Trampled Underfoot / Black Mountain Side / Kashmir / Guitar Solo (including The Star-Spangled Banner) / Achilles Last Stand / Stairway To Heaven

Possibly the most bizarre show ever in the concert history of Led Zeppelin. Certainly a strong contender for their worst ever show. The concert was due to start at 8:00 p.m., but was delayed to 9:00 p.m., with no reason given for the late start. Page, who was normally quite animated onstage was standing still for most of the performance. "White Summer" is not played, and Page goes straight into "Black Mountain Side" for ten seconds before going into "Kashmir." It takes a few seconds for the rest of the band to realize what is happening and come in late, one by one. The whole band appear tired, but Page is in worse state than the rest, missing notes and making mistakes. He is totally uninspired tonight. To add insult to injury, during "Achilles Last Stand" Page stood too close to the flash pots that let off loud, bright explosions. When one went off right in front of him, he was thrown back against the stage. He was entirely to blame, as he knew where they were, but he was really out of it tonight. There was no "Moby Dick" and the band ended their

Poster advertising two Led Zeppelin concerts at the Oakland Stadium on 23 and 24 July 1977. These would turn out to be the band's last-ever US shows.

truncated set with "Stairway To Heaven" and did not come back for an encore.

23 July 1977, Day on the Green, Alameda County Coliseum, Oakland, California (11:00 a.m. Support from Judas Priest and Rick Derringer.)

SETLIST: The Song Remains The Same / The Rover Intro / Sick Again / Nobody's Fault But Mine / Over The Hills And Far Away / Since I've Been Loving You / No Quarter / Ten Years Gone / The Battle Of Evermore / Going To California / Black Country Woman / Bron-Yr-Aur Stomp / Trampled Underfoot / White Summer / Black Mountain Side / Kashmir / Guitar Solo / Achilles Last Stand / Stairway To Heaven / Whole Lotta Love / Rock And Roll / Black Dog

The massive stage had a fabulous eye-catching backdrop incorporating the famous Stonehenge stones. The band play in the afternoon and Plant greets the crowd with a cheery "Good afternoon. So this is what they call daylight!" The band deliver a strong set, although Page is a little wobbly at times. The band play a rare, for 1977, "Black Dog" as a second and final encore.

Unfortunately, this show will always be remembered for what happened backstage rather than the performance onstage. It was after this show that John Bonham, Peter Grant, Richard Cole, and John Bindon were accused of beating a member of Bill Graham's security staff. It arose when Peter Grant's son had wanted a sign from one of the backstage trailers, and his request was turned down by James Matzorkis, who worked as security for Bill Graham. People have reported that he had to remove the kid's hands from the sign to stop him, but there was no evidence of him hitting the kid. The completely over-the-top reaction from Led Zeppelin's people was ferocious and unforgivable. John Bonham had kicked the guy in the balls, and later Bindon and Grant cornered the security man in a caravan, where they proceeded to kick the shit out of him. It was like something out of the movie *A Clockwork Orange.*

As mentioned at the beginning of the 1977 chapter, having a manager high on cocaine and hiring criminals on drugs for your security was never a good idea. This despicable episode rightly tarnished Led Zeppelin's organizational reputation throughout the music industry. Bill Graham stated that he would never book the band again. As it turns out, it was all academic of course, because after 24 July 1977 the band would never return to America. It was a sad way to end their American journey that had started so innocently and full of promise eight years earlier in Denver.

In February 1978, John Bonham, Peter Grant, Richard Cole, and John Bindon entered a plea of *nolo contendere*, which means they did not accept or deny responsibility for the charges, but agreed to accept punishment. It also meant that they could defend themselves in any subsequent civil suit that might arise. They were found guilty in their absence and given fines along with suspended jail sentences. Bill Graham was furious at what he saw as lenient sentences. He wanted them all incarcerated for their crime. In his later life, Peter Grant bitterly regretted the incident when reading Bill Graham's detailed account of it in his autobiography. Had Peter not been using cocaine so heavily at the time, he would no doubt have acted very differently.

24 July 1977, Day on the Green, Alameda County Coliseum, Oakland, California (11:00 a.m. Support from Judas Priest and Rick Derringer.)

SETLIST: The Song Remains The Same / The Rover Intro / Sick Again / Nobody's Fault But Mine / Over The Hills And Far Away / Since I've Been Loving You / No Quarter / Ten Years Gone / The Battle Of Evermore / Going To California / Mystery Train / Black Country Woman / Bron-Yr-Aur Stomp / Trampled Underfoot / White Summer / Black Mountain Side / Kashmir / Guitar Solo / Achilles Last Stand / Stairway To Heaven / Whole Lotta Love / Rock And Roll

Amazingly, after the events of the 23rd July, today's show goes ahead but starts an hour and a half late due to some quick legal preshow negotiations. A mixed show, but some much needed laughter happened when a local dancer named Betty rushes onstage and dances with Plant during "No Quarter." The show seems rushed and sloppy at times, and clearly the band understandably want to get away from California and the media circus surrounding the beating incident.

Robert Plant arrived in New Orleans on 26 July in preparation for the band's concert at the Superdome when he received a telephone call from his wife, Maureen, who told him that their son Karac had been

taken to hospital with a respiratory infection and that he was not responding to treatment. She told Robert that she would contact him again when she had more news. Unfortunately, when she called him two hours later, it was with the devastating news that their five-year-old son had died. The remainder of the tour was immediately canceled, and Robert Plant, John Bonham, and Richard Cole flew back to England via New York. Karac's funeral took place a week later and was not attended by Peter Grant, Jimmy Page, and John Paul Jones, who were all still in America. Richard Cole and John Bonham were in attendance, lending their support to a shattered family.

30 July 1977, Louisiana Superdome, New Orleans, Louisiana (Tonight's show and all the remainder of shows for the 1977 tour were canceled due to the death of Robert Plant's son.)

AUGUST 1977

2 August 1977, Chicago Stadium, Chicago, Illinois (canceled)

3 August 1977, Chicago Stadium, Chicago, Illinois (canceled)

6 August 1977, Rich Stadium, Orchard Park, New York (canceled)

8 August 1977, Buffalo Memorial Auditorium, Buffalo, New York (canceled)

9 August 1977, Civic Arena, Pittsburgh, Pennsylvania (canceled)

10 August 1977, Civic Arena, Pittsburgh, Pennsylvania (canceled)

13 August 1977, John F. Kennedy Stadium, Philadelphia, Pennsylvania (canceled)

14 August 1977, the Half Moon Pub, Ditchling Road, Plumpton, Sussex (Jimmy Page joins Ron Wood for a jam with a local band called Arms and Legs in aid of the Goaldiggers football charity, which provided play areas for underprivileged children.)

SEPTEMBER 1977

8 September 1977, Metropole Hotel, Kings Road, Brighton, Sussex (Jimmy Page is a guest at the annual Warner-Elektra–Atlantic sales conference. He takes the stage with Phil Carson and Liverpool Express's Billy Kinsley for some classic rock 'n' roll numbers.)

19 1978: New Beginnings

Robert Plant understandably kept himself pretty much to himself after the death of his son. It was devastating and life changing. Led Zeppelin naturally became unimportant to him in the short term, as did the lifestyle that accompanied being in the band. He seriously looked into the possibility of becoming a teacher and leaving the music industry behind him. But really all he wanted was to be away from the band and the whole over-the-top scene associated with it. Family life was far more appealing than the surreal life with Led Zeppelin. The band naturally understood the situation and gave Plant and his family space and time to grieve. Bonham was the only member to keep in regular contact with him during this period.

In the meantime, the press was hounding Jimmy Page to ask if Led Zeppelin were splitting up. It was a constant barrage as each eager reporter wanted to be the first to get that exclusive headline, "Led Zeppelin Splits!" They never got it of course . . . well, not yet anyway. A press statement was issued saying that Robert Plant needed time be alone with his family, but there was categorically no question of Led Zeppelin splitting up. On a creative front, Page had completed work on a new home studio at the end of 1977, and now set about slowly compiling a live chronological retrospective collection on Led Zeppelin with tapes, which according to him went back as far as the Royal Albert Hall in 1969. He also started demoing some potential new material for a future Led Zeppelin album.

In the meantime, Peter Grant was under constant pressure trying to keep the Swan Song label going, as well as attempting to sort out the Oakland public relations disaster that could cost him dearly in America. On top of that, it looked like the band may never get back together, and he would lose his main source of income. He also had to go through a bitter custody battle for his children. Whichever way he turned there were problems, and not surprisingly he suffered a mild heart attack. He had not been in the best of health anyway, but the heart scare had a positive impact on him. He decided to clean up his act. He stopped taking drugs and drinking alcohol and started eating a healthier diet.

By April 1978, Peter Grant called Robert Plant and suggested to him that there should be an informal band meeting at Clearwell Castle in the Forest of Dean, with a view of having a jam to see what happens. This was clearly too early to even consider, but Plant was almost badgered into coming. After several attempts to get him to attend, he finally agreed as long as it was just a jam and nothing more. Not surprisingly, the resultant jam was a mess. Nobody was prepared mentally or physically. Plant in particular wondered why on earth he had attended this aimless get-together. In his mind at least, he had no thought of re-joining the band anytime soon, if at all. Later on he started to go out and play with some local friends, which he enjoyed without any pressure. But Led Zeppelin still seemed far away in his mind. After six more months, he finally felt that he would be ready to give rehearsals with Led Zeppelin a try, but any return would be on his terms. Page and Grant would no longer be the decision-making force of the band. Plant would have his say.

By October the band were rehearsing new material at a London rehearsal space for an album that would soon be recorded at Abba's Polar Studios in Stockholm,

Sweden. Once again, the taxman had reared his ugly head and the band could not record in the UK or America, if they wanted to avoid a huge tax bill. So off to a cold and dark Sweden it was.

INFORMAL JAMMING

MAY 1978
CLEARWELL CASTLE
Clearwell, Forest of Dean, Gloucestershire

The 1977 US tour had put Led Zeppelin back on top and in the full spotlight of the press. The death of Robert Plant's son instantly changed his priorities. He gave up drugs and decided that Led Zeppelin would no longer be allowed to dominate his life. From that point onward, his family would be given first priority. In fact, he seriously considered going to teacher-training college and give up the music scene altogether. By 1978, it seemed like the whole of the Led Zeppelin family was disintegrating. Peter Grant, Jimmy Page, and John Bonham all had drug problems, which invariably had a negative impact on business decisions as well as creative ones. The arrival of punk and New Wave, along with the popularity of disco, had radically changed the music scene in England from 1976 to 1979. Led Zeppelin were very aware of this new scene and even embraced the music of bands like the Damned.

By May 1978, Robert Plant had been persuaded to meet up with the other members of the band for some informal jamming to see how things would develop. Peter Grant suggested Clearwater Castle, a venue that Swan Song label mates Bad Company had used. In reality none of the band were ready mentally or physically to return to any kind of serious playing. When Plant also announced at frequent intervals during rehearsal jams that he would never sing "Stairway To Heaven" again, everyone knew it would be some time before he would feel comfortable in re-joining the group. On the positive side, the Clearwater sessions did provide some much needed renewed kinship between band members. The impatient and naturally inquisitive press had heard about the rehearsals, even though they were supposedly done in secret, and wanted details. The 6 June 1978 *Melody Maker* had a spokesperson from Atlantic stating: "I don't know what will come of the rehearsals, an album, a tour or what, but I expect things will be clarified in the next few weeks."

All sorts of wild rumors starting appearing in the July music press, such as Led Zeppelin supposedly opening for Maggie Bell at a show at the Royal Festival Hall in London, or that they would be playing a series of pub gigs under an assumed name. Not surprisingly, none of the above happened. What did happen was Robert Plant joining Dave Edmunds onstage for an impromptu jam, and he also attended Simon Kirke's wedding and sang a couple of songs. It was good to see him slowly getting back into music.

REHEARSALS FOR *IN THROUGH THE OUT DOOR*

OCTOBER 1978–NOVEMBER 1978
E-ZEE HIRE, Market Road, London N7

Led Zeppelin hired a rehearsal studio in Islington, North London, for an intense six-week period to try out new material for their next studio album. Although some ideas had been worked on at the loose jams at Clearwater Castle earlier in the year, these were a lot more formal. Jimmy Page brought along a new toy to the sessions, a Gizmotron. Invented by 10CC's Kevin Godley and Lol Creme, the unit was attached to the guitar body giving the player an automatic bowing device. It could pluck a string up to 100 times per second. Despite high-profile advertising, the Gizmotron faded into obscurity. Page used it to great effect, especially on the atmospheric intro to "In the Evening."

20 1978: Recording Sessions

SESSIONS FOR *IN THROUGH THE OUT DOOR*

POLAR STUDIOS
Sankt Eriksgatan 58-60,
Kungsholmen, Stockholm

NOVEMBER 1978-DECEMBER 1978

Polar Studios were opened by Abba's Bjorn Ulvaeus and Benny Andersson in May 1978. They were keen to increase the studio's international presence by attracting some high-profile artists to their complex. Led Zeppelin were one of the first, and they were offered some free studio time as an incentive to use the studios. As they were also forced to record outside of the UK for tax reasons, why not do it in Sweden? The band flew over on 13 November to a snowbound and bitterly cold Stockholm. Although Polar Studios were state of the art, Page found that the studio room was not particularly ambient, and it took a couple of days for everyone to get used to the sound.

The band's weekly schedule would consist of flying out to Stockholm at midday on a Monday and flying back home the following Friday so that they could all spend the weekend in the UK. Jimmy Page would usually have the week's recordings with him for mixing and overdubbing at his home studio in Plumpton, Sussex. The band had four suites at the Sheraton in Stockholm for the whole period, and it became their home away from home when in Sweden. Recording

time was usually allocated between Tuesday and Thursday every week between the middle of November and the end of December.

Jimmy Page, who had always been the guiding creative force in the studio, was not in great shape health-wise, and as a result a lot of the creative decisions had to be made by Robert Plant and John Paul Jones. Page and Bonham would often arrive late at the studio, so rather than just sit around Plant and Jones would lay their tracks down, which would later be overdubbed by Page at his home studio on the weekend. "In The Evening" and "Carouselambra" in particular started out as just keyboards and drums with Page adding his parts later. Sound-wise, it was quite a shift in direction from previous work the band had produced. When Page brought back the tapes to the studio after the weekend, they sounded very different from how they had the Thursday before.

"In The Evening" was a long, brooding number that worked well in the live arena. Page starts the intro on his Fender Stratocaster with the Gizmotron. The sessions ended just before Christmas, allowing the band to spend the holidays with their respective families. Jimmy Page would do final mixes and work out the running order at his home studio in Plumpton during January 1979. He made no secret of the fact that he found the album a little lightweight. But at least some of the blame must lay at his door for not being focused enough. After all the album's biggest letdown was that the guitar tone was very thin throughout. Where was the archetypal fat sound of the Les Pauls and Marshalls? Was this really an album showing the band moving with the times or was it more of a desperate bid to get some new product out on the market? In the end, it is an album very much of its time, and certainly the weakest of all the Led Zeppelin albums released. It is also the only one that sounds dated.

14 NOVEMBER 1978–16 NOVEMBER 1978

21 NOVEMBER 1978–23 NOVEMBER 1978

28 NOVEMBER 1978–30 NOVEMBER 1978

5 DECEMBER 1978–7 DECEMBER 1978

12 DECEMBER 1978–14 DECEMBER 1978

19 DECEMBER 1978–21 DECEMBER 1978

OZONE BABY (Jimmy Page / Robert Plant) Available on vinyl *Coda* US Swan Song 90051, released 19 November 1982 / UK Swan Song A 0051, released 22 November 1982.

DARLENE (John Bonham / John Paul Jones / Jimmy Page / Robert Plant) Available on vinyl *Coda* US Swan Song 90051, released 19 November 1982 / UK Swan Song A 0051, released 22 November 1982.

WEARING AND TEARING (Jimmy Page / Robert Plant) Available on vinyl *Coda* US Swan Song 90051, released 19 November 1982 / UK Swan Song A 0051, released 22 November 1982.

IN THE EVENING (Jimmy Page / Robert Plant / John Paul Jones) Available on vinyl *In Through the Out Door* US Swan Song SS-16002, released 15 August 1979 / UK Swan Song SSK 59410, released 20 August 1979.

SOUTH BOUND PIANO (Later retitled "South Bound Saurez") (John Paul Jones / Robert Plant) Available on vinyl *In Through the Out Door* US Swan Song SS-16002, released 15 August 1979 / UK Swan Song SSK 59410, released 20 August 1979.

FOOL IN THE RAIN (Jimmy Page / Robert Plant / John Paul Jones) Available on vinyl *In Through the Out Door* US Swan Song SS-16002, released 15 August 1979 / UK Swan Song SSK 59410, released 20 August 1979.

HOT DOG (Jimmy Page / Robert Plant) Available on vinyl *In Through the Out Door* US Swan Song SS-16002, released 15 August 1979 / UK Swan Song SSK 59410, released 20 August 1979.

THE EPIC (Later retiled "Carouselambra") (Jimmy Page / Robert Plant / John Paul Jones) Available on vinyl *In Through the Out Door* US Swan Song SS-16002, released 15 August 1979 / UK Swan Song SSK 59410, released 20 August 1979.

THE HOOK (Later retitled "All My Love") (Robert Plant / John Paul Jones) Available on vinyl *In Through the Out Door* US Swan Song SS-16002, released 15 August 1979 / UK Swan Song SSK 59410, released 20 August 1979.

EVERY LITTLE BIT OF MY LOVE (Blot) (Later retiled "I'm Gonna Crawl") (Robert Plant / John Paul Jones) Available on vinyl *In Through the Out Door* US Swan Song SS-16002, released 15 August 1979 / UK Swan Song SSK 59410, released 20 August 1979.

PRODUCER: JIMMY PAGE
ENGINEER: LEIF MASES
MIXED AT JIMMY PAGE'S HOME STUDIO AT PLUMPTON PLACE, DITCHLING ROAD, PLUMPTON, NR. LEWES, SUSSEX

66 Polar Studios in Stockholm had been set up by Abba's Bjorn and Benny in 1977. They were keen to have an international group record there and I was personally contacted by a representative of the studios who offered three weeks free recording time. This seemed a sound idea to go there to produce what was to become our eighth studio album—In Through the Out Door. We'd been playing around with some ideas at Clearwell Castle in Gloucestershire, UK but then went into Easy Hire, a rehearsal studio in North London, where most of the material that would surface on the album was routined. When we arrived in Stockholm, it was well into their winter, there was heavy snow in the streets and very, very cold. Polar was a state of the art studio for its time, but not particularly ambient. It took a couple of days to get used to this. We worked on the first track that was to become 'Ozone Baby' and on this day (14 November) 'South Bound Saurez' had been recorded. Juices were flowing and the recording process was now fully underway. 99

—JIMMY PAGE (From his website)

GUEST RECORDING SESSIONS

John Bonham Session for Roy Wood

UNKNOWN STUDIO

OCTOBER 1978

KEEP YOUR HANDS ON THE WHEEL (Roy Wood) Available on vinyl *On the Road Again* Warner Brothers BSK 3247 released 1979.

ROY WOOD: LEAD VOCALS, BACKING VOCALS, ELECTRIC GUITAR, SITAR
JOHN BONHAM: DRUMS

Robert Plant and John Paul Jones backstage at the Knebworth Festival in 1979. (Rex)

BILLY PAUL: ALTO SAXOPHONE
PAUL ROBBINS: ELECTRIC GUITAR, PIANO, BACKING VOCALS
CARL WAYNE: BACKING VOCALS
PETE MACKIE: BASS, BACKING VOCALS
PRODUCER: ROY WOOD

John Bonham and John Paul Jones Guest Session for Paul McCartney and Wings

ABBEY ROAD STUDIOS
3 Abbey Road, St Johns Wood,
London NW8

3 OCTOBER 1978

Paul McCartney had been working for sometime on the idea of forming a large rock supergroup orchestra to record together. The original demo was made at Lympne Castle on 24-track tape with Wings triple-tracking themselves. McCartney loved the huge rock 'n' roll orchestra sound so much that he wanted to do it again at Abbey Road studios with all the best rock musicians of the time in one room together with minimal overdubbing. In all they recorded just two numbers, both of which appear on Wings' *Back to the Egg* album.

ROCKESTRA THEME (Paul McCartney) Available on *Back to the Egg* album MPL Records PCTC 257 released June 1979.

PAUL MCCARTNEY: VOCALS, BASS, PIANO
LINDA MCCARTNEY: BACKING VOCALS, KEYBOARDS
DENNY LAINE: ELECTRIC GUITAR
LAURENCE JUBER: ELECTRIC GUITAR
DAVID GILMOUR: ELECTRIC GUITAR
HANK MARVIN: ELECTRIC GUITAR
PETE TOWNSHEND: ELECTRIC GUITAR
STEVE HOLLY: DRUMS
KENNY JONES: DRUMS
JOHN BONHAM: DRUMS
JOHN PAUL JONES: BASS, PIANO
RONNIE LANE: BASS
BRUCE THOMAS: BASS
TONY ASHTON: KEYBOARDS
GARY BROOKER: PIANO
SPEEDY ACQUAYE: PERCUSSION
TONY CARR: PERCUSSION
RAY COOPER: PERCUSSION
MORRIS PERT: PERCUSSION
HOWIE CASEY: HORNS
TONY DORSEY: HORNS
STEVE HOWARD: HORNS
THADDEUS RICHARD: HORNS

SO GLAD TO SEE YOU HERE (Paul McCartney) Available on *Back to the Egg* album MPL Records PCTC 257 released June 1979.

PAUL MCCARTNEY: VOCALS, BASS, PIANO
LINDA MCCARTNEY: BACKING VOCALS, KEYBOARDS
DENNY LAINE: ELECTRIC GUITAR
LAURENCE JUBER: ELECTRIC GUITAR
DAVID GILMOUR: ELECTRIC GUITAR
HANK MARVIN: ELECTRIC GUITAR
PETE TOWNSHEND: ELECTRIC GUITAR
STEVE HOLLY: DRUMS
KENNY JONES: DRUMS
JOHN BONHAM: DRUMS
JOHN PAUL JONES: BASS, PIANO
RONNIE LANE: BASS
BRUCE THOMAS: BASS
TONY ASHTON: KEYBOARDS
GARY BROOKER: PIANO
SPEEDY ACQUAYE: PERCUSSION
TONY CARR: PERCUSSION
RAY COOPER: PERCUSSION
MORRIS PERT: PERCUSSION
HOWIE CASEY: HORNS
TONY DORSEY: HORNS
STEVE HOWARD: HORNS
THADDEUS RICHARD: HORNS
PRODUCER: PAUL MCCARTNEY
ENGINEER: PHIL MCDONALD

1979: Can You Do the Dinosaur Rock?

21

The year was all about getting the band back together and on the road. Peter Grant wanted it to be a spectacular comeback, rather than simply doing a tour of England in smaller venues. Promoter Freddie Bannister, who had organized the two Bath Festivals in 1969 and 1970, had approached Grant several times over the years about getting the band to headline at Knebworth, but was always turned down. By 1979, several major acts had already headlined successfully at Knebworth, such as Bob Dylan, the Rolling Stones, and Pink Floyd, among others. It was seen as a prestigious festival to play at. And 1979 would be Led Zeppelin's turn. Jack Calmes from Swan Song and Peter Grant negotiated a deal for £1 million with Bannister to play a show in the grounds of Knebworth House that could easily accommodate over 200,000 people. It would be their largest ever audience. A show was advertised for 4 August 1979, and when 150,000 tickets were sold within hours of tickets going on sale, Grant persuaded Bannister to add a second date for the following weekend, on 11 August 1979. Quite an achievement for a band that had not played in England since 1975.

The band were nervous about playing such a high-profile event and booked Bray Studios for over a month of rehearsals, as well as booking two low-key warm-up shows in Copenhagen, Denmark. They wanted to make sure that everything was going to be perfect on the night.

LED ZEPPELIN

JUNE 1979–JULY 1979

Rehearsals at Bray Studios, Bray, Berkshire

COPENHAGEN WARM-UPS

23 JULY 1979– 24 JULY 1979

JULY 1979

With the band ready to return to the live arena, it made sense to do a couple of warm-up shows for the upcoming Knebworth concerts to test the light show, effects, and sound system, as well as seeing how the setlist went down with an audience. The two shows in Copenhagen had to be done in complete secrecy to avoid any press intrusion, and were organized within fourteen days of the dates being announced. They were certainly low-key, with the Falkoner Theatre's capacity being a mere 2,000 seats. Incredibly, you could still buy tickets at the door on the night of the show due to lack of any publicity. Unfortunately, the band were far from ready. Some people refer to the shows as being loose. In reality they were sloppy and a far cry from their best years.

23 July 1979, Falkoner Theatre, Copenhagen, Denmark
    (8:00 p.m.)

SETLIST: The Song Remains The Same / Celebration Day / Out On The Tiles Intro / Black Dog / Nobody's Fault But Mine / Over The Hills And Far Away / Misty Mountain Hop / Since I've Been Loving You / No Quarter / Hot Dog / The Rain Song / White Summer / Black Mountain Side / Kashmir / Trampled Underfoot / Achilles Last Stand / Guitar Solo / Drum Solo / In The Evening / Stairway To Heaven / Rock And Roll

Technical issues with any new production are to be expected, especially when the venue size is not known. To start with, the ambitious new light show, which was designed for the huge stage at Knebworth, was way too large for the venue. Then there were issues with the generator, which caused a long delay in allowing people into the venue, frustrating everyone. The Danish newspapers, who along with anyone else from the press worldwide, were not allowed to attend. Somehow they managed to get in, and made their feelings pretty clear. Splashed across the headlines in bold was, "Led Zeppelin—Fiasko." Not the ideal headline if you want to make an impressive return to live work.

The concert featured the first ever public performances of "Hot Dog" and "In The Evening" from their forthcoming album. Plant's vocals appear to be hoarse, but that is probably more down to first-night nerves than any health issues. The setlist tries too hard to please everyone and is basically a greatest hits live from the various stages of their career up to that point. The groove is simply not there and overall the night was a letdown with some average playing. A few overseas reporters also managed to sneak in, and a review in *Sounds* magazine by Erik Von Lustbaden tells the story in accurate detail: "Dazzling, staggering and sometimes awful. The subdued lights were still much better than most bands will ever have! The powerful ascending riff of 'Kashmir' and the group's sense of simple melody and repetition combine to at least give an inkling of why they've attained such a legendary status. Dazzling. Another Page solo, all without any backing. I went for a piss, bought a bar of chocolate, ate it, had a sit down, made some notes, went back in, and he was still playing it!"

An even more bitter review was made by Eric Kornfeld in the *New Musical Express*: "They appeared sloppy and unrehearsed, sometimes seeming awkwardly lost, bewildered, stiff and reluctant to play. They were no more than a quartet of uninspired old men, a relic from the past. There was so little feeling

inherent in the set that for the most part it was like watching a fully automated factory producing an endless string of chords that neither musicians nor audience cared about." It should be pointed out that by this point in 1979, the *NME* were staunch supporters of the punk movement and viewed bands like Led Zeppelin as fossils from a bygone age. That said, the reviewer had some valid points, however painful they may have been to fans.

24 July 1979, Falkoner Theatre, Copenhagen, Denmark (8:00 p.m.)

SETLIST: The Song Remains The Same / Celebration Day / Out On The Tiles Intro / Black Dog / Nobody's Fault But Mine / Over The Hills And Far Away / Misty Mountain Hop / Since I've Been Loving You / No Quarter / Ten Years Gone / Hot Dog / The Rain Song / White Summer / Black Mountain Side / Kashmir / Trampled Underfoot / Sick Again / Achilles Last Stand / Guitar Solo / Drum Solo / In The Evening / Stairway To Heaven / Whole Lotta Love

All in all, a much better show than the previous day, although there were some technical issues during the concert. Problems with John Paul Jones's effects pedals prior to playing "Ten Years Gone" prompts Plant to tell the audience, "We'll very shortly be doing 'Eleven Years Gone.'"

Despite a strict embargo on the press for the Danish shows, Jon Carlsson manages to get a review for the 4 August 1979 issue of *Melody Maker*. The headline for the review, "Warming Up in Denmark: Duck-Walks and Lasers," sounded pretty exciting. He goes on to describe Page's instrumental solo spot at the show: "The bow began glowing with an eerie green light that you could read a book by. It made Page look like a Crowleyite elf or perhaps Obi-Wan Kenobi on exotic snuff. Page was then enclosed by a green pyramid of thin laser light, which on every fourth beat rotated through 90 degrees. It became faster in its rotations until it became a glowing green cone, Page stepped back into it and let the color wash over him."

"Achilles Last Stand" and "In The Evening" are played with energy and enthusiasm, as was the new arrangement for "Whole Lotta Love." On the other hand, "Stairway To Heaven" sounds more like a dirge, which appears rushed and has no life to it. In short, both the shows in Copenhagen were contradictions, with some good playing mixed in with some inexcusable mistakes, which were reflected in the reviews.

Led Zeppelin at the
Knebworth Festival
August 1979. (Rex)

LED ZEPPELIN KNEBWORTH FESTIVAL

4 August 1979, Knebworth Festival, Knebworth, Stevenage (Show due to start at 11:00 a.m. Support from Fairport Convention, Todd Rundgren and Utopia, Southside Johnny and the Asbury Jukes, Marshall Tucker Band, and Chas and Dave. Concert was professionally recorded and filmed. "Ten Years Gone" was used for the 1990 *Remasters* compilation promo and was used by MTV for their special *Whole Lotta Led* program in late 1990.)

SETLIST: The Song Remains The Same / Celebration Day / Out On The Tiles Intro / Black Dog / Nobody's Fault But Mine / Over The Hills And Far Away / Misty Mountain Hop / Since I've Been Loving You / No Quarter / Ten Years Gone / Hot Dog / The Rain Song / White Summer / Black Mountain Side / Kashmir / Trampled Underfoot / Sick Again / Achilles Last Stand / Guitar Solo / Drum Solo / In The Evening / Stairway To Heaven / Rock And Roll / Whole Lotta Love / Heartbreaker

For the shows at Knebworth, Page had quite an arsenal of guitars on the side of the stage. Along with the same guitars he used on the 1977 US tour, he also had a blue Lake Placid Fender Stratocaster for "In The Evening," a "Botswana Brown" 1953 Fender Telecaster with rosewood neck for "Hot Dog" and "Ten Years Gone," and a 1977 Gibson RD Artist for "Misty Mountain Hop." Both shows were professionally filmed, with the sound being recorded by the Rolling Stones Mobile by engineer George Chkiantz. Great care had been taken to ensure things were right as Page told the *NME*, "We've actually been down there and worked things out relative to the actual site. But then again it's like a natural amphitheatre, so I would imagine it's actually quite a good gig to be at."

Peter Grant had brought in a 100,000-watt sound system and a 600,000-watt light system, both of which were handled by Showco, who had worked with the band on several US tours as well as at Earls Court. The concert was good, but not amazing, but the light show was spectacular; especially during Page's solo segment, which featured a beam of light shooting out from his violin bow as a laser pyramid swirled around him. Ultimately, though, however ambitious the light show was, the band struggled to find a groove and it felt in some instances that they were simply going through the motions.

The problems found in the Copenhagen shows were still present here. Plant messes up the lyrics to "Hot Dog," which can be forgiven as it was only the third public performance of the song and in front of a huge home crowd. There were a few technical issues also, which caused Plant to come out with a strange statement: "So we get all the way here, and the equipment blows up! Never mind, it's got to be better than Earls Court." One has to wonder if Plant was being rational in his thinking, because to describe the Knebworth show as being better than Earls Court is delusional.

The best numbers from the Knebworth shows are actually the ones that made the *Led Zeppelin* DVD in 2003, all of which are taken from this evening's show. "Rock and Roll," "Nobody's Fault But Mine," "Sick Again," "Achilles Last Stand," "In The Evening," and "Kashmir" all made the cut and sound far better than all of the bootlegs because the guitar has been beefed up with some reverb during the mixing process for the release. The fact that the whole show was not released to the general public speaks volumes. The most energetic numbers are "Rock And Roll" and a new arrangement of "Whole Lotta Love," both of which go down well with the crowd. A short "Heartbreaker" as a final encore seems almost anticlimactic with a short final comment from Plant: "All you people that have come so far. It's been kinda like a blind date. Thanks for eleven years!"

11 August 1979, Knebworth Festival, Knebworth, Stevenage (Show due to start at 11:00 a.m. Support from the New Barbarians, Todd Rundgren and Utopia, Southside Johnny and the Asbury Jukes, the Marshall Tucker Band, Fairport Convention, and Chas and Dave. Concert was professionally recorded and filmed. "Hot Dog" and "Kashmir" were used for the 1990 *Remasters* compilation promo and by MTV for their special *Whole Lotta Led* program in late 1990.)

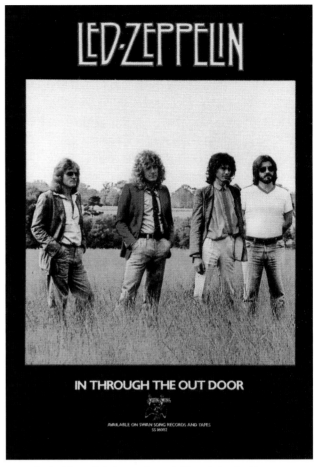

Advert for Led Zeppelin's latest album, *In Though the Out Door.*

SETLIST: The Song Remains The Same / Celebration Day / Out On The Tiles Intro / Black Dog / Nobody's Fault But Mine / Over The Hills And Far Away / Misty Mountain Hop / Since I've Been Loving You / No Quarter / Hot Dog / The Rain Song / White Summer / Black Mountain Side / Kashmir / Trampled Underfoot / Sick Again / Achilles Last Stand / Guitar Solo / Drum Solo / In The Evening / Stairway To Heaven / Rock And Roll / Whole Lotta Love / Communication Breakdown

The press were not exactly glowing in their reviews of the first show, although there were some positive ones as well. An unhappy Plant commented to the crowd, "Well, it didn't rain. But it rained on us during the week from one or two sources, and we're really gonna stick it right where it really belongs." Sadly, the band's second performance didn't stick it to the critics, and pretty much confirmed why the reviews were not exactly favorable. The other problem was that the crowds at both shows were worn out from having listened to a host of other bands during the afternoon in a festival setting. Their response to the headliners was lukewarm as a result. Had the festival only featured Led Zeppelin on the bill, the audiences at both shows would have had a lot more energy reserved for them.

Perhaps having got the first show over and done with gave the band more confidence for their second and final Knebworth concert. It appeared that way for the first quarter of the set, which had a lot more energy than the first show, but lacked emotion. Plant managed to mess up the lyrics to "Hot Dog" again, and pretty soon the band started to flag, and some numbers were sounding very sloppy. Overall, it seemed like the band were unsure of their position in the world of rock. Plant even stated sarcastically before playing the encores, "Can you do the dinosaur rock?" At least he had a sense of humor about it. A final encore of "Communication Breakdown" was a surprise, and replaced "Heartbreaker," which was played at the first show. To the crowd's pleasure and surprise, it sounded like the band would soon be touring, according to Plant, who announced at the end of the show, "We'll see you soon. Very soon. Don't know about the Marquee, but somewhere soon."

Nick Kent reviewed the second show for the *NME* and was less than complimentary: "The mixture of Robert Plant's frequent snipes at their less-than-totally-adulatory press coverage and the elongated virtuosity of the likes of 'No Quarter' and 'Dazed And Confused' [he clearly must have been referring to Page's solo bow piece, as 'Dazed' was not played at either show] ultimately left me cold and bored.

Zeppelin, for all their virtuosity, had very little to say beyond the bombastic power. Zep are like a behemoth, impressive but something from the past—almost a museum piece."

DECEMBER 1979

29 December 1979, Concert for the People of Kampuchea, Hammersmith Odeon, Hammersmith, London (The Concerts for the People of Kampuchea were put together by Paul McCartney. The shows were held over four days and would benefit the starving people of Kampuchea. The concerts included some of the best British talent at the time. Three members of Led Zeppelin appeared on the final night in Paul McCartney's Rockestra all-star band, who closed the evening's show in fine style. Robert Plant had also made a guest appearance with Rockpile for a version of "Little Sister" earlier in the evening. The members of the Rockestra all-stars included Paul McCartney, Linda McCartney, Denny Laine, Laurence Juber, Steve Holly, John Bonham, Billy Bremner, Gary Brooker, Howie Casey, Tony Dorsey, Dave Edmunds, James Honeyman-Scott, Steve Howard, Kenney Jones, John Paul Jones, Ronnie Lane, Robert Plant, Thadeus Richard, Bruce Thomas, and Pete Townshend. Together they played the following songs: "Rockestra Theme," "Let It Be," "Lucille," and "Rockestra Theme (Reprise)." The RAK Mobile Recording Studio recorded the show, and all the above numbers were released on the double album titled *Concerts for the People of Kampuchea* on Atlantic Records in June 1981. Sadly, the album has never been released officially on CD.)

22 1980: The End of the Road

Almost a year after the two massive Knebworth shows, Led Zeppelin announced a low-key tour of Europe playing smaller venues with a capacity of around 4,000 seats. It seemed like the machine was destined to carry on working no matter what problems existed. Although parts of the two Knebworth shows were sluggish and tired, the group's popularity did not appear to have diminished. It made sense to tour in Europe in a low-key fashion, if only to promote *In Through the Out Door*, their latest album, which had sold extremely well in England, Europe, and America. More importantly, it would hopefully unite and rekindle the group's passion for live playing before heading back to the USA for a lengthy tour, their first since 1977.

Peter Grant felt that the only way for the group to survive was to head back to America, where their huge fan base was hungry to see the band onstage. Unfortunately, by 1980 Robert Plant had lost any taste for touring the US, John Paul Jones was ambivalent, and John Bonham was drinking too much. Jimmy Page in particular was not in the best of health, and many industry friends and music journalists who saw him backstage and at hotel parties on the European tour were commenting in the press and privately how stick-thin and unkempt he was. His gums and teeth showed all the signs of cocaine and heroin abuse. It was incredibly sad to see him in such a state, and ultimately the band having reached these low depths.

There really was no support system to help them, which can be blamed on their successful insular lives over many years. Nobody from the outside could get close, and anyone on the inside was either too messed up themselves, or would not dare to voice an opinion.

Led Zeppelin were close to burning out and were falling apart. Grant was unwise to book a massive two-part US tour under such circumstances. It is doubtful they would have survived the tour. Was he really unable to see how bad things were on the inside? The only way they could have survived was to have taken a two year sabbatical to spend some quality time with family and friends and more importantly, get clean, both physically and mentally. If they could have done that, there is every possibility that their creative juices would have started flowing again and given them the impetus to record a much needed new, decent, riff-laden hard-rock album. Unfortunately history has shown us it was not meant to be.

As for the 1980 Europe tour, it was a back-to-basics approach with the band wisely dropping the lengthy marathons like "Dazed And Confused" and "No Quarter," concentrating on more concise numbers such as the surprise opener, 'The Train Kept A Rollin." It had not been played since Oakland on 2 September 1970. In the era of punk where bands like Led Zeppelin were being criticized for being out of touch, Plant, in particular, was keen to reduce "the guitar solos that lasted an hour." Also dropped was the acoustic set, which helped the flow of the new show as well as reducing the chance of equipment problems. Some favorites were still included of course, such as "Stairway To Heaven," but Robert Plant could barely hide his boredom during the song. He seemed to amuse himself on the tour by shouting, "Eye Thank Yew!" to the crowd at regular intervals whilst inviting them to copy his "dickhead gestures" by placing his cupped hand on his forehead and then moving it downward in a semi-circle. Most of the tour can be summed up as being sluggish, with several moments of apathy and a far cry from the momentous peaks in 1975. The enthusiasm of their earlier tours was simply not there. This was far from being anything close to a rebirth for the band. More a death knell.

The band spent over a month rehearsing at the Rainbow in Finsbury Park and at the New Victoria Theatre in London before moving to Shepperton Studios in May for a final run-through. The new set was basically a scaled-down version of their 1979 Knebworth shows. The only new numbers from *In Through the Out Door* to be rehearsed were "In The Evening," "Hot Dog," and "All My Love." Only the latter had not been played in public before.

FEBRUARY 1980

3 February 1980, Top Rank, Birmingham, Midlands (Robert Plant joins Dave Edmunds and Rockpile for their encore.)

LED ZEPPELIN OVER EUROPE TOUR

17 JUNE 1980–8 JULY 1980

The equipment for the tour was a stripped-down set up from the 1979 dates, with Showco handling the sound and lights as usual. Jimmy Page's guitars consisted of his usual Gibson Les Pauls, the "Botswana Brown" Fender Telecaster, used for "Hot Dog" and "All My Love," the double-neck Gibson, a cream Fender Telecaster, and his Danelectro guitar.

22 May 1980, Stadhalle, Vienna, Austria (Canceled. Rescheduled for 26 June 1980.)

23 May 1980, Olympiahalle, Munich, Germany (Canceled. Rescheduled for 5 July 1980.)

25 May 1980, Westfalenhalle, Dortmund, Germany (Canceled. Rescheduled for 17 June 1980.)

26 May 1980, Sporthalle, Cologne, Germany (Canceled. Rescheduled for 18 June 1980.)

28 May 1980, Stadhalle, Bremen, Germany (Canceled. Rescheduled for 23 June 1980.)

29 May 1980, Eissporthalle, Berlin, Germany (Canceled. Rescheduled for 7 July 1980.)

31 May 1980, Eisstadion Am Freidrichspark, Mannheim, Germany (Canceled. Rescheduled for 2 June 1980.)

JUNE 1980

1 June 1980, Hallenstadion, Zurich, Switzerland (Canceled. Rescheduled for 29 June 1980.)

5 June 1980, Forest National, Brussels, Belgium (Canceled. Rescheduled for 20 June 1980.)

14 June 1980, Palais Des Sports, Paris, France (Canceled. Not rescheduled.)

17 June 1980, Westfalenhalle, Dortmund, Germany (8:00 p.m. Rescheduled from 25 May 1980.)

SETLIST: The Train Kept A Rollin' / Nobody's Fault But Mine / Out On The Tiles Intro / Black Dog / In The Evening / The Rain Song / Hot Dog / All My Love / Trampled Underfoot / Since I've Been Loving You / Achilles Last Stand / White Summer / Black Mountain Side / Kashmir / Stairway To Heaven / Rock And Roll / Whole Lotta Love (including Heartbreaker)

A bizarre show that starts off pretty well with an enthusiastic performance that is sadly let down by Page from "White Summer" onward, where he sounds out of tune and out of time at different stages in the show.

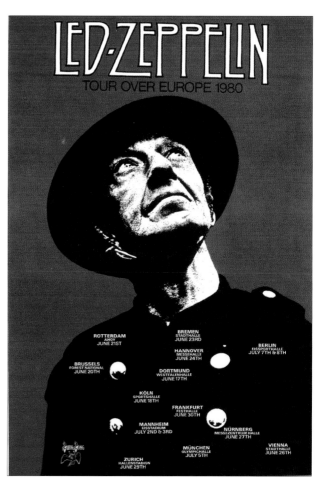

Poster advertising Led Zeppelin's 1980 tour of Europe.

18 June 1980, Sporthalle, Cologne, Germany

SETLIST: The Train Kept A Rollin' / Nobody's Fault But Mine / Out On The Tiles Intro / Black Dog / In The Evening / The Rain Song / Hot Dog / All My Love / Trampled Underfoot / Since I've Been Loving You / Achilles Last Stand / White Summer / Black Mountain Side / Kashmir / Stairway To Heaven / Rock And Roll / Communication Breakdown

20 June 1980, Forest National, Brussels, Belgium (8:30 p m Rescheduled from 5 June 1980.)

SETLIST: The Train Kept A Rollin' / Nobody's Fault But Mine / Out On The Tiles Intro / Black Dog / In The Evening / The Rain Song / Hot Dog / All My Love / Trampled Underfoot / Since I've Been Loving You / Achilles Last Stand / White Summer / Black Mountain Side / Kashmir / Stairway To Heaven / Rock And Roll / Whole Lotta Love (including Boogie Chillun')

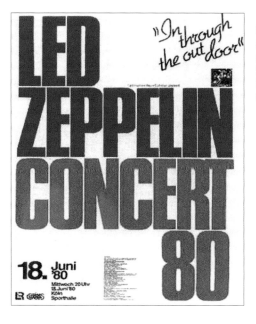

Poster for Led Zeppelin's appearance at the Sporthalle in Cologne, Germany, on 18 June 1980.

One of the better shows on the Europe 1980 tour. In fact, this could arguably be the best night of the tour in terms of performance and setlist. The boisterous crowd, many from England and France, ruined Page's concentration during "White Summer," and he has to stop the song halfway through and ask them to be quiet. Fantastic version of "Whole Lotta Love" drives the crowd wild.

21 June 1980, Ahoy, Rotterdam, Holland (8:00 p.m.)

SETLIST: The Train Kept A Rollin' / Nobody's Fault But Mine / Out On The Tiles Intro / Black Dog / In The Evening / The Rain Song / Hot Dog / All My Love / Trampled Underfoot / Since I've Been Loving You / Achilles Last Stand / White Summer / Black Mountain Side / Kashmir / Stairway To Heaven / Rock And Roll / Heartbreaker

For some reason, the band fail to capture the hearts of the crowd tonight. Even a knockout encore version of "Heartbreaker" does not liven the crowd. Quite a few people made the trip from England to support the band.

23 June 1980, Stadhalle, Bremen, Germany (8:00 p.m. Rescheduled from 28 May 1980.)

SETLIST: The Train Kept A Rollin' / Nobody's Fault But Mine / Out On The Tiles Intro / Black Dog / In The Evening / The Rain Song / Hot Dog / All My Love / Trampled Underfoot / Since I've Been Loving You / Achilles Last Stand / White Summer / Black Mountain Side / Kashmir / Stairway To Heaven / Rock And Roll / Communication Breakdown

Uneven show tonight with Page missing notes here and there. A concise version of "Communication Breakdown" closes the show.

24 June 1980, Messehalle, Hanover, Germany (8:30 p.m.)

SETLIST: The Train Kept A Rollin' / Nobody's Fault But Mine / Out On The Tiles Intro / Black Dog / In The Evening / The Rain Song / Hot Dog / All My Love / Trampled Underfoot / Since I've Been Loving You / Achilles Last Stand / White Summer / Black Mountain Side / Kashmir / Stairway To Heaven / Rock And Roll / Communication Breakdown

Another low-key show. Plant is not happy with the apparent ambivalence of the crowd. He can clearly be heard off-mic saying, "Hanover, fucking horrible place!" before the band play "In The Evening." The show is not a disaster, though, with fine performances on "Since I've Been Loving You" and "All My Love." Plant tries to get John Bonham to play "Moby Dick" as a way of livening the crowd, but all to no avail as Bonham refuses point blank, "No way, mate. No way."

26 June 1980, Stadhalle, Vienna, Austria (7:30 p.m. Rescheduled from 22 May 1980.)

SETLIST: The Train Kept A Rollin' / Nobody's Fault But Mine / Out On The Tiles Intro / Black Dog / In The Evening / The Rain Song / Hot Dog / All My Love / Trampled Underfoot / Since I've Been Loving You / Achilles Last Stand / White Summer / Kashmir / Stairway To Heaven / Rock And Roll / Whole Lotta Love (including Boogie Chillun')

Despite a very boisterous audience, the band put in a pretty good performance overall, which is only marred by some irresponsible idiot throwing a firecracker, hitting Page in the face during "White Summer." The song is ended and the band makes a quick exit from the stage. A little while later, the angry promoter of the concert comes out front to make an announcement (translated):

> We have a group here that is giving their all and cannot be interrupted by idiots who throw something onto the stage! A firecracker that hit him in the eye has injured Jimmy Page! I would like to ask you for one thing: if someone is standing next to you and does this kind of nonsense, give him a quick rap over the knuckles! I can't set up concerts in Vienna, and I've been promoting concerts here for fifteen years, if I can't guarantee the safety of my acts and performers. So now I must request your patience in order for us to clear this situation. We can't just forget what just happened, that's why we want the person who threw this to come up here onstage, or to be brought here by his neighbors. We want to meet him; we want to talk to him. And if he himself doesn't have the courage to come up here, because we can't continue with the concert until we talked to him, I hope his neighbors can get him up on to the stage. After that, the concert will continue. We'll have to talk to this man. I want him here because this idiot is messing up the show for everyone.

When the band does come back onstage to resume the show, they perform with energy and power, probably out of anger. Page wickedly plays a few bars of "Deutschland Uber Alles" before playing the intro to "Stairway To Heaven." The delay due to the firecracker incident resulted in "Achilles Last Stand" being dropped from the set due to time restrictions.

27 June 1980, Messhalle, Nuremburg, Germany (8:00 p.m.)

SETLIST: The Train Kept A Rollin' / Nobody's Fault But Mine / Out On The Tiles Intro / Black Dog

Jimmy Page steps to the microphone after "Nobody's Fault But Mine" to inform the crowd that two members of the band are not feeing well. After fifteen minutes, the show comes to an end after John Bonham collapses onstage. The official line was that he had supposedly eaten a ridiculous amount of bananas, which gave him severe stomach cramp.

29 June 1980, Hallenstadion, Zurich, Switzerland (7:00 p.m. Rescheduled from 1 June 1980.)

SETLIST: The Train Kept A Rollin' / Nobody's Fault But Mine / Out On The Tiles Intro / Black Dog / In The Evening / The Rain Song / Hot Dog / All My Love / Trampled Underfoot / Since I've Been Loving You / Achilles Last Stand / White Summer /

Black Mountain Side / Kashmir / Stairway To Heaven / Rock And Roll / Heartbreaker

Led Zeppelin fans rate this show highly. Certainly some inspired playing throughout the show, but there are several mistakes as well, notably at the end of "Kashmir," which causes Plant to remark, "If anybody's bootlegging that, you'll have to scratch that number 'cause it wasn't completely correct—somehow we got through it."

30 June 1980, Festhalle, Frankfurt, Germany (9:00 p.m.)

SETLIST: The Train Kept A Rollin' / Nobody's Fault But Mine / Out On The Tiles Intro / Black Dog / In The Evening / The Rain Song / Hot Dog / All My Love / Trampled Underfoot / Since I've Been Loving You / Achilles Last Stand / White Summer / Black Mountain Side / Kashmir / Stairway To Heaven / Rock And Roll / Money / Whole Lotta Love (including Boogie Chillun', Frankfurt Special)

Another fan favorite for the title of best show from the Europe 1980 tour. Clearly the band are in high spirits. Page has to ask for calm again as he plays "White Summer," as he did at most shows in Europe. The band's old friend, Phil Carson, is here tonight and joins the band for an inspired cover of Barrett Strong's "Money (That's What I Want)."

JULY 1980

1 July 1980, Festhalle, Frankfurt, Germany (Jimmy Page joins Santana for their encore, "Shake Your Moneymaker." A perfect soundboard recording of the show circulates among fans.)

2 July 1980, Eisstadion, Mannheim, Germany (7:30 p.m. Rescheduled from 31 May 1980.)

SETLIST: The Train Kept A Rollin' / Nobody's Fault But Mine / Out On The Tiles Intro / Black Dog / In The Evening / The Rain Song / Hot Dog / All My Love / Trampled Underfoot / Since I've Been Loving You / Achilles Last Stand / White Summer / Black Mountain Side / Kashmir / Stairway To Heaven / Rock And Roll / Whole Lotta Love

Led Zeppelin are almost on auto-pilot tonight, putting in a very average show. The band are not in a good place and it shows.

3 July 1980, Eisstadion, Mannheim, Germany (7:30 p.m.)

SETLIST: The Train Kept A Rollin' / Nobody's Fault But Mine / Out On The Tiles Intro / Black Dog / In The Evening / The Rain

Song / Hot Dog / All My Love / Trampled Underfoot / Since I've Been Loving You / Achilles Last Stand / White Summer / Black Mountain Side / Kashmir / Stairway To Heaven / Communication Breakdown / Rock And Roll

Only marginally better than the night before. The band are clearly wanting the tour to end and return home. "White Summer" meanders on too long and the solo in "Stairway To Heaven" is all over the place.

5 July 1980, Olympiahalle, Munich, Germany (9:00 p.m. Rescheduled from 23 May 1980.)

SETLIST: The Train Kept A Rollin' / Nobody's Fault But Mine / Out On The Tiles Intro / Black Dog / In The Evening / The Rain Song / Hot Dog / All My Love / Trampled Underfoot / Since I've Been Loving You / Achilles Last Stand / White Summer / Black Mountain Side / Kashmir / Stairway To Heaven / Rock And Roll / Whole Lotta Love (including Boogie Chillun')

Reasonable performance, but the best part of the show was the encore. As the lights dimmed, members of the road crew could be seen wheeling a second drum kit on to the stage. It was for Bad Company's Simon Kirke, who joined the band for an enthusiastic, high-energy version of "Whole Lotta Love."

7 July 1980, Eissporthalle, Berlin, Germany (8:00 p.m. Rescheduled from 29 May 1980.)

SETLIST: The Train Kept A Rollin' / Nobody's Fault But Mine / Out On The Tiles Intro / Black Dog / In The Evening / The Rain Song / Hot Dog / All My Love / Trampled Underfoot / Since I've Been Loving You / White Summer / Black Mountain Side / Kashmir / Stairway To Heaven / Rock And Roll / Whole Lotta Love

Not only was this the last show of the tour, it turned out to be the last ever Led Zeppelin concert with John Bonham. The playing at this show pretty much followed in the same vein as the others with moments of greatness peppered with mistakes and boredom. The highlight is a longer than usual "Trampled Underfoot." In fact, many numbers were longer at this show compared to the previous nights, which would explain why "Achilles Last Stand" was dropped. "Stairway To Heaven" was stretched out to fourteen minutes, the longest version of the tour, with a lengthy meandering Jimmy Page solo. "Whole Lotta Love," their last number, was turned into a marathon jam that lasted over seventeen minutes. Maybe this was the way forward again with the band extending certain

numbers as they had done in the past and finding a good groove. America soon beckoned, but we never had the chance to find out the direction they would take as fate intervened.

SEPTEMBER–OCTOBER 1980

After a summer break, Robert Plant finally agreed to go on a tour in the US, providing it was no more than thirty days in duration. It was a surprising decision on his part as privately he was seriously considering a solo career, but did not have the nerve to actually break away yet. Peter Grant announced via a press release on the 11th September 1980 that Led Zeppelin would perform a series of concerts in North America, their first since the 1977 tour. It was called "The 1980s Part One" and would largely take place on the East Coast, and Part Two would concentrate on West Coast dates to be announced at a later time. Peter Grant assumed that Plant would have mellowed in his views after being on the road and sanction the second leg. As much as Plant loved Led Zeppelin, he no longer felt obliged to do anything he did not like.

By mid-September Jimmy Page had approved the new stage design and lighting for the forthcoming US tour. Bray Studios were booked for later that month and rehearsals began. It was interesting to note that "Carouselambra" was on the proposed setlist for America. This would have been the first time this song from *In Through the Out Door* would have been played in public.

On 24 September John Bonham left his Worcestershire home accompanied by his friend and assistant, Rex King. They were en route to Bray for rehearsals, but stopped off for breakfast at a pub where he downed four quadruple measures of vodka. He continued the binge drinking at Bray and the unproductive rehearsal ended in the early evening. The band and various assistants then headed off to Jimmy Page's home, the Old Mill House in Clewer, Windsor. Bonham continued drinking until finally falling asleep around midnight. All in all, he had consumed forty measures of vodka that day. These were not the actions of a happy man. He had been pretty apprehensive about the thought of heading off to America, being away from home and family once again, and the booze helped him with his anxieties and depression.

Jimmy Page's aide checked in on Bonham at around 8:00 a.m. on the morning of 25 September. He was still sleeping normally and it was decided to let him sleep off the previous day's alcohol abuse. When Benji Le Fevre, soundman for the group, along with John Paul Jones, went to awake Bonham at 1:45 p.m., they found he did not stir after repeated banging on his door. Upon entering the room, they went over to the bed and checked his pulse and realized he was dead. John Paul Jones had the unenviable job of telling Jimmy Page and Robert Plant the news. He had died of asphyxiation after vomiting in his sleep. What a tragic, senseless loss. He was only thirty-two years old. From that moment on Led Zeppelin ceased to exist. It is to their credit and integrity that they made the following statement and actually stuck to it:

On 4 December Led Zeppelin issued a statement:

We wish it to be known that the loss of our dear friend and the deep respect we have for his family, together with the sense of undivided harmony felt by ourselves and our manager, have led us to decide that we could not continue as we were.

LED ZEPPELIN THE 1980S PART 1 US TOUR

17 OCTOBER 1980–15 NOVEMBER 1980

17 October 1980, Montreal Forum, Montreal, Canada (The show was canceled due to the death of drummer John Bonham.)

19 October 1980, Capitol Centre, Landover, Maryland (The show was canceled due to the death of drummer John Bonham.)

21 October 1980, Capitol Centre Landover, Maryland (The show was canceled due to the death of drummer John Bonham.)

22 October 1980, Spectrum, Philadelphia, Pennsylvania (The show was canceled due to the death of drummer John Bonham.)

23 October 1980, Capitol Centre, Landover, Maryland (The show was canceled due to the death of drummer John Bonham.)

26 October 1980, Richfield Coliseum, Cleveland, Ohio (The show was canceled due to the death of drummer John Bonham.)

27 October 1980, Richfield Coliseum, Cleveland, Ohio (The show was canceled due to the death of drummer John Bonham.)

29 October 1980, Joe Louis Stadium, Detroit, Michigan (The show was canceled due to the death of drummer John Bonham.)

30 October 1980, Joe Louis Stadium, Detroit, Michigan (The show was canceled due to the death of drummer John Bonham.)

NOVEMBER 1980

1 November 1980, War Memorial Auditorium, Buffalo, New York (The show was canceled due to the death of drummer John Bonham.)

3 November 1980, Spectrum, Philadelphia, Pennsylvania (The show was canceled due to the death of drummer John Bonham.)

4 November 1980, Spectrum, Philadelphia, Pennsylvania (The show was canceled due to the death of drummer John Bonham.)

6 November 1980, Civic Arena, Pittsburgh, Pennsylvania (The show was canceled due to the death of drummer John Bonham.)

7 November 1980, Civic Arena, Pittsburgh, Pennsylvania (The show was canceled due to the death of drummer John Bonham.)

9 November 1980, Civic Centre, St. Paul, Minnesota (The show was canceled due to the death of drummer John Bonham.)

10 November 1980, Chicago Stadium, Chicago, Illinois (The show was canceled due to the death of drummer John Bonham.)

12 November 1980, Chicago Stadium, Chicago, Illinois (The show was canceled due to the death of drummer John Bonham.)

13 November 1980, Chicago Stadium, Chicago, Illinois (The show was canceled due to the death of drummer John Bonham.)

15 November 1980, Chicago Stadium, Chicago, Illinois (The show was canceled due to the death of drummer John Bonham.)

WHAT HAPPENED NEXT

There was a sense of disbelief in the Led Zeppelin camp. They had lost their drummer and friend and it had signaled the end of the band. Nobody knew what to do with themselves. The lives they had led for the last twelve years suddenly stopped. Crucially, they also realized that together, Led Zeppelin was always greater than the sum of its parts. Without Bonham, there was no Led Zeppelin.

After John Bonham's death, Jimmy Page was a broken man and continued his descent into drug addiction. When he stumbled onstage to join his old mate Jeff Beck at London's Hammersmith Odeon on 10 March 1981 for an encore of "Going Down," everybody was shocked to see the state he was in. Backstage it was obvious he could not even stand up un-aided and had to be helped to a waiting car before being driven off by a family member. Several well-known friends came to his aide and attempted to get him clean. It would be a long and painful process. Recording-wise, he was offered the soundtrack to Michael Winner's *Death Wish* film, which he recorded in the summer of 1981. It was not particularly revelatory in sonic terms, but at least it got him working again, albeit slowly. There were a few public appearances in 1983, one with Eric Clapton at a show in Guildford, along with the ARMS shows at the Royal Albert Hall and in America the same year. He still looked in a bad way, and his playing was tentative. It would take awhile longer before he was in better shape and able to work properly. But the ARMS shows did give him the confidence boost he needed when he realized how much people wanted to see and hear him play.

In 1984 he played a few shows with Roy Harper as well as recording an album with him. This was really a stepping-stone to him forming a new band with Paul Rogers called the Firm. On paper it looked as though this combination should have been amazing. In reality it was an experiment that did not work particularly well, and certainly did not enamor the fans of Led Zeppelin, who wanted a return to heavy riffs. But it was good to see Page in much better health. He would pursue a solo career in 1988, touring in the UK and America promoting his first solo album, *Outrider*. The highlight for many was the instrumental version of "Stairway To Heaven" that usually ended the shows. During this time he had made various approaches to Robert Plant about working together again, but Plant was not ready and would naturally want a major input in any possible collaboration. But by 1991, frustrated that Robert Plant was still pursuing a solo path and showing no interest in getting back with him for a collaboration, Page made an ill-judged alliance with David Coverdale, which later resulted in a dodgy album and even dodgier tour in Japan. What was he thinking?

Finally, in 1994 the music world paid attention when it was announced that Jimmy Page and Robert Plant would be making music together again. It started with an MTV show based on their successful "Unplugged" brand, except that for Page and Plant it would be re-titled "Unledded." Two shows were filmed and recorded in London on 25 and 26 August 1994, which were edited for later broadcast and release on CD and DVD. This was no nostalgia trip. What they categorically did not want was this pairing to be called Led Zeppelin and did not invite their old bandmate John Paul Jones for that reason. It was a decidedly concerted effort to produce new material as well as dramatically changing arrangements of Led Zeppelin classics backed by a Middle Eastern orchestra. The only stipulation Plant made ahead of them getting together was that "Stairway To Heaven" would not be played. Page and Plant traveled the world on a PR campaign for the CD and video release, appearing on numerous television shows and giving countless press interviews. This was followed by a hugely successful year-long tour by the pair taking in the USA, Canada, Europe, UK, Ireland, South America, Japan, and Australia. After a new studio album and another huge tour in 1998, Plant informed Page he would not be playing any more shows with him. He explained that he'd had enough, and after a few months break formed a low-key band with some mates who would call themselves the Priory of Brion. They largely played '60s West Coast covers by the likes of Love and Moby Grape. Plant was having fun again, and would be away from any annoying ego clashes. He continued on his solo path with varying degrees of commercial success, but one suspects that it is the positive critical success achieved that is what he appreciates far more.

As for Jimmy Page, well, he was often seen at Black Crowes shows and liked their music. It made sense that he would inevitably collaborate with them. Although they did not record a studio album together, they went out on two tours in 1999 and 2000. Page injured his back during the tour in 2000, and it had to be curtailed as a result. A hugely successful live double album recorded at their two 1999 Los Angeles shows was released. In between the odd public appearance, he has concentrated in keeping the legacy of Led Zeppelin in good shape and has done an admirable job. But since 2000 he has also told various reporters that he is working on some exciting new material and will be going out on the road with a new band. Sixteen

Jimmy Page back in the public eye, playing at Royal Albert Hall in London on 20 September 1983. (Rex)

years on and we are all still waiting on hearing and seeing this new material and new band.

John Paul Jones, always the most versatile musician in Led Zeppelin, has also pursued a solo career, which has been far more eclectic than that of his two ex-colleagues. He worked on soundtracks initially and later made several guest sessions, both in the studio and in concert. He was part of the critically acclaimed supergroup called Them Crooked Vultures, along with Dave Grohl from the Foo Fighters and Josh Homme from the Queens of the Stone Age. He has also produced several albums by the likes of the Datsuns, the Mission, and Uncle Earl.

LED ZEPPELIN

The surviving members of the band have only reunited using the Led Zeppelin name publicly for a handful of occasions for charity, and one for an award ceremony.

LIVE AID

JULY 1985

The surviving members of Led Zeppelin came together for one of the biggest worldwide charity events ever hosted, Live Aid. Robert Plant, Jimmy Page, and John Paul Jones played a three-song set of iconic numbers from Led Zeppelin's back catalogue backed by Phil Collins and Tony Thompson (ex-Chic drummer) on drums. Paul Martinez, from Plant's touring band, joined in on bass for "Stairway To Heaven." Despite little rehearsal time and major sound problems, the 90,000 odd present at the venue and just about every living room around the world welcomed three-quarters of Led Zeppelin back onstage. But musically speaking, it was pretty atrocious.

13 July 1985, Live Aid, JFK Stadium, Philadelphia, Pennsylvania

SETLIST: Rock And Roll / Whole Lotta Love / Stairway To Heaven

The actual performance was not without problems. As well as being under-rehearsed, Robert Plant's voice was hoarse and Jimmy Page had monitor problems, which made it difficult for him to hear what was going on. On top of that, Phil Collins and Tony Thompson were out of sync, and overall the performance was erratic and uneven. Before starting their third and last number, Plant shouts out, "Any requests?" which was quickly followed by "Stairway To Heaven," to the delight of everyone in attendance. Because of the issues with the performance, the members of Led Zeppelin refused permission for the footage to be used in the *Live Aid* DVD box set.

ATLANTIC RECORDS 40th ANNIVERSARY

MAY 1988

Atlantic Records celebrate their 40th Anniversary in style with some of their major acts over the last forty years playing short sets of their greatest hits on Atlantic. They were introduced by Ahmet Ertegun, who signed many of them to the label. Led Zeppelin were represented by Robert Plant, Jimmy Page, John Paul Jones, and Jason Bonham. Other artists appearing were Average White Band, Bee Gees, Ruth Brown, Peabo Bryson, the Coasters, Phil Collins, Steve Cropper and Donald Duckdan, Crosby, Stills and Nash, Emerson, Lake and Palmer, Roberta Flack, Foreigner, Bob Geldof, Genesis, Debbie Gibson, Mickie Howard, Iron Butterfly, Ben E. King, LaVern Baker, Manhattan Transfer, Sam Moore and Elwood Blues, Wilson Pickett, the Rascals, Paul Rodgers, Paul Schaeffer, the Spinners, Carla Thomas, Rufus Thomas, 3, Robert Plant, and Yes.

13 May 1988, Madison Square Garden, New York City, New York (Led Zeppelin soundcheck in preparation for their spot on the Atlantic Records 40th Anniversary concert on 14 May 1988.)

14 MAY 1988 Madison Square Garden, New York City, New York (Atlantic Records 40th Anniversary)

SETLIST: Kashmir / Heartbreaker / Whole Lotta Love / Misty Mountain Hop / Stairway To Heaven

The curse of television continued at this show for Led Zeppelin. It should have been a wonderful performance, but Jason Bonham's kit was not properly mixed, as there was no real power coming from the drums. Zeppelin was always about that huge drum sound pushing the songs to greatness. It just was not happening tonight. "Kashmir" in particular suffered, and that was the opening number. Robert Plant also messed up some of the lyrics. "Heartbreaker" was disappointing with some uninspired playing by Page during his solo. "Stairway To Heaven" was also average with more messed-up lyrics and Page's solo was short. This sort of environment was clearly not one that worked for Led Zeppelin. If Peter Grant had still been managing them, none of these embarrassing television appearances would have happened. And if they did, he would have made sure that the band and all the technical aspects of the broadcast were in perfect shape to avoid any problems. As such, both their Live Aid and Atlantic Records appearances were shambolic and did nothing to enhance their reputation.

1995 10th ANNUAL ROCK AND ROLL HALL OF FAME AWARDS

JANUARY 1995

12 January 1995, Waldorf Astoria Hotel, New York City, New York (10th Rock and Roll Hall of Fame Awards)

The three surviving members of Led Zeppelin reunited for the annual Rock and Roll Hall of Fame induction ceremony. It would be the last to be held at the Waldorf-Astoria hotel after ten years. Future events would be held at the new Hall of Fame's permanent museum, which opened on 1 September 1995, in Cleveland. Steven Tyler and Joe Perry of Aerosmith inducted Led Zeppelin. John Bonham's children, Zoe and Jason, were there to receive the award on behalf of their father. Joe Perry said this about Bonham, "Even today, nobody can take his place."

The inductions and speeches finished at around midnight. The music then started, with Led Zeppelin and Steven Tyler and Joe Perry from Aerosmith playing a short, high-octane set of standards and Led

Zeppelin numbers. There was a second jam without Perry and Tyler that included Michael Lee on drums and Neil Young on guitar, playing their rendition of "When the Levee Breaks." Robert Plant briefly strapped on Jimmy Page's cherry red Gibson Les Paul Standard for his three chords of wisdom.

Jimmy Page and Robert Plant, who had got together in 1994 for a hugely successful MTV "Unledded" show, were now preparing to launch their first tour together since playing in Led Zeppelin. There had been the occasional jam, but never a full-blown tour with a group. Unfortunately John Paul Jones had not been told about it, nor invited to participate, and naturally was upset. During his short speech he turned to Page and Plant and said, "I would also like to say thank you to my friends for finally remembering my phone number!" Ouch! Plant and Page looked uncomfortable. Nevertheless they managed to put aside the obvious tensions and played an epic set. For the induction, Joe Perry summed it up best: "Everything you ever heard about Led Zeppelin was true. . . . No way was it for the faint of heart. Led Zeppelin was the real deal."

SETLIST: The Train Kept A Rollin' / For Your Love / Bring It On Home / Blues Jam (including Prison Blues, Gamblers Blues, Baby Please Don't Go) / When The Levee Breaks (including a snippet of For What It's Worth)

At last Led Zeppelin nail their televison appearance after the two previous shaky sets in 1985 and 1988 and play an amazing off-the-scale set. The real surprise is the quickie performance of the classic Yardbirds hit "For Your Love."

2007 AHMET ERTEGUN TRIBUTE SHOW

DECEMBER 2007

12 December 2007, O2 Arena, London (Led Zeppelin took to the stage at 9:00 p.m.)

Robert Plant, Jimmy Page, and John Paul Jones, along with Jason Bonham, reunite as Led Zeppelin as a tribute to the man who signed them to Atlantic Records in 1968, and had recently passed away. Originally the plan was for a concert to take place at the Royal Albert Hall with British acts who had been with the Atlantic family. Cream was going to do a set,

Poster advertising Led Zeppelin's appearance at the Rock and Roll Hall of Fame awards show at the Waldorf Astoria hotel in New York on 12 January 1995.

Program cover for Led Zeppelin's appearance at the Ahmet Ertegun tribute concert at London's O2 Arena on 10 December 2007.

The surviving members of Led Zeppelin attend the 35th Annual Kennedy Center Honors on 2 December 2012. (Rex)

as was Led Zeppelin, along with other acts. Eventually it was decided to make this a bigger event with Led Zeppelin headlining in their own right at the huge O2 Arena in London. The original date for the show was 26 November 2007, but it had to be rescheduled because Jimmy Page had fractured his ring finger on his left hand while gardening. Support acts for the show were a mixture of old and new Atlantic acts, Bill Wyman and Rhythm Kings with Keith Emerson and Albert Lee, Maggie Bell, Paolo Nutini, Paul Rodgers, and Foreigner. The event was introduced by well-known UK promoter Harvey Goldsmith, who had organized the show. The entire event was professionally recorded and filmed.

SETLIST: Good Times Bad Times / Ramble On / Black Dog / In My Time Of Dying / For Your Life / Trampled Underfoot / Nobody's Fault But Mine / No Quarter / Since I've Been Loving You / Dazed And Confused / Stairway To Heaven / The Song Remains The Same / Misty Mountain Hop / Kashmir / Whole Lotta Love / Rock And Roll

At long last, the surviving members of Led Zeppelin play a full set in front of a large crowd. Other than some minor irritating feedback in the opening song, the evening is pretty flawless with everyone in great shape. Far more enjoyable than anything post-1977, the set was just the right combination of crowd-pleasers, and even a rarity in the form of a complete live version of "For Your Life" from the *Presence* album.

An evening of nostalgia for some, but largely an opportunity for many people to witness the mighty Led Zeppelin experience for the first time. The band had worked very hard to make this a perfect evening with extensive rehearsals at Shepperton Studios, and it paid off. This would clearly have been the ideal opportunity to do a series of swan-song shows at the venue, as everything was in place and the band finely tuned. Hundreds of thousands of people had applied for just 20,000 tickets, so they could easily have sold out the venue for several months had they chose to, just as Michael Jackson had planned. Plant had commitments with Alison Krauss and it was not to be, much to the frustration of Jimmy Page, who had felt that Plant may have been persuaded to continue after this successful performance at the O2. Realistic fans have now pretty much resigned themselves to the fact they will not see the band again.

A lot of fingers are constantly pointed in Plant's direction when it comes to the blame game as to why the band will not play together again. He has no real wish or desire to go back there. To confuse fans even more, Plant plays numerous Led Zeppelin hits during his own solo shows, albeit in a dramatically rearranged style. Fans have difficulty in appreciating that Plant loves the music that Led Zeppelin produced in its lifetime, so why should he not be allowed to play it during his solo concerts? It would be absurd to assume that he does not have any right to play those songs unless it were under the banner of Led Zeppelin. In 2014 a clearly irate Page started to tell the press about his frustrations with Plant's apparent intransigence about playing together again. It backfired somewhat when an equally irate and exasperated Plant quickly issued a rebuttal saying that he in fact told Page he been amenable to a collaboration with him, provided the material was more acoustic based. Page simply walked away.

Led Zeppelin Discography

Front cover of Led Zeppelin's debut album.

Front cover of Led Zeppelin's second album.

Led Zeppelin

Released 12 January 1969, US Atlantic SD 8216 / released 28 March 1969, UK Atlantic 588 171

SIDE 1
1. Good Times, Bad Times (2:46)
2. Babe, I'm Gonna Leave You (6:41)
3. You Shook Me (6:28)
4. Dazed And Confused (6:26)

SIDE 2
1. Your Time Is Gonna Come (4:34)
2. Black Mountain Side (2:05)
3. Communication Breakdown (2:27)
4. I Can't Quit You Baby (4:42)
5. How Many More Times (8:28)

LINEUP:
JIMMY PAGE: ACOUSTIC, ELECTRIC, AND PEDAL-STEEL GUITAR, BACKING VOCALS
ROBERT PLANT: VOCALS, HARMONICA
JOHN PAUL JONES: BASS GUITAR, ORGAN, KEYBOARDS, BACKING VOCALS
JOHN BONHAM: DRUMS, TYMPANI, BACKING VOCALS
ADDITIONAL MUSICIAN:
VIRAM JASANI: TABLA DRUMS (ON BLACK MOUNTAIN SIDE)
PRODUCER: JIMMY PAGE

Led Zeppelin II

Released 22 October 1969, US Atlantic SD 8236 / released 31 October 1969, UK Atlantic 588 198

SIDE 1
1. Whole Lotta Love (5:34)
2. What Is And What Should Never Be (4:46)
3. The Lemon Song (6:18)
4. Thank You (4:47)

SIDE 2
1. Heartbreaker (4:14)
2. Living Loving Maid (She's Just A Woman) (2:38)
3. Ramble On (4:24)
4. Moby Dick (4:21)
5. Bring It On Home (4:21)

LINEUP:
JIMMY PAGE: ACOUSTIC, ELECTRIC, AND PEDAL-STEEL GUITAR, BACKING VOCALS
ROBERT PLANT: VOCALS, HARMONICA
JOHN PAUL JONES: BASS GUITAR, ORGAN, BACKING VOCALS
JOHN BONHAM: DRUMS, BACKING VOCALS
PRODUCER: JIMMY PAGE
RECORDING ENGINEERS: EDDIE KRAMER, GEORGE CHKIANTZ, ANDREW JOHNS, CHRIS HUSTON

Front cover of Led Zeppelin's third album.

Original artwork of wheel found on the inside of *Led Zeppelin III*'s front album sleeve.

Led Zeppelin III

Released 5 October 1970, US Atlantic SD 7201 / released 23 October 1970, UK Atlantic 2401 002

SIDE 1

1. Immigrant Song (2:25)
2. Friends (3:54)
3. Celebration Day (3:29)
4. Since I've Been Loving You (7:23)
5. Out On The Tiles (4:07)

SIDE 2

1. Gallows Pole (4:56)
2. Tangerine (3:10)
3. That's The Way (5:37)
4. Bron-Y-Aur Stomp (4:16)
5. Hats Off To (Roy) Harper (3:42)

> LINEUP:
> JIMMY PAGE: ACOUSTIC GUITAR, ELECTRIC GUITAR, PEDAL-STEEL
> GUITAR, BACKING VOCALS
> ROBERT PLANT: VOCALS, HARMONICA
> JOHN PAUL JONES: BASS, ORGAN, SYNTHS, MANDOLIN,
> BACKING VOCALS
> JOHN BONHAM: DRUMS, PERCUSSION, BACKING VOCALS,
> BANJO

Led Zeppelin IV (Untitled)

Released 8 November 1971, US Atlantic SD 7208 / released 12 November 1971, UK Atlantic 2401 012

SIDE 1

1. Black Dog (4:56)
2. Rock And Roll (3:41)
3. The Battle Of Evermore (5:52)
4. Stairway To Heaven (8:02)

SIDE 2

1. Misty Mountain Hop (4:39)
2. Four Sticks (4:45)
3. Going To California (3:32)
4. When The Levee Breaks (7:08)

> LINEUP:
> JIMMY PAGE: ACOUSTIC AND ELECTRIC GUITARS, MANDOLIN,
> VOCALS
> ROBERT PLANT: LEAD VOCALS, HARMONICA
> JOHN PAUL JONES: SYNTHESIZERS, BASS GUITAR, KEYBOARDS,
> MANDOLIN, RECORDERS
> JOHN BONHAM: DRUMS
> ADDITIONAL MUSICIAN:
> SANDY DENNY: VOCALS (ON THE BATTLE OF EVERMORE)
> PRODUCER: JIMMY PAGE
> ENGINEER: ANDY JOHNS

Front cover of Led Zeppelin's fourth album.

Front cover of Led Zeppelin's *Houses of the Holy* album.

Houses of the Holy

Released 18 March 1973, US Atlantic SD 7255 / released 26 March 1973, UK Atlantic 2401 012

SIDE 1
1. The Song Remains The Same (5:29)
2. The Rain Song (7:39)
3. Over The Hills And Far Away (4:49)
4. The Crunge (3:17)

SIDE 2
1. Dancing Days (3:43)
2. D'yer Ma'ker (4:22)
3. No Quarter (7:00)
4. The Ocean (4:30)

LINEUP:
JIMMY PAGE: ALL GUITARS
ROBERT PLANT: VOCALS
JOHN PAUL JONES: BASS, GRAND PIANO, ORGAN, MELLOTRON,
  SYNTHESIZERS
JOHN BONHAM: DRUMS, PERCUSSION
PRODUCER: JIMMY PAGE

Physical Graffiti (Double Album)

Released 24 February 1975, US Swan Song SS-2-200 / released 24 February 1975, UK Swan Song SSK 89400

SIDE 1
1. Custard Pie (4:13)
2. The Rover (5:36)
3. In My Time Of Dying (11:04)

SIDE 2
1. Houses Of The Holy (4:01)
2. Trampled Under Foot (5:35)
3. Kashmir (8:31)

SIDE 3
1. In The Light (8:44)
2. Bron-Yr-Aur (2:06)

3. Down By The Seaside (5:14)
4. Ten Years Gone (6:31)

SIDE 4
1. Night Flight (3:36)
2. The Wanton Song (4:06)
3. Boogie With Stu (3:51)
4. Black Country Woman (4:24)
5. Sick Again (4:43)

LINEUP:
JIMMY PAGE: ACOUSTIC GUITARS, ELECTRIC GUITARS, MANDOLIN
ROBERT PLANT: HARMONICA, VOCALS
JOHN PAUL JONES: BASS, KEYBOARDS, MELLOTRON, GUITAR,
  MANDOLIN
JOHN BONHAM: DRUMS, PERCUSSION
ADDITIONAL MUSICIAN:
IAN STEWART: PIANO (SIDE 4, TRACK 3)
PRODUCER: JIMMY PAGE

Presence

Released 31 March 1976, US Swan Song SS-8416 / released 5 April 1976, UK Swan Song SSK 59402

SIDE 1
1. Achilles Last Stand (10:25)
2. For Your Life (6:20)
3. Royal Orleans (2:58)

SIDE 2
1. Nobody's Fault But Mine (5:27)
2. Candy Store Rock (4:07)
3. Hots On For Nowhere (4:43)
4. Tea For One (9:27)

LINEUP:
JIMMY PAGE: ELECTRIC GUITARS
ROBERT PLANT: VOCALS, HARMONICA
JOHN PAUL JONES: 4-, 5-, AND 8-STRING BASS GUITARS
JOHN BONHAM: DRUMS, PERCUSSION
PRODUCER: JIMMY PAGE

Front cover of Led Zeppelin's *Physical Graffiti* cover.

Front cover of Led Zeppelin's *Presence* cover.

Front cover of Led Zeppelin's *The Song Remains the Same* cover.

The Song Remains the Same (Double Album)

Released 22 October 1976, US Swan Song SS-2-201 / released 22 October 1976, UK Swan Song SSK 89402

SIDE 1
1. Rock And Roll (4:03)
2. Celebration Day (3:49)
3. The Song Remains The Same (6:00)
4. The Rain Song (8:25)

SIDE 2
1. Dazed And Confused (26:53)
Side 3
1. No Quarter (12:30)
2. Stairway To Heaven (10:58)
Side 4
1. Moby Dick (12:47)
2. Whole Lotta Love (14:25)

   PRODUCER: JIMMY PAGE

The Song Remains the Same (Double Expanded Remastered CD)

Released 20 November 2007, US Swan Song R2 328252 / released 19 November 2007, UK Swan Song 8122-79961-1
Tracks on 2007 Remaster:

CD 1 (60:30):
1. Rock And Roll (3:56)
2. Celebration Day (3:37)
3.* Black Dog (3:46)
4.* Over The Hills And Far Away (6:11)
5.* Misty Mountain Hop (4:43)
6.* Since I've Been Loving You (8:23)
7. No Quarter (10:38)
8. The Song Remains The Same (5:39)
9. The Rain Song (8:20)

10.* The Ocean (5.13)

CD 2 (71:25):
1. Dazed And Confused (29:18)
2. Stairway To Heaven (10:52)
3. Moby Dick (11:02)
4.* Heartbreaker (6:19)
5. Whole Lotta Love (13:51)
Total Time 131:55   *previously unreleased
(2007, remastered, with 6 previously unreleased tracks)
   JIMMY PAGE: ELECTRIC AND ACOUSTIC GUITARS, THEREMIN
   ROBERT PLANT: VOCALS
   JOHN PAUL JONES: BASS GUITAR, KEYBOARDS, MELLOTRON
   JOHN BONHAM: DRUMS, PERCUSSION
   RECORDED LIVE BETWEEN JULY 27, JULY 28 AND JULY 29, 1973
    AT MADISON SQUARE GARDEN, NEW YORK
   PRODUCER: JIMMY PAGE

In Through the Out Door (Released in Six Different Sleeves)

Released 15 August 1979, US Swan Song SS-16002 / released 20 August 1979, UK Swan Song SSK 59410

SIDE 1
1. In The Evening (6:49)
2. South Bound Saurez (4:12)
3. Fool In The Rain (6:12)
4. Hot Dog (3:17)

SIDE 2
1. Carouselambra (10:31)
2. All My Love (5:53)
3. I'm Gonna Crawl (5:30)

   LINEUP:
   JIMMY PAGE: ACOUSTIC GUITAR, ELECTRIC GUITAR
   ROBERT PLANT: VOCALS
   JOHN PAUL JONES: BASS GUITAR, KEYBOARDS
   JOHN BONHAM: DRUMS
   PRODUCER: JIMMY PAGE

Outer sleeve that housed the *In Through the Out Door* album.

Front cover for jacket A of Led Zeppelin's *In Through the Out Door*.

Back cover for jacket A of Led Zeppelin's *In Through the Out Door*.

Front cover for jacket B of Led Zeppelin's *In Through the Out Door*.

Back cover for jacket B of Led Zeppelin's *In Through the Out Door*.

Front cover for jacket C of Led Zeppelin's *In Through the Out Door*.

Back cover for jacket C of Led Zeppelin's *In Through the Out Door*.

Front cover for jacket D of Led Zeppelin's *In Through the Out Door*.

Back cover for jacket D of Led Zeppelin's *In Through the Out Door*.

Front cover for jacket E of Led Zeppelin's *In Through the Out Door*.

Back cover for jacket E of Led Zeppelin's *In Through the Out Door*.

Front cover for jacket F of Led Zeppelin's *In Through the Out Door*.

Back cover for jacket F of Led Zeppelin's *In Through the Out Door*.

Coda

Released 19 November 1982, US Swan Song 90051-1 / released 22 November 1982, UK Swan Song A 0051

SIDE 1
1. We're Gonna Groove (2:40)
2. Poor Tom (3:01)
3. I Can't Quit You Baby (4:17)
4. Walter's Walk (4:31)

SIDE 2
1. Ozone Baby (3:35)
2. Darlene (5:06)

Front cover of Led Zeppelin's *Coda* album.

3. Bonzo's Montreux (4:17)
4. Wearing and Tearing (5:31)

CD Bonus Tracks available on the version of *Coda* found in the *Complete Led Zeppelin Studio Recordings* box set:
1. Baby Come on Home (4:30)
2. Travelling Riverside Blues (5:11)
3. White Summer/Black Mountain Side (8:01)
4. Hey Hey What Can I Do (3:55)

> JOHN BONHAM: DRUMS
> JOHN PAUL JONES: BASS, PIANO, KEYBOARDS
> JIMMY PAGE: ACOUSTIC GUITAR, ELECTRIC GUITAR
> ROBERT PLANT: VOCALS, HARMONICA
> RECORDED: JANUARY 9, 1970–NOVEMBER 21, 1978
> PRODUCER: JIMMY PAGE

BBC Sessions

Released 18 November 1997, US Atlantic 7567-83061-2 / released 17 November 1997, UK Atlantic 7567-83061-2

CD 1:
1. You Shook Me (5:14)
2. I Can't Quit You Baby (4:22)
3. Communication Breakdown (3:12)
4. Dazed and Confused (6:39)
5. The Girl I Love She Got Long Black Wavy Hair (3:00)
6. What Is and What Should Never Be (4:20)

7. Communication Breakdown (2:40)
8. Travelling Riverside Blues (5:12)
9. Whole Lotta Love (6:09)
10. Somethin' Else (2:06)
11. Communication Breakdown (3:05)
12. Can't Quit You Baby (6:21)
13. You Shook Me (Live) (10:19)
14. How Many More Times (11:51)
Tracks 1, 2, and 4 recorded 3 March 1969.
Tracks 3, 5, and 10 recorded 16 June 1969.
Tracks 6–9 recorded 24 June 1969.
Tracks 11–14 recorded 27 June 1969.

CD 2:

1. Immigrant Song (3:20)
2. Heartbreaker (5:16)
3. Since I've Been Loving You (6:56)
4. Black Dog (5:17)
5. Dazed And Confused (18:36)
6. Stairway To Heaven (Live) (8:49)
7. Going To California (Live) (3:54)
8. That's The Way (5:43)
9. Whole Lotta Love (13:45)
10. Thank You (6:37)
Tracks 1–10 recorded April 1, 1971, at the Paris Theatre, London

PRODUCER: JIMMY PAGE

How the West Was Won

Released 27 May 2003, US/UK Atlantic 7567-83587-2

CD 1 :

1. LA Drone (0:14)
2. Immigrant Song (3:42)
3. Heartbreaker (7:25)
4. Black Dog (5:41)
5. Over The Hills And Far Away (5:08)
6. Since I've Been Loving You (8:02)
7. Stairway To Heaven (9:38)
8. Going To California (5:37)
9. That's The Way (5:54)
10. Bron-Yr-Aur Stomp (4:55)

CD 2:

1. Dazed And Confused (25:25)
2. What Is And What Should Never Be (4:41)
3. Dancing Days (3:42)
4. Moby Dick (19:20)

CD 3:

1. Whole Lotta Love (Medley) (23:08)
2. Rock And Roll (3:56)
3. The Ocean (4:21)
4. Bring It On Home (9:30)

JIMMY PAGE: ACOUSTIC AND ELECTRIC GUITARS
ROBERT PLANT: VOCALS AND HARMONICA
JOHN PAUL JONES: BASS GUITAR, KEYBOARDS, AND MANDOLIN
JOHN BONHAM: DRUMS AND PERCUSSION
RECORDED LIVE AT THE LA FORUM 25 JUNE 1972 AND LONG
  BEACH ARENA 27 JUNE 1972.
PRODUCER: JIMMY PAGE

Celebration Day

Released 19 November 2012
2CD Atlantic/Swan Song (2012)
3LP Atlantic/Swan Song (2012, 180-gram vinyl)
Blu-ray audio Atlantic/Swan Song (2012, 48 K 24-bit PCM
Stereo and DTS-HD Master Audio 5.1)
2CD + DVD Atlantic/Swan Song (2012, CD-size digipack)
2CD + DVD Atlantic/Swan Song (2012, DVD size digipack)
2CD + Blu-ray + DVD Atlantic/Swan Song
(2012, CD-size digipack)
2CD + 2DVD Atlantic/Swan Song (2012, CD-size digipack)

CD 1:

1. Good Times Bad Times (3:10)
2. Ramble On (5:44)
3. Black Dog (5:53)
4. In My Time of Dying (11:08)
5. For Your Life (6:42)
6. Trampled Under Foot (6:19)
7. Nobody's Fault But Mine (6:43)
8. No Quarter (9:19)
9. Since I've Been Loving You (7:51)
Total time 62:49

CD 2:

1. Dazed And Confused (11:43)
2. Stairway To Heaven (8:49)
3. The Song Remains The Same (5:46)
4. Misty Mountain Hop (5:08)
5. Kashmir (9:06)
6. Whole Lotta Love (7:26)
7. Rock And Roll (4:33)
Total time 52:31
DVD/Blu-ray—full-show video: 1. Good Times Bad Times
2. Ramble On 3. Black Dog 4. In My Time Of Dying
5. For Your Life 6. Trampled Under Foot 7. Nobody's Fault
But Mine 8. No Quarter 9. Since I've Been Loving You
10. Dazed And Confused 11. Stairway To Heaven
12. The Song Remains The Same 13. Misty Mountain Hop
14. Kashmir 15. Whole Lotta Love 16. Rock And Roll
(Total time 124:05)
Bonus DVD (on 2CD + Blu-ray + DVD and 2CD + 2DVD
editions) 1. Full Dress Rehearsal at Shepperton Studios

JIMMY PAGE: GUITARS
ROBERT PLANT: VOCALS, HARMONICA ON
  "NOBODY'S FAULT BUT MINE"

JOHN PAUL JONES: BASS, KEYBOARDS
JASON BONHAM: DRUMS, BACKING VOCALS ON "GOOD TIMES
  BAD TIMES" AND "MISTY MOUNTAIN HOP"
RECORDED IN 2007 AT THE O2 ARENA IN LONDON FOR A
  CHARITY CONCERT IN HONOR OF THE FOUNDER OF ATLANTIC
  RECORDS, AHMET ERTEGUN.
PRODUCER: JIMMY PAGE

LED ZEPPELIN 2014-2015 REMASTERS

Led Zeppelin (Deluxe Edition)

DISC 1:
1. Good Times Bad Times
2. Babe I'm Gonna Leave You
3. You Shook Me
4. Dazed and Confused
5. Your Time Is Gonna Come
6. Black Mountain Side
7. Communication Breakdown
8. I Can't Quit You Baby
9. How Many More Times

Disc 2: Live at the Olympia—Paris, France, 10 October 1969:
1. Good Times Bad Times/Communication Breakdown
2. I Can't Quit You Baby
3. Heartbreaker
4. Dazed And Confused
5. White Summer/Black Mountain Side
6. You Shook Me
7. Moby Dick
8. How Many More Times

PRODUCER: JIMMY PAGE

Led Zeppelin II (Deluxe Edition)

DISC 1:
1. Whole Lotta Love
2. What Is and What Should Never Be
3. The Lemon Song
4. Thank You
5. Heartbreaker
6. Living Loving Maid (She's Just A Woman)
7. Ramble On
8. Moby Dick
9. Bring It on Home

DISC 2:
1. Whole Lotta Love (alternate mix)
2. What Is and What Should Never Be (alternate mix)
3. Thank You (backing track)
4. Heartbreaker (alternate mix)

5. Living Loving Maid (She's Just A Woman) (backing track)
6. Ramble On (alternate mix)
7. Moby Dick (alternate mix)
8. La La (previously unreleased)

PRODUCER: JIMMY PAGE

Led Zeppelin III (Deluxe Edition)

DISC 1:
1. Immigrant Song
2. Friends
3. Celebration Day
4. Since I've Been Loving You
5. Out On The Tiles
6. Gallows Pole
7. Tangerine
8. That's The Way
9. Bron-Yr-Aur Stomp
10. Hats Off To (Roy) Harper

Disc 2:
1. Immigrant Song (studio outtake)
2. Friends (studio outtake)
3. Celebration Day (studio outtake)
4. Since I've Been Loving You (studio outtake)
5. Bathroom Sound (previously unreleased instrumental version of "Out On The Tiles")
6. Gallows Pole (studio outtake)
7. That's the Way (studio outtake)
8. Jennings Farm Blues (previously unreleased instrumental forerunner to "Bron-Yr-Aur Stomp")
9. Keys To The Highway/Trouble In Mind (previously unreleased rendition of blues standards)

PRODUCER: JIMMY PAGE

Led Zeppelin IV (Deluxe Edition)

DISC 1:
1. Black Dog
2. Rock And Roll
3. The Battle Of Evermore
4. Stairway To Heaven
5. Misty Mountain Hop
6. Four Sticks
7. Going To California
8. When The Levee Breaks

DISC 2:
1. Black Dog (basic track with guitar overdubs)
2. Rock And Roll (alternate mix)
3. The Battle Of Evermore (mandolin/guitar mix from Headley Grange)
4. Stairway To Heaven (Sunset Sound mix)

5. Misty Mountain Hop (alternate mix)
6. Four Sticks (alternate mix)
7. Going To California (mandolin/guitar mix)
8. When The Levee Breaks (alternate UK mix)

PRODUCER: JIMMY PAGE

Houses of the Holy (Deluxe Edition)

DISC 1:
1. The Song Remains The Same
2. The Rain Song
3. Over The Hills And Far Away
4. The Crunge
5. Dancing Days
6. D'yer Mak'er
7. No Quarter
8. The Ocean

DISC 2:
1. The Song Remains The Same (guitar overdub reference mix)
2. The Rain Song (mix minus piano)
3. Over The Hills And Far Away (guitar mix backing track)
4. The Crunge (rough mix—keys up)
5. Dancing Days (rough mix with vocal)
6. No Quarter (rough mix with John Paul Jones keyboard overdubs—no vocal)
7. The Ocean (working mix)

PRODUCER: JIMMY PAGE

Physical Graffiti (Deluxe Edition)

DISC 1:
1. Custard Pie
2. The Rover
3. In My Time Of Dying
4. Houses Of The Holy
5. Trampled Under Foot
6. Kashmir

DISC 2:
1. In The Light
2. Bron-Yr-Aur
3. Down By The Seaside
4. Ten Years Gone
5. Night Flight
6. The Wanton Song
7. Boogie With Stu
8. Black Country Woman
9. Sick Again

DISC 3: (deluxe and box set only):
1. Brandy & Coke (Trampled Under Foot–initial rough mix)

2. Sick Again (early version)
3. In My Time Of Dying (initial rough mix)
4. Houses Of The Holy (rough mix with overdubs)
5. Everybody Makes It Through (In The Light early version/in transit)
6. Boogie With Stu (Sunset Sound mix)
7. Driving Through Kashmir (Kashmir rough orchestra mix)

Presence (Deluxe Edition)

DISC 1:
1. Achilles Last Stand
2. For Your Life
3. Royal Orleans
4. Nobody's Fault But Mine
5. Candy Store Rock
6. Hots On For Nowhere
7. Tea For One

DISC 2:
1. Two Ones Are Won (Achilles Last Stand—reference mix)
2. For Your Life (reference mix)
3. 10 Ribs & All/Carrot Pod Pod (Pod) (reference mix)
4. Royal Orleans (reference mix)
5. Hots On For Nowhere (reference mix)

In Through the Out Door (Deluxe Edition)

DISC 1:
1. In The Evening
2. South Bound Saurez
3. Fool In The Rain
4. Hot Dog
5. Carouselambra
6. All My Love
7. I'm Gonna Crawl

DISC 2:
1. In The Evening (rough mix)
2. Southbound Piano (South Bound Saurez—rough mix)
3. Fool In The Rain (rough mix)
4. Hot Dog (rough mix)
5. The Epic (Carouselambra—rough mix)
6. The Hook (All My Love—rough mix)
7. Blot (I'm Gonna Crawl—rough mix)

Coda (Deluxe Edition)

DISC 1:
1. We're Gonna Groove

2. Poor Tom
3. I Can't Quit You Baby
4. Walter's Walk
5. Ozone Baby
6. Darlene
7. Bonzo's Montreux
8. Wearing And Tearing

DISC 2:
1. We're Gonna Groove (alternate mix)
2. If It Keeps On Raining (When The Levee Breaks—rough mix)
3. Bonzo's Montreux (mix construction in progress)
4. Baby Come On Home
5. Sugar Mama (mix)
6. Poor Tom (instrumental mix)
7. Travelling Riverside Blues (BBC session)
8. Hey, Hey, What Can I Do

DISC 3:
COMPANION AUDIO / DISC 2
1. Four Hands (Four Sticks—Bombay Orchestra)
2. Friends (Bombay Orchestra)
3. St. Tristan's Sword (rough mix)
4. Desire (The Wanton Song—rough mix)
5. Bring It On Home (rough mix)
6. Walter's Walk (rough mix)
7. Everybody Makes It Through (In The Light—rough mix)

COMPILATIONS

Led Zeppelin Remasters Box Set

Released in US and UK 29 October 1990, Atlantic
7567-8214-4
54 tracks digitally remastered 1990 Atlantic

CD 1:
1. Whole Lotta Love (5:34)
2. Heartbreaker (4:14)
3. Communication Breakdown (2:27)
4. Babe I'm Gonna Leave You (6:41)
5. What Is And What Should Never Be (4:44)
6. Thank You (4:47)
7. I Can't Quit You Baby (4:16)
8. Dazed And Confused (6:26)
9. Your Time Is Gonna Come (4:14)
10. Ramble On (4:23)
11. Travelling Riverside Blues (5:09)
12. Friends (3:54)
13. Celebration Day (3:28)
14. Hey Hey What Can I Do (3:56)
15. White Summer/Black Mountain Side (8:01)

CD 2:
1. Black Dog (4:54)
2. Over The Hills And Far Away (4:47)
3. Immigrant Song (2:23)
4. The Battle Of Evermore (5:51)
5. Bron-Y-Aur Stomp (4:16)
6. Tangerine (2:57)
7. Going To California (3:31)
8. Since I've Been Loving You (7:24)
9. D'yer Mak'er (4:22)
10. Gallows Pole (4:56)
11. Custard Pie (4:13)
12. Misty Mountain Hop (4:58)
13. Rock And Roll (3:40)
14. The Rain Song (7:39)
15. Stairway To Heaven (8:00)

CD 3:
1. Kashmir (8:31)
2. Trampled Underfoot (5:35)
3. For Your Life (6:20)
4. No Quarter (6:59)
5. Dancing Days (3:41)
6. When The Levee Breaks (7:07)
7. Achilles Last Stand (10:22)
8. The Song Remains The Same (5:28)
9. Ten Years Gone (6:31)
10. In My Time Of Dying (11:04)

CD 4:
1. In The Evening (6:49)
2. Candy Store Rock (4:07)
3. The Ocean (4:30)
4. Ozone Baby (3:35)
5. Houses Of The Holy (4:01)
6. Wearing And Tearing (5:28)
7. Poor Tom (3:02)
8. Nobody's Fault But Mine (6:27)
9. Fool In The Rain (6:12)
10. In The Light (8:44)
11. The Wanton Song (4:06)
12. Moby Dick/Bonzo's Montreux (3:50)
13. I'm Gonna Crawl (5:30)
14. All My Love (5:53)

PRODUCER: JIMMY PAGE

Led Zeppelin Remasters Box Set 2

Released in US and UK 19 March 1993, Atlantic 7567-82477-2

CD 1:
1. Good Times Bad Times
2. We're Gonna Groove
3. Night Flight

4. That's The Way
5. Baby Come On Home (previously unreleased)
6. The Lemon Song
7. You Shook Me
8. Boogie With Stu
9. Bron-Yr-Aur
10. Down By The Seaside
11. Out On The Tiles
12. Black Mountain Side
13. Moby Dick
14. Sick Again
15. Hot Dog
16. Carouselambra

CD 2:
1. South Bound Saurez
2. Walter's Walk
3. Darlene
4. Black Country Woman
5. How Many More Times
6. The Rover
7. Four Sticks
8. Hats Off To (Roy) Harper
9. I Can't Quit You Baby
10. Hots On For Nowhere
11. Living Loving Maid (She's Just A Woman)
12. Royal Orleans
13. Bonzo's Montreux
14. The Crunge
15. Bring It On Home
16. Tea For One

PRODUCER: JIMMY PAGE

Early Days:
The Best Of Led Zeppelin, Volume 1

Released in US and UK 23 November 1999, Atlantic 83268-2

1. Good Times, Bad Times (2:48)
2. Babe, I'm Gonna Leave You (6:28)
3. Dazed And Confused (6:27)
4. Communication Breakdown (2:29)
5. Whole Lotta Love (5:34)
6. What Is And What Should Never Be (4:44)
7. Immigrant Song (2:25)
8. Since I've Been Loving You (7:24)
9. Black Dog (4:54)
10. Rock And Roll (3:41)
11. The Battle Of Evermore (5:52)
12. When The Levee Breaks (7:08)
13. Stairway To Heaven (8:02)

PRODUCER: JIMMY PAGE

Latter Days:
The Best Of Led Zeppelin, Volume 2

Released in US and UK 21 March 2000, Atlantic 83278-2

1. The Song Remains The Same (5:28)
2. No Quarter (6:59)
3. Houses Of The Holy (4:01)
4 Trampled Underfoot (5:35)
5. Kashmir (8:31)
6. Ten Years Gone (6:31)
7. Achilles Last Stand (10:22)
8. Nobody's Fault But Mine (6:27)
9. All My Love (5:53)
10. In The Evening (6:49)

Mothership (2CDs+DVD)

Released 13 November 2007 US Atlantic R2 313212 /
released 12 November 2007 UK Atlantic 8122-79961-3

CD 1:
1. Good Times Bad Times (2:47)
2. Communication Breakdown (2:28)
3. Dazed And Confused (6:28)
4. Babe I'm Gonna Leave You (6:41)
5. Whole Lotta Love (5:32)
6. Ramble On (4:22)
7. Heartbreaker (4:15)
8. Immigrant Song (2:26)
9. Since I've Been Loving You (7:23)
10. Rock And Roll (3:41)
11. Black Dog (4:54)
12. When The Levee Breaks (7:10)
13. Stairway To Heaven (8:02)

CD 2:
1. Song Remains The Same (5:32)
2. Over The Hills And Far Away (4:49)
3. D'yer Maker (4:23)
4. No Quarter (7:00)
5. Trampled Under Foot (5:36)
6. Houses Of The Holy (4:04)
7. Kashmir (8:29)
8. Nobody's Fault But Mine (6:16)
9. Achilles Last Stand (10:23)
10. In The Evening (6:51)
11. All My Love (5:53)
DVD
Contains excerpts from *Led Zeppelin* DVD.

US Singles

GOOD TIMES BAD TIMES (2:46) / Communication Breakdown (2:27) (Atlantic 45-2613, released 10 March 1969)
Whole Lotta Love (5:34) / Living Loving Maid (She's Just A Woman) (2:38) (Atlantic 45-2690, released 7 November 1969)
IMMIGRANT SONG (2:21) / Hey Hey What Can I Do (3:53) (Atlantic 45-2777, released 5 November 1970)
BLACK DOG (4:56) / Misty Mountain Hop (4:38) (Atlantic 45-2849, released 2 December 1971)
ROCK AND ROLL (3:40) / Four Sticks (4:42) (Atlantic 45-2865, released 21 February 1972)
OVER THE HILLS AND FAR AWAY (4:42) / Dancing Days (3:40) (Atlantic 45-2970, released 24 May 1973)
D'yer Mak'er (4:19) / The Crunge (3:10) (Atlantic 45-2986, released 17 September 1973)
TRAMPLED UNDERFOOT (5:38) / Black Country Woman (4:30) (Atlantic SS 70102, released 2 April 1975)
CANDY STORE ROCK (4:10) / Royal Orleans (2:58) (Atlantic SS 70110, released 18 June 1976)
FOOL IN THE RAIN (6.08) / Hot Dog (3.15) (Atlantic SS 71003, released 7 December 1979)

DVD/VIDEO

The Song Remains the Same

Originally released for cinema in 1976.
Released on Warner DVD 7321900 113892, US 21 December 1999 / UK 5 June 2000
Live footage from Madison Square Garden July 1973 along with fantasy sequences and incidental footage from 1973.

DVD SCENE LISTING:
1. Mob Rubout
2. Mob Town Credits
3. Country Life (Autumn Lake)
4. Bron-Yr-Aur
5. Rock And Roll
6. Black Dog
7. Since I've Been Loving You
8. No Quarter
9. Who's Responsible?
10. The Song Remains The Same
11. The Rain Song
12. Fire And Sword
13. Capturing The Castle
14. Not Quite Backstage Pass
15. Dazed And Confused
16. Strung Out
17. Magic In The Night

18. Gate Crasher
19. No Comment
20. Stairway To Heaven
21. Moby Dick
22. Country Squire Bonham
23. Heartbreaker
24. Grand Theft
25. Whole Lotta Love
26. End Credits (with studio version of '"Stairway to Heaven" playing over)

DIRECTED BY PETER CLIFTON, JOE MASSOT
SOUND PRODUCED BY JIMMY PAGE

Led Zeppelin

Released on Warner DVD 0349 70198-2, US 26 May 2003 / UK 5 June 2003

DISC 1:
Recorded live at the Royal Albert Hall, London 9 January 1970

1. We're Gonna Groove
2. I Can't Quit You Baby
3. Dazed And Confused
4. White Summer
5. What Is And What Should Never Be
6. How Many More Times
7. Moby Dick
8. Whole Lotta Love
9. Communication Breakdown
10. C'mon Everybody
12. Something Else
13. Bring It On Home

1969 PROMO FILM
14. Communication Breakdown
Danish Television, 14 March 1969
15. Communication Breakdown
16. Dazed And Confused
17. Babe I'm Gonna Leave You
18. How Many More Times
Supershow, 18 March 1969
19. Dazed And Confused
Tous En Scene, Paris, 19 June 1969
20. Communication Breakdown
21. Dazed And Confused

DISC 2:
Footage from Sydney Showground on 27 February 1972 with overdubbed sound from Long Beach Area, 27 June 1972.
1. Immigrant Song

MADISON SQUARE GARDEN, JULY 1973
2. Black Dog
3. Misty Mountain Hop
4. Since I've Been Loving You
5. The Ocean

EARLS COURT, MAY 1975
6. Going To California
7. That's The Way
8. Bron-Y-Aur Stomp
9. In My Time Of Dying
10. Trampled Underfoot
11. Stairway To Heaven

KNEBWORTH, AUGUST 1979
12. Rock And Roll
13. Nobody's Fault But Mine

14. Sick Again
15. Achilles Last Stand
16. In The Evening
17. Kashmir
18. Whole Lotta Love
Footage from Sydney Showground on 27 February 1972
19. Rock And Roll
Total Running time: 320 minutes